Best Buy Bargain Plus

Skills & Practice

Grade 4

DISCARD

Frank Schaffer Publications®

Editor: Karen Thompson

Frank Schaffer Publications®

Send all inquiries to:
Frank Schaffer Publications
8720 Orion Place
Columbus, OH 43240-2111

Best Buy Bargain Plus Books: Skills & Practice Grade 4

ISBN 0-7682-3794-7

1 2 3 4 5 6 7 8 9 10 MAZ 09 08 07

Table of Contents

Published by Frank Schaffer Publications. Copyright protected.

Name _____

The National Pastime

Print the names of the National League Baseball Teams in ABC order on the lines below. Then write the letters in the circles on the lines at the bottom of the page to decode the message.

1.

2.

3.

4.

5.

6.

7.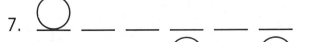

8.

9.

10.

11.

12.

13.

14.

Teams
- Marlins
- Padres
- Phillies
- Giants
- Rockies
- Cardinals
- Reds
- Dodgers
- Braves
- Mets
- Astros
- Expos
- Pirates
- Cubs

These teams belong to the:

8^2 10 12 14 5 3 1 8^1 11 13 2 7 4 6

8^1 = 1st circled letter 8^2 = 2nd circled letter

Name _____

Are You Alphabetically Inclined?

Below are several groups of words. If the group is in the correct alphabetical order, draw a star around it. If it is incorrect, write it correctly in the blanks provided at the bottom of the page.

slithering	dialect	tomahawk	mingle
Seminole	doleful	thatch	metallic
sorrowful	deafen	tourniquet	mythical
salvage	defiance	turban	muslin

platform	abrupt	strewn	capable
pompadour	askew	superintendent	college
prominent	accordion	suspend	comprehend
protrude	arthritis	swamp	cymbal

gig	hammock	awaken	bloodhound
garfish	hoist	astonishment	bellow
gawk	horde	adz	bespeak
glum	inaudible	atmospheric	bewilder

_____ _____ _____ _____

_____ _____ _____ _____

_____ _____ _____ _____

_____ _____ _____ _____

_____ _____ _____ _____

_____ _____ _____ _____

Name _____

Compound Checkup

Write the compound word from the Word Box that matches each definition.

1. physical examination – _____

2. a giant Pacific coast evergreen – _____

3. difficult thing to bear – _____

4. an outdoor advertising sign – _____

5. small metal pot for cooking – _____

6. on a lower floor – _____

7. a glass container used for measuring time – _____

8. a movable ramp to a ship – _____

9. to betray – _____

10. a person with a quick temper – _____

11. to intimidate – _____

12. delighted – _____

13. a logger – _____

14. lower half of a chicken leg – _____

15. a very clever person – _____

16. a robbery – _____

17. a limited-access highway – _____

18. an insect with brightly-colored wings – _____

19. a large area for dancing – _____

20. a path in the street marked for pedestrians – _____

Word Box

ballroom	billboard	browbeat	butterfly	checkup
crosswalk	double-cross	downstairs	drumstick	freeway
gangplank	hardship	hold up	hothead	hourglass
lumberjack	mastermind	overjoyed	redwood	saucepan

Name _____

Compound It!

Help Rufus find as many compound words as you can by using the grid. First give the location and then write the word. Use the back of this sheet if you run out of room.

	R	U	F	U	S
1	light	foot	class	house	some
2	birth	her	tooth	snow	base
3	thing	man	side	him	day
4	room	one	work	out	bare
5	boat	roar	every	in	ball
6	self	time	no	mail	paste
7	stairs	to	shop	mate	up

location   **word**
Example: F-2, S-6   toothpaste

location	**word**		**location**	**word**
1. _____	_____		10. _____	_____
2. _____	_____		11. _____	_____
3. _____	_____		12. _____	_____
4. _____	_____		13. _____	_____
5. _____	_____		14. _____	_____
6. _____	_____		15. _____	_____
7. _____	_____		16. _____	_____
8. _____	_____		17. _____	_____
9. _____	_____		18. _____	_____

Bonus

How many of your words can you draw rebus clues for? Trade your drawings with friends and ask them to guess the words.

Example: basketball

   4   0-7682-3794-7 *Skills & Practice Gr. 4*

Name _____

Words That Break

Divide each word into two words with a slash (/). Then choose one of the two words and combine it with a word from the Word Bank to form a different word.

Example: side/walk→boardwalk

1. afternoon _____
2. junkyard _____
3. handkerchief _____
4. football _____
5. downstairs _____
6. eggshell _____
7. understand _____
8. heartbreak _____

9. outgrow _____
10. without _____
11. everybody _____
12. inside _____
13. overripe _____
14. teapot _____
15. lighthouse _____
16. cowboy _____

Word Bank

back	day	in	town
base	heat	off	wear
bell	flash	sea	where
board	thought	spoon	some

Take two unrelated words to create a whole new compound word. Then tell what it means and use it in a sentence.

Example: junktea — a blend of tea made from garbage. We bought our junktea at a reduced price.

1. _____
_____

2. _____
_____

3. _____
_____

4. _____
_____

Name _____

Comma Quandary

Look at the underlined parts in each sentence. If each is a complete thought, place a comma in the box. If it is not a complete thought, place an X in the box.

Oh, now I get it!

1. <u>Squanto crawled up a sand hill</u> ☐ and <u>looked over the top.</u>

2. <u>He was not afraid</u> ☐ but <u>he remembered what his mother had said.</u>

3. <u>It was good to see the sky again</u> ☐ and <u>to breathe the fresh air.</u>

4. <u>They sailed along the shore</u> ☐ and <u>into the port of Málaga.</u>

5. <u>The Brothers took Squanto to their home</u> ☐ and <u>soon he was well enough to work in the gardens.</u>

6. <u>The captain said that Squanto could sail with him</u> ☐ but <u>the ship was going to London, not America.</u>

7. <u>The Indian was hungry</u> ☐ but <u>he had no money to buy food.</u>

8. <u>That night Squanto ate</u> ☐ and <u>slept in the home of John Slanie.</u>

Copy these sentences adding capitals and punctuation as needed.

9. squanto liked living in london at mistress robbins' house but he still wanted to go back to america to see his family

_____

_____

10. squanto wanted to help the people from england but some of them were not very kind to him

_____

_____

_____

Name _____

The Prisoner's Sentence Is Imperative!

Match each sentence with the correct type by drawing a line.

"I don't want a slave in my room!"   interrogative

"Are you a freedman?"   declarative

"Go to the cellar and get some food."   exclamatory

The fall sunshine felt nice.   imperative

Use vocabulary words in the Word Bank to help you write each type of sentence.

Word Bank			
apologize	doubtfully	confided	maddening
rudeness	impatiently	enthusiastically	sprawled
cantered	scornfully	dumbfounded	defiantly
convince	lurking	denser	good-humored
collided	exhausted		

Imperative _____

_____

Declarative _____

_____

Exclamatory _____

_____

Interrogative _____

_____

Name _____

Makin' Room

An apostrophe is used in contractions to represent missing letters and in possessive forms of singular and plural nouns to show ownership. Add an apostrophe where it is needed in each sentence.

1. The doctors decision was helpful to Sadako.

2. Sadakos classmates sent her a Kokeshi doll.

3. Sadako wasnt very hungry when her mother brought the food.

4. The golden cranes wings blew in the wind.

5. Eijis paper donation smelled of candy.

6. Sadakos good luck cranes became a symbol for peace and hope.

7. "Ill get better," said Sadako over and over.

8. There wasnt enough room on the table for all of the paper cranes so Masahiro hung Sadakos cranes from the ceiling.

9. Chizuko really didnt believe in superstitions like Sadako did.

10. Sadako couldnt sleep very well after she was told she could go home for a visit.

11. Mrs. Sasakis slippers slapped softly on the floor.

12. "Heres your first crane," said Chizuko.

Name _____

Keep It Simple

Underline the simple subject in each sentence. Then on the line write a synonym for the simple subject using the thesaurus or dictionary if necessary.

1. The voyage took many long, hot days to achieve. _____

2. Lanterns were used to guide the spirits home. _____

3. The ballast of the ship was the passengers themselves. _____

4. Many refugees were very lonely in Hong Kong and after awhile wanted to go home. _____

5. The kerosene was used to fuel a lamp so Mai could study when it became dark. _____

6. The ceremonial altar was an important part of Mai's household.

_____

7. The huge temple was empty because the government had removed the Buddhist priests. _____

8. The seasonal monsoon would be over the area soon. _____

9. Great pyramids seemed to rise into the sky as they neared the city.

_____

10. Chrysanthemums made a lovely border on the plate. _____

Name _____

That's Mine!

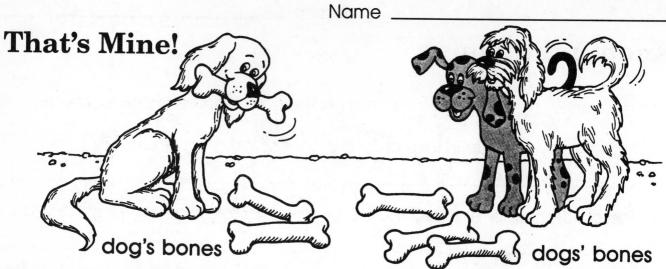

dog's bones   dogs' bones

Change the underlined word to show possession by adding an apostrophe or apostrophe and **s**. Write the possessive form on the line.

Possessive

1. Mother took me to <u>Tony</u> house. _____

2. The <u>chickens</u> eggs were large. _____

3. <u>Jonathan</u> bicycle needs new brakes. _____

4. Follow the <u>team</u> rules. _____

5. The <u>shoes</u> soles need repair. _____

6. Mrs. <u>Thomas</u> car was in the driveway. _____

7. My <u>brother</u> story won first prize. _____

8. Our <u>neighbors</u> lawns need cutting. _____

9. <u>Ellen</u> paintings were on display. _____

10. The truck <u>drivers</u> routes were long. _____

11. The <u>babies</u> toys are put away. _____

12. The <u>principal</u> office is small. _____

13. The <u>bird</u> nest is completed. _____

14. The <u>doctors</u> hours were long. _____

15. The <u>painter</u> brushes were clean. _____

16. The <u>skunk</u> scent was not pleasant. _____

17. The <u>aliens</u> spaceship had landed. _____

Name _____

Know Your Nouns

Find and circle the proper nouns in each sentence. Then write them correctly.

1. Miss brophy grew up in lake champlain, new york.

   _____

2. The children really enjoyed the stories mr. fency told them when he visited.

   _____

3. Addie had to visit the settlement of ree heights to see tilla.

   _____

4. Addie carried her doll ruby lillian everywhere she went.

   _____

5. Addie and her family were living in hutchinson county.

   _____

6. The mills had moved from sabula to oak hollow.

   _____

7. Malcolm and daniel connolly were very mischievous boys.

   _____

8. Addie wrote a poem titled "the wild prairie rose."

   _____

9. Miss brophy often recited poetry written by henry wadsworth longfellow.

   _____

10. Tilla, katya, addie, and nellie all went on a picnic down by the creek.

   _____

Name _____

A View of the Past?

In each sentence below, change the underlined verb to the past tense.

1. Martin <u>will escape</u> to the North to find freedom. _____

2. Laura and Martin <u>will run</u> through the woods at great speed. _____

3. Bert <u>was hiding</u> Martin while the sheriff searched the house. _____

4. People <u>were watching</u> the Eastman home for runaway slaves. _____

5. Laura <u>was looking</u> out the window at the dark, still night. _____

6. Laura <u>will sew</u> a ruffle at the bottom of her green cotton dress. _____

7. Joel <u>will catch</u> Laura helping Martin escape. _____

8. The horse <u>will dash</u> through the street pulling the carriage. _____

Now rewrite the sentences using a present tense verb.

1. _____

2. _____

3. _____

4. _____

5. _____

6. _____

7. _____

8. _____

Name _____

Are You in the Past or Present?

Underline the verb in each sentence. On the line after each sentence write if the verb is past or present tense.

1. Sadako ran home from school every day. _____

2. The wind almost blew the light out of the ceremonial lantern on

   Peace Day. _____

3. Sadako dreamed of good health. _____

4. The wind caught the paper cranes. _____

5. Sadako's gums were swollen. _____

6. Sadako read all of the letters. _____

7. The sun shines brightly on the balcony of the hospital. _____

8. Sadako slept very soundly after the shot of medication. _____

9. Sadako runs faster than almost anyone. _____

10. Kenji knew about leukemia. _____

Name _____

Three Playful Kittens

Rule An **adjective** is a word that describes a noun or a pronoun. It tells **what kind**, **how many**, or **which one**.

Example *All of these adjectives can be used to describe kittens : black, several, these, playful, furry, three, many, young.*

Exercise Place an **X** in the blanks in front of the adjectives. Then complete the sentence with those adjectives.

1. ____ striped ____ one ____ carefully ____ soon _____ zebra ran through the jungle.	2. ____ powerful ____ ahead ____ two ____ cautiously _____ elephants trudged along the path.
3. ____ yesterday ____ quickly ____ scaly ____ spotted A _____ , _____ snake darted through the grass.	4. ____ colorful ____ graceful ____ happily ____ however The _____ , _____ birds soared through the air.

• Underline the nouns in the sentences below. Circle the adjectives.

1. The huge, gray elephant lumbered through the hot jungle.
2. Three swift lions raced through the long, green grass.
3. The playful monkeys swung from the high tree branches.
4. The lazy, green turtle slept under the hot tropical sun.
5. The large, horned rhinoceros slipped into the muddy river.
6. The scaly, old crocodile blinked its large, dark eyes.

Name _____

The Fragrant Flowers

Rule **Adjectives** answer these specific questions about the nouns they modify.

Which one?	What kind?	How many?

Example

these, those, that, this	tall, colorful, red, majestic	three, many, several, few, one

Exercise   Underline the nouns in the sentences below. Circle the adjectives that modify these nouns. Then write the adjectives you circled in the correct column.

1. Those fragrant pink carnations have five ruffled blossoms.
2. These vibrant white roses have a sweet fragrance.
3. Each flower has several dainty petals.
4. The refreshing aroma of the sweet-scented lavender filled the air.
5. That large, colorful canna is a tall, ornamental plant.
6. It has many large leaves and bright red flowers.

Which one?	What kind?	How many?
1. _____	_____	_____
_____	_____	_____
2. _____	_____	_____
_____	_____	_____
3. _____	_____	_____
_____	_____	_____
4. _____	_____	_____
_____	_____	_____
5. _____	_____	_____
_____	_____	_____
6. _____	_____	_____
_____	_____	_____

Name _____

Adverbs Answer

Adverbs modify verbs or adjectives and tell
how, **when**, or **where**.

> **How**—I read **slowly**.
> **Where**—I read **inside**.
> **When**—I was reading **today**.

Write either **how**, **when**, or **where** after each adverb.

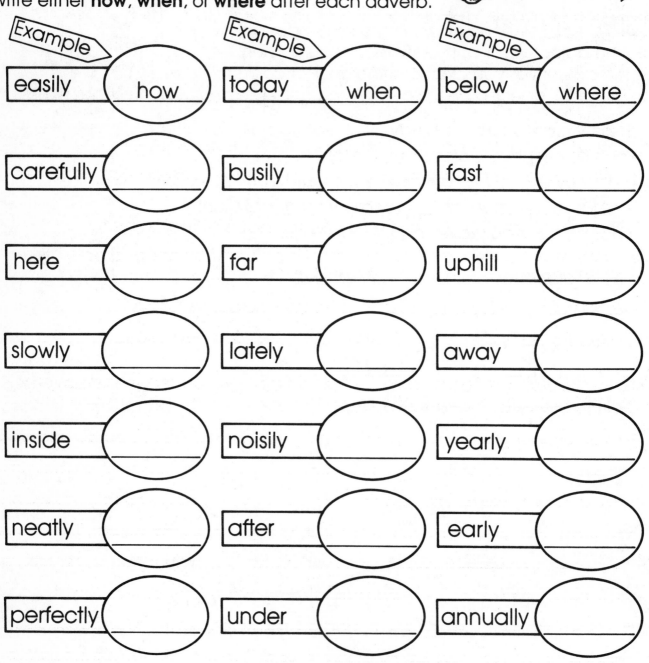

Example	Example	Example
easily — how	today — when	below — where
carefully	busily	fast
here	far	uphill
slowly	lately	away
inside	noisily	yearly
neatly	after	early
perfectly	under	annually

Name _____

That's How It's Done!

Adverbs answer the questions **when**, **where**, and **how**. The adverbs in the sentences below answer **how**. Underline the adverb(s) in each sentence. Then circle the verb it describes. The first one is done for you.

1. The two boys <u>solemnly</u> (shook) hands.

2. Chip looked down incredulously at the fallen shingle which landed softly at his feet.

3. "I don't salvage," remarked Rudy calmly when his counselor glared at him.

4. "Rudy," whispered Mike warningly. Chip was glaring in their direction.

5. The door opened and Mr. Warden emerged, smartly dressed in a white tennis outfit.

6. "Harold, you have no soul," explained Rudy pleasantly.

7. "Why do you immediately assume that I'm guilty?" asked Rudy in a hurt tone.

8. "I'd rather go back to arts and crafts," nodded Mike sheepishly.

9. "Tomorrow," Rudy said thoughtfully as they carefully daubed pale blue paint onto their creation, "we'll go earlier."

10. Arms flailing wildly, Chip rushed anxiously toward his cabin.

11. "Let's just walk directly away from the lake," decided Rudy.

Write four sentences of your own containing adverbs. Underline the adverbs and circle the verbs that are described.

1. _____

_____

2. _____

_____

3. _____

_____

4. _____

_____

Name _____

They're Coming!

Circle the 24 pronouns in the following story.

 A Scary Dream

"They are coming after us," Rhonda said to her brother, Scott. Believe me, Scott, I saw them with their funny-looking faces. The two of them had long, orange hair, and they had gigantic feet. I thought they could be from Mars because they spoke a funny language.

One of them glared at me with his strange-looking face. The other one looked like she had on her clothes from outer space.

Scott, you can't imagine my thoughts as I saw them coming after me with their weird looks and their weird clothes.

Finish this story. Use at least six different pronouns. Circle the pronouns you use.

_____

_____

_____

_____

_____

_____

_____

_____

_____

Name _____

Listen to the Music

In the sentences below, label each of the following.

N—noun	**Adj**—adjective
P—pronoun	**Adv**—adverb
V—verb	

Example:

Adj Adj N V Adv
The little girl ran outside.

1. We feed the birds regularly.

2. Derek planted a maple tree yesterday.

3. Charles wrote them a letter.

4. They have two small dogs.

5. Rosie will be dancing tomorrow.

6. The toys were everywhere.

7. The three children are going swimming today.

8. You can eat now.

9. They washed the car carefully.

10. Several thirsty children drank cold lemonade.

11. We run three miles often.

12. The chorus has been singing beautifully.

13. He gave Chuck five dollars.

14. Pam washed the dishes slowly.

15. That tiny baby was sleeping soundly.

0-7682-3794-7 *Skills & Practice Gr. 4*

Name _____

Break It Up!

For each word given below, give the base word and the prefix and/or suffix. Remember, some base words' spellings have been changed before adding suffixes. Not all words will have a prefix and a suffix.

Word	Prefix	Base Word	Suffix
resourceful			
accomplishment			
numbness			
convincing			
merciless			
sturdiest			
disobeying			
unmistakable			
disinfecting			
disclaimed			
reopening			
inventive			
restless			
precaution			
imitating			

Name _____

Fore and Aft

Fill in the blanks with the appropriate affixes. Some will be used more than once.

Prefixes: dis- im- mis- re- un-   Suffixes: -ful -ish -ist -less -ly -ness -ward

Meaning	Root Word + Affix	New Word
1. having no fear	fear ___ ___ ___ ___	_____
2. to vanish	___ ___ ___ appear	_____
3. toward a lower level	down ___ ___ ___ ___	_____
4. having no friends	friend ___ ___ ___ ___	_____
5. an error in action	___ ___ ___ take	_____
6. to enter again	___ ___ enter	_____
7. too many to count	count ___ ___ ___ ___	_____
8. not happy	___ ___ happy	_____
9. perfection seeker	perfection ___ ___ ___	_____
10. quality of being dark	dark ___ ___ ___ ___	_____
11. not possible	___ ___ possible	_____
12. having doubts	doubt ___ ___ ___	_____
13. without a care	care ___ ___ ___ ___	_____
14. sad from being alone	lone ___ ___ ___	_____
15. not thinking	___ ___ thinking	_____
16. without shoes	shoe ___ ___ ___ ___	_____
17. in a mysterious way	mysterious ___ ___	_____
18. appear again	___ ___ appear	_____
19. in a quiet manner	quiet ___ ___	_____
20. call by wrong name	___ ___ ___ call	_____
21. somewhat yellow	yellow ___ ___ ___	_____
22. cautious	care ___ ___ ___	_____
23. to release	___ ___ ___ engage	_____

Name _____

Don't Miss This!

The prefix **mis** – means wrong or *wrongly, bad* or *badly, no* or *not*. Underline the base words in the following list. Then circle the base words in the wordsearch. Words may go → ← ↑ ↓ ↘ ↗ ↙.

misadventure
misapply
misbehave
miscall
miscast
mischance
misconduct
miscount
misdeal
misdeed
misdirect
misfile
misfire

misfit
misfortune
misgovern
misguide
mishandle
mishear
mislay
mislead
misname
misplay
misread
misrule

S	F	A	P	P	L	Y	G	F	R	E
A	I	O	D	E	A	L	I	N	E	L
T	L	E	C	V	O	R	E	M	A	U
L	E	V	A	H	E	B	A	Y	D	R
D	E	P	L	A	Y	N	S	T	I	F
I	L	A	L	C	A	S	T	C	R	M
R	D	S	D	L	E	D	I	U	G	T
E	N	U	T	R	O	F	S	D	R	H
C	A	O	H	M	C	H	A	N	C	E
T	H	B	L	K	T	N	U	O	C	A
G	O	V	E	R	N	T	N	C	O	R

Choose a word from the list above to correctly complete each sentence.

1. Jeremy is _____ in the play – he should have been the villain.

2. Did I _____ the car keys?

3. It was my _____ to be the first to be called on in class.

4. I think I saw you _____ the cards.

5. Did the cannon _____ ?

6. Our vacation turned out to be one _____ after another.

7. Don't _____ that crystal vase or you might break it.

8. I think I _____ that paragraph – I didn't understand it at all.

9. Robbing a bank is a _____ .

10. The drawings of the beautiful vacation resort _____ us – it wasn't even half finished.

Similar in Some Way

Name _____

 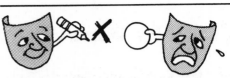

Put an **X** in the circle by the phrase to correctly complete each analogy.

1. conductor is to orchestra as . . .	○ scene is to actor ○ director is to play
2. absent is to present as . . .	○ adult is to child ○ levy is to tax
3. button is to blouse as . . .	○ coat is to hat ○ zipper is to skirt
4. pork is to hog as . . .	○ bacon is to eggs ○ beef is to cattle
5. allow is to permit as . . .	○ alter is to change ○ refute is to confirm
6. mirror is to reflect as . . .	○ scissors is to cut ○ read is to book
7. aide is to assistant as . . .	○ brash is to cautious ○ convince is to persuade
8. autumn is to season as . . .	○ winter is to summer ○ Halloween is to holiday
9. shirt is to collar as . . .	○ sock is to shoes ○ trousers is to cuffs
10. ice cream is to dessert as . . .	○ cereal is to breakfast ○ supper is to dinner
11. graph is to chart as . . .	○ present is to past ○ explore is to investigate

Name _____

Daffy Definitions!

If you know baseball, then you probably know what a *grand slam* is. It's a home run with the bases loaded. But if you like word play, you can come up with a daffy definition: A *grand slam* is someone who slaps $1,000 onto a table. A thousand dollars is sometimes called a *grand*. By using that meaning of *grand*, you can get the daffy definition of *grand slam*.

How daffy are you? See if you can match the expressions below with their crazy definitions. Write your answers on the lines.

rock garden	**capital punishment**	**New Jersey**
diamond cutter	**net profit**	**bank balance**

1. The person who mows the grass on a baseball field
_____

2. A place where outdoor music concerts are held
_____

3. Having to stay after school in Washington, D.C.
_____

4. What is left after the fishing boat owner pays all expenses
_____

5. A replacement for a worn-out turtleneck sweater
_____

6. What keeps a building full of money from tipping over _____

Now try the same thing with single words. Think about the sound of each word, as well as its meaning.

bamboo	**cartoon**	**pharmacy**	**watchdog**	**footnotes**

7. A school where you learn to be a farmer
_____

8. An animal that knows how to tell time _____

9. Music that is written and played for dancing
_____

10. A song you might hum while you're driving
_____

Name _____

Let's Change Laura's Disposition

Antonyms are words that mean almost the opposite. Replace the underlined word in each sentence with an antonym from the Word Bank.

1. Laura stood by the door with a <u>mournful</u> look on her face. _____

2. Laura <u>retreated</u> at the sound of voices outside the springhouse.

   _____

3. Laura <u>scornfully</u> accepted the fact that they would be hiding a runaway

   slave. _____

4. When Joel asked Laura to read a book of his, she was very <u>resentful</u> .

   _____

5. Bert asked Laura to look in the wardrobe for Martin. She was very <u>impatient</u>

   in her search. _____

6. Laura <u>swiftly</u> went to her room and firmly closed the door. _____

7. Martin quickly <u>descended</u> the stairs when they heard a wagon out front.

   _____

8. Laura was very <u>indignant</u> about the idea of having Martin hiding in her

   room. _____

Word Bank			
respectfully	tolerant	cheerful	gratified
sluggishly	happy	climbed	advanced

Choose three of the vocabulary words underlined above and use each one in a sentence.

1. _____

2. _____

3. _____

Name _____

Antonym Action

Using the words from the Word Box, write a word that means the opposite of each numbered word. Then circle each word from the Word Box in the wordsearch. Words may go → ← ↑ ↓ ↘ ↖ ↙.

Word Box				
hero	deny	clean	bright	ancient
exit	stale	rebel	compel	divulge
raze	solid	greedy	corrupt	educated

1. approve – _____

2. coax – _____

3. conform – _____

4. construct – _____

5. coward – _____

6. dreary – _____

7. enter – _____

8. fresh – _____

9. generous – _____

10. hide – _____

11. honest – _____

12. ignorant – _____

13. liquid – _____

14. modern – _____

15. soiled – _____

```
T E D U C A T E D
H S O L I D A E I
G O T I X E N E V
I R S A N Y C Z U
R E B E L A I A L
B H O Y D E E R G
L E P M O C N L E
C O R R U P T O C
```

0-7682-3794-7 *Skills & Practice Gr. 4*

Name _____

Code Names

Use the code to write a synonym for each word.

a	c	e	g	h	o	p	r	t	y
1	2	3	4	5	6	7	8	9	10

1. enclose – $\underline{}_{2}\ \underline{}_{1}\ \underline{}_{4}\ \underline{}_{3}$

2. inexpensive – $\underline{}_{2}\ \underline{}_{5}\ \underline{}_{3}\ \underline{}_{1}\ \underline{}_{7}$

3. right – $\underline{}_{2}\ \underline{}_{6}\ \underline{}_{8}\ \underline{}_{8}\ \underline{}_{3}\ \underline{}_{2}\ \underline{}_{9}$

4. transport – $\underline{}_{2}\ \underline{}_{1}\ \underline{}_{8}\ \underline{}_{8}\ \underline{}_{10}$

5. center – $\underline{}_{2}\ \underline{}_{6}\ \underline{}_{8}\ \underline{}_{3}$

6. duplicate – $\underline{}_{2}\ \underline{}_{6}\ \underline{}_{7}\ \underline{}_{10}$

7. pen – $\underline{}_{2}\ \underline{}_{6}\ \underline{}_{6}\ \underline{}_{7}$

8. table – $\underline{}_{2}\ \underline{}_{5}\ \underline{}_{1}\ \underline{}_{8}\ \underline{}_{9}$

9. conversation – $\underline{}_{2}\ \underline{}_{5}\ \underline{}_{1}\ \underline{}_{9}$

10. applaud – $\underline{}_{2}\ \underline{}_{5}\ \underline{}_{3}\ \underline{}_{3}\ \underline{}_{8}$

11. harvest – $\underline{}_{2}\ \underline{}_{8}\ \underline{}_{6}\ \underline{}_{7}$

12. crawl – $\underline{}_{2}\ \underline{}_{8}\ \underline{}_{3}\ \underline{}_{3}\ \underline{}_{7}$

13. concern – $\underline{}_{2}\ \underline{}_{1}\ \underline{}_{8}\ \underline{}_{3}$

14. capture – $\underline{}_{2}\ \underline{}_{1}\ \underline{}_{9}\ \underline{}_{2}\ \underline{}_{5}$

15. class – $\underline{}_{2}\ \underline{}_{1}\ \underline{}_{9}\ \underline{}_{3}\ \underline{}_{4}\ \underline{}_{6}\ \underline{}_{8}\ \underline{}_{10}$

16. price – $\underline{}_{2}\ \underline{}_{5}\ \underline{}_{1}\ \underline{}_{8}\ \underline{}_{4}\ \underline{}_{3}$

17. stick – $\underline{}_{2}\ \underline{}_{6}\ \underline{}_{5}\ \underline{}_{3}\ \underline{}_{8}\ \underline{}_{3}$

18. force – $\underline{}_{2}\ \underline{}_{6}\ \underline{}_{3}\ \underline{}_{8}\ \underline{}_{2}\ \underline{}_{3}$

19. task – $\underline{}_{2}\ \underline{}_{5}\ \underline{}_{6}\ \underline{}_{8}\ \underline{}_{3}$

20. swindle – $\underline{}_{2}\ \underline{}_{5}\ \underline{}_{3}\ \underline{}_{1}\ \underline{}_{9}$

Write ten new words. Then use the code to write the numbers to spell synonyms for each word. Trade your paper with a classmate to see if he or she can decipher your code.

Example: deed – $\underline{}_{1}\ \underline{}_{2}\ \underline{}_{9}$

1. _____
2. _____
3. _____
4. _____
5. _____

6. _____
7. _____
8. _____
9. _____
10. _____

Name _____

The Synonymous Sleuth

Write the synonym for the backwards word in each sentence. Decode and use the backwards synonyms at the bottom.

1. Miss Whitehead's feet look regral this year. _____

2. I kniht Miss Elson is one of those people you don't bother to think about twice. _____

3. It's just what Ole Golly says, hcir people are boring. _____

4. When I look at him, I could tae 1,000 tomato sandwiches. _____

5. He looks yppah except I wouldn't like all those cats. _____

6. Is he a tnereffid person when he's with someone else? _____

7. She snworf when she looks at things close. _____

8. I just feel ynnuf all over. _____

9. Spies should not get thguac. _____

10. It was just too suoregnad to go there. _____

11. Every time I have a dab dream, I feel like leaving town. _____

12. Sometimes Sport is like a little old namow. _____

13. I have deman him the boy with the purple socks. _____

14. Maybe they think I'm a gnilkaew, but I'm trained for this kind of fight.

_____

15. There is no rest for the yraew. _____

16. This cook certainly makes a lot of esion. _____

17. Ole Golly is thgir, sometimes you have to lie. _____

18. They're trying to lortnoc me and make me give up. _____

19. I will never give up this notebook, but it is raelc that they are going to be as mean as they can. _____

20. I will be the tseb spy there ever was and I will know everything. _____

Clues						
egnarts	ydal	reggib	slwocs	delebal	derit	tekcar
yksir	ruoved	eveileb	yhtlaew	pmiw	elur	tcerroc
tnetnoc	tcnitsid	derutpac	nialp	tsetaerg	elbirret	

Name _____

Super Synonyms

Read each sentence below. Write a synonym for each underlined word. You may want to use a thesaurus.

1. Mattie and Toni find a <u>beautiful</u> pin for Mattie's mother. _____

2. Matt is <u>thrilled</u> to be on the basketball team. _____

3. Mrs. Benson works very hard to keep everything <u>done</u> around the apartment building. _____

4. Mrs. Stamps is a <u>friendly</u> person to visit. _____

5. Mr. Ashby tries to be a <u>fair</u> teacher. _____

6. Angel is <u>wicked</u> toward everyone around her. _____

7. The Bacon family really <u>enjoyed</u> Mattie's babysitting service. _____

8. Charlene took the bracelet from Angel because she was <u>envious</u> of Angel. _____

9. Mr. Phillips was <u>amazed</u> by Mattie's story. _____

10. Mattie had been very <u>helpful</u> to her mother. _____

Now use the thesaurus to find an antonym for each synonym you wrote above.

1. _____   6. _____

2. _____   7. _____

3. _____   8. _____

4. _____   9. _____

5. _____   10. _____

Name _____

You Can Count on the Count

Homographs are words that are spelled the same but have different meanings. Write the correct homograph for the underlined word(s) in each sentence.

Word Bank		
bank	spruce	pupil
flag	hide	stake
brush	arms	bay

1. She hid the gold by the <u>evergreen</u> tree. _____

2. The soldiers carried <u>weapons</u>. _____

3. I have a <u>dark center in my eye</u>. _____

4. The children had a lot at <u>risk</u> if they were caught with the gold. _____

5. The kids could <u>signal</u> for help if needed. _____

6. The <u>skin</u> on the alligator was thick and dark. _____

7. The ship docked in the <u>inlet</u>. _____

8. The <u>tentacles</u> on the octopus moved constantly. _____

9. The dog suddenly began to <u>howl</u>. _____

10. The children could <u>conceal</u> the gold in the snow. _____

11. Uncle Victor had a <u>banner</u> hanging in his ship. _____

12. Someone was hiding in the <u>bushes</u> by the Snake River. _____

13. The <u>land along the river</u> was covered with brush. _____

14. She had a close <u>encounter</u> with danger. _____

15. The snow <u>pile</u> was as tall as a tree. _____

16. She was a quiet <u>student</u>. _____

17. I will help you <u>fix</u> up things around here. _____

18. They drove a <u>post</u> in the ground to mark the spot. _____

Name _____

Help with Homophones

Circle the correct homophones in each sentence.

1. I'd like to (halve, have) a piece when you (halve, have) that apple.
2. Please give me the (real, reel) fishing rod (real, reel).
3. Our (guessed, guest) (guessed, guest) the correct answer.
4. I heard (him, hymn) sing the (him, hymn).
5. The robber was (scene, seen) at the (scene, seen) of the crime.
6. The (band, banned) could not play the (band, banned) song.
7. I heard Alex (moan, mown) when he was reminded he had not yet (moan, mown) the grass.
8. The weather forecaster said the (missed, mist) had (missed, mist) our area.
9. When the knight hurled his (soared, sword), it (soared, sword) into the air.
10. It's so (chili, chilly) today, let's have (chili, chilly) for supper.

On the lines below, write a sentence for each pair of homophones.

ate, eight _____

_____

dear, deer _____

_____

we'd, weed _____

_____

hoarse, horse _____

_____

scent, sent _____

_____

Name _____

Homophone Hype

For each word given below find and circle the homophone(s) in the wordsearch. List the homophones in the spaces provided. Then write a sentence using the given word and at least one homophone.

```
W  R  I  T  E  L  D  U  E  R  C
G  N  I  R  R  A  B  L  N  I  B
R  M  E  T  O  D  S  Y  A  H  E
O  I  H  E  R  I  S  R  M  G  A
T  N  E  C  F  R  Y  E  O  I  R
H  E  I  S  L  B  A  A  D  E  I
G  R  D  E  W  A  G  F  T  W  N
I  A  Y  E  H  O  O  E  O  A  G
R  H  K  P  O  W  T  L  G  W  L
G  N  I  R  E  B  R  O  U  T  E
```

1. **Main** _____ _____

   Sentence: _____

2. **Liar** _____

   Sentence: _____

3. **Farrow** _____ _____

   Sentence: _____

4. **Bridle** _____

   Sentence: _____

5. **I'll** _____ _____

   Sentence: _____

6. **Graze** (Hint: plural form of a color) _____

   Sentence: _____

7. **Here** _____

   Sentence: _____

8. **Way** _____ _____

   Sentence: _____

9. **Do** _____ _____

   Sentence: _____

10. **Sent** _____ _____

    Sentence: _____

Name _____

Indefatigable Idioms

Use the code to find idioms for each phrase.

Code	
A	N
B	O
C	P
D	Q
E	R
F	S
G	T
H	U
I	V
J	W
K	X
L	Y
M	Z

1. wasting time

___ ___ ___ ___ ___ ___ ___   ___ ___ ___ ___
X   V   Y   Y   V   A   T   G   V   Z   R

2. start to think

___ ___ ___ ___ ___ ___   ___ ___ ___ ___ ___
J   U   R   R   Y   F   O   R   T   V   A

___ ___   ___ ___ ___ ___
G   B   G   H   E   A

3. become weak and weary

___ ___ ___   ___ ___ ___ ___
E   H   A   Q   B   J   A

4. self-evident

___ ___   ___ ___ ___ ___   ___ ___ ___ ___ ___ ___ ___
V   G   T   B   R   F   J   V   G   U   B   H   G

___ ___ ___ ___ ___ ___
F   N   L   V   A   T

5. take back what he said

___ ___ ___   ___ ___ ___   ___ ___ ___ ___ ___
R   N   G   U   V   F   J   B   E   Q   F

6. what a person deserves

___ ___ ___ ___   ___ ___ ___ ___ ___ ___ ___
W   H   F   G   Q   R   F   F   R   E   G   F

7. she attempts to do too much

___ ___ ___ ___ ___   ___ ___ ___   ___ ___ ___   ___ ___ ___ ___
O   V   G   R   F   B   S   S   Z   B   E   G   U   N   A

___ ___ ___   ___ ___ ___   ___ ___ ___ ___
F   U   R   P   N   A   P   U   R   J

8. poorly planned

___ ___ ___ ___ ___ ___ ___ ___ ___ ___
U   N   Y   S   –   O   N   X   R   Q

Challenge: Write a story using as many idioms as possible. You might want to include: play it by ear, child's play, eyes peeled, double cross, ham it up, see red, over a barrel, wound up, down in the dumps, time flies, make ends meet, on the tip of my tongue.

Name _____

Watch for Grandpa's Watch

Each "watch" in the title of this worksheet has a different meaning. One means "to look for," and the other means "time piece." Write two meanings for the words below.

	Meaning 1	**Meaning 2**
1. spring	_____	_____
2. run	_____	_____
3. ruler	_____	_____
4. duck	_____	_____
5. suit	_____	_____
6. cold	_____	_____
7. fall	_____	_____
8. tire	_____	_____
9. rose	_____	_____
10. face	_____	_____
11. train	_____	_____
12. play	_____	_____
13. foot	_____	_____
14. pen	_____	_____
15. box	_____	_____
16. dice	_____	_____
17. fly	_____	_____
18. seal	_____	_____
19. bowl	_____	_____
20. ride	_____	_____
21. line	_____	_____

Challenge: Choose some of the above words and illustrate their two meanings on another piece of paper.

Name _____

Double Trouble

Fill in the blanks with the correct definition number for each underlined word.

Example: __3__ I was covered with <u>pitch</u> after climbing the pine tree.

winding	1. having bends or curves
	2. the act of turning something around a central core
wolf	1. to gulp down
	2. a large carnivorous member of the dog family
pitch	1. to sell or persuade
	2. to throw a ball from the mound to the batter
	3. a resin that comes from the sap of pine trees

_____ 1. Do girl scouts <u>pitch</u> cookies?

_____ 2. We are <u>winding</u> the top's string tightly.

_____ 3. The adult <u>wolf</u> returned to her lair.

_____ 4. Red didn't <u>pitch</u> after the fourth inning.

_____ 5. The Mather family had a <u>winding</u> driveway.

_____ 6. The young ball player <u>wolfed</u> down his lunch.

choke	1. to strangle
	2. to bring the hands up on the bat
hitch	1. obstacle
	2. to fasten or tie temporarily
wind-up	1. the swing of the pitcher's arm just before the pitch
	2. to close or conclude

_____ 1. We <u>hitched</u> the mule to the cart.

_____ 2. Tip would not <u>choke</u> up on his bat.

_____ 3. Paul wished to play, but there was just one <u>hitch</u>.

_____ 4. We wish to <u>wind-up</u> our program with more music.

_____ 5. Mom was afraid the dog would <u>choke</u> itself on its leash.

_____ 6. He has a great <u>wind-up</u> and curve ball.

Name _____

Words We Can Hear ... Onomatopoeia

Words that imitate the sounds that they are associated with are onomatopoeic. Use words from the Word Bank to write a poem or short story.

Word Bank					
whack	buzz	hiss	creak	squeal	honk
twang	cuckoo	grind	clink	ping	crack
thump	crash	bow wow	chug	moo	blip
flip flop	squish	beep	smack	chug	chirp
ding dong	rustle	clomp			

_____

_____

_____

_____

_____

_____

_____

_____

_____

_____

_____

_____

_____

_____

_____

_____

_____

LANGUAGE ARTS

Name _____

Describe It Please!

Decide in which category each word from the Word Bank belongs.

Word Bank

robust	slimy	sour	energetic	forgiving
aggravated	devoted	enormous	outraged	prickly
affectionate	delighted	tart	spiteful	silky
enraged	happy	gooey	well	depressed
miserable	adorable	fit	ecstatic	
gloomy	gigantic			

Anger

_____

_____

_____

_____

Sadness   **Joy**

_____   _____

_____   _____

_____   _____

Love   **Feel (Touch)**

_____   _____

_____   _____

_____   _____

Taste   **Size**

_____   _____

_____   _____

Name _____

As Sharp As a Tack

Similes use **like** or **as** to compare two unlike things that share a characteristic. Draw a red line under the two things being compared in each sentence.

1. The snow reached high into the sky like a mountain peak.

2. The barn door felt like a lost friend.

3. The Connolly brothers are as mean as skunks.

4. The huge hill climbed into the sky like a giant's belly as he lay on his back.

5. The wood stovepipe was as red as a fire engine.

6. Tilla's eyes were as blue as a cornflower.

7. The barn was dark like a cave.

8. The warm cow was like a comfortable blanket.

9. George looked like a coyote peering into a henhouse.

10. Tilla's brother was as strong as an ox.

Draw lines to make similes from the following sets of words.

1. Blowing snow is . . .   like contented cows.

2. Miss Brophy is . . .   as friendly as a lost puppy.

3. The boys moved their jaws . . .   like a white blanket.

4. Mr. Fency is . . .   as slippery as worms.

5. Oysters are . . .   as pretty as a china doll.

Name _____

Like . . . a Simile!

In the sentences below, underline the two objects, persons, etc., being compared. In the blank, write if the comparison is a simile or a metaphor. Remember, a simile uses **like** or **as**; metaphors do not.

1. Angel was as mean as a wild bull. _____

2. Toni and Mattie were like toast and jam. _____

3. Mr. Ashby expected the students to be as busy as beavers. _____

4. The pin was a masterpiece in Mattie's mind. _____

5. The park's peacefulness was a friend to Mattie. _____

6. The words came as slow as molasses into Mattie's mind. _____

7. Mrs. Stamps's apartment was like a museum. _____

8. Mrs. Benson was as happy as a lark when Mattie won the contest.

_____

9. Mr. Phillip's smile was a glowing beam to Mattie and Mrs. Benson.

_____

10. Mattie ran as fast as the wind to get her money. _____

11. Angel's mean words cut through Charlene like glass. _____

12. Mr. Bacon was a fairy godmother to Mattie. _____

13. The gingko tree's leaves were like fans. _____

Complete the following sentences using similes.

1. Matt was as artistic as _____

2. Hannibal's teeth were like _____

3. Toni's mind worked fast like _____

4. Mattie was as sad as _____

5. Mrs. Stamps was like _____

Name _____

Snacking in the U.S.A.

Ned's award for losing weight was a trip to Disney World. Travel to these vacation spots in the U.S.A. and list the foods you could eat there that begin with the same first letter as the place. For example, Disney World = doughnuts, dill pickles.

Niagara Falls
1. _____
2. _____
3. _____

Hollywood
1. _____
2. _____
3. _____

Grand Canyon
1. _____
2. _____
3. _____

Washington, D.C.
1. _____
2. _____
3. _____

Mount Rushmore
1. _____
2. _____
3. _____

Disneyland
1. _____
2. _____
3. _____

Busch Gardens
1. _____
2. _____
3. _____

Statue of Liberty
1. _____
2. _____
3. _____

Rocky Mountains
1. _____
2. _____
3. _____

Lincoln Memorial
1. _____
2. _____
3. _____

Pike's Peak
1. _____
2. _____
3. _____

Empire State Building
1. _____
2. _____
3. _____

Carlsbad Caverns
1. _____
2. _____
3. _____

Indianapolis Speedway
1. _____
2. _____
3. _____

Sea World
1. _____
2. _____
3. _____

Name _____

Abracadabra Magical Sentences

Make magical sentences by using words that begin with each of the letters in the animal names given below.

For example: FROG = Foxes Run Over Grasslands.
                       BEAR = Blue Elephants Are Rare!

1. SNAKE = _____
   _____

2. LION = _____
   _____

3. GORILLA = _____

4. CROW = _____

5. SHEEP = _____

6. PIG = _____
   _____

7. PYTHON = _____

8. RABBIT = _____
   _____

9. HORSE = _____
   _____

10. WOLF = _____
    _____

11. CAMEL = _____
    _____

12. MOUSE = _____

13. HAMSTER = _____
    _____

Challenge: Illustrate your best abracadabra sentences on drawing paper.

Published by Frank Schaffer Publications. Copyright protected.   0-7682-3794-7 *Skills & Practice Gr. 4*

R.I.P.

Not all epitaphs are serious or sentimental. Some are humorous. Below are two examples.

Epitaph for a Dachshund

The bone he fetched
Was still atteched
...To a bulldog

Epitaph for a School Crossing Guard

Oh, Mrs. Toots, our crossing guard
Why didn't you use your head?
We wish you hadn't o'er stepped the curb
But looked both ways instead

Try your hand at writing an epitaph. Here are some ideas of characters for whom you might write:

a sports announcer
a waiter or waitress
a carpenter
a professional wrestler
a talkative parrot

a bank teller
an aerial performer
a pet boa constrictor
a lawyer
a minister, rabbi or priest

Here lies _____
name

_____ - _____
born   died
(month, day, year)   (month, day, year)

epitaph

_____
_____
_____
_____
_____

Name _____

Publishing House

Theodor Seuss Geisel was best known by his pen name, Dr. Seuss. His children's books are usually written in verse and combine nonsense with humor. Draw a picture of a nonsensical being in the box below. Give it a name. Then, write a poem about it on the lines to the right.

Norman Rockwell was an illustrator of everyday people involved in everyday situations. His pictures told stories. They were filled with actions, feeling and details. Think of something you just did with your family, or a feeling you just experienced. Draw a detailed account of the situation in the box to the right.

43

Name _____

Dear . . .

november 30,

dear mr henshaw

   i would like to learn how to right letters like leigh botts. can we be pun plas two   i ve never

red Moose on Toast or Weighs to Amuse a Dog, but i will soon i liked when you signed that letter

Messing a round have you written eny more books lately who is your favrit author i will sind you

a story with this letter. right back and tell me how you like it

                                                  yours 'til niagara falls,

Follow the directions to correct this letter to Mr. Henshaw. Use colored pencils or crayons.
Put a check in each box as you correct each item.

☐   1. Put periods and question marks in the letter where needed in **red.**

☐   2. Add commas and apostrophes in **green.**

☐   3. Underline any misspelled words in **orange.**

☐   4. Circle in **purple** letters that should be capitals.

☐   5. Write the year after the date in pencil.

☐   6. Write your name in cursive for the signature.

☐   7. Circle the entire body of this letter in **yellow.**

☐   8. Draw a **brown** box around the greeting of the letter.

☐   9. Underline the closing with **blue.**

☐   10. Draw two **pink** lines under the signature.

☐   11. Draw a **red** happy face above the date.

Bonus

On another paper write a story to send to Mr. Henshaw.

Name _____

Mistake'n Letter

The letter below has several mistakes in punctuation, capitalization, and in form. Write it correctly below.

september 9 1868

dear laura.

I was so sorry to hear of your move to virginia we used to have so much fun together i will really miss the opportunity to spend time with you i hope you will enjoy living with your aunt and uncle I hope you return soon in the meantime please write often

sincerely joel.

_____

_____

_____

_____

_____

_____

_____

_____

_____

Name _____

Matching Before and After

Match the first part of each sentence with its last part. Write the matching parts on the lines below the boxes.

First Part	**Before**	Second Part

First Part

Call the store to see if they have turkey
It's better to have insurance
I had my hair cut
My room was cleaned
Refill the water jar

Second Part

you need it.
hot weather set in.
you could count to three.
we drive there to get it.
you put it back in the refrigerator.

_____ before _____
_____ before _____
_____ before _____
_____ before _____
_____ before _____

First Part **After** **Second Part**

We had plenty of hot water
Let's have a party
My mom and dad ordered new carpet
We were suntanned
Sam's golf game improved by several points

he took some hitting lessons.
we finish our tests.
we bought a larger water heater.
we came back from a long vacation.
the puppy was trained.

_____ after _____
_____ after _____
_____ after _____
_____ after _____
_____ after _____

• Write what comes next.

at   bat   cat   eat   fat   hat _____

Name _____

When Do You Do It?

Write the listed activities that you do under the appropriate heading. If you do any activities more than once a day, write them more than once. Cross out the ones you don't do.

Activities		
make my bed	take care of a pet	turn off alarm clock
go to school	carry out trash	organized sports
go to scouts	go to dentist	go to lunchroom
eat brunch	watch cartoons	play with friend after school
homework	take bath or shower	sleep a long time
do the dishes	go to Sunday school	go home from school
go to bed	have pleasant dreams	go to dance lessons
have lunch recess	play after school	kiss mom and/or dad goodnight

Between Dinner and Breakfast

_____

_____

_____

_____

_____

Between Breakfast and Lunch

_____

_____

_____

_____

_____

Between Lunch and Dinner

_____

_____

_____

_____

_____

• Write what comes next.

     _____

Name _____

If – Then

Match the sentence parts that go together best. Write the number of the first sentence part on the line in front of the last sentence part for each one.

1. If you baby-sit for me Saturday night
2. If you are nice
3. If we leave work by 4:30
4. If you leave a note on your door
5. If you don't have enough money for the movie
6. If my father isn't too tired
7. If the wind keeps up
8. If you want to get a seat at the concert
9. If our neighbor cuts the grass early Sunday morning
10. If the plant doesn't feel damp
11. If my house were painted white
12. If everyone talked at the same time
13. If you don't get a haircut
14. If the tea kettle whistles
15. If no one answers the door
16. If the little boy crosses the street
17. If the horse is tired
18. If you have a long fork
19. If you don't want any dessert
20. If a king comes into a room
21. If it snows a lot tomorrow

___ the delivery man will leave the package.
___ it needs to be watered.
___ you could roast marshmallows.
___ probably no one is at home.
___ everyone will rise.
___ I'll pay you double.
___ the water is boiling.
___ tomorrow will be a great kite-flying day.
___ let him rest.
___ no one could hear directions.
___ we will avoid rush hour.
___ say "No thank you."
___ the noise will wake me up.
___ we can build an igloo.
___ he said he would show me how to shoot baskets.
___ it would look like a miniature White House.
___ I'll loan you the rest.
___ he must hold onto his mother's hand.
___ you will have many friends.
___ you will have to be at the auditorium early.
___ you will have long hair.

• Write what comes next.

A ꓭ Ɔ ◠ E _____

Name _____

Putting It in Perspective

Cut along the dotted lines to divide the events related to the life of Michelangelo listed below. Then rearrange them in chronological order to put the events in historical perspective. Glue the ordered events to your own paper.

1508–1512 Michelangelo works on the Sistine Chapel Ceiling project.

1564 Having worked on projects until his very last days, Michelangelo dies at the age of 89. His contemporaries describe his death as the passing of a "divine angel."

---

c.1515 Michelangelo completes one of his most famous sculptures, *Moses*.

1386 Donatello is born. His techniques will influence Michelangelo, and one of his former students will serve as Michelangelo's teacher at art school.

1475 Michelangelo Buonarroti is born to a distinguished Florentine family.

1488–1489 Michelangelo apprentices with Domenico Ghirlandaio.

1501–1504 Michelangelo works on the marble figure of *David*.

1452 Leonardo da Vinci is born. His work and Michelangelo's work will be displayed side by side at least once in their lifetimes.

1350 The Renaissance era in art, music, literature, and religion is born. Michelangelo will contribute substantially to the High Renaissance period within this era.

1517 The Reformation is initiated when Martin Luther nails his 95 Theses to the door of a German cathedral, criticizing practices of the Catholic church. The resulting split in the church and beginning of the Protestant faith affects the religious Michelangelo, whose works display more sorrow and disillusionment.

1498–1500 Michelangelo works on the *Pietà*.

1541 Michelangelo completes the *Last Judgment* mural.

1492 Michelangelo's first patron, Lorenzo de Medici, dies, his family falls out of favor in Florence, and Michelangelo finds himself in exile in Bologna two years later.

1505–1516 The Vatican is the primary patron of Michelangelo's work.

1550 Michelangelo begins work on a sculpture many believe he wished to be placed at his own burial site. Out of depression or disappointment in the quality of the work, he destroys his own work, which is later repaired.

Name _____

Time for Titles

Choose the word or phrase from the Word Box that best completes the heading for each group of words.

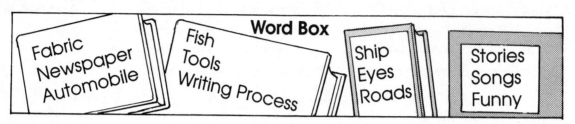

Word Box

Fabric
Newspaper
Automobile

Fish
Tools
Writing Process

Ship
Eyes
Roads

Stories
Songs
Funny

Parts of a . . .	Kinds of . . .	Things for . . .
_____	_____	_____
helm rudder gunwale	boulevard freeway avenue	goggles spectacles contacts
Other words for . . .	Parts of an . . .	Kinds of . . .
_____	_____	_____
witty hilarious humorous	headlight windshield seatbelt	satin velvet flannel
Kinds of . . .	Kinds of . . .	Parts of a . . .
_____	_____	_____
legend myth parable	pliers chisel crowbar	headline column article
Kinds of . . .	Part of the . . .	Kinds of . . .
_____	_____	_____
lullaby anthem hymn	edit proofread revise	flounder sardine salmon

Name _____

Row, Row, Row Your Boat

In the wordsearch, circle words from the list that name **types of boats**. Cross out words that do not belong in that category. Words may go → ← ↑ ↓ ↗.

ark	schooner	battleship	boat	canoe
dory	destroyer	dinghy	liner	sarong
skiff	submarine	mirage	sloop	kayak
raft	rowboat	sailboat	ferry	barge
ship	freighter	carrier	yacht	hinge
tug	tanker	steamer		

```
W O R R O W B O A T A B
R E N O O H C S D F E D
S U B M A R I N E A T I
U C A R R I E R S R R N
T R T E D A R K T M E G
A E T N O Y M A R B T H
O M L I R N N Y O C H Y
B A E L P K R A Y A G A
L E S I E O T K E N I C
I T H R D H U B R O E H
A S I B A R G E B E R T
S I P O O L S K I F F S
```

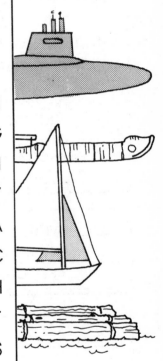

Use a dictionary to help answer the questions.

1. Which boat has the ability to travel underwater: a skiff or a submarine?

   _____

2. Which boat would more likely be used in a war: a carrier or a liner?

   _____

3. Which boat is more like a canoe: a sloop or a kayak? _____

4. Which vessel is a type of fishing boat: a barge or a dory? _____

Name _____

Classification

Read the paragraph. Write each sentence in the correct category.

The civilians of the town had a strange disease. The disease was somewhat like scarlet fever, and it spread through the town like a plague. However, the disease only affected small children. All of the small children who had the disease had to be quarantined. The children did not lose their appetite and did not have a temperature. The Commandant ordered that they keep a careful quarantine. He was afraid his infantrymen might contract the disease. The German army had ammunition, but none to fight this type of war. The lieutenant did not want his sentries around the diseased children, so they did not go into town. The witty doctor created a disease for the children and it was a success! The children moved the gold safely.

Sentences relating to the townspeople

_____

_____

_____

_____

_____

_____

Sentences relating to the German army

_____

_____

_____

_____

_____

_____

Name _____

Scaredy-Cat!

What do you fear? Rate these fears from greatest to least, with one being the greatest.

Fear	Rating
dark	_____
fire	_____
strangers	_____
thunder	_____
snakes	_____
school grades	_____
not having friends	_____
monsters	_____
bees	_____
dogs	_____
death	_____
moving	_____
cemeteries	_____
superstitions	_____
crying in public	_____
being unloved	_____

Think about a fear that you have now or might have in the future. Write a diary entry describing this fear.

date _____

Dear Diary,

_____

_____

_____

_____

_____

_____

_____

Name _____

In Other Words . . .

On the line in front of each sentence, write the letter of the phrase that best defines, describes or explains the underlined part of each sentence.

_____ 1. Mom decided it was a perfect day to <u>capture Minnesota on film</u>.

_____ 2. Lenny thought Huckleberry Heights looked like <u>uncharted territory</u>.

_____ 3. Once they got the door open, they could see that Huckleberry Heights looked like a <u>desert of snow</u>.

_____ 4. Aunt Fluffy always said, "<u>Let's sleep on it</u>."

_____ 5. Edgar thought Mr. Cummings had <u>bitten off more than he could chew</u>.

_____ 6. When Lenny walked Gladys onto the stage, it <u>brought the house down</u>.

_____ 7. Mom said that little Rosalie should be <u>welcomed into their circle</u>.

_____ 8. Tony brushed Smiley's fur so that he <u>shone like tinsel</u>.

_____ 9. Aunt Fluffy's new boyfriend was the <u>last cloud hanging over Tony's holidays</u>.

_____ 10. The whole house <u>smelled like Christmas</u>.

A. think about something overnight and see how you feel about it in the morning

B. the air was filled with scents that remind you of Christmas

C. to make everyone feel like they belong

D. take photographs of Minnesota

E. took on a project that is more than he can handle

F. the audience clapped and cheered

G. was very shiny

H. somewhere no one has ever been before

I. a gloomy thing to think about

J. there was snow everywhere

I guess we're just a pair of "good skates."

A
NOW . . .
D

A "good skate" is someone who is cooperative and gets along well with other people. Choose a classmate who you think is a good skate and write down reasons that explain why you feel this way. Share these "warm fuzzies" (nice thoughts) with your class.

Name _____

What a Tragedy!

Drama is a play performed by actors. A drama tells a story. Drama can be serious, or funny, or sometimes both. There are three basic kinds of drama: tragedy, comedy and melodrama.

A tragedy is a drama about a serious subject. Tragedies often deal with the meaning of life, and how people treat each other.

A comedy is a drama that uses feelings of joy. Comedy can also show very exaggerated and ridiculous behavior.

A melodrama is a drama which tells a story of good against evil. A melodrama features an evil villain who tries to destroy the good characters.

Drama is believed to have begun in ancient Greece. The

Greeks performed their plays in outdoor theaters. Many of the Greek tragedies were about myths. Drama was later popular in many countries: Italy, England, Spain, France, India, China and Japan. Today, drama is popular in practically every country in the world.

Circle and check.

Drama

. . . is a   costume
         play   performed by actors.

. . . tells a: ☐ joke   ☐ part   ☐ story

. . . can be serious, or funny, or both.   T   F

Write.

Drama is believed to have begun in ancient _____.

The Greeks performed their dramas in _____ theaters.

Many of the Greek tragedies were about _____.

• Write a plot or story for each of the three kinds of drama.

Name _____

Scrambled Words

Unscramble the letters in parentheses to spell a word that makes sense in each sentence.

1. Cookies don't _____ to me; I prefer candy.
   (papale)

2. The desert is a good place to see a _____ .
   (saccut)

3. When is Halley's _____ supposed to appear again?
   (tomec)

4. Take a deep breath and then _____ .
   (elahex)

5. Place the _____ in the can before pouring the gasoline.
   (nenulf)

6. I am learning how to do _____ tricks.
   (gicam)

7. "I don't have a _____ thing to wear!" complained Jill.
   (gilens)

8. An _____ home is made of sun-dried bricks.
   (bedoa)

9. Is _____ ice cream your favorite?
   (alaviln)

10. This word scramble is _____ too difficult for me.
    (splimy)

11. Mother set the china on the _____ tablecloth.
    (ennil)

12. I am _____ for chocolate chip cookies.
    (gurhyn)

13. I wish you much _____ on your new job.
    (usseccs)

14. How many people are employed at that _____ ?
    (tarfocy)

15. Hold your breath to help get rid of the _____ .
    (spuchic)

Perfect Pairs 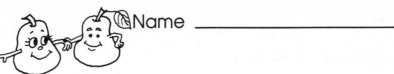 Name _____

Some words just seem to belong together. See how many word pairs you can make by using words from Column B to complete the phrases in Column A.

Example: salt and **pepper**

Column A

1. Rocky and _____
2. cup and _____
3. pencil and _____
4. cookies and _____
5. cats and _____
6. rock and _____
7. hammer and _____
8. Batman and _____
9. mustard and _____
10. song and _____
11. shoes and _____
12. hat and _____
13. ham and _____
14. peanut butter and _____
15. bacon and _____
16. Jack and _____
17. night and _____
18. table and _____
19. comb and _____
20. bread and _____
21. apples and _____
22. fruits and _____
23. bride and _____

Column B

brush
Bullwinkle
butter
chairs
cheese
coat
dance
day
dogs
eggs
vegetables
groom
jelly
Jill
ketchup
milk
nails
oranges
paper
Robin
roll
saucer
socks

Name _____

Babes in Arms

Situation: It's five o'clock p.m., and you are babysitting for a family with three young children. Before the adults leave, what questions should you ask?

Number these questions in importance, listing 1 as the most important.
Cross out any questions you feel are inappropriate.

____ Does your stereo system work well?

____ How much does the job pay?

____ How long do you expect to be out?

____ Where is your telephone?

____ Are you expecting any phone calls?

____ Do you have a VCR?

____ Do I have to wash the dishes?

____ What is an appropriate bedtime for the children?

____ Where do you keep snacks?

____ May I invite a friend over to stay with me?

____ How much money do you make?

____ How might I reach you in an emergency?

____ When was the last time you vacuumed your carpet?

____ What shall I feed the children?

____ Has your dog been tested for rabies?

____ May I share some candy with the children?

Comment on either a question you crossed out as inappropriate or a question you rated very high.

_____

_____

On another sheet of paper, provide a list of ten tips for prospective babysitters.

Ride with the Wind

Name _____

Size: 22-inch frame
Weight: 37 lbs.
Tire Size: 26" x 1 3/8"

Tire Pressure: 65 lbs
Gears: 3

The tires provide good grip on both wet and dry road surfaces. The narrow tires decrease friction and allow for greater speed.

The side basket is useful for carrying a wide variety of items from newspapers to groceries.

The frame is lighter than most bikes of this time. It is painted maroon or "icky brick."

With the bike's three gears, the rider can easily adjust pedal speed to match the road conditions.

The streamers and raccoon tail are just two ways for a rider to give her or his individual touch.

When these caliper brake levers are depressed, "shoes" or pads on both sides of the wheel rim press in to bring the wheel to a halt.

Use the diagram above to answer these questions about Addie's bike.

1. Why does Addie's bike go faster than other children's bikes? _____

_____

2. Where can Addie carry her flowers? _____

3. How many gears does Addie's bike have? _____

4. Where does the raccoon tail hang? _____

5. What is the color of the bike? _____

6. How do the brakes work? _____

_____

7. How heavy is this bike? _____

8. How many more pounds of pressure are in Addie's bike tires than are in Carla Mae's which has 41 pounds of pressure? _____

9. Does this bike have a chain guard? _____ Why does this help? _____

_____

10. How is this bike different from many bikes today? _____

_____

Name _____

Jumping to Conclusions

Write your own conclusion to each situation in the space provided.

Situations   Conclusions

1. Your brother just turned five. He has
   chocolate all over his face and he
   looks sheepish.
   _____
   _____
   _____

2. Your parents are gone. It's 9:00 p.m. and
   you hear a thump and a cry.
   _____
   _____
   _____

3. You are making a cake. You hear the
   sound of beating wings and a thin,
   shrill squeal.
   _____
   _____
   _____

4. You are outdoors after dark during summer
   vacation. You see a sudden flash of light
   and smell a smoky odor.
   _____
   _____
   _____

5. One morning at school you see your friend
   looking dreamy-eyed. On her paper, she
   writes SW + SD.
   _____
   _____
   _____

6. A large column of clouds appears
   in the western sky, and a strong wind
   starts blowing.
   _____
   _____
   _____

7. You hear a noise in your parents' bedroom.
   Then you see a broken window and a
   baseball rolling across the floor.
   _____
   _____
   _____

8. In the classroom next door you see a desk
   tipped over, text books scattered, and one
   boy crying.
   _____
   _____
   _____

Challenge: Describe a new situation on another paper. Include four
important details and make up a conclusion in your head. Then let a friend
read what you've written and guess your conclusion. Does your friend draw
the same conclusion?

It's Greek to Me

Name _____

Anti – is a prefix from the Greek word **anti** which means *against.*
Look up each word in the dictionary and write its definition.

1. antibiotic _____

2. antidote _____

3. antiknock _____

4. antipathy _____

5. antiperspirant _____

6. antiseptic _____

Answer the questions in complete sentences.

1. If a person were accidentally poisoned, would he or she be given an
   antidote or an antiseptic? _____
   _____

2. If you strongly disliked fish, would you have an antibiotic or an antipathy
   toward it? _____
   _____

3. Which would a person more likely use on his or her body: an antiperspirant
   or an antipathy? _____
   _____

4. To prevent infection from a cut, would you use an antiperspirant or an
   antiseptic? _____
   _____

5. Is penicillin an example of an antibiotic or an antiseptic? _____
   _____

Name _____

Borrowed from Abroad

Many words in the English language have come from other languages. For example, **garage** comes from a French word meaning *protect*.

Use a dictionary to find the language from which each of the following words was taken. Write the name of the language and a short meaning for each word.

1. gimlet: _____

   _____

2. hacienda: _____

   _____

3. javelin: _____

   _____

4. jerky: _____

   _____

5. morgue: _____

   _____

6. terrazzo: _____

   _____

Answer the following questions in complete sentences.

1. Which two words above are from Spanish?

   _____

2. Which two words are French in origin?

   _____

3. Which word is the name of something to eat?

   _____

4. Where would you likely find terrazzo – in a morgue or a hacienda?

   _____

5. Which might an athlete use: a javelin or a gimlet?

   _____

Name _____

My Own Secret Kingdom

Create your own kingdom by following these directions. Use a large sheet of drawing paper.

1. Draw a directional compass in the southeast corner of the paper.

2. Draw your castle in the northeast corner of the kingdom. Add plenty of details.

3. There is a river that runs north and south through your kingdom. Color the river blue and write its name beside it.

4. Two bridges cross the river. One crosses the northern section and one crosses the southern section. Draw them.

5. Draw a moat around your castle.

6. Add a large forest south of the castle.

7. Horses and chariots are stabled in a barn surrounded by a corral. The corral is between the forest and the river.

8. There are four lookout towers protecting your land. Place one in each of the corners of the kingdom. Add different colored flags at the top of each.

9. A pond lies in the southeast part of the kingdom, west of the river and east of the tower and directional compass.

10. Your guardian dog, _____ (name), is napping by the pond. He is a _____ (breed).

11. Secret evergreen groves are north of the pond. In the center of the grove is a meeting place built with rocks.

12. In the northwest corner by the tower, draw your kingdom's crest or symbol.

13. Now add four more features to your kingdom. List them here.

   _____

   _____

   _____

   _____

14. Name your kingdom.

   _____

Name _____

Pictures from the Palace

Fold a piece of drawing paper into four parts and draw a picture for each descriptive paragraph below. Number the pictures to match the paragraphs.

1. The Emperor sat on a golden throne. The huge chair was taller than any man and carved with dragons and snakes. Multicolored jewels were embedded in the gold. The Emperor wore a royal blue and gold robe. His hat resembled a blue graduation cap with several strands of multicolored beads hanging from the brim. His shoes were black. He held a paper scroll in both hands.

2. The Princess was beautiful. Her long black hair was knotted into several sections. A pink butterfly hair clip was fastened off to one side. She had black, almond-shaped eyes and rosy cheeks. Her flowered pink, green, and yellow silk gown was tied with a green sash. Pink slippers adorned her feet. She carried a pink fan decorated with Chinese nature scenes.

3. The palace kitchen had a long wooden table in the middle of the room, filled with steaming pots of food. The back wall was made of brick. Long-handled copper and silver pans and skillets hung near the top of this brick wall. Huge ovens covered the left wall. On the right, several cooks chopped and diced fresh vegetables. Vegetable baskets lined the floor.

4. The summer palace was small, built high up on bamboo poles. The roof was made of straw and bamboo with upward curving edges. Its long, vertical windows were covered with paper and colorful Chinese murals. A balcony was built around the outside.

Name _____

Hamsterology

Carefully read the following paragraph about golden hamsters. Then follow the directions.

Native to Central Asia and Europe, the golden hamster is a nocturnal animal that makes its home in complex tunnels under the ground. It is a rodent, related to mice and rats. It eats mostly vegetables, grains and seeds which it stores in its cheek pouches to take back to its tunnel. In the wild, the hamster will also prey upon small animals and birds. It grows to be about 5 inches long and has a short tail. It weighs 4 to 5 ounces and has golden brown fur. The female breeds when she is seven to eight weeks old, producing litters of six to seven babies. Golden hamsters make good pets. Their life span is two to three years.

Directions:
1. Circle in yellow every "hamster" in the paragraph.
2. Make blue boxes around the places where golden hamsters originated.
3. Underline in red the plant foods that golden hamsters eat.
4. Draw an orange **X** over the animals a hamster will eat.
5. Draw a purple, wiggly line under the word that means hamsters sleep during the day and are awake at night.
6. Put a green **R** over the word that tells what type of animal the hamster is.
7. Draw a brown star over the place where hamsters store their food.
8. Make a pink line below the hamster's habitat.
9. Draw a red line on top of the word that describes their tails.
10. Circle in red the number of babies most female hamsters have.
11. Underline in black how long hamsters live.
12. Draw an orange box around how long hamsters grow to be.
13. Put a green heart around the verb that as a noun means an animal eaten by a meat-eating animal.
14. Draw a brown, wiggly line under the color of the hamster's fur.

Challenge: Use the encyclopedia to write a report on field mice, gerbils, kangaroo rats or guinea pigs, comparing them to golden hamsters. Share your findings with the rest of the class.

Name _____

Answering Questions

Within each group draw a line from each question on the left to the answer that matches it best on the right.

Where will you stay if the hotel can't take you?
Who has the lead part in the play?
Why didn't you complete your homework last night?
When was the last time you saw the gerbil?
What time do you want to meet?
How many people will be at the game?

Whenever is best for you.
I had to go to my grandmother's birthday dinner.
I'll make that decision then.
If it's raining, there will be very few.
They are posting the roles after lunch.
Last Friday when he climbed into the wastebasket.

Are there any holes in that sieve?
Why are the dishes still in the sink?
Would you show me how to play?
How well do you know him?
What did you tell her?
Why didn't you go to the concert?

I was too tired.
He has lived next to me for two years.
It's a secret.
It's in perfect condition.
I will when there is time.
Dad said he'd do them.

Why aren't you eating dinner?
What is the boy saying?
Why isn't the new boy playing kickball?
When will it be ready?
Did anyone send a thank-you note to our room mother?
Does she have good handwriting?

I mailed it to her yesterday.
It is supposed to be available now.
We had a late lunch.
He's giving the score.
It's the best I've seen.
He doesn't know how.

Has anyone heard anything about the new play?
How are the flowers?
Why did Tom stay after school?
How old is the antique dresser?
Is there any cake left?
Where did you find the ball?

They need water.
The teacher wanted to see him.
Jean said it was very long.
Barbara finished the crumbs.
It was caught in the fence.
It was my great grandmother's.

Name _____

What's the Point?

Locate and underline the main idea in each group of sentences.

1. Bert returned with half a baked ham, butter, and a jug of milk. Martin had not eaten since the night before last. Laura set the table for their late night snack.

2. When Laura woke up, Martin looked like a different boy. He was wearing a pair of Bert's pants and one of his old shirts. He looked as though he had taken a bath.

3. Humming, Laura began to scrape and stack the dishes. She put water on the stove to heat. Laura enjoyed working in the kitchen.

4. The sheriff and slave hunters stormed through the house. Laura heard the crash of a chair. They searched every room and closet. The men were looking for a fugitive slave.

5. The field behind the vegetable garden was aglow with goldenrod and wild flowers. The autumn sun shone brightly in the yard. Laura looked out the window. She longed to go outside on this beautiful autumn day.

Now write one detail sentence from each group on the lines below.

1. _____
2. _____
3. _____
4. _____
5. _____

Name _____

Camp Rules

Donald, Arnold and Jack are all at Camp Explore-It-All this week. They think camp is a lot of fun, but they have also learned from their instructors that there are some very important rules all campers must obey so that everyone has a good time.

All campers had to take swimming tests to see what depth of water they will be allowed to swim in. Donald and Jack passed the advanced test and can swim in the deep water. Arnold, however, only passed the intermediate test. He is supposed to stay in the area where the water is waist deep. When it is time to swim, Arnold decides to sneak into advanced with Donald and Jack. After all, he has been swimming in deep water for three years. No way is he going to stay in the shallow water with the sissies.

Donald and Jack don't think Arnold should come into the deep water, but they can't tell him anything. So the boys jump into the water and start swimming and playing. Fifteen minutes later, Arnold is yelling, "Help!" He swam out too far and is too tired to make it back in. The lifeguard jumps in and pulls him out. Everyone stops to see what is happening. Arnold feels very foolish.

Check.

The main idea of this story is . . .

☐ Arnold ends up feeling foolish.　　　　☐ Camp is fun.

☐ All campers take swimming tests.　　　☐ Rules are made for good reasons.

☐ You can learn a lot from instructors.　　☐ Rules are made to be broken.

Underline.

Arnold got himself into a(n) _____ situation.

　　amusing　　　　　　funny　　　　　　　dangerous　　　　　ambiguous

Circle.

Arnold thought the guys in the shallow area were (bullies/sissies). However, he should have (stayed with them/gone to the advanced area).

Write.

What lesson do you think Arnold learned? _____

_____

What do you think the other campers learned? _____

_____

Name _____

From Whose Point of View?

Read each sentence below. Decide if it is the first or third person's point of view. If it is a first person's point of view, rewrite the sentence to make it a third person's point of view. If it is a third person's point of view, rewrite it to make it a first person's point of view.

1. I wanted to tell Anh and Thant the secret of our leaving, but I had given my word.

   _____

2. The grandmother did not want to go aboard the boat.

   _____

3. The people on shore were pushing to get on the deck of the boat.

   _____

4. Though I had worked many days in the rice paddies watching planes fly over, I never thought I'd be on one.

   _____

5. Loi made a net from pieces of string and caught a turtle with his new device.

   _____

6. I know of a place where we can wash our clothes.

   _____

7. The officer looked at them with great interest.

   _____

8. When I looked into the harbor, I could see the shape of the sampan boats.

   _____

9. This is my duck and I choose to share it with everyone on the boat for the celebration of Tet.

   _____

Name _____

Make Your Mark Here

Use the proofreader marks shown to the right to correct the sentences below.

apostrophe ˇ	end marks ⊙ ? !
quotation marks " "	comma ∧
capitalize ≡	

1. lucy wailed i can t go to the party i told everyone what a great costume i was going to have

2. carla said okay meet me at my place the basement apartment of the eucalyptus arms do you know where that is

3. are you a real vampire lucy demanded

4. hold it lucy i dropped my fangs down your neck mumbled the embarrassed knievel

5. knievel howled don t you have more that s the best chocolate cupcake i ever ate why it s got everything

6. stay right there squeaked the rabbit i ll get you something don t move

7. where s the tv questioned susannah looking around i m sure i heard one before we came in

8. mr mordecai rubbed his hands and smiled shyly i ll be back he whispered then he vanished

9. i m pretty sure knievel got the poisoned candy when he was with us susannah said i don t think he had done any trick-or-treating before he met us

10. forgot my key shouted aunt louise how are you girl where s that niece of mine

Draw a picture to go with one of the quotes above. Write the quote next to it.

Quote: _____

_____

_____

Name _____

Fish Facts

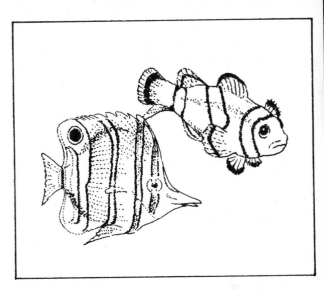

All of the fourth graders in Miss Freed's class did reports on animals. Jackie did hers on fish. She learned so much about these fascinating animals. She can't wait to share the information with her class.

Jackie didn't know much about fish when she started. She has since learned that fish are vertebrates because they have backbones. She was also amazed to learn that there are more kinds of fish than all other kinds of water and land vertebrates put together. The kinds of fish differ so greatly in shape, color and size that Jackie can hardly believe they all belong to the same group of animals.

Some fish, Jackie found out, look like lumpy rocks. Others look like wriggly worms. Some can blow themselves up like balloons, and others are as flat as pancakes. Fish can be all the colors of the rainbow, and also striped and polka-dotted. The one fish Jackie definitely never wants to run into is the stonefish. Though it is small, it can kill a person in a few minutes. The subject of fish turned out to be a lot more interesting than Jackie ever imagined.

Circle.

Fish are (invertebrates/vertebrates) because they (do not have/have) backbones.

Underline.

Fish differ greatly in . . .

taste.   size.   shape.   color.   length.

Check.

Fish can be . . .

☐ lumpy.   ☐ depressed.   ☐ colorful.   ☐ striped.

☐ smart.   ☐ flat.   ☐ polka-dotted.   ☐ sad.

Write.

Describe the kinds of fish found in aquariums. Use adjectives relating to size, shape and color.

_____

_____

What kinds of fish have you eaten? _____

_____

Name _____

Mixed-Up Recipe

In a story, Laura decides to make a batch of homemade applesauce. Below is a recipe she may have followed. However, by looking at the directions, it is easy to see that something is mixed-up.

Applesauce

12 to 16 medium pears
3 cups vinegar
1 to 1 1/2 cups of flour

Directions:

Add water to pan. Peel and slice the apples into quarters. Simmer over low heat for 20 to 30 minutes or until soft. Stir occasionally. Stir in sugar and heat through. Add 1 teaspoon cinnamon if you wish.

Makes 12 servings.

Correct Directions:

_____

_____

_____

_____

_____

_____

_____

_____

Name _____

Weekend Fun

Number each group of sentences in the correct order.

____ I had a hamburger, but everyone else had a salad.

____ My parents picked us up after the movie.

____ A horse-drawn carriage took us for a ride through the park to the zoo.

____ I didn't buy any popcorn during the movie.

____ We spent a couple of hours at the zoo before we took a bus to meet our friends for lunch.

____ We walked to the movie after lunch.

____ A wind lifted the kite high in the air.

____ Father let out the string while I ran with the kite.

____ The park was crowded with people flying kites when we got there.

____ We found a spot to fly the kite away from the other people.

____ Father and I took a kite to the park.

____ We had to tie a tail on the kite before it was ready to be flown.

____ I took an atlas home with me on Friday.

____ I wrote down important facts about each country.

____ I turned in my report on Monday morning.

____ After I watched cartoons Saturday morning, I looked up England and Germany in the atlas.

____ I wrote a report about England and Germany from my notes.

____ Friday morning the teacher said our reports on different countries were due on Monday.

____ We decided what kind of cones we wanted while standing in line.

____ Larry fell down and the cone flew into the air.

____ While walking down the street with our cones, a large dog charged Larry.

____ There was a long line at the ice-cream shop when Larry and I got there.

____ The dog caught the cone and ran away with it.

____ We stood behind the last person in line.

Name _____

Putting Them in Order

Rewrite the sentences in each paragraph below in the correct order.

There was a loud crack and the ice Elizabeth was on began to sink. Her mother warned her not to go too far out on the ice, but she forgot. Elizabeth asked her mother if she could go skating on the pond. Elizabeth's cries for help were answered, and some other skaters pulled her to safety.

_____

_____

_____

_____

_____

_____

_____

When Marcy and Tony were walking home from school he suggested they go a different way. The stream twisted and turned, and it eventually led them back to school. They followed the stream in the direction they thought would take them home. They cut across a farmer's field and down a hill to a stream.

_____

_____

_____

_____

_____

_____

_____

_____

• Write what comes next.

VI   VOI   VOIVI   _____

_____

Name _____

Moving Time

David's family is buying a new house. Their old house is just too small. However, there are two houses that they like equally as much. The first one is in the neighborhood in which they live now. David's family would still be around all their same friends, and David could still ride to school with his best friend. The only problem is that this house doesn't have a playroom where David and his friends could go, which was one of the reasons for moving. It also needs a lot of painting, which David's dad is not happy about. But, it's a good buy.

The second house is across town. David could still go to the same school, but he wouldn't be close to his old friends. This house is really big with a huge playroom, and it has just been freshly painted. Even though it costs more than the other one, it's still a good deal.

So now David's family has to decide if they want less room, more work and the same neighborhood, or more room and less work. Both houses have 3 bedrooms and big family rooms, so his parents are happy about that. What a decision!

Underline.

David and his family have found two houses that they like . . .

    equally as well.   almost as much as their old one.   in his neighborhood.   a little.

Circle.

David would want to buy the second house except that it . . .

    has a big playroom.   needs to be painted.   isn't close to his friends.

Check.

The first house is different from the second one because it . . .

☐ has three bedrooms.   ☐ has a family room.

☐ is in David's same neighborhood.   ☐ needs to be painted.

☐ doesn't have a play room.   ☐ is a good buy.

Write.

List at least 3 reasons David's family is having a hard time deciding which house to buy.

1. _____

2. _____

3. _____

If you ever had to move, how would you feel about it? List five positive things and five negative things about moving.

_____

Name _____

Yesterday and Today

Read each sentence. If it tells about a past event, write **THEN** on the line. If it tells about an event that is happening in the present, write **NOW** on the line.

_____ The forest fire is burning out of control.

_____ We sent money to help feed and clothe the flood victims.

_____ The river rushing past my window keeps me up at night.

_____ I am taking a series of tennis lessons on Wednesdays.

_____ Glaciers covered over one-fifth of the world.

_____ The student council sets rules for the student body to follow.

_____ I bought enough glue to last a lifetime.

_____ The third grade had the best attendance record.

_____ The picnic was cancelled because of the heavy downpour.

_____ I belong to the scouts.

_____ The forest floor is covered with ferns and moss.

_____ The Hopi Indians live within the Navajo Indian nation.

_____ My aunt and uncle stayed with us for a week.

_____ The day started out sunny.

_____ My grade in penmanship indicates great improvement.

_____ I baked banana bread for the room mother's tea.

_____ I watch television every night for an hour before going to bed.

_____ Melissa is the fastest runner in the class.

_____ I made a deposit in my savings account.

_____ I cut my birthday cake after I blew out all the candles.

_____ The patrol boys and girls help younger children cross the street.

_____ The snow is continuing to fall.

_____ I save my pennies for rainy days.

_____ The chandelier swayed during the earthquake.

_____ We fastened our seat belts before father started the car.

_____ The native dancers' clothes were colorful.

• Write what comes next.

BA   ED   IH   ON   _____

Name _____

Keeping in Touch

On the lines next to the letter, write the correct category **(who, what, when, where** or **why)** for each underlined word or phrase in Genevieve's letter.

Dear Mom and Dad,

I have been very busy (1) <u>here in the United States</u> taking care of Lucas and the twins. (2) <u>A few weeks ago</u> (3) <u>Lucas and his friends</u> (4) <u>climbed up onto the roof</u> of the Cotts' home (5) <u>to get a better view of the neighborhood</u>. (6) <u>He</u> has spent a lot of time with me (7) <u>since then</u>.

(8) <u>Today,</u> I (9) <u>taught him how to dance</u> (10) <u>so he can have a girlfriend</u> (11) <u>when he gets older</u>. (12) <u>Julio</u> danced with us (13) <u>in the living room,</u> too. (14) <u>I</u> miss you both.

Love,

Genevieve

1. _____

2. _____

3. _____

4. _____

5. _____

6. _____

7. _____

8. _____

9. _____

10. _____

11. _____

12. _____

13. _____

14. _____

A NOW ... D   Write an essay titled, "The Importance of Being Trustworthy." Share it with your classmates and discuss what each of you thinks about *being* trustworthy and *expecting* trust from others.

Name _____

Are You Mixed Up?

I see Good Grades in Your Future!

Unscramble the letters on the left to create words which match the meanings on the right.

	Word	**Word Meaning**
1. degfti	_____	To move restlessly or nervously
2. spygy	_____	A member of a wandering people believed to have come out of India
3. pureto	_____	A group of actors or dancers
4. tayjun	_____	Having a self-confident manner
5. nastioyrta	_____	Not capable of being moved
6. caottitep	_____	A woman's slip or underskirt
7. ever	_____	To swerve
8. rylub	_____	Heavy, strong and muscular
9. merba	_____	A brownish-yellow color
10. laiggnl	_____	Very annoying

Write sentences using four of the words you unscrambled.

1. _____

_____

2. _____

_____

3. _____

_____

4. _____

_____

Name _____

Say It Again

Add a letter to each word to make a new word. Use letters from the Letter Bank and the clues to help. The letter may be added anywhere to the word.

Example:

word		letter		new word	clue
hove	+	l	=	hovel	a hut

Word	Letter	New Word	Clue
gain	_____	_____	Small seed
rate	_____	_____	Used in fireplaces
par	_____	_____	A fruit
rip	_____	_____	Ready for harvest
sing	_____	_____	To burn at the edges
tick	_____	_____	Slow witted
pear	_____	_____	Weapon that can be thrown
ad	_____	_____	Fuss or bother
mat	_____	_____	Important to sailing ships
boar	_____	_____	Two-by-four
die	_____	_____	Urgent
men	_____	_____	Sign of a future event
yarn	_____	_____	To want
tool	_____	_____	Place to sit
toe	_____	_____	To carry
single	_____	_____	Roofing material

Letter Bank
d   e   e   e   e   g   h   h   o   o   r   r   s   s   t

Name _____

Guide-Worthy Words

Use a pencil to write ten vocabulary words from the Word Bank under each of the guide words. Remember to put them in alphabetical order.

Reflection	Syllable

Abrupt	Authority

Babyhood	Crest

Defense	Exult

Word Bank

burrow	commence	cordial	corporal	accustom
accidentally	barracks	barometer	explosive	schoolmaster
stealth	allow	calamity	stance	defiant
epidemic	ancient	scowl	discard	ammunition
disturbance	subside	salute	reindeer	consternation
assign	demoralize	disposition	appoint	beneficial
resolute	enormous	ashamed	retort	entirely
earthenware	additional	commotion	almanac	surpass

Name _____

Hey, Look Me Over

Use the dictionary pronunciations to answer the questions below.

concoction (kən kok´ shən) *noun.* something prepared by mixing ingredients.

1. Which syllable is accented? _____

2. How many syllables have a "schwa" sound? _____

3. How many syllables are in "concoction?" _____

hover (huv´ ər) *verb. hovered hovering.* to flutter over or about.

1. How many syllables are in *hover*? _____

2. Which syllable is accented? _____

3. How many syllables are found in *hovering*? _____

eternity (i tur´ nə tē) *noun.* an endless length of time.

1. Which syllable has a long "e" sound? _____

2. Which syllable is accented? _____

3. How many syllables are in *eternity*? _____

honeysuckle (hun´ ē suk´ əl) *noun.* a climbing shrub with pleasant-smelling flowers.

1. How many syllables are in "honeysuckle?" _____

2. Which syllable has a primary accent? _____

3. Which syllable has a secondary accent? _____

4. Which syllable has a "schwa" sound? _____

5. Which two syllables have the same vowel sound? _____

Challenge: Write the phonetic spellings of these words.

audible _____   camouflage _____

pneumonia _____   municipal _____

supernatural _____

Name _____

Weird Words

Use a dictionary to help you answer the questions using complete sentences.

1. Which would you use to treat a sore throat: a **gargoyle** or a **gargle**?

_____

2. Which might be used on a gravestone: an **epiphyte** or an **epitaph**?

_____

3. Which is an instrument: **calligraphy** or a **calliope**?

_____

4. Would a building have a **gargoyle** or an **argyle** on it?

_____

5. If you trick someone, do you **bamboozle** him or **barcarole** him?

_____

6. if you studied handwriting, would you learn **calligraphy** or **cajolery**?

_____

7. What would a gondolier sing: a **barcarole** or an **argyle**?

_____

8. If you tried to coax someone, would you be using **cajolery** or **calamity**?

_____

9. Which might you wear: **argyles** or **calliopes**?

_____

10. In Venice, Italy, would you travel in a **gondola** or a **calamity**?

_____

Name _____

From the Diary of Milo

Use a dictionary to help you circle the correct definition for each underlined word. In the space, write the dictionary page number.

_____ 1. We saw <u>debris</u> scattered everywhere after the fortress fell.

    smoke   rubble   vegetation

_____ 2. The beautiful island <u>beckoned</u> us to its rich bounty.

    warned   darkened   lured

_____ 3. The strange creature <u>doffed</u> his hat and welcomed us to Digitopolis.

    pounded   washed   tipped

_____ 4. We ducked our heads to avoid the cave's <u>stalactites</u>.

    pitfalls   icicle-shaped mineral   dripping water
                      deposits

_____ 5. The soup's pot loosed a <u>savory</u> steam into the air.

    boiling   safe   appetizing

_____ 6. If I continue to add ones, I could count into <u>infinity</u>.

    endlessness   a secret chamber   wee hours of the night

_____ 7. The <u>sheer</u> mountain walls made climbing difficult for our traveling band.

    icy   very steep   sharply spiked

_____ 8. The giant whined <u>peevishly</u> when we asked him to assist us.

    crossly   weakly   foolishly

_____ 9. As the demons drew near, we noted their <u>loathsome</u> odors.

    powerful   angry   disgusting

_____ 10. The ugly demon, whose <u>bulbous</u> nose honked constantly, fell from his perch.

    reddened   wart-covered   bulb-shaped

Name _____

Hang Tough, Student

Write the letter of the resource book which would best help you answer each question.

A. general encyclopedia

C. science encyclopedia

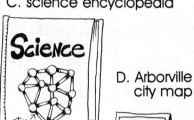

B. dictionary

E. medical encyclopedia

D. Arborville city map

F. Little League Baseball regulations booklet

_____ 1. What is a *coati*?

_____ 2. What does a geologist do?

_____ 3. May a runner lead off a base in Little League?

_____ 4. When did the game of soccer originate?

_____ 5. What is the easiest way to get to Sampson Park from the expressway?

_____ 6. Would you say that Mr. and Mrs. Mather were *overtly tactless* with Jim Anderson?

_____ 7. How large is the baseball strike zone?

_____ 8. What causes acne?

_____ 9. How is a lunar eclipse formed?

_____ 10. How far is it from Ferdon Street to the Clinton School diamond?

_____ 11. What are some symptoms of leukemia?

_____ 12. How many states border Michigan?

_____ 13. How long must a pitcher rest between games pitched?

_____ 14. How many calories are found in a meal consisting of two slices of salami on whole wheat bread, a 2-ounce wedge of Swiss cheese, one apple and 14 ounces of milk?

Challenge   Answer one of the above questions using a resource book.

Question Number	Source Used	Page in Source	Answer
_____		_____	

Jimminy Cricket!

Underline the key word in each question. Then write the encyclopedia volume number you would use to find information to answer each question.

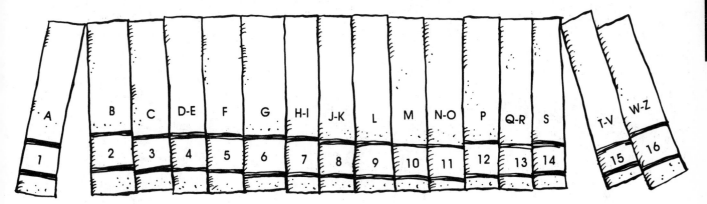

_____ 1. How are cattle branded?

_____ 2. What were some names of early American airplanes?

_____ 3. How should you care for your hair?

_____ 4. How large can a collie become?

_____ 5. Who invented the x-ray machine?

_____ 6. When did Vermont become a state?

_____ 7. What is the life of a cowboy like?

_____ 8. How many ways may a ball be kicked in the game of football?

_____ 9. Which state mines the most tin?

_____ 10. Where was tobacco first grown?

_____ 11. Name the different parts of the corn plant.

_____ 12. Where can daisies be found?

_____ 13. Do tornadoes occur in New England?

_____ 14. When were knickers popular in the United States?

_____ 15. How many bones are found in the human foot?

<u>Challenge</u>   Look up three of the key words from above in an encyclopedia index. How many references are made to it?

_____ (word) _____ (number of references)

_____ (word) _____ (number of references)

_____ (word) _____ (number of references)

Name _____

Furoshiki Bundle

Sadako's mother wrapped all of Sadako's favorite foods in a *furoshiki* bundle. The bundle contained an egg roll, rice, chicken, plums, and bean cakes. List the heading under which you might find information on these foods in a recipe book.

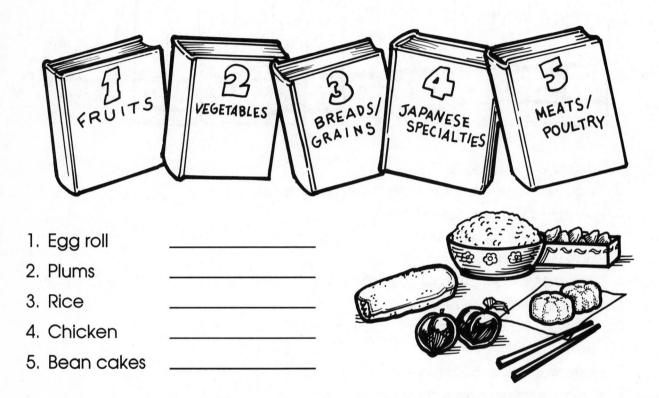

1. Egg roll   _____
2. Plums   _____
3. Rice   _____
4. Chicken   _____
5. Bean cakes   _____

Now, list five foods that someone might bring to you in a *furoshiki* bundle. Then list the heading under which each would be found in a recipe book.

1. _____
2. _____
3. _____
4. _____
5. _____

Name _____

Mumps, Measles, and Other Diseases

Index Sample

diptheria
    description, 17
    contagion, 19
    recovery rate, 20

measles
    rubella, 61-63
    three-day, 64-65
    treatment, 68

mumps
    description, 72
    prevention, 75

scarlet fever
    cause, 85
    danger, 87
    prevention, 88

small pox
    history, 94-95
    contagion, 96
    prevention, 98

tetanus
    cause, 103
    incubation period, 105

whooping cough
    symptoms, 123
    incubation period, 105
    treatment, 127-128

Use the index sample to write the page numbers you would turn to in order to answer each question below.

_____ 1. How are people treated for whooping cough?

_____ 2. How did small pox affect people 400 years ago?

_____ 3. What is rubella?

_____ 4. How can mumps be prevented?

_____ 5. What are some of the dangers of scarlet fever?

_____ 6. How quickly does a person recover from diptheria?

_____ 7. What is mumps?

_____ 8. How can scarlet fever be prevented?

_____ 9. Is small pox highly contagious?

_____ 10. How does a person become infected with tetanus?

Challenge: Compare the dangers of these seven diseases today. Which diseases are still serious threats in North America? Which are very rare?

Name _____

Place Value

$$1\,,\,2\quad3\quad4\,,\,5\quad6\quad7$$

↑ millions
↑ hundred-thousands
↑ ten-thousands
↑ thousands
↑ hundreds
↑ tens
↑ ones

1. The number 8,672,019 has:

   _____ thousands   _____ millions

   _____ ten   _____ ones

   _____ hundred-thousands   _____ ten-thousands

                    _____ hundreds

2. What number has:

   6 ones   9 tens   8 thousands

   3 millions   7 hundreds   5 hundred-thousands

                   4 ten-thousands

   The number is _____ .

3. The number 6,792,510 has:

   _____ ten-thousands   _____ ones

   _____ millions   _____ thousands

   _____ hundreds   _____ ten

                    _____ hundred-thousands

4. What number has:

   5 millions   6 thousands   4 ones

   3 tens   1 hundred   8 ten-thousands

                   0 hundred-thousands

   The number is _____ .

Name _____

The First State

What state is known as the first state? Follow the directions below to find out.

1. Put an A above number 2 if 31,842 rounded to the nearest thousand is 31,000.

2. Put an E above number 2 if 62 rounded to the nearest ten is 60.

3. Put an R above number 7 if 4,234 rounded to the nearest hundred is 4,200.

4. Put an L above number 3 if 677 rounded to the nearest hundred is 600.

5. Put an E above number 5 if 344 rounded to the nearest ten is 350.

6. Put an A above number 4 if 5,599 rounded to the nearest thousand is 6,000.

7. Put an A above number 6 if 1,549 rounded to the nearest hundred is 1,500.

8. Put a W above number 2 if 885 rounded to the nearest hundred is 800.

9. Put an E above number 8 if 521 rounded to the nearest ten is 520.

10. Put an R above number 6 if 74 rounded to the nearest ten is 80.

11. Put an L above number 3 if 3,291 rounded to the nearest thousand is 3,000.

12. Put an R above number 4 if 248 rounded to the nearest hundred is 300.

13. Put a D above number 1 if 615 rounded to the nearest ten is 620.

14. Put a W above number 1 if 188 rounded to the nearest ten is 200.

15. Put a W above number 5 if 6,817 rounded to the nearest thousand is 7,000.

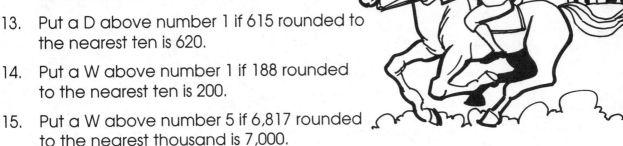

___ ___ ___ ___ ___ ___ ___ ___
 1   2   3   4   5   6   7   8

Name _____

Underwater Addition

$$446 + 489$$

$$476 + 527$$

$$509 + 375$$

$$708 + 507$$

$$438 + 419$$

$$334 + 278$$

$$251 + 368$$

$$464 + 456$$

$$589 + 322$$

$$288 + 377$$

$$811 + 386$$

$$445 + 476$$

$$831 + 483$$

$$810 + 428$$

$$531 + 249$$

$$714 + 185$$

$$609 + 475$$

$$319 + 287$$

$$767 + 246$$

$$230 + 284$$

$$211 + 396$$

$$911 + 427$$

Name _____

Grand Prix Addition

Solve each problem. Beginning at 7,000, run through this racetrack to find out the path the race car took. When you reach 7,023, you're ready to exit and gas up for the next race.

3792 + 3225 *7017*	1838 + 5178 *6916*	3767 + 3248 *7015*	1874 + 5140 *7014*	4809 + 2204 *7013*
1536 + 5482 *7018*	3561 + 3458 *7019*	3771 + 4213 *7984*	2435 + 5214 *649*	1725 + 5287 *7012*
1157 + 6412 *75*	4162 + 2858 *7020*	4853 + 2156 *09*	4123 + 2887	5879 + 1132
3544 + 3478	1273 + 5748	3589 + 3419	5218 + 1789	4658 + 2348
5997 + 1026	5289 + 1713	3698 + 3305	4756 + 2248	4248 + 2757
4853 + 2147	2216 + 4785	3720 + 3698	3612 + 3552	1687 + 5662

Published by Frank Schaffer Publications. Copyright protected.   91   0-7682-3794-7 *Skills & Practice Gr. 4*

MATH

Name _____

Fishy Problems

Solve each problem. Locate the fish in the aquarium that has the sum for each
problem floating around in its stomach. Write the letter to match each answer in
the box above each problem.

□	□	□	□	□
1. 31,604 + 29,217	2. 47,215 + 23,094	3. 92,185 + 18,293	4. 20,815 + 19,903	5. 49,248 + 27,181

□	□	□	□	□
6. 53,614 + 29,193	7. 21,385 + 23,492	8. 45,218 + 12,649	9. 64,218 + 13,924	10. 81,346 + 13,497

□	□	□	□	□
11. 30,249 + 28,926	12. 42,618 + 34,193	13. 50,006 + 29,999	14. 26,149 + 81,224	15. 76,415 + 21,248

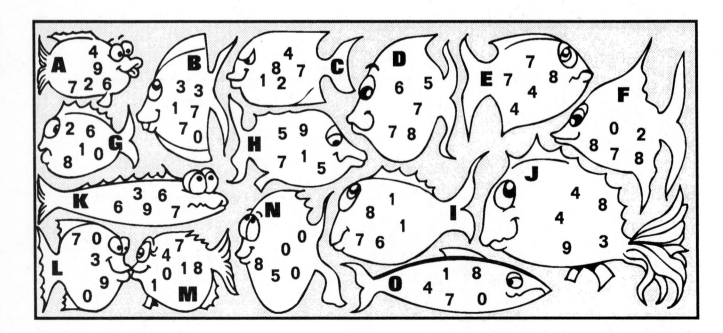

Name _____

Batter Up!

Complete each addition box.

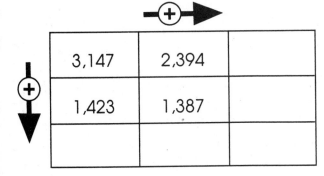

+ →		
3,147	2,394	
1,423	1,387	

+ →		
492	224	
118	303	

+ →		
7,540	2,918	
1,387	2,913	

+ →		
1,435	2,916	
3,192	2,921	

+ →		
721	519	
908	286	

+ →		
5,642	1,829	
2,819	6,425	

+ →		
4,256	1,487	
1,842	2,143	

0-7682-3794-7 *Skills & Practice Gr. 4*

Name _____

Addition Slides

```
              213      206
    825       641      413
    132     + 823    + 227
  + 691
```

```
    462
    381              603
  + 253              247
                   + 314        485            420
                                232            382          321
                              + 126          + 156          643
                                                          + 284
```

```
                                               462
                                               310
                                             + 293
                  629      523
                  312      146
                + 438    + 384
    426
    559       569
  + 675       243                            540
             + 284        803                262
                          261              + 351
                        + 342
```

```
    549      542      326      643
    261      681      243      251
  + 341    + 346    + 814    + 382
```

Pinball Mathematics

Solve the problems in the pinball machine.

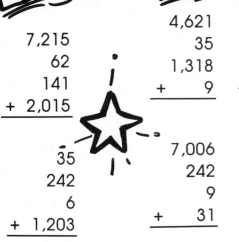

HOG HEAVEN

SCORE BIG!

```
  7,215          4,621        8,143
     62             35           60
    141          1,318          235
+ 2,015        +     9      + 1,423
```

```
     35          7,006          521
    242            242        3,134
      6              9           64
+ 1,203        +    31      +   243
```

DING   **PONG**   **BUZZ**

```
    496
  8,172        6,201        5,242        4,162        6,425
     83          325          342          328           41
+   199           41            8           41          324
             + 2,136        +    51      +   503      +     3
  6,117
     24
    315        4,205
+ 2,136           81
                   3        2,516        5,426        2,481        3,204
             +   414          310          310        2,514          182
                               82          512            2           23
                          +      3      +      4      +     43      +     5
```

Name _____

Knowing When to Add

Circle the key addition words and solve the problems.

1. The choir at Madison School is made up of 26 girls and 18 boys. What is the total choir membership?

____ 〇 ____ = ____

2. The band at Madison School is composed of 19 girls and 22 boys. How many band members are there in all?

3. There are 214 girls and 263 boys attending Madison School. How many students altogether attend Madison School?

4. Next fall, in addition to the 477 students already at Madison, 248 more will be bussed in. Altogether, how many students will be at Madison School?

5. Mr. Mill's bus route is 14 miles long. Mrs. Albert's route is 17 miles long. Ms. Byrne's route is 15 miles long. How many miles altogether do these 3 bus routes cover?

6. The book rental at Madison is $8.00. The supplies cost $14.00. The locker fee is $3.00. What is the sum of these expenses?

7. The staff at Madison is made up of 24 teachers, 3 custodians and 2 administrators. How many staff members in all are there?

Name _____

Math Cranes

Across

```
2.    517        7.    535        11.    845        14.    356
    - 228             - 248            - 599             - 168
```

```
3.    428        8.    857        13.    325
    - 249             - 389             - 186
```

```
4.    562        9.    561
    - 274             - 247
```

```
5.    924
    - 348
```

```
6.    923
    - 346
```

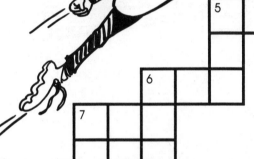

```
4.    582        8.    721
    - 346             - 240
```

Down

```
1.    421        5.    824        10.    768
    - 342             - 247             - 292
```

```
2.    627        6.    921        12.    826
    - 348             - 346             - 337
```

```
3.    362        7.    926        13.    247
    - 194             - 718             - 129
```

Name _____

Timely Zeros

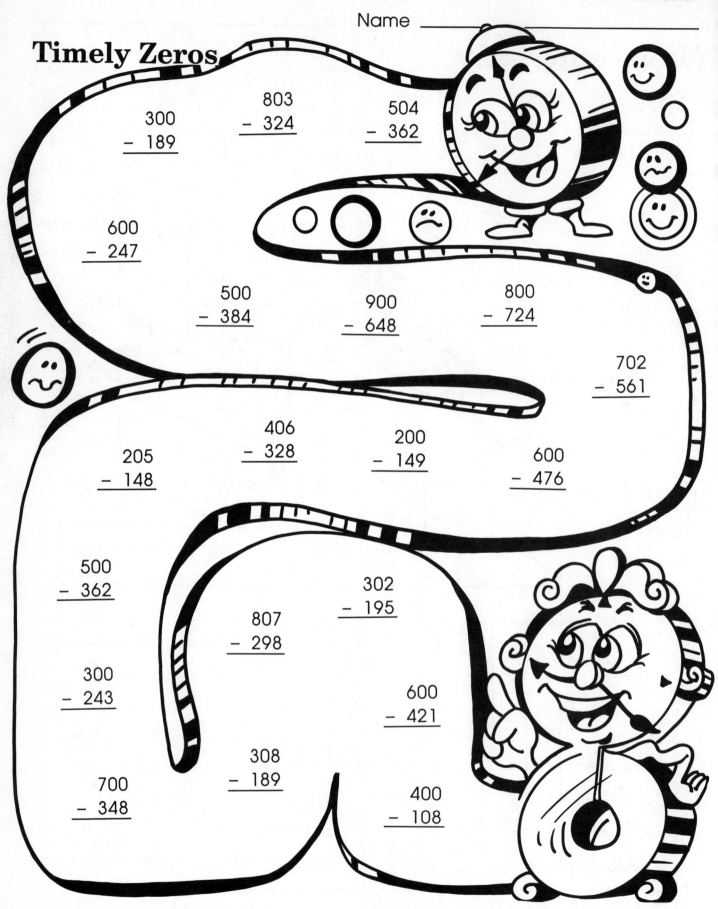

$$\begin{array}{r} 300 \\ -\ 189 \\ \hline \end{array}$$

$$\begin{array}{r} 803 \\ -\ 324 \\ \hline \end{array}$$

$$\begin{array}{r} 504 \\ -\ 362 \\ \hline \end{array}$$

$$\begin{array}{r} 600 \\ -\ 247 \\ \hline \end{array}$$

$$\begin{array}{r} 500 \\ -\ 384 \\ \hline \end{array}$$

$$\begin{array}{r} 900 \\ -\ 648 \\ \hline \end{array}$$

$$\begin{array}{r} 800 \\ -\ 724 \\ \hline \end{array}$$

$$\begin{array}{r} 702 \\ -\ 561 \\ \hline \end{array}$$

$$\begin{array}{r} 205 \\ -\ 148 \\ \hline \end{array}$$

$$\begin{array}{r} 406 \\ -\ 328 \\ \hline \end{array}$$

$$\begin{array}{r} 200 \\ -\ 149 \\ \hline \end{array}$$

$$\begin{array}{r} 600 \\ -\ 476 \\ \hline \end{array}$$

$$\begin{array}{r} 500 \\ -\ 362 \\ \hline \end{array}$$

$$\begin{array}{r} 807 \\ -\ 298 \\ \hline \end{array}$$

$$\begin{array}{r} 302 \\ -\ 195 \\ \hline \end{array}$$

$$\begin{array}{r} 300 \\ -\ 243 \\ \hline \end{array}$$

$$\begin{array}{r} 600 \\ -\ 421 \\ \hline \end{array}$$

$$\begin{array}{r} 700 \\ -\ 348 \\ \hline \end{array}$$

$$\begin{array}{r} 308 \\ -\ 189 \\ \hline \end{array}$$

$$\begin{array}{r} 400 \\ -\ 108 \\ \hline \end{array}$$

0-7682-3794-7 *Skills & Practice Gr. 4*

Name _____

Subtraction Maze

Work problems.

4172	6723	547	834	562	7146
− 1536	− 2586	− 259	− 463	− 325	− 3498

9427	8149	5389	421	7456	818
− 6648	− 5372	− 1652	− 275	− 3724	− 639

772	6529	5379	6275	5612	8355
− 586	− 4538	− 2835	− 3761	− 1505	− 5366

MATH

Shade in answers to find path.

	2514	288	186	3732	2989
	2779	156	1901	2414	4137
3748	3337	2777	371	179	1991
3048	3737	146	2717		
679	237	374	4107		
886	2636	2544	3648		

 0-7682-3794-7 Skills & Practice Gr. 4

High Class Math

Name _____

$$3{,}270 - 1{,}529$$

$$8{,}248 - 1{,}513$$

$$7{,}648 - 3{,}291 \qquad 4{,}321 - 1{,}809 \qquad 8{,}241 - 3{,}516 \qquad 3{,}002 - 1{,}231$$

$$9{,}200 - 3{,}146$$

$$8{,}254 - 3{,}187 \qquad 7{,}265 - 2{,}134 \qquad 3{,}846 - 1{,}359 \qquad 8{,}006 - 3{,}084$$

$$5{,}017 - 2{,}408$$

$$6{,}265 - 4{,}189 \qquad 4{,}824 - 1{,}913 \qquad 6{,}205 - 1{,}054 \qquad 5{,}253 - 4{,}428$$

$$3{,}084 - 1{,}926$$

$$9{,}205 - 3{,}187 \qquad 5{,}809 - 3{,}913 \qquad 5{,}642 - 2{,}408$$

Published by Frank Schaffer Publications. Copyright protected.

0-7682-3794-7 *Skills & Practice Gr. 4*

Name _____

Under the Big Top!

43	x	4	=	
x				
2	x	58	=	
=	////	x		
	x	7	=	
		=		

65	x	4	=	
x	////	x		
5	x	77	=	
=		=		

0-7682-3794-7 *Skills & Practice Gr. 4*

MATH

Name _____

More Multiplication

Put numbers in
the ▢ 's to get
correct answer.

```
  4 7 5        7 7 9        8 7 9
  [5][4]       [ ][ ]       [ ][ ]
     [7]          [ ]          [ ]
× _____     × _____     × _____
  3 7 8        6 7 9        6 3 2
```

```
  4 8 7        7 6 3        6 9 4        7 3 9        5 2 9
  [ ][ ]       [ ][ ]       [ ][ ]       [ ][ ]       [ ][ ]
     [ ]          [ ]          [ ]          [ ]          [ ]
× _____     × _____     × _____     × _____     × _____
  5 8 8        4 3 8        5 6 4        3 3 3        4 6 0
```

```
  9 5 6        2 7 5        4 5 6        5 7 6        3 6 9
  [ ][ ]       [ ][ ]       [ ][ ]       [ ][ ]       [ ][ ]
     [ ]          [ ]          [ ]          [ ]          [ ]
× _____     × _____     × _____     × _____     × _____
  3 4 5        1 7 5        2 2 4        3 8 0        2 3 4
```

```
  4 8 7        6 6 7        5 5 4        2 3 3        7 8 4
  [ ][ ]       [ ][ ]       [ ][ ]       [ ][ ]       [ ][ ]
     [ ]          [ ]          [ ]          [ ]          [ ]
× _____     × _____     × _____     × _____     × _____
  3 3 6        4 0 2        2 7 0          9 6        5 9 2
```

```
  6 5 7        9 4 2        3 8 4        7 8 4        3 8 2
  [ ][ ]       [ ][ ]       [ ][ ]       [ ][ ]       [ ][ ]
     [ ]          [ ]          [ ]          [ ]          [ ]
× _____     × _____     × _____     × _____     × _____
  3 8 0          9 8        3 4 4        5 9 2        1 8 4
```

Name _____

Solve It!

What set of ridges, loops and whirls are different on every person? To find out, solve the following problems and put the corresponding letter above the answer at the bottom of the page.

I.   303
    x 3

R.   214
    x 2

N.   413
    x 2

N.   142
    x 2

R.   211
    x 4

F.   104
    x 2

T.   131
    x 2

E.   301
    x 2

I.   134
    x 1

G.   244
    x 2

S.   334
    x 2

P.   232
    x 3

208   909   826   488   602   844   696   428   134   284   262   668

Name _____

Space Math

Complete this space-walking mission!

204
x 8

817
x 6

923
x 2

326
x 5

281
x 4

406
x 3

231
x 6

262
x 7

214
x 2

218
x 5

126
x 9

306
x 7

241
x 8

329
x 6

310
x 5

421
x 6

431
x 3

814
x 9

231
x 4

624
x 7

896
x 1

742
x 8

525
x 4

606
x 7

Name _____

Amazing Arms

What will happen to a starfish that loses an arm? To find out, solve the following problems and put the corresponding letter above the answer at the bottom of the page.

O. 2,893
    x 4
    _____

W. 1,763
    x 3
    _____

W. 7,665
    x 5
    _____

A. 1,935
    x 6
    _____

W. 3,097
    x 3
    _____

E. 2,929
    x 4
    _____

G. 6,366
    x 5
    _____

T. 7,821
    x 8
    _____

L. 6,283
    x 7
    _____

I. 5,257
    x 3
    _____

R. 3,019
    x 6
    _____

N. 2,908
    x 7
    _____

I. 6,507
    x 8
    _____

N. 5,527
    x 2
    _____

L. 6,626
    x 3
    _____

O. 7,219
    x 9
    _____

E. 3,406
    x 6
    _____

___ ___   ___ ___ ___ ___   ___ ___ ___ ___
52,056 62,568   5,289 15,771 43,981 19,878   31,830 18,114 64,971 9,291

                                                                    !

    ___   ___ ___ ___   ___ ___ ___
    11,610   20,356 20,436 38,325   11,572 11,054 11,716

0-7682-3794-7 *Skills & Practice Gr. 4*

Name _____

Multiplication Drill

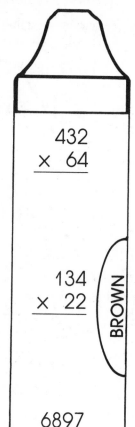

$$\begin{array}{r} 82 \\ \times\ 4 \\ \hline \end{array}$$

$$\begin{array}{r} 48 \\ \times 66 \\ \hline \end{array}$$

BLACK

$$\begin{array}{r} 876 \\ \times 13 \\ \hline \end{array}$$

$$\begin{array}{r} 432 \\ \times 64 \\ \hline \end{array}$$

$$\begin{array}{r} 134 \\ \times 22 \\ \hline \end{array}$$

BROWN

$$\begin{array}{r} 6897 \\ \times\ 6 \\ \hline \end{array}$$

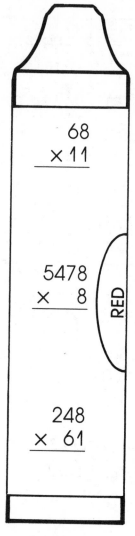

$$\begin{array}{r} 68 \\ \times 11 \\ \hline \end{array}$$

$$\begin{array}{r} 5478 \\ \times\ 8 \\ \hline \end{array}$$

RED

$$\begin{array}{r} 248 \\ \times 61 \\ \hline \end{array}$$

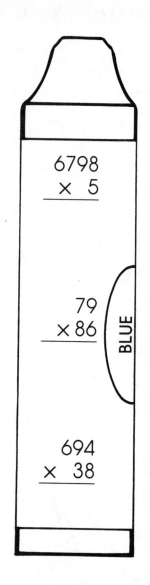

$$\begin{array}{r} 6798 \\ \times\ 5 \\ \hline \end{array}$$

$$\begin{array}{r} 79 \\ \times 86 \\ \hline \end{array}$$

BLUE

$$\begin{array}{r} 694 \\ \times 38 \\ \hline \end{array}$$

Color picture by matching answers with crayons.

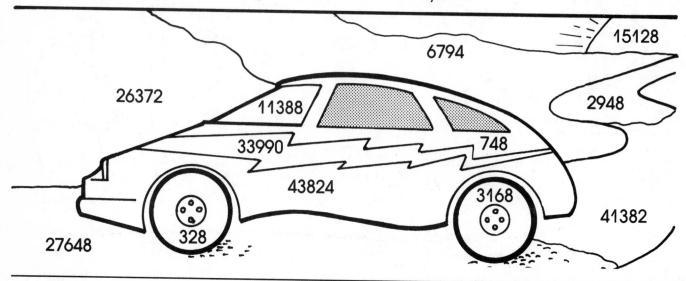

Name _____

Elephant Escapades

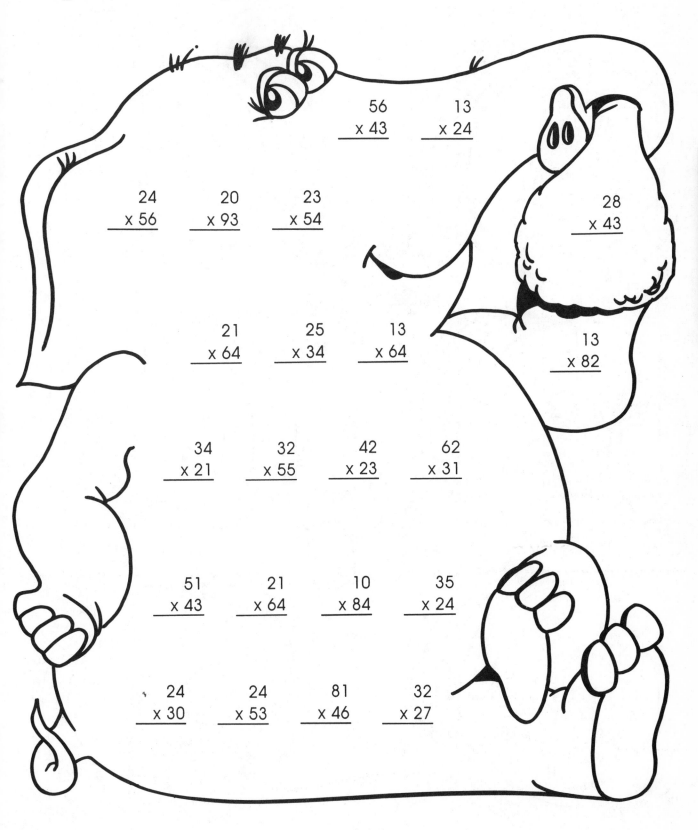

```
          56        13
        x 43      x 24
```

```
   24         20         23
 x 56       x 93       x 54
```

```
                                        28
                                      x 43
```

```
        21         25         13
      x 64       x 34       x 64
```

```
                                        13
                                      x 82
```

```
     34         32         42         62
   x 21       x 55       x 23       x 31
```

```
     51         21         10         35
   x 43       x 64       x 84       x 24
```

```
     24         24         81         32
   x 30       x 53       x 46       x 27
```

Name _____

Wheels of Wonder

Solve the following problems by multiplying each number by the power of 10 in the center.

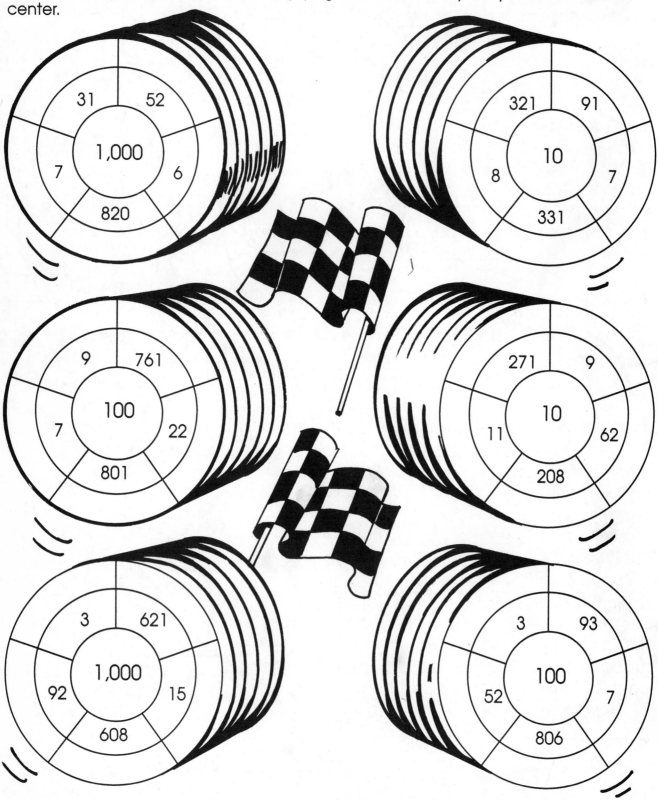

0-7682-3794-7 *Skills & Practice Gr. 4*

Step by Step

Name _____

Read the problems below. Solve each in the space provided.

Work space

1. Mr. Lundstrom knew they would have to be careful moving the gold. He had the Defense Club only move a small amount at a time. They moved 137 gold bars on Monday and on Tuesday. On Wednesday they moved 150 gold bars. They moved 121 gold bars on Thursday, on Friday, and on Saturday. How many bars were moved in the entire week? _____

2. The German soldiers moved quickly into Norway on the night of the blackout. 1,259 troops came in by parachute, 2,067 came to shore by boat, and 1,099 came in by truck. How many troops came to Norway on that first night? _____

3. Pretend that Peter and Helga could each carry 25 bars of gold on their sleds. They made 35 trips down to the fiord with their loads. How many bars did they move? _____

4. The children saw many small groups of soldiers marching. In one group they counted 53 soldiers. In another group, they counted 69 soldiers. In each of three groups, they counted 77. How many soldiers did they see?

_____

MATH

Name _____

Wacky Waldo's Snow Show

Wacky Waldo's Snow Show is an exciting and fantastic sight. Waldo has trained whales and bears to skate together on the ice. There is a hockey game between a team of sharks and a pack of wolves. Elephants ride sleds down steep hills. Horses and buffaloes ski swiftly down mountains.

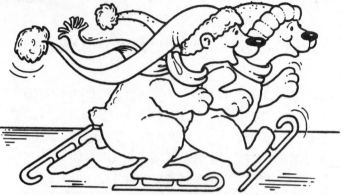

1. Wacky Waldo has 4 ice-skating whales. He has 4 times as many bears who ice skate. How many bears can ice skate?

2. **Waldo's Snow Show** has 4 shows on Thursday, but it has 6 times as many shows on Saturday. How many shows are there on Saturday?

3. The Sharks' hockey team has 3 white sharks. It has 6 times as many tiger sharks. How many tiger sharks does it have?

4. The Wolves' hockey team has 4 gray wolves. It has 8 times as many red wolves. How many red wolves does it have?

5. Waldo taught 6 buffaloes to ski. He was able to teach 5 times as many horses to ski. How many horses did he teach?

6. Buff, a skiing buffalo, took 7 nasty spills when he was learning to ski. His friend Harry Horse fell down 8 times as often. How many times did Harry fall?

0-7682-3794-7 *Skills & Practice Gr. 4*

Name _____

Molly Mugwumps

Molly Mugwumps is the toughest kid in school. She picks fights with kindergarteners and spends more time in the office than the principal does.

1. Molly is the toughest football player in her school. She ran for 23 yards on one play and went 3 times as far on the next play. How far did she run the second time?

2. Molly keeps a rock collection. She has 31 rocks in one sack. She has 7 times as many under her bed. How many rocks are under her bed?

3. Molly had 42 marbles when she came to school. She went home with 4 times as many. How many did she go home with?

4. Molly stuffed 21 sticks of gum in her mouth in the morning. In the afternoon, she crammed 9 times as many sticks into her mouth. How many sticks did she have in the afternoon?

5. Molly got 51 problems wrong in math last week. This week, she missed 8 times as many. How many did she miss this week?

6. Molly was sent to the office 21 days last year. This year, she was sent 7 times as often. How many days did she go this year?

Name _____

Snowball Bash

Help Pete climb down this
mound of giant snowballs!

7) 84

5) 75

3) 45

9) 99

4) 88

5) 80

4) 64

3) 57

3) 78

3) 72

8) 96

2) 86

2) 38

6) 66

5) 65

4) 52

4) 68

6) 78

7) 91

2) 42

6) 72

0-7682-3794-7 *Skills & Practice Gr. 4*

Name _____

Scaling the Heights

Work the problems. To find the path to the top, the answers should match the problem number. Color the path.

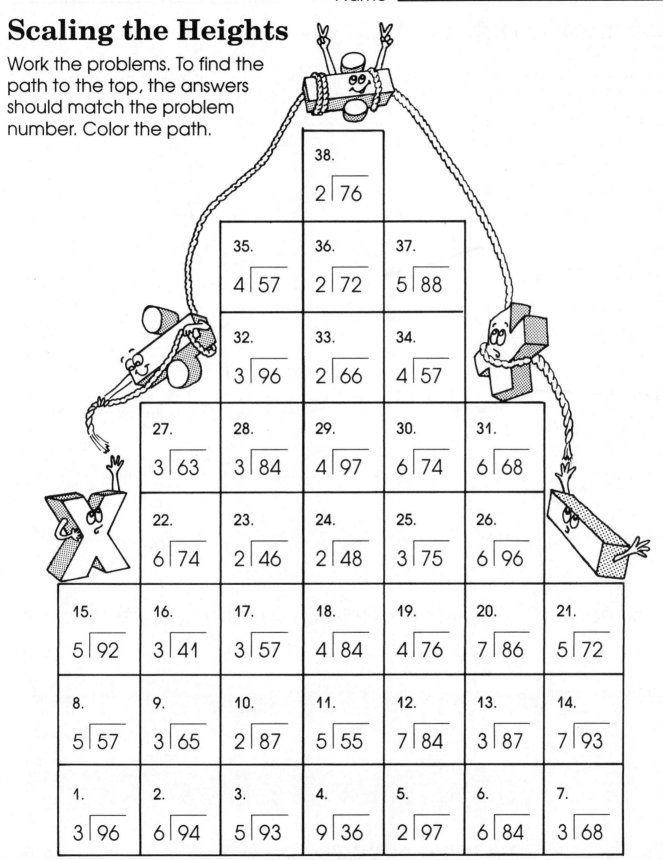

38.
2)‾76‾

35.
4)‾57‾

36.
2)‾72‾

37.
5)‾88‾

32.
3)‾96‾

33.
2)‾66‾

34.
4)‾57‾

27.
3)‾63‾

28.
3)‾84‾

29.
4)‾97‾

30.
6)‾74‾

31.
6)‾68‾

22.
6)‾74‾

23.
2)‾46‾

24.
2)‾48‾

25.
3)‾75‾

26.
6)‾96‾

15.
5)‾92‾

16.
3)‾41‾

17.
3)‾57‾

18.
4)‾84‾

19.
4)‾76‾

20.
7)‾86‾

21.
5)‾72‾

8.
5)‾57‾

9.
3)‾65‾

10.
2)‾87‾

11.
5)‾55‾

12.
7)‾84‾

13.
3)‾87‾

14.
7)‾93‾

1.
3)‾96‾

2.
6)‾94‾

3.
5)‾93‾

4.
9)‾36‾

5.
2)‾97‾

6.
6)‾84‾

7.
3)‾68‾

0-7682-3794-7 *Skills & Practice Gr. 4*

Name _____

Geometric Division!

Solve the division problems below and color each shape according to the matching problem and quotient (b = blue, r = red, y = yellow, g = green and p = purple).

Name seven shapes that are in the design.
1. _____
2. _____
3. _____
4. _____
5. _____
6. _____
7. _____

19 R3
13 R2
14 R1
23 R1
21 R2
47 R1
17 R3
12 R3
11 R4
15 R3
18 R1
24 R1
32 R1
31 R2
14 R3
32 R1
38 R1
17 R2
36 R1
26 R2
27 R2
14 R4

1. $2\overline{)65}$ (b)   2. $4\overline{)86}$ (b)

3. $3\overline{)80}$ (r)   4. $5\overline{)88}$ (g)   5. $7\overline{)93}$ (g)   6. $2\overline{)65}$ (y)   7. $2\overline{)73}$ (p)

8. $4\overline{)79}$ (y)   9. $3\overline{)55}$ (y)   10. $6\overline{)88}$ (g)   11. $2\overline{)77}$ (r)   12. $3\overline{)70}$ (y)

13. $6\overline{)70}$ (g)   14. $5\overline{)73}$ (y)   15. $4\overline{)57}$ (p)   16. $2\overline{)49}$ (b)   17. $4\overline{)70}$ (r)

18. $5\overline{)78}$ (r)   19. $3\overline{)95}$ (y)   20. $8\overline{)99}$ (p)   21. $2\overline{)95}$ (r)   22. $3\overline{)83}$ (p)

On-Stage Division

$6\overline{)888}$ $2\overline{)956}$ $2\overline{)712}$

$4\overline{)860}$ $6\overline{)750}$ $9\overline{)999}$

$8\overline{)968}$ $3\overline{)774}$ $5\overline{)735}$ $8\overline{)920}$ $5\overline{)845}$

$7\overline{)805}$ $8\overline{)984}$ $4\overline{)500}$ $2\overline{)846}$ $4\overline{)712}$

$6\overline{)810}$ $7\overline{)882}$

$3\overline{)642}$ $3\overline{)477}$

MATH

Published by Frank Schaffer Publications. Copyright protected. 0-7682-3794-7 *Skills & Practice Gr. 4*

Name _____

Puzzling Problems

Solve the following problems. Write the answers in the puzzle.
Hint: Remainders (R) take up their own box.

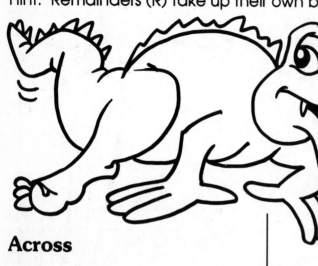

Across

2. $2\overline{)917}$ 4. $6\overline{)830}$

7. $4\overline{)975}$ 8. $2\overline{)859}$

12. $2\overline{)779}$ 14. $3\overline{)475}$

16. $3\overline{)680}$ 17. $8\overline{)988}$

18. $3\overline{)971}$ 19. $5\overline{)927}$

Down

1. $3\overline{)776}$ 3. $7\overline{)948}$ 5. $3\overline{)740}$

6. $7\overline{)897}$ 9. $4\overline{)751}$ 10. $5\overline{)714}$

11. $4\overline{)639}$ 13. $6\overline{)749}$ 15. $5\overline{)634}$

0-7682-3794-7 *Skills & Practice Gr. 4*

Name _____

Division Checklist

Work the problems. Draw a line
from the division problem to the
matching checking problem.

$$3\overline{)56} \quad\text{———}\quad \begin{array}{r} 18 \\ \times\ 3 \\ \hline \end{array}$$

$$3\overline{)64} \qquad \begin{array}{r} 92 \\ \times\ 3 \\ \hline \end{array} \qquad 3\overline{)276}$$

$$3\overline{)127} \qquad \begin{array}{r} 59 \\ \times\ 3 \\ \hline \end{array} \qquad 3\overline{)178} \qquad \begin{array}{r} 21 \\ \times\ 3 \\ \hline \end{array} \qquad 3\overline{)175}$$

$$\begin{array}{r} 42 \\ \times\ 3 \\ \hline \end{array} \qquad 3\overline{)236} \qquad \begin{array}{r} 10 \\ \times\ 3 \\ \hline \end{array} \qquad 3\overline{)32} \qquad \begin{array}{r} 58 \\ \times\ 3 \\ \hline \end{array}$$

$$\begin{array}{r} 28 \\ \times\ 3 \\ \hline \end{array} \qquad 3\overline{)86} \qquad \begin{array}{r} 78 \\ \times\ 3 \\ \hline \end{array} \qquad 3\overline{)247} \qquad \begin{array}{r} 82 \\ \times\ 3 \\ \hline \end{array}$$

Name _____

From Cocoons to Butterflies

Work problems. Draw line connecting cocoon with butterfly.

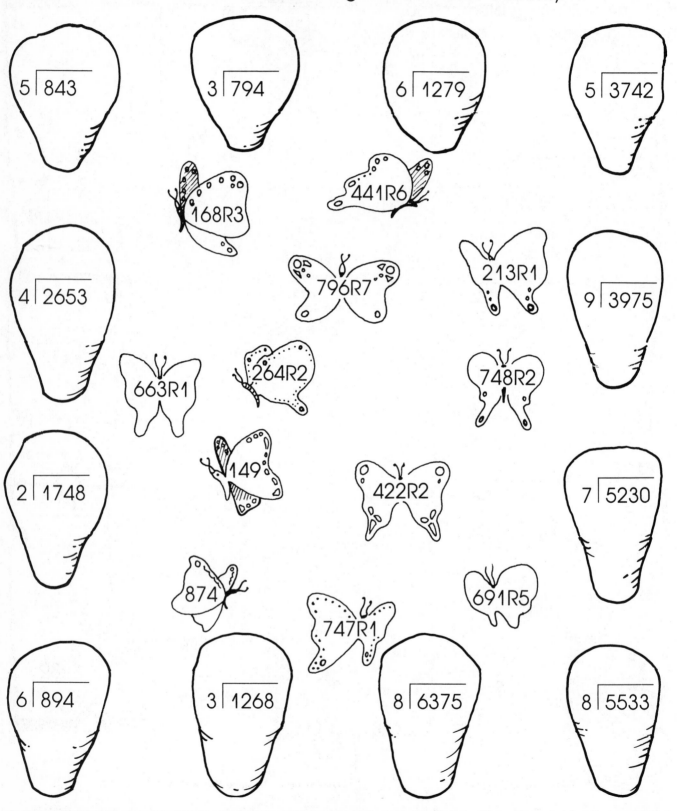

$5\overline{)843}$

$3\overline{)794}$

$6\overline{)1279}$

$5\overline{)3742}$

441R6

168R3

$4\overline{)2653}$

796R7

213R1

$9\overline{)3975}$

663R1

264R2

748R2

$2\overline{)1748}$

149

422R2

$7\overline{)5230}$

874

691R5

747R1

$6\overline{)894}$

$3\overline{)1268}$

$8\overline{)6375}$

$8\overline{)5533}$

Published by Frank Schaffer Publications. Copyright protected. 0-7682-3794-7 *Skills & Practice Gr. 4*

Name _____

Marty's Mania

Help Marty eat all the cheese by traveling the route.

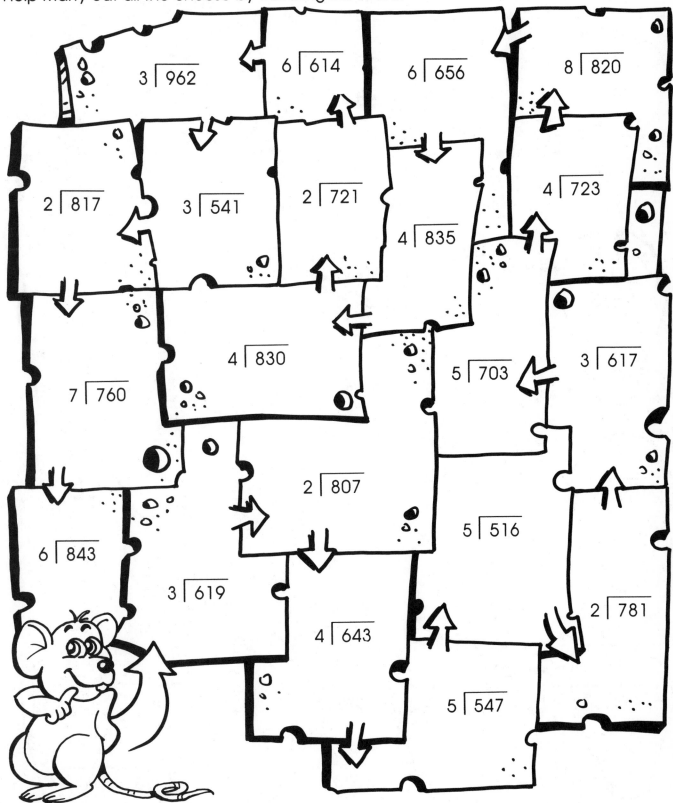

$3\overline{)962}$ $6\overline{)614}$ $6\overline{)656}$ $8\overline{)820}$

$2\overline{)817}$ $3\overline{)541}$ $2\overline{)721}$ $4\overline{)723}$

$4\overline{)835}$

$7\overline{)760}$ $4\overline{)830}$ $5\overline{)703}$ $3\overline{)617}$

$2\overline{)807}$

$6\overline{)843}$ $5\overline{)516}$

$3\overline{)619}$ $2\overline{)781}$

$4\overline{)643}$

$5\overline{)547}$

0-7682-3794-7 *Skills & Practice Gr. 4*

MATH

Name _____

Yum! Yum!

What edible fungus is occasionally found on pizzas or in omelets? To find out, solve the problems. Then, write the corresponding letter above the answer at the bottom of the page.

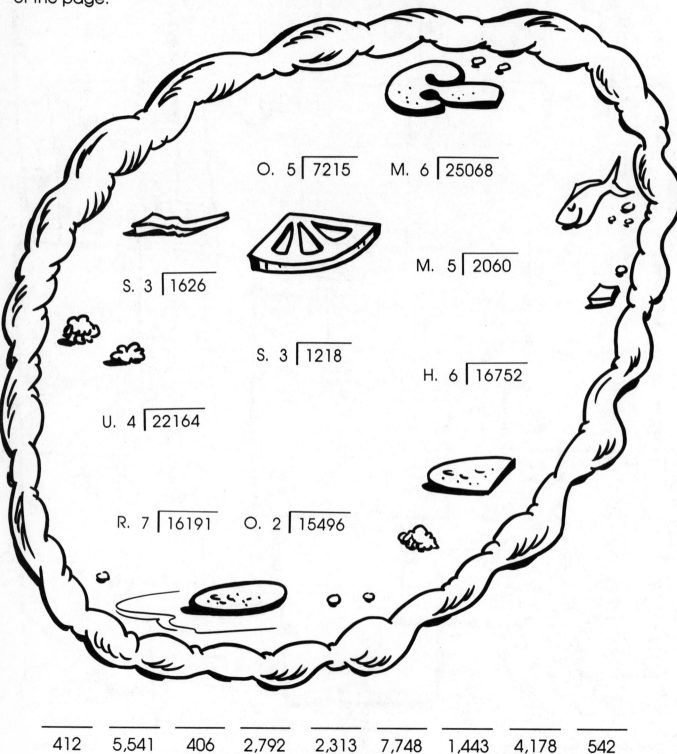

O. $5\overline{)7215}$ M. $6\overline{)25068}$

S. $3\overline{)1626}$

M. $5\overline{)2060}$

S. $3\overline{)1218}$

H. $6\overline{)16752}$

U. $4\overline{)22164}$

R. $7\overline{)16191}$ O. $2\overline{)15496}$

| 412 | 5,541 | 406 | 2,792 | 2,313 | 7,748 | 1,443 | 4,178 | 542 |

Name _____

Flying High

Solve the problems in this incredible dragon kite!

18 ⟌ 130   45 ⟌ 140   13 ⟌ 92

24 ⟌ 164

53 ⟌ 320   42 ⟌ 90   24 ⟌ 98

22 ⟌ 70

41 ⟌ 92   17 ⟌ 104   35 ⟌ 42   18 ⟌ 75

26 ⟌ 80

12 ⟌ 75   19 ⟌ 100   43 ⟌ 221

61 ⟌ 185

32 ⟌ 193

16 ⟌ 90   23 ⟌ 74

121   0-7682-3794-7 *Skills & Practice Gr. 4*

Name _____

Lizzy the Lizard Bags Her Bugs

Lizzy the Lizard is a great hunter
of insects. She separates her
bugs into separate bags so that
her lunch is ready for the week.
Help her decide how to divide
the bugs.

1. Lizzy bagged 45 cockroaches.
She put 5 into each bag. How
many bags did she use?

2. Lizzy found 32 termites. She
put 4 into each bag. How
many bags did she need?

3. Lizzy captured 49 stinkbugs.
She put them into 7 bags. How
many stinkbugs were in each
bag?

4. Lizzy captured 27 horn
beetles. She used 3 bags.
How many beetles went into
each bag?

5. Lizzy lassoed 36 butterflies.
She put 9 into each bag. How
many bags did she need?

6. Lizzy went fishing and caught
48 water beetles. She used 6
bags for her catch. How many
beetles went into each bag?

122

0-7682-3794-7 *Skills & Practice Gr. 4*

Name _____

Bargain Bonanza at Pat's Pet Place

Pat is having a gigantic sale at his place. Help him divide his animals into groups for the sale.

1. Pat got 84 rabbits. He is putting 4 rabbits in each cage. How many cages does he need?

2. Pat sells guppies in plastic bags with 5 guppies in each bag. He has 195 guppies. How many plastic bags does he need?

3. Pat has 392 white mice. They are kept in cages of 7 mice each. How many cages does Pat need?

4. Pat has 324 goldfish. If he puts 6 goldfish in each bag, how many plastic bags will he need?

5. Pat received 116 hamsters. He keeps them in cages of 4 each. How many cages does he need for his hamsters?

6. Pat has 120 parrots. They live in bird cages with 3 to each cage. How many bird cages does Pat need?

MATH

Name _____

Number Puzzles

1

Write your age. ____

Multiply it by 3. ____

Add 18. ____

Multiply by 2. ____

Subtract 36. ____

Divide by 6. (your age) ____

2

Write any number. ____

Double that number. ____

Add 15. ____

Double again. ____

Subtract 30. ____

Divide by 2. ____

Divide by 2 again. ____

3

Write any two-digit
number. ____

Double that number. ____

Add 43. ____

Subtract 18. ____

Add 11. ____

Divide by 2. ____

Subtract 18. ____

4

Write the number of
children in your class. ____

Double that number. ____

Add 15. ____

Double it again. ____

Subtract 30. ____

Divide by 4. ____

Name _____

Which Problem Is Correct?

One of the methods of solution at the left is correct for the problem. Pick the correct method of solution and finish solving the problem.

1. $\begin{array}{r} 56 \\ +17 \end{array}$ $\begin{array}{r} 56 \\ -17 \end{array}$ Bill and his friends collect baseball cards. Bill has 17 fewer cards than Mack. Bill has 56 cards. How many baseball cards does Mack have?

2. $\begin{array}{r} 54 \\ \times\ 3 \end{array}$ $3\overline{)54}$ Amos bought 54 baseball cards. He already had 3 times as many. How many baseball cards did Amos have before his latest purchase?

3. $\begin{array}{r} 3.80 \\ +3.50 \end{array}$ $\begin{array}{r} 3.80 \\ -3.50 \end{array}$ Joe paid $3.50 for a "Mickey Mantle" baseball card. "Ted Williams" cost him $3.80. How much more did he pay for "Ted Williams" than for "Mickey Mantle"?

4. $\begin{array}{r} 3.60 \\ \times\ 9 \end{array}$ $9\overline{)3.60}$ Will bought 9 baseball cards for $3.60. How much did he pay per card?

5. $\begin{array}{r} 8.00 \\ +\ .50 \end{array}$ $\begin{array}{r} 8.00 \\ -\ .50 \end{array}$ "Babe Ruth" baseball cards were selling for $8.00. "Herb Score" baseball cards sold for 50¢. "Herb Score" cards sold for how much less than "Babe Ruth" cards?

6. $\begin{array}{r} 0.75 \\ \times\ 8 \end{array}$ $8\overline{)0.75}$ Andy bought 8 baseball cards at 75¢ each. How much did Andy pay in all?

0-7682-3794-7 *Skills & Practice Gr. 4*

Name _____

Identifying Operations

Decide which sign is correct for
each problem and put in blank.

5 ◯ 5 = 10   14 ◯ 59 = 73   21 ◯ 9 = 30   36 ◯ 63 = 99

9 ◯ 9 = 81   56 ◯ 17 = 73   64 ◯ 8 = 8   6 ◯ 9 = 54

56 ◯ 8 = 48   40 ◯ 5 = 8   7 ◯ 8 = 56   33 ◯ 57 = 90

91 ◯ 16 = 75   9 ◯ 3 = 27   76 ◯ 19 = 57   27 ◯ 3 = 9

54 ◯ 6 = 9   29 ◯ 37 = 66   43 ◯ 7 = 50   63 ◯ 9 = 54

28 ◯ 17 = 11   6 ◯ 5 = 30   4 ◯ 9 = 36   8 ◯ 38 = 46

25 ◯ 5 = 5   36 ◯ 5 = 31   48 ◯ 8 = 6   2 ◯ 9 = 18

72 ◯ 9 = 63   56 ◯ 8 = 7   9 ◯ 1 = 9   55 ◯ 37 = 92

64 ◯ 8 = 56   7 ◯ 1 = 7   45 ◯ 5 = 9   81 ◯ 9 = 9

36 ◯ 4 = 9   57 ◯ 9 = 48   36 ◯ 27 = 63   80 ◯ 17 = 63

45 ◯ 5 = 40   7 ◯ 6 = 42   48 ◯ 6 = 42   32 ◯ 4 = 8

82 ◯ 9 = 91   8 ◯ 8 = 64   9 ◯ 8 = 72   71 ◯ 15 = 86

17 ◯ 77 = 94   40 ◯ 6 = 34   47 ◯ 38 = 9   56 ◯ 9 = 47

36 ◯ 6 = 30   15 ◯ 38 = 53   3 ◯ 6 = 18   6 ◯ 6 = 36

72 ◯ 8 = 9   43 ◯ 48 = 91   27 ◯ 18 = 45   5 ◯ 9 = 45

49 ◯ 7 = 7   7 ◯ 7 = 49   8 ◯ 3 = 24   16 ◯ 16 = 32

126   0-7682-3794-7 *Skills & Practice Gr. 4*

Work It Out

The average is the result of dividing the sum of addends by the number of addends. Match the problem with its answer.

$$\begin{array}{r} 62 \\ 79 \\ +\,87 \\ \hline 228 \end{array} \qquad 3\overline{)228}^{\,76}$$

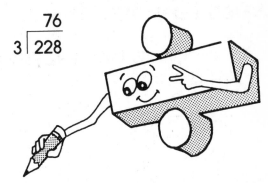

1. 80 + 100 + 90 + 95 + 100 •   A. 53

2. 52 + 56 + 51 •   B. 190

3. 85 + 80 + 95 + 95 + 100 •   C. 410

4. 782 + 276 + 172 •   D. 91

5. 125 + 248 + 214 + 173 •   E. 93

6. 81 + 82 + 91 + 78 •   F. 55

7. 40 + 60 + 75 + 45 •   G. 83

8. 278 + 246 •   H. 33

9. 75 + 100 + 100 + 70 + 100 •   I. 3

10. 0 + 0 + 0 + 0 + 15 •   J. 262

11. 21 + 34 + 44 •   K. 89

12. 437 + 509 + 864 + 274 •   L. 94

13. 80 + 80 + 100 + 95 + 95 •   M. 8

14. 4 + 6 + 7 + 12 + 11 •   N. 90

15. 75 + 100 + 100 + 100 + 95 •   O. 521

Published by Frank Schaffer Publications. Copyright protected.

127

0-7682-3794-7 *Skills & Practice Gr. 4*

MATH

Name _____

Sport Problems

Work problems by averaging. Shade in answers.

$$54 + 75 + 16 + 28 + 32$$

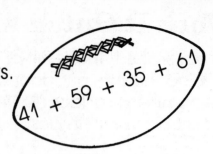

$$41 + 59 + 35 + 61$$

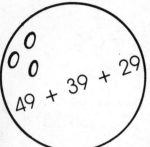

$$49 + 39 + 29$$

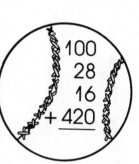

100
28
16
+ 420

$$25 + 30 + 68$$

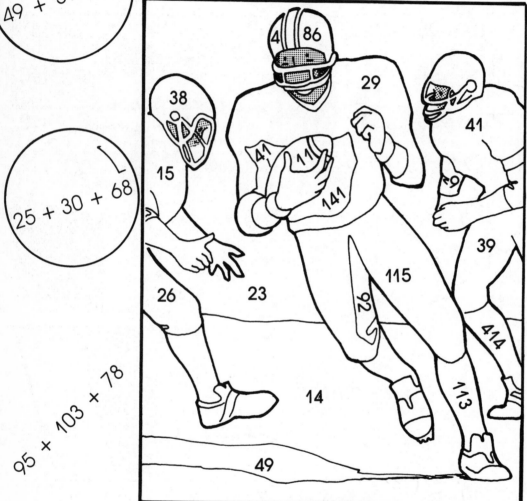

$$95 + 103 + 78$$

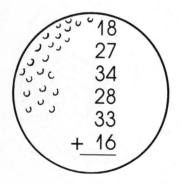

18
27
34
28
33
+ 16

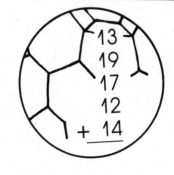

13
19
17
12
+ 14

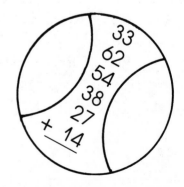

33
62
54
38
27
+ 14

Name _____

What Fraction Am I?

Identify the fraction for each shaded section.

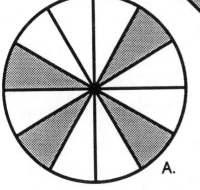

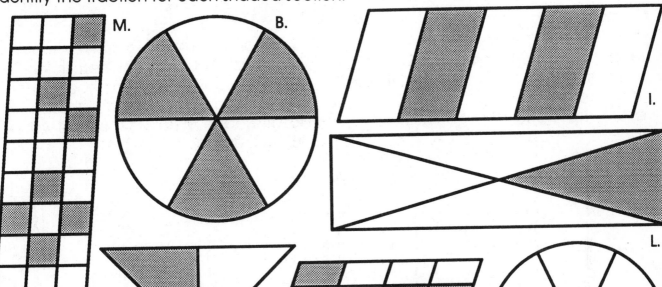

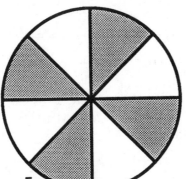

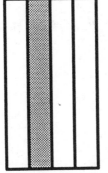
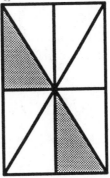
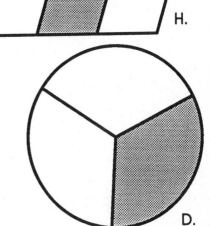

A. _____

B. _____   H. _____

C. _____   I. _____

D. _____   J. _____

E. _____   K. _____

F. _____   L. _____

G. _____   M. _____

0-7682-3794-7 *Skills & Practice Gr. 4*

Name _____

Picture the Problem

Draw a picture of each problem. Then solve the problem.

1. Andy had two ropes of the same length. He cut one rope into 2 equal parts and gave the 2 halves to Bill. The other rope he cut into 4ths and gave 2 of the 4ths to Sue. Who got the most rope?

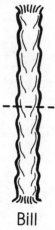 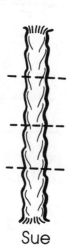

Bill   Sue

2. Henry cut an 8-foot log into 4 equal pieces and burned 2 of them in the fireplace. Joseph cut an 8-foot log into 8 equal pieces and put 3 of them in the fireplace. Who put the most wood in the fireplace?

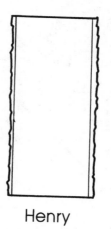 

Henry   Joseph

3. Mr. Johns built an office building with an aisle down the middle. He divided one side into 6 equal spaces. He divided the other side into 9 equal spaces. The Ace Company rented 5 of the 9ths. The Best Company rented 4 of the 6ths. Which company rented the larger space?

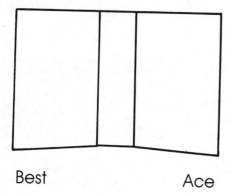

Best   Ace

4. The 4-H Club display area at the state fair was divided into 2 equal areas. One of these sections had 12 booths, the other 9 booths. The flower display covered 3 of the 9ths, and the melon display covered 4 of the 12ths. Which display had the most room?

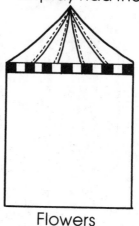 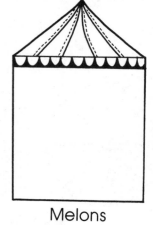

Flowers   Melons

Name _____

Dare to Compare

Compare the fractions below. Use >, < and =.

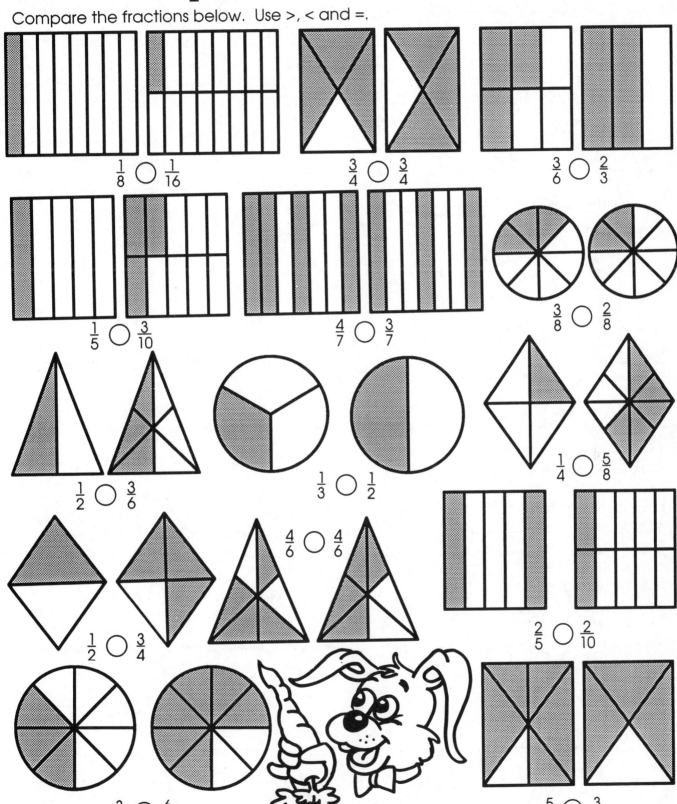

0-7682-3794-7 *Skills & Practice Gr. 4*

More Than Peanuts

Use >, < and = to compare the fractions below.

 $\frac{3}{8} \bigcirc \frac{2}{8}$

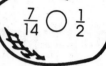 $\frac{1}{2} \bigcirc \frac{3}{6}$

 $\frac{2}{3} \bigcirc \frac{3}{6}$

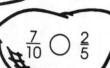 $\frac{3}{6} \bigcirc \frac{1}{2}$

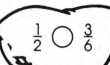 $\frac{7}{14} \bigcirc \frac{1}{2}$

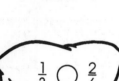 $\frac{4}{7} \bigcirc \frac{4}{14}$

 $\frac{8}{12} \bigcirc \frac{3}{6}$

 $\frac{4}{7} \bigcirc \frac{3}{7}$

 $\frac{7}{10} \bigcirc \frac{2}{5}$

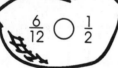 $\frac{1}{3} \bigcirc \frac{6}{9}$

 $\frac{3}{4} \bigcirc \frac{3}{4}$

 $\frac{4}{8} \bigcirc \frac{8}{16}$ $\frac{1}{3} \bigcirc \frac{2}{6}$ $\frac{2}{8} \bigcirc \frac{1}{2}$ 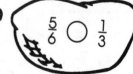 $\frac{4}{7} \bigcirc \frac{4}{14}$ $\frac{1}{5} \bigcirc \frac{3}{10}$

$\frac{6}{11} \bigcirc \frac{5}{11}$ $\frac{6}{12} \bigcirc \frac{1}{2}$ $\frac{2}{3} \bigcirc \frac{2}{6}$  $\frac{7}{12} \bigcirc \frac{2}{4}$ $\frac{5}{6} \bigcirc \frac{1}{3}$

 $\frac{7}{10} \bigcirc \frac{3}{10}$ $\frac{1}{2} \bigcirc \frac{8}{12}$ $\frac{1}{5} \bigcirc \frac{8}{10}$  $\frac{7}{8} \bigcirc \frac{2}{4}$ $\frac{1}{3} \bigcirc \frac{5}{6}$

 $\frac{3}{8} \bigcirc \frac{1}{4}$ $\frac{2}{5} \bigcirc \frac{5}{10}$ $\frac{5}{6} \bigcirc \frac{2}{3}$ 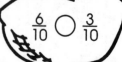 $\frac{6}{10} \bigcirc \frac{2}{5}$ $\frac{6}{10} \bigcirc \frac{3}{10}$

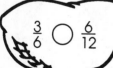 $\frac{3}{6} \bigcirc \frac{6}{12}$ $\frac{1}{8} \bigcirc \frac{1}{4}$  $\frac{1}{2} \bigcirc \frac{1}{4}$ 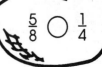 $\frac{5}{6} \bigcirc \frac{2}{3}$ $\frac{5}{8} \bigcirc \frac{1}{4}$

Name _____

Match the Fractions

Under each bar, write a fraction for the shaded part. Then, match each fraction on the left with its equivalent fraction on the right.

1. 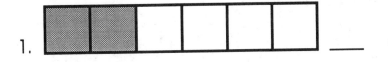 ___

a. 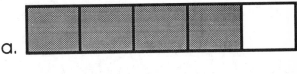 ___

2.  ___

b. 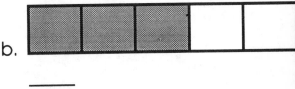 ___

3. 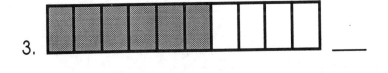 ___

c.  ___

4.  ___

d.  ___

5. 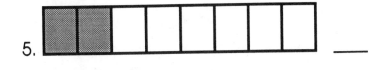 ___

e.  ___

6. 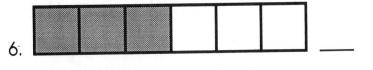 ___

f.  ___

7. 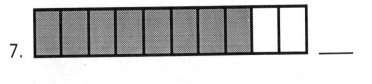 ___

g. 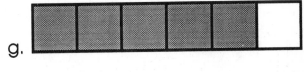 ___

8. ___

h. ___

0-7682-3794-7 *Skills & Practice Gr. 4*

Name _____

Oh, My!

Draw the correct mouths on the animals by finding the whole number for each fraction.

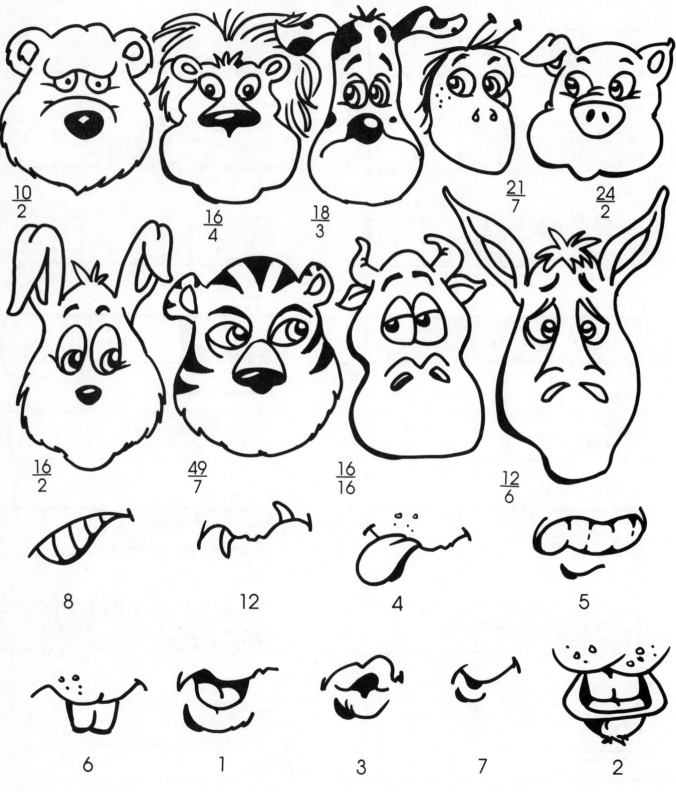

0-7682-3794-7 *Skills & Practice Gr. 4*

Name _____

Reduce the Fat Grams

Help this reducing machine function properly! Reduce each fraction.

$\frac{5}{25}$ = $\frac{8}{16}$ = $\frac{12}{18}$ = $\frac{10}{25}$ = $\frac{12}{30}$ = $\frac{3}{30}$ =

$\frac{6}{30}$ = $\frac{12}{20}$ = $\frac{3}{18}$ = $\frac{3}{9}$ = $\frac{4}{26}$ = $\frac{4}{28}$ =

$\frac{7}{21}$ = $\frac{16}{20}$ = $\frac{2}{10}$ = $\frac{3}{27}$ = $\frac{5}{60}$ =

$\frac{21}{35}$ = $\frac{3}{12}$ = $\frac{24}{40}$ = $\frac{8}{24}$ =

$\frac{16}{40}$ = $\frac{9}{36}$ = $\frac{15}{25}$ = $\frac{7}{35}$ =

NO CAL

Name _____

"Gator Aid"

Climb these obstacle ledges to the top.

$$\frac{3}{7} = \frac{}{21}$$

$$\frac{4}{5} = \frac{}{20}$$

$$\frac{4}{6} = \frac{}{18}$$

$$\frac{1}{3} = \frac{}{24}$$

$$\frac{2}{3} = \frac{}{15}$$

$$\frac{2}{3} = \frac{4}{}$$

$$\frac{1}{2} = \frac{6}{}$$

$$\frac{5}{7} = \frac{}{49}$$

$$\frac{7}{9} = \frac{14}{}$$

$$\frac{2}{3} = \frac{}{12}$$

$$\frac{4}{9} = \frac{}{27}$$

$$\frac{1}{6} = \frac{}{24}$$

$$\frac{4}{7} = \frac{}{28}$$

$$\frac{1}{2} = \frac{4}{}$$

$$\frac{5}{10} = \frac{}{20}$$

$$\frac{1}{8} = \frac{}{16}$$

$$\frac{1}{6} = \frac{}{36}$$

$$\frac{2}{5} = \frac{4}{}$$

$$\frac{1}{3} = \frac{}{12}$$

$$\frac{2}{3} = \frac{}{9}$$

$$\frac{4}{9} = \frac{}{27}$$

$$\frac{3}{8} = \frac{}{24}$$

$$\frac{1}{2} = \frac{}{16}$$

$$\frac{1}{4} = \frac{4}{}$$

$$\frac{2}{5} = \frac{}{25}$$

$$\frac{3}{6} = \frac{}{12}$$

$$\frac{2}{7} = \frac{}{14}$$

Name _____

Figure It Out

Work problems. Connect the
dots in order of answers.

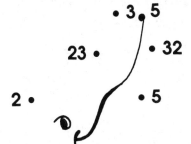

1. $3\frac{3}{4} = \frac{}{4}$

2. $\frac{9}{2} = 4\frac{}{2}$

3. $\frac{30}{11} = 2\frac{}{11}$

4. $8\frac{1}{2} = \frac{}{2}$

5. $\frac{10}{6} = 1\frac{}{6}$

6. $4\frac{3}{8} = \frac{}{8}$

7. $4\frac{1}{5} = \frac{}{5}$

8. $\frac{11}{3} = 3\frac{}{3}$

9. $\frac{13}{7} = 1\frac{}{7}$

10. $3\frac{5}{6} = \frac{}{6}$

11. $1\frac{5}{6} = \frac{}{6}$

12. $\frac{13}{5} = 2\frac{}{5}$

13. $4\frac{1}{3} = \frac{}{3}$

14. $\frac{12}{7} = 1\frac{}{7}$

15. $2\frac{2}{5} = \frac{}{5}$

16. $6\frac{2}{5} = \frac{}{5}$

17. $1\frac{1}{9} = \frac{}{9}$

18. $\frac{13}{8} = 1\frac{}{8}$

19. $1\frac{2}{5} = \frac{}{5}$

20. $1\frac{1}{8} = \frac{}{8}$

MATH

0-7682-3794-7 *Skills & Practice Gr. 4*

Name _____

Make the Move

Lighten the load by solving the puzzle.

Down

1. $\frac{3}{4}$ of 12

3. $\frac{1}{5}$ of 25

5. $\frac{8}{9}$ of 27

6. $\frac{3}{6}$ of 18

7. $\frac{3}{8}$ of 16

12. $\frac{2}{11}$ of 22

13. $\frac{3}{4}$ of 24

15. $\frac{1}{8}$ of 16

Across

2. $\frac{3}{10}$ of 20

4. $\frac{9}{10}$ of 20

8. $\frac{1}{3}$ of 15

9. $\frac{7}{9}$ of 9

10. $\frac{1}{3}$ of 12

11. $\frac{1}{8}$ of 16

12. $\frac{7}{8}$ of 16

14. $\frac{1}{5}$ of 15

15. $\frac{1}{6}$ of 18

16. $\frac{2}{5}$ of 10

Published by Frank Schaffer Publications. Copyright protected.   0-7682-3794-7 *Skills & Practice Gr. 4*

Name _____

Make a Wish

Begin this acrobatic challenge of mathematics and skill. Work your way to the top and make a little magic for Marty the mouse.

MAGIC LAMP

$\frac{7}{8}$ of 16 $\frac{3}{7}$ of 49 $\frac{4}{6}$ of 60

$\frac{3}{6}$ of 54 $\frac{6}{8}$ of 24 $\frac{9}{12}$ of 36

$\frac{9}{12}$ of 24 $\frac{2}{5}$ of 25 $\frac{3}{8}$ of 32

$\frac{5}{7}$ of 42 $\frac{3}{4}$ of 48 $\frac{3}{7}$ of 35

$\frac{7}{9}$ of 36 $\frac{6}{8}$ of 64 $\frac{8}{9}$ of 81

$\frac{3}{6}$ of 24 $\frac{5}{6}$ of 30 $\frac{9}{10}$ of 40

$\frac{6}{8}$ of 72 $\frac{9}{11}$ of 33 $\frac{3}{8}$ of 48

MATH

139   0-7682-3794-7 *Skills & Practice Gr. 4*

Name _____

The Ultimate Adding Machine

Find the sum for each problem. Reduce to lowest terms.

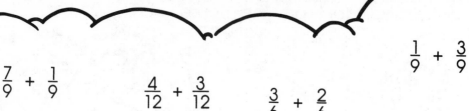

$$\frac{1}{9} + \frac{3}{9}$$

$$\frac{7}{9} + \frac{1}{9}$$

$$\frac{4}{12} + \frac{3}{12}$$

$$\frac{3}{6} + \frac{2}{6}$$

$$\frac{4}{10} + \frac{2}{10}$$

$$\frac{3}{6} + \frac{2}{6}$$

$$\frac{5}{9} + \frac{3}{9}$$

$$\frac{2}{5} + \frac{1}{5}$$

$$\frac{5}{11} + \frac{5}{11}$$

$$\frac{3}{7} + \frac{2}{7}$$

$$\frac{4}{8} + \frac{1}{8}$$

$$\frac{4}{12} + \frac{1}{12}$$

$$\frac{5}{8} + \frac{2}{8}$$

$$\frac{6}{12} + \frac{4}{12}$$

$$\frac{4}{11} + \frac{4}{11}$$

$$\frac{5}{8} + \frac{1}{8}$$

$$\frac{2}{5} + \frac{2}{5}$$

$$\frac{1}{9} + \frac{2}{9}$$

$$\frac{7}{10} + \frac{2}{10}$$

$$\frac{4}{6} + \frac{1}{6}$$

Name _____

Bubble Math

Reduce each sum to a whole number or a mixed number in lowest terms.

$\frac{6}{9} + \frac{6}{9}$

$\frac{5}{11} + \frac{8}{11}$

$\frac{3}{4} + \frac{2}{4}$

$\frac{8}{11} + \frac{8}{11}$

$\frac{2}{5} + \frac{3}{5}$

$\frac{4}{5} + \frac{6}{5}$

$\frac{5}{9} + \frac{5}{9}$

$\frac{8}{9} + \frac{3}{9}$

$\frac{4}{8} + \frac{6}{8}$

$\frac{5}{4} + \frac{2}{4}$

$\frac{4}{3} + \frac{2}{3}$

$\frac{5}{7} + \frac{6}{7}$

$\frac{2}{4} + \frac{2}{4}$

$\frac{3}{6} + \frac{3}{6}$

$\frac{7}{14} + \frac{8}{14}$

$\frac{4}{8} + \frac{4}{8}$

$\frac{8}{11} + \frac{3}{11}$

$\frac{3}{12} + \frac{10}{12}$

$\frac{6}{12} + \frac{8}{12}$

$\frac{7}{12} + \frac{7}{12}$

$\frac{6}{8} + \frac{6}{8}$

$\frac{5}{12} + \frac{8}{12}$

$\frac{7}{11} + \frac{7}{11}$

$\frac{5}{12} + \frac{10}{12}$

$\frac{3}{9} + \frac{7}{9}$

$\frac{7}{13} + \frac{6}{13}$

$\frac{13}{16} + \frac{7}{16}$

$\frac{8}{15} + \frac{14}{15}$

$\frac{5}{7} + \frac{6}{7}$

$\frac{4}{11} + \frac{9}{11}$

MATH

   0-7682-3794-7 *Skills & Practice Gr. 4*

Name _____

Bug Me!

Solve the puzzle.

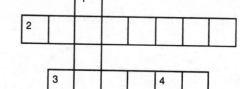

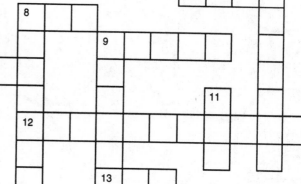

Across

2. $\frac{1}{12} + \frac{1}{3}$ = five _____

3. $\frac{5}{10} + \frac{2}{5}$ = nine _____

5. $\frac{7}{15} + \frac{1}{5}$ = _____ thirds

6. $\frac{1}{2} + \frac{2}{6}$ = _____ sixths

8. $\frac{1}{6} + \frac{1}{2}$ = _____ thirds

9. $\frac{1}{5} + \frac{4}{10}$ = _____ fifths

10. $\frac{1}{3} + \frac{3}{6}$ = _____ sixths

12. $\frac{2}{7} + \frac{1}{14}$ = five _____

13. $\frac{8}{14} + \frac{2}{7}$ = _____ sevenths

Down

1. $\frac{1}{15} + \frac{2}{5}$ = _____ fifteenths

4. $\frac{2}{12} + \frac{2}{6}$ = one _____

5. $\frac{3}{10} + \frac{7}{20}$ = thirteen _____

7. $\frac{1}{8} + \frac{1}{4}$ = three _____

8. $\frac{3}{6} + \frac{1}{12}$ = seven _____

9. $\frac{3}{9} + \frac{1}{3}$ = two _____

11. $\frac{1}{8} + \frac{2}{16}$ = _____ fourth

Published by Frank Schaffer Publications. Copyright protected.

0-7682-3794-7 *Skills & Practice Gr. 4*

Name _____

Soaring Subtraction

Solve each subtraction problem. Reduce each difference to lowest terms.

$$\frac{7}{10} - \frac{3}{10}$$

$$\frac{14}{16} - \frac{7}{16}$$

$$\frac{7}{7} - \frac{3}{7}$$

$$\frac{6}{8} - \frac{2}{8}$$

$$\frac{9}{11} - \frac{7}{11}$$

$$\frac{16}{21} - \frac{9}{21}$$

$$\frac{9}{10} - \frac{6}{10}$$

$$\frac{17}{18} - \frac{6}{18}$$

$$\frac{9}{12} - \frac{7}{12}$$

$$\frac{17}{20} - \frac{9}{20}$$

$$\frac{15}{18} - \frac{7}{18}$$

$$\frac{11}{14} - \frac{8}{14}$$

$$\frac{17}{17} - \frac{8}{17}$$

$$\frac{14}{15} - \frac{8}{15}$$

$$\frac{11}{12} - \frac{2}{12}$$

$$\frac{9}{10} - \frac{5}{10}$$

$$\frac{5}{7} - \frac{2}{7}$$

$$\frac{8}{9} - \frac{7}{9}$$

$$\frac{4}{5} - \frac{3}{5}$$

$$\frac{8}{10} - \frac{5}{10}$$

$$\frac{2}{3} - \frac{1}{3}$$

$$\frac{4}{6} - \frac{3}{6}$$

$$\frac{8}{9} - \frac{5}{9}$$

$$\frac{5}{10} - \frac{3}{10}$$

143

0-7682-3794-7 *Skills & Practice Gr. 4*

MATH

Name _____

Take a Closer Look

| What is a stamp collector called? |

To find out, solve the following subtraction problems, reduce to lowest terms, and then put the letter above its corresponding answer at the bottom of the page.

I. $\dfrac{10}{11} - \dfrac{9}{11}$ H. $\dfrac{12}{12} - \dfrac{3}{12}$ E. $\dfrac{13}{14} - \dfrac{8}{14}$

A. $\dfrac{6}{8} - \dfrac{4}{8}$ I. $\dfrac{6}{7} - \dfrac{5}{7}$ P. $\dfrac{6}{6} - \dfrac{2}{6}$

T. $\dfrac{13}{14} - \dfrac{6}{14}$ L. $\dfrac{17}{20} - \dfrac{8}{20}$ S. $\dfrac{10}{14} - \dfrac{6}{14}$

T. $\dfrac{8}{10} - \dfrac{2}{10}$ L. $\dfrac{14}{18} - \dfrac{8}{18}$

$\dfrac{2}{3}$ $\dfrac{3}{4}$ $\dfrac{1}{7}$ $\dfrac{1}{3}$ $\dfrac{1}{4}$ $\dfrac{1}{2}$ $\dfrac{5}{14}$ $\dfrac{9}{20}$ $\dfrac{1}{11}$ $\dfrac{2}{7}$ $\dfrac{3}{5}$

0-7682-3794-7 *Skills & Practice Gr. 4*

Name _____

Numeral Nibblers

Finish these number sentences.

MATH

$\frac{15}{16}$	$-$	$\frac{1}{2}$	$=$	
$-$				
$\frac{3}{4}$	$-$	$\frac{10}{16}$	$=$	
$=$	▨	$-$		
	$-$	$\frac{1}{8}$	$=$	
		$=$		$-$
$\frac{2}{3}$	$-$	$\frac{2}{12}$	$=$		$\frac{1}{48}$
$-$				$=$
$\frac{2}{9}$		$\frac{21}{24}$	$-$	$\frac{5}{6}$	$=$
$=$		$-$	▨	$-$	
		$\frac{3}{4}$	$-$	$\frac{7}{12}$	$=$
		$=$		$=$	

0-7682-3794-7 *Skills & Practice Gr. 4*

Name _____

Figuring Distance

Find the perimeter of each figure.

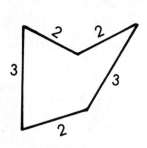

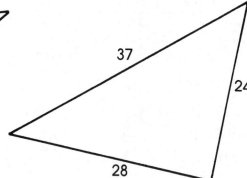

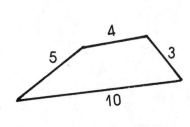

_____

_____

_____

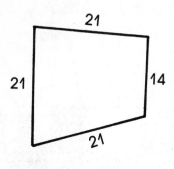

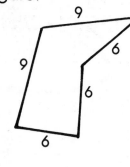

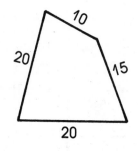

_____

_____

_____

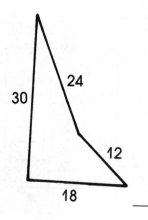

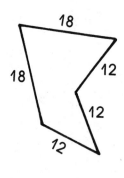

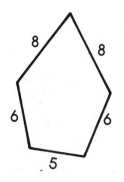

_____

_____

_____

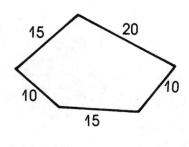

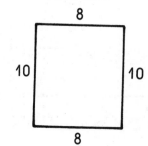

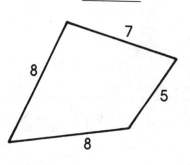

_____

_____

_____

0-7682-3794-7 *Skills & Practice Gr. 4*

Name _____

Quilt Math

Find the perimeter and area of each quilt.

1.

perimeter _____   area _____

2.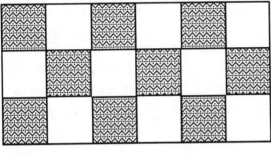

perimeter _____   area _____

3.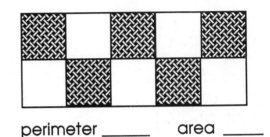

perimeter _____   area _____

4.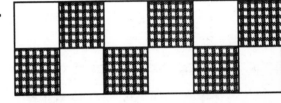

perimeter _____   area _____

5.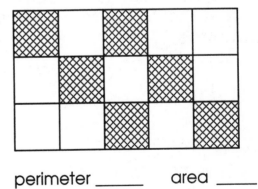

perimeter _____   area _____

6.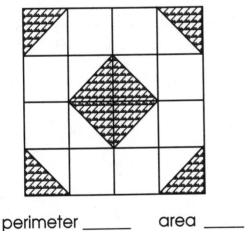

perimeter _____   area _____

7.

perimeter _____   area _____

8. What did you notice about the perimeter in problems 4, 5, 6 and 7? _____

_____

9. On the back of this paper, lay out and then sketch a quilt so that it has 30 blocks in it.

10. On the back, lay out and sketch a quilt that has a perimeter of 14 units.

Name _____

Suzy Spider, Interior Decorator

Suzy Spider is decorating her house. She is a very clever decorator, but she needs your help figuring out the area and perimeter.

1. Suzy is putting a silk fence around her garden. It is 12 cm long and 10 cm wide. What is the perimeter of the garden?

2. Suzy Spider wants to surround her house with a silk thread. Her house is 17 cm long and 12 cm wide. What is its perimeter?

3. Suzy wants to carpet her living room. It is 5 cm long and 4 cm wide. How much carpet should she buy for her living room?

4. Suzy wants to put wallpaper on a kitchen wall. The wall is 7 cm tall and 4 cm wide. What is its area?

5. Suzy has decided to hang a silk thread all the way around her porch. The porch is 4 cm long and 3 cm wide. How long should the thread be?

6. Suzy's bedroom is 6 cm long and 5 cm wide. How much carpet should she buy for it?

Name _____

Turn Up the Volume

The **volume** is the measure of the inside of a space figure. Find the volume. Count the boxes.

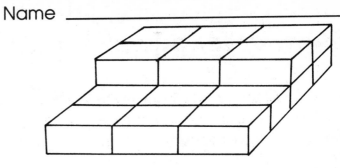

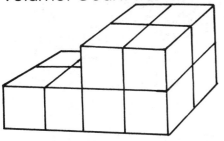

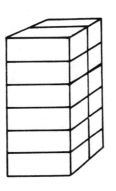

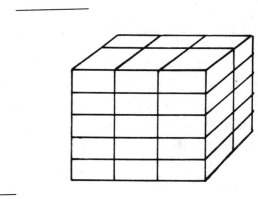

_____

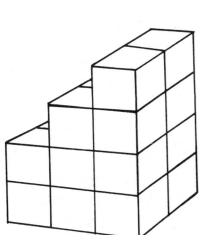

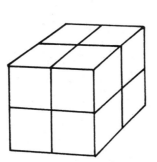

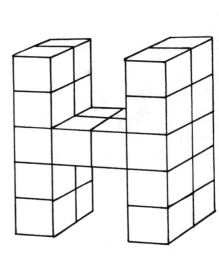

_____

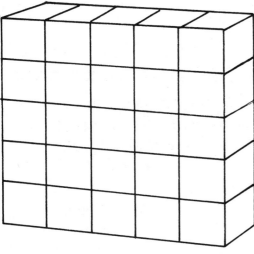

_____

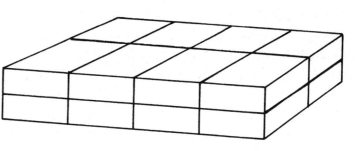

_____

0-7682-3794-7 *Skills & Practice Gr. 4*

Name _____

Krab E. Krabby

Krab E. Krabby carries a yardstick
with him everywhere he goes, and
he measures everything that he can.

Key Facts:
   12 inches = 1 foot
   36 inches = 3 feet = 1 yard

1. Krab E. Krabby wanted to
measure the length of a
grasshopper. Would he use a
ruler or a yardstick?

2. Krab E. Krabby scolded Rollo
Rattlesnake because Rollo
wouldn't straighten out and
cooperate. Should Krab E. Krabby
use a ruler or a yardstick to
measure Rollo?

3. Mr. Krabby measured a
garter snake that was 44
inches long. How many yards
and inches was this?
_____ yard _____ inches left over

4. Krab E. measured a tomato
hornworm that was 5 inches
long. How many inches less than
a foot was this?

5. Mr. Krabby measured a
monarch butterfly that was 4
inches wide. How many inches
less than a foot was the butterfly?

6. Krab E. Krabby measured a
lazy tuna that was 1 foot 11
inches long. How many total
inches was the tuna?

Name _____

Animal Math

The chart below lists some of the body statistics of 15 endangered animals. Use these measurements to solve the problems below the chart.

Animal	Height	Weight	Length
Mountain gorilla	6 feet	450 pounds	
Brown hyena	25 inches	70 pounds	3 feet
Black rhinoceros	5.5 feet	4000 pounds	12 feet
Cheetah	2.5 feet	100 pounds	5 feet
Leopard	2 feet	150 pounds	4.5 feet
Spectacled bear	2.5 feet	300 pounds	5 feet
Giant armadillo		100 pounds	4 feet
Vicuna	2.5 feet	100 pounds	
Central American tapir	3.5 feet	500 pounds	8 feet
Black-footed ferret		1.5 pounds	20 inches
Siberian tiger	38 inches	600 pounds	6 feet
Orangutan	4.5 feet	200 pounds	
Giant panda		300 pounds	6 feet
Polar Bear		1600 pounds	8 feet
Yak	5.5 feet	1200 pounds	

Problems to solve:

1. What is the total height of a mountain gorilla, a vicuna and a yak? _____

2. What is the total weight of a leopard, a cheetah and a polar bear? _____

3. What is the total weight of a giant panda and a giant armadillo? _____

4. Add the lengths of a black rhinoceros, a spectacled bear and a Siberian tiger. _____

5. Add the heights of two leopards, three yaks and four orangutans. _____

6. Subtract the height of a vicuna from the height of a cheetah. _____

7. Multiply the height of a Central American tapir by the height of a mountain gorilla. _____

8. Add the heights of a brown hyena and a Siberian tiger. _____

9. Add the weights of all the animals. _____

10. For the animals whose lengths are given, arrange the lengths of the animals from longest to shortest on another sheet of paper.

Name _____

It Suits Me to a Tee!

How many centimeters from the tee to the flag? Stay on "course"!

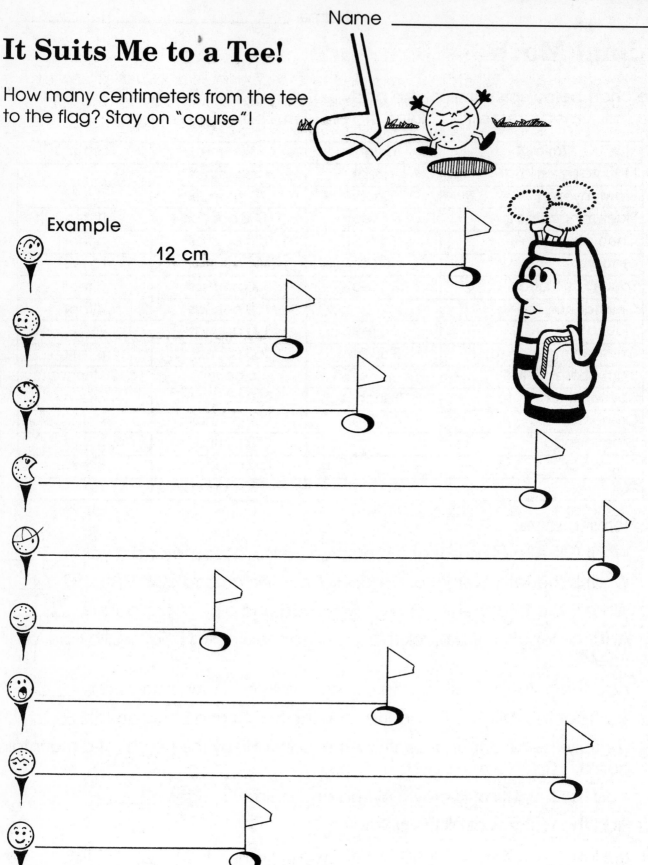

Example

12 cm

Name _____

Digging for Lost Treasure

While vacationing on Octopus Island in the Caribbean Sea, you discover an old treasure map in a bottle on the beach. Using a metric ruler, follow the directions below by plotting your movements to the location of the buried treasure using vertical and horizontal lines. Mark the spot on the map where you locate the treasure. You will be rewarded if you are correct!

1. From the starting point, go 8 centimeters east.
2. Go 6 centimeters north.
3. Go 9 centimeters east.
4. Go 3 centimeters south.
5. Go 7 centimeters west.
6. Go 5 centimeters north.
7. Go 7.5 centimeters west.
8. Go 2 centimeters north.
9. Go 9.5 centimeters east.
10. Go 10 centimeters south. Dig for treasure!

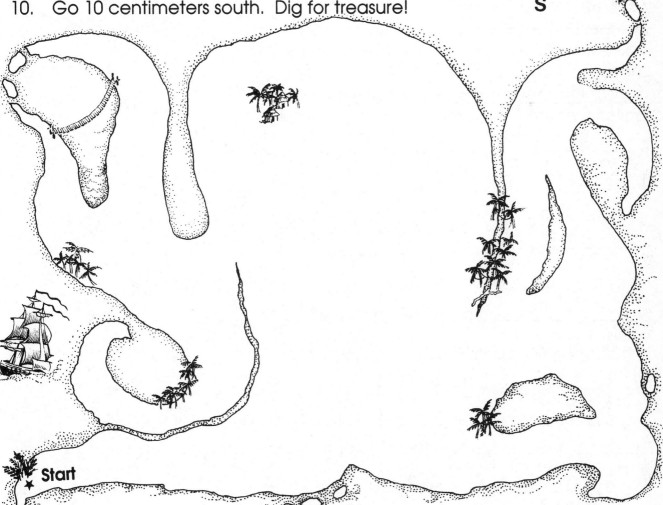

Start

0-7682-3794-7 *Skills & Practice Gr. 4*

Name _____

Discovering Metric Equivalents

Isn't it fun to estimate and guess? How many times a day do you guess how much bubble gum it will take to fill that hole, or how much oatmeal it will take to fill that crack? How about how much milk it will take to cover your crunchy, poppity cereal? We're always making guesses!

Materials Needed

1 cup capacity measuring cup
500 mL capacity measuring cup
2 one-gallon capacity plastic jugs
water

Directions

Set the 2 one-gallon jugs beside each other. Fill one with water. You will then take turns filling the measuring cups with water from one jug to determine the number of cups, pints, quarts and gallons of water it will take to fill the other jug.

1 cup - How many mL do you think it will take? _____

The actual amount _____

1 pint (2 cups) - How many mL do you think it will take? _____

_____ The actual amount _____

1 quart (2 pints) - How many L and mL do you think it will take?

_____ L _____ mL   The actual amounts _____ L _____ mL

1 half gallon (2 quarts) - How many L and mL do you think it will take?

_____ L _____ mL   The actual amounts _____ L _____ mL

1 gallon (4 quarts) - How many L and mL do you think it will take?

_____ L _____ mL   The actual amounts _____ L _____ mL

Were you close in your estimates? _____

Name _____

Gliding Graphics

Draw the lines as directed from point to point for each graph.

Draw a line from:
F,7 to D,1
D,1 to I,6
I,6 to N,8
N,8 to M,3
M,3 to F,1
F,1 to G,4
G,4 to E,4
E,4 to B,1
B,1 to A,8
A,8 to D,11
D,11 to F,9
F,9 to F,7
F,7 to I,9
I,9 to I,6
I,6 to F,7

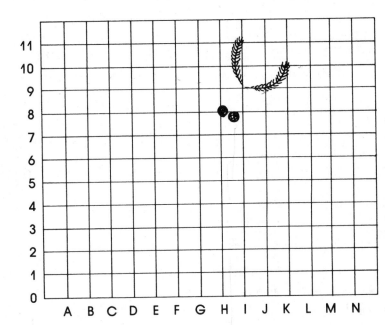

Draw a line from:
J,⊙ to N,☾
N,☾ to U,☾
U,☾ to Z,■
Z,■ to X,♡
X,♡ to U,☾
U,☾ to S,☆
S,☆ to N,☾
N,☾ to N,☆
N,☆ to J,⊙
J,⊙ to L,•
L,• to Y•
Y,• to Z,■
Z,■ to L,■
L,■ to J,⊙

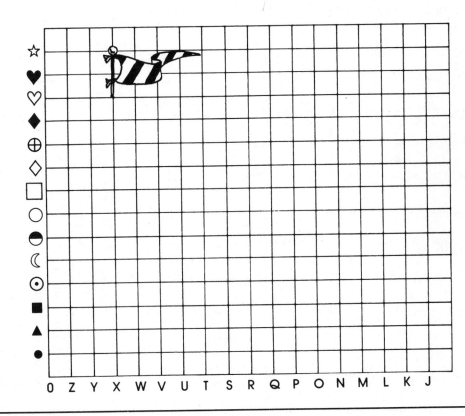

• Write what comes next.

SAD   SBF   SCH   SDJ   SEL   _____

Name _____

School Statistics

Read each graph and do as directed.

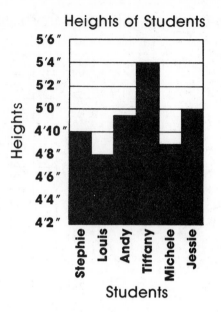

Heights of Students

List the names of the
students from the shortest
to the tallest.

1. _____   4. _____

2. _____   5. _____

3. _____   6. _____

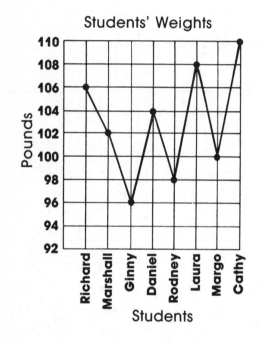

Students' Weights

List the names of the
students from the heaviest
to the lightest.

1. _____   5. _____

2. _____   6. _____

3. _____   7. _____

4. _____   8. _____

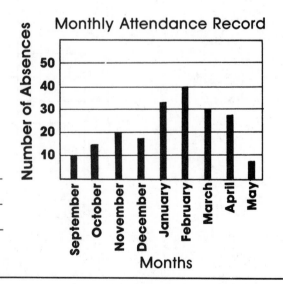

Monthly Attendance Record

List the months in the order
of the least number of
absences to the greatest
number of absences.

1. _____ 4. _____ 7. _____

2. _____ 5. _____ 8. _____

3. _____ 6. _____ 9. _____

• Draw what comes next.

    _____

156   0-7682-3794-7 *Skills & Practice Gr. 4*

Name _____

It's About Time!

Write the letter of the card that matches the clock on the line under the clock.

Example

H

___

___

___

___

___

___

___

___

___

| A 4:05 | B 5:40 | C 11:10 | D 10:15 | E 8:25 |

| F 12:55 | G 5:20 | H 2:50 | I 3:20 | J 1:45 |

Name _____

Father Time Teasers

Father Time doesn't want to tease you with these. He just wants you to work a little harder to figure out: "What time was it?" or "What time will it be?"

Example

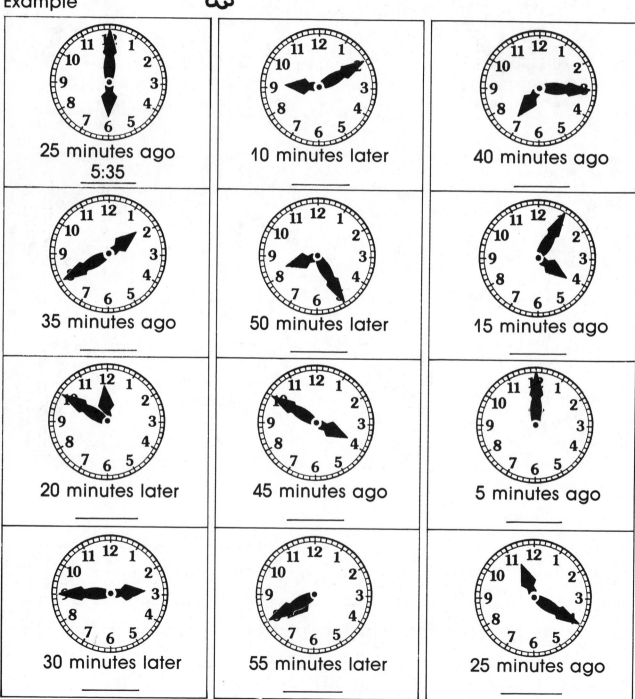

25 minutes ago
5:35

10 minutes later
_____

40 minutes ago
_____

35 minutes ago
_____

50 minutes later
_____

15 minutes ago
_____

20 minutes later
_____

45 minutes ago
_____

5 minutes ago
_____

30 minutes later
_____

55 minutes later
_____

25 minutes ago
_____

0-7682-3794-7 *Skills & Practice Gr. 4*

Name _____

Time "Tables"

"Set" these tables by drawing the hands on these clocks.

Example

10 minutes **before**
12:17

36 minutes **after**
8:19

8 minutes **before**
1:05

21 minutes **after**
8:40

16 minutes **before**
4:30

46 minutes **after**
10:11

32 minutes **before**
5:25

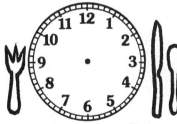

11 minutes **after**
3:16

24 minutes **before**
12:30

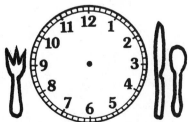

17 minutes **after**
1:31

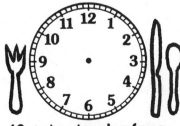

43 minutes **before**
2:01

18 minutes **after**
6:45

0-7682-3794-7 *Skills & Practice Gr. 4*

MATH

Name _____

Time Problems

Draw the hands on the clocks to show the starting time and the ending time.
Then write the answer to the problem.

1. The bike race started at 2:55 p.m. and lasted 2 hours and 10 minutes. What time did the race end?

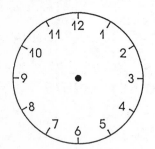 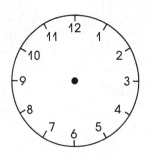

Answer:

2. Sherry walked in the 12-mile Hunger Walk. She started at 12:30 p.m. and finished at 4:50 p.m. How long did she walk?

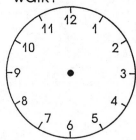 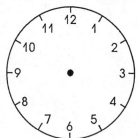

Answer:

3. The 500-mile auto race started at 11:00 a.m. and lasted 2 hours and 25 minutes. What time did the race end?

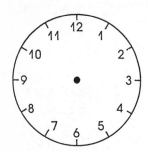 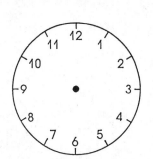

Answer:

4. The train left Indianapolis at 7:25 a.m. and arrived in Chicago at 10:50 a.m. How long did the trip take?

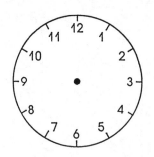 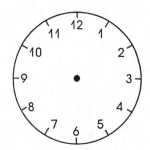

Answer:

5. The chili cook-off started at 10:00 a.m., and all the chili was cooked by 4:30 p.m. How long did it take to cook the chili?

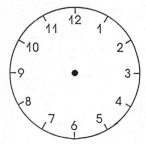 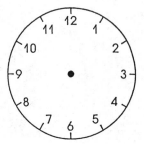

Answer:

6. The chili judging began at 4:30 p.m. After 3 hours and 45 minutes the chili had all been eaten. At what time was the chili judging finished?

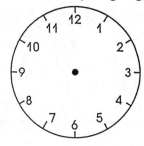 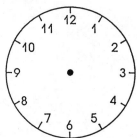

Answer:

Name _____

Super Savers!

Adding money means you're saving money! Keep saving. It adds up. Here are a few success stories. Add 'em up!

Sam's Account	Debbie's Account	Sarah's Account	Roberto's Account	Cheryl's Account
$8.03	$45.32	$85.42	$41.46	$54.26
.84	2.41	12.58	+ 8.89	3.04
+ 5.47	+ 34.28	+ 2.21		+ .25

Alex's Account	Eva's Account	Bill's Account	Monica's Account	David's Account
$ 4.06	$89.42	$62.41	$20.04	$56.04
81.23	3.06	3.84	3.42	2.81
+ 2.84	+ .94	+ 64.21	+ 25.81	+ .94

Tom's Account	Andy's Account	Earl's Account	Mark's Account	Michele's Account
$ 8.05	$ .47	$50.42	$21.46	$ .55
21.21	31.24	3.84	20.00	30.24
+ .98	+ 2.38	+ .98	+ 5.58	+ 3.49

Katelyn's Account	Kimberly's Account	Gwen's Account
$ .42	$ 5.42	$60.42
.59	40.64	3.84
+ 3.42	+ 3.89	+ 21.25

Whose account is the largest?

_____

Whose is the smallest?

_____

Whose is closest to $50?

_____

MATH

161

0-7682-3794-7 *Skills & Practice Gr. 4*

Name _____

Match the $ale

Which item did each of the kids purchase? Calculate the amount. Write the purchase price in each blank.

Jessica:

$17.43
–
_____
$9.14

Tammy:

$43.21
–
_____
$34.86

Heather:

$10.06
–
_____
$1.64

Mark:

$52.46
–
_____
$14.17

Eva:

$65.04
–
_____
$36.94

Roger:

$3.45
–
_____
$2.56

Monica:

$6.99
–
_____
$3.56

Katelyn:

$9.06
–
_____
$5.24

David:

$15.25
–
_____
$6.82

Curt:

$63.45
–
_____
$46.16

Michele:

$32.45
–
_____
$13.50

Carolyn:

$18.46
–
_____
$14.49

Gwen:

$19.24
–
_____
$6.38

Thomas:

$9.43
–
_____
$5.59

162

0-7682-3794-7 *Skills & Practice Gr. 4*

Name _____

McMealworm

McMealworm's is the latest restaurant of that famous fast food creator, Buggs I. Lyke. His McMealworm Burger costs $1.69. An order of Roasted Roaches costs $.59 for the regular size and $.79 for the large size. A Cricket Cola is $.89.

1. You buy a McMealworm Burger and a regular order of Roasted Roaches. What is the total?

2. Your best friend in class orders a McMealworm Burger, a large order of Roasted Roaches and a Cricket Cola. How much will it cost?

3. Your teacher buys a Cricket Cola and a regular order of Roasted Roaches. What does it cost?

4. The principal is very hungry, so his bill comes to $14.37. How much change will he get from $20.00?

5. Your mom goes to McMealworm's to buy your dinner. She spends $3.37. How much change does she get from a $5.00 bill?

6. You have $1.17 in your bank. How much more do you need to pay for a McMealworm Burger?

MATH

Name _____

One-Stop Shopping

Stash McCash is shopping! Find the total cost of the items. Then find how much change Stash should receive.

$3.36 Stickers $.94 $.27 $2.68 $4.25

$3.99 $1.54 $3.15 $1.49

$3.61 $.88 Soccer $1.27 $2.49 $2.55

$.77

Example

Stash has $5.00	Stash has $8.50
Buys	Buys

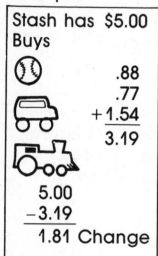

```
      .88
      .77
   + 1.54
     3.19

    5.00
   -3.19
    1.81  Change
```

Stash has $8.50
Buys

Change

Stash has $7.04
Buys

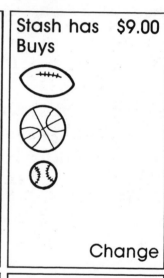

Change

Stash has $9.00
Buys

Change

Stash has $10.95
Buys

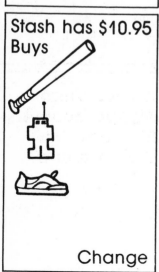

Change

Stash has $10.00
Buys

Change

Stash has $9.24
Buys

Change

Stash has $8.09
Buys

Change

0-7682-3794-7 Skills & Practice Gr. 4

Name _____

Shifty Sam's Shop

Shifty Sam's store is a messy jumble of things. Anything a child could want is there if it can be found under the piles of junk and stuff. But be careful if you buy anything. Check Sam's multiplication!

1. Mighty Man comics cost 13¢ at Shifty Sam's. You buy 4 of these comics. How much should you pay?

2. Your sister decides to buy 2 copies of the latest hit record by the Bird Brains. Each copy costs 89¢. How much will she pay?

3. Your best friend bought 9 marbles at Shifty's. Each marble cost 19¢. How much money did he spend?

4. Crazy stickers cost 21¢ each at Sam's. You buy 7 of them. How much should you pay?

5. Baseball cards are 11¢ each at Shifty Sam's. How much will it cost you for 8 cards?

6. Stinky Stickers have a skunk odor. Your best friend bought 7 Stinky Stickers which cost 18¢ each. How much did he spend?

MATH

Name _____

What a Great Catch!

This is "fishy" business! Use your money "sense" to solve these problems.

$2.47

$1.69

$2.18

$3.29

$2.36

$4.39

$3.62

$1.77

$2.54

$3.76

Buy fish $2.47 A, C and H. 2.18 +2.54 Total Cost $7.19	You have $4.00. Buy fish D. How much money is left?

You have $10.00.
Buy fish E and J.
How much money
is left?

Buy 4 of fish I.

Total Cost

You have $5.75
Buy fish G and C.

How much money
is left?

Buy fish
D, F, J and B.

Total Cost

Buy 6 of fish E.

Total Cost

Buy 3 of fish J
and 6 of fish D.

Total Cost

You have $10.76
Buy 3 of fish A.

How much money
is left?

0-7682-3794-7 *Skills & Practice Gr. 4*

Name _____

Money Math

MATH

$3.42
x 27

$2.45
x 34

$6.42
x 56

$8.43
x 30

$5.41
x 24

$1.24
x 48

$5.42
x 28

$2.43
x 17

$.49
x 56

$2.53
x 41

$8.21
x 37

$4.21
x 36

$5.41
x 42

$.21
x 84

$1.06
x 93

$3.42
x 26

$1.23
x 46

$5.43
x 24

$.89
x 32

$4.25
x 31

0-7682-3794-7 *Skills & Practice Gr. 4*

Name _____

Sam Sillicook's Doughnut Shoppe

Sam Sillicook believes that you should put a little jelly in your belly. He has invented the Super Duper Jelly Doughnuts that are so full of jelly, they leak. His Twisted Circles are drenched in sugar. He has also invented the Banana Cream Doughnut and Jam-jammed Cream Puffs.

1. Your teacher bought 32 Jam-jammed Cream Puffs. They cost $.89 each. How much did your teacher spend?

2. Harry D. Hulk bought 14 Banana Cream Doughnuts for his breakfast at $.65 each. How much did they cost Harry?

3. Your best friend bought 12 Twisted Circles at $.29 each. How much did he spend?

4. You love Jam-jammed Cream Puffs. Your mother buys 17 for your birthday party at $.89 each. How much do they cost?

5. Your principal decided to treat the teachers. He bought 24 Super Duper Jelly Doughnuts at $.49 each. What was the total cost?

6. Your class was treated to 40 Banana Cream Doughnuts which cost $.65 each. What was the total?

Name _____

Perplexing Problems

Heather and Gwen went to the water park. How much did each of them pay?

Total: $ _____
$9.68

On Saturday, James, Gary, Ted and Raul went to the zoo. What was their individual cost to get in?

Total: $ _____
$8.72

Mark, David, Curt and Sam rented a motorized skateboard for 1 hour. What was the cost for each of them — split equally 4 ways?

Total: $ _____
$7.36

Five students pitched in to buy Mr. Jokestopper a birthday gift. How much did each of them contribute?

Total: $ _____
$9.60

All 6 members of the volleyball team received a special shirt for being in the final game. What was the amount of each shirt?

Total: $ _____
$8.16

Mary, Cheryl and Betty went to the skating rink. What was their individual cost?

$ _____

Total:
$7.44

Carol, Katelyn and Kimberly bought lunch at their favorite salad shop. What did each of them pay for lunch?

Total: $ _____
$8.52

Debbie, Sarah, Michele and Kelly earned $6.56 altogether for collecting cans. How much did each of them earn individually?

Total: $ _____
$6.56

Five friends went to the Hamburger Hot Spot Cafe for lunch. They all ordered the special. What did it cost?

Total: $ _____
$7.45

Lee and Ricardo purchased an awesome model rocket together. What was the cost for each of them?

Total: $ _____
$9.52

The total fee for Erik, Bill and Steve to enter the science museum was $8.76. What amount did each of them pay?

Total: $ _____
$8.76

MATH

Name _____

Too Much Information

Underline the **distractor** and solve the problems.

1. All 20 of the students from Sandy's class went to the movies. Tickets cost $1.50 each. Drinks cost 55¢ each. How much altogether did the students spend on tickets?

2. Of the students, 11 were girls and 9 were boys. At $1.50 per ticket, how much did the boys' tickets cost altogether?

3. While 5 students had ice cream, 12 others had candy. Ice cream cost 75¢ per cup. How much did the students spend on ice cream?

4. 7 of the 20 students did not like the movie. 3 of the 20 students had seen the movie before. How many students had not seen the movie before?

5. Mary paid 55¢ for an orange drink and 65¢ for a candy bar. Sarah paid 45¢ for popcorn. How much did Mary's refreshments cost her?

6. 6 of the students spent a total of $16.50 for refreshments and $9.00 for their tickets. How much did each spend for refreshments?

7. 10 of the students went back to see the movie again the next day. Each student paid $1.50 for a ticket, 45¢ for popcorn and 55¢ for a soft drink. How much did each student pay?

0-7682-3794-7 *Skills & Practice Gr. 4*

Name _____

Get the Point

When you add or subtract decimals, remember to "include the point."

Add	Subtract
3.6	6.8
+ 3.3	− 2.6
6.9	4.2

$$\begin{array}{r} 4.2 \\ + 5.2 \end{array} \quad \begin{array}{r} 6.4 \\ + 1.4 \end{array} \quad \begin{array}{r} 3.1 \\ + 7.8 \end{array} \quad \begin{array}{r} 4.7 \\ + 3.2 \end{array} \quad \begin{array}{r} 4.9 \\ + 2.0 \end{array} \quad \begin{array}{r} 3.4 \\ + 1.2 \end{array}$$

$$\begin{array}{r} 5.9 \\ - 3.2 \end{array} \quad \begin{array}{r} 6.7 \\ - 5.6 \end{array} \quad \begin{array}{r} 7.8 \\ - 2.5 \end{array} \quad \begin{array}{r} 5.8 \\ - 3.3 \end{array} \quad \begin{array}{r} 3.9 \\ - 1.5 \end{array} \quad \begin{array}{r} 5.8 \\ - 2.2 \end{array}$$

$$\begin{array}{r} .23 \\ + .25 \end{array} \quad \begin{array}{r} .43 \\ + .16 \end{array} \quad \begin{array}{r} .26 \\ + .42 \end{array} \quad \begin{array}{r} .64 \\ + .15 \end{array} \quad \begin{array}{r} .68 \\ + .31 \end{array} \quad \begin{array}{r} .26 \\ + .31 \end{array}$$

$$\begin{array}{r} .87 \\ - .42 \end{array} \quad \begin{array}{r} .98 \\ - .35 \end{array} \quad \begin{array}{r} .79 \\ - .15 \end{array} \quad \begin{array}{r} .87 \\ - .67 \end{array} \quad \begin{array}{r} .83 \\ - .12 \end{array} \quad \begin{array}{r} .96 \\ - .12 \end{array}$$

$$\begin{array}{r} 3.13 \\ + 2.26 \end{array} \quad \begin{array}{r} 4.72 \\ + 1.15 \end{array} \quad \begin{array}{r} 6.87 \\ + 2.11 \end{array} \quad \begin{array}{r} 4.98 \\ - 2.32 \end{array} \quad \begin{array}{r} 5.97 \\ - 2.54 \end{array} \quad \begin{array}{r} 5.89 \\ - 1.35 \end{array}$$

$$\begin{array}{r} 4.86 \\ - 1.76 \end{array} \quad \begin{array}{r} 5.86 \\ - 3.83 \end{array} \quad \begin{array}{r} 6.98 \\ - 1.45 \end{array} \quad \begin{array}{r} 6.73 \\ + 1.15 \end{array} \quad \begin{array}{r} 4.27 \\ + 5.52 \end{array} \quad \begin{array}{r} 3.46 \\ + 2.31 \end{array}$$

Published by Frank Schaffer Publications. Copyright protected. 0-7682-3794-7 *Skills & Practice Gr. 4*

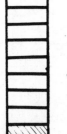

Doing Decimals

Name _____

DECIMAL POINT—A dot placed between the ones
place and the tenths place

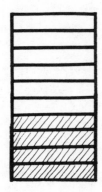

.2 is read as
two tenths.

.4
four tenths

Write answer as decimal for shaded parts.

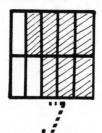

.7
_____

_____

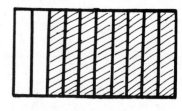

_____

_____

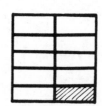

_____

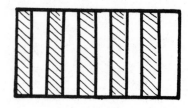

_____

Color parts that match decimals.

.4

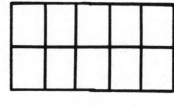

.3

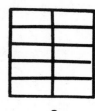

.2

Name _____

Animal Trivia

1. A wood rat has a tail which is 23.6 cm long. A deer mouse has a tail 12.2 cm long. What is the difference?

2. A rock mouse is 26.1 cm long. His tail adds another 14.4 cm. What is his total length from his nose to the tip of his tail?

3. A spotted bat has a tail 4.9 cm long. An evening bat has a tail 3.7 cm long. What is the difference?

4. A pocket gopher has a hind foot 3.5 cm long. A ground squirrel's hind foot is 6.4 cm long. How much longer is the ground squirrel's foot?

5. A cottontail rabbit has ears which are 6.8 cm long. A jackrabbit has ears 12.9 cm long. How much shorter is the cottontail's ear?

6. A porcupine has a tail 30.0 cm long. A possum has a tail 53.5 cm long. How much longer is the possum's tail?

7. The hind foot of a river otter is 14.6 cm long. The hind foot of a hog-nosed skunk is 9.0 cm long. What is the difference?

0-7682-3794-7 *Skills & Practice Gr. 4*

MATH

Name _____

Living History Books

You can learn a lot about a tree by reading its special calendar of rings. Every year a tree grows a new layer of wood. This makes the tree trunk get fatter and fatter. The new layer makes a ring.

You can see the rings on a freshly cut tree stump. When the growing season is wet, the tree grows a lot and the rings are wide. When the season is dry, the tree grows very little. Then the rings are narrow.

This tree was planted in 1973. Use the picture clues to color the rings of the tree stump. Where will the very first ring be?

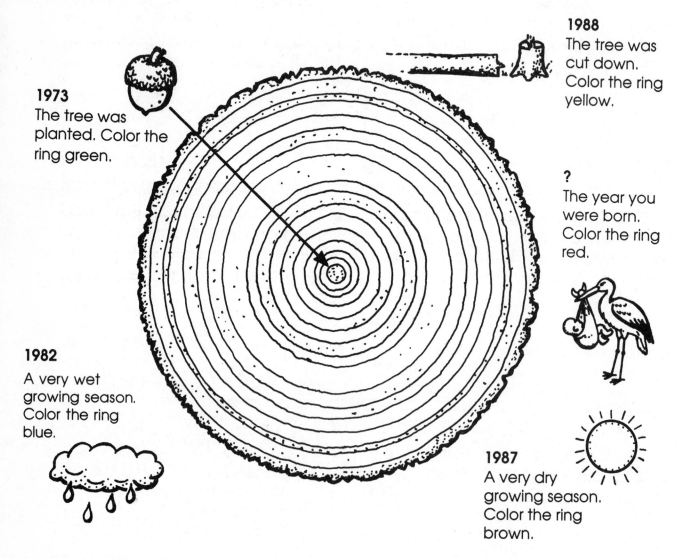

1973
The tree was planted. Color the ring green.

1988
The tree was cut down. Color the ring yellow.

?
The year you were born. Color the ring red.

1982
A very wet growing season. Color the ring blue.

1987
A very dry growing season. Color the ring brown.

Many of the giant sequoia trees in California are more than 2,000 years old. How many rings would a 2,000-year-old tree have?

Name _____

Jogging Geraniums

You will probably never see a flower running down the sidewalk, but you might see one climbing a fence. Most plants are rooted in one place, but they still move.

Roots, stems, leaves, and even flowers move in different ways. The leaves grow toward the light. Roots will grow toward water. Even gravity will make a plant grow straight up in the air, away from the center of the earth.

Look at the three plants below. Tell what made the plants "move" or grow the way they did.

_____ _____ _____

_____ _____ _____

_____ _____ _____

Scientists give special names to the three kinds of plant movements above. The names come from combining two words. Put the correct puzzle pieces together to make the new word. Write the new word. Label the pictures above with the correct new word.

	New Word	Meaning
photo "light" + tropism "turn"	_____	To turn toward the light.
geo "earth" + tropism "turn"	_____	To turn because of of earth's gravity.
hydro "water" + tropism "turn"	_____	To turn toward the water.

Name _____

Cruising Coconuts

"Look at this coconut!" Amy called to Matt as they walked along the beach. Safe inside its thick husk, the coconut had floated across the water. Once it washed up on shore, the green leaves sprouted from this large seed.

Seeds travel in many ways. Below are five ways that seeds travel. Tell how each seed travels.

_____
_____
_____
_____
_____
_____
_____
_____
_____
_____
_____
_____
_____
_____
_____
_____
_____

Fun Fact

Blast Off
The seed pod of the "touch-me-not" swells as it gets ripe. Finally the seed pod bursts and launches seeds in all directions.

0-7682-3794-7 *Skills & Practice Gr. 4*

Name _____

Corny Medicine

Use the words from the Word Bank to complete the puzzle. Cross out each word in the Word Bank as you use it. The remaining words in the Word Bank will help you answer the "Corny Medicine" riddle.

Across
4. Deep growing type of root
6. Beautiful, seed-making part of plant
7. Brightly colored "leafy" parts of the flower
9. Large part of seed that supplies food
10. Sweet food made by the leaves

Down
1. Making food with the help of light
2. Green food-making material in a leaf
3. Plant's "food factory"
5. Plant's anchor
8. Plants get their energy from the

_____.

Corny Medicine
Why did the cornstalk go to the doctor's office?

_____

Word Bank

petals	because	cotyledon	it	root
had	flower	leaf	an	sugar
chlorophyll	sun	photosynthesis	ear	tap
ache				

Name _____

Guess What?

Use the following hints and the Word Bank to decide what insect each riddle describes.

1. I have stout, spiny forelegs.
   I eat insects, including some of my own kind.
   I camouflage well in my surroundings.
   My forelegs make me appear to be praying.

   What am I? _____

2. I have clear wings.
   My body is quite round.
   The males of my species make long, shrill sounds in summer.
   Some of us take 17 years to develop.

   What am I? _____

3. I have two pairs of long, thin wings.
   I eat mosquitoes and other small insects.
   I live near lakes, ponds, streams and rivers.
   My abdomen is very long . . . as long as a darning needle.

   What am I? _____

4. I am a type of beetle.
   My young are often called glowworms.
   My abdomen produces light.

   What am I? _____

5. I like warm, damp and dark places and come out at night.
   Humans hate me.
   I am a destructive household pest.
   I am closely related to grasshoppers and crickets.

   What am I? _____

Word Bank			
lightning bug	cicada	dragonfly	termite
mosquito	ladybug	aphid	praying mantis
bumblebee	cockroach		

Challenge: Research an insect. Draw a detailed picture and write a report about it.

Name _____

Going Places

Looking at a bird's feet can tell you a lot about how they are used. Look at the bird's feet below. Unscramble the bird's name. Write the bird's name by the best sentence. Can you match the pictures with the names?

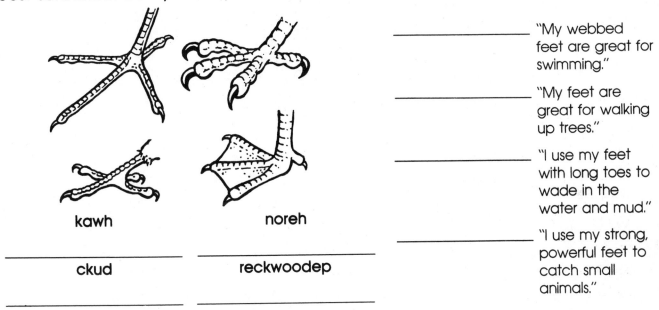

kawh

noreh

_____

ckud

_____

reckwoodep

_____

_____ "My webbed feet are great for swimming."

_____ "My feet are great for walking up trees."

_____ "I use my feet with long toes to wade in the water and mud."

_____ "I use my strong, powerful feet to catch small animals."

Can the shape of a bird's bill tell you anything about what it eats? Look closely at the bills below. Unscramble the bird's name. Write the bird's name by the best sentence. Can you match the pictures with the names?

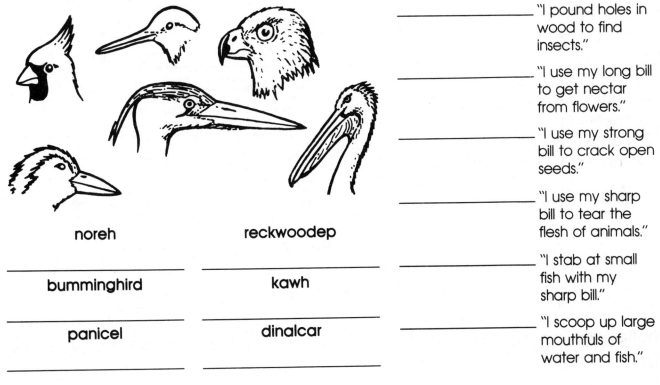

noreh

reckwoodep

_____

bumminghird

_____

kawh

_____

_____

panicel

_____

dinalcar

_____

_____ "I pound holes in wood to find insects."

_____ "I use my long bill to get nectar from flowers."

_____ "I use my strong bill to crack open seeds."

_____ "I use my sharp bill to tear the flesh of animals."

_____ "I stab at small fish with my sharp bill."

_____ "I scoop up large mouthfuls of water and fish."

SCIENCE

Name _____

Family Ties

Unscramble the names of the mom, pop, and baby of these animal families. The coordinates in front of each scrambled name tell where to write it on the chart.

(J-2) nhe   (B-2) woc   (A-1) obc   (C-1) roba

(E-2) ckdu   (G-3) ignolgs   (B-3) plewh   (I-1) arm

(F-2) exvin   (D-3) wfna   (I-3)balm   (G-1) greadn

(I-2) wee   (C-2) ows   (A-3)gentyc   (E-1) kared

(H-2) ream   (D-1) bcku   (F-3) ucb   (J-1) mot

(H-3) loaf   (B-1) lulb   (G-2) sogeo   (A-2) nep

(D-2) eod   (C-3) buc   (J-3) tupol   (H-1) lastonil

(E-3) gludcink   (F-1) odg

		1 Male	2 Female	3 Baby
A	swan			
B	seal			
C	bear			
D	deer			
E	duck			
F	fox			
G	goose			
H	horse			
I	sheep			
J	turkey		hen	

Challenge: Find the group names of these animals and write them on another sheet of paper.

Name _____

Adopt an Animal

The seas of the world are filled with an amazing variety of life. Starfish, crabs, flying fish, angelfish, worms, turtles, sharks and whales all make their home underwater. The shape, color and size of most sea animals depend on their lifestyle and where they live in the seas. Select a sea animal and become an expert on it. Research your animal and complete the profile below.

Common Name _____

Scientific Name _____

Description

weight:

length:

body shape:

tail shape:

color:

unusual characteristics:

Picture

Behaviors

Description of Habitat: _____

_____

_____

Food and Feeding Habits: _____

_____

_____

Migration (if applicable): _____

_____

_____

SCIENCE

Name _____

Food Chains

All living things in the seas depend on each other for food. The food chain begins with sea plants called phytoplankton. A huge variety of tiny animals called zooplankton, feed on the phytoplankton. These animals include shrimp, copepods, and jellyfish. Some of the most common fish—herring, anchovies, and sprats—feed on zooplankton. These fish are eaten by others, such as tuna and mackerel, which in turn are eaten by the superpredators, such as sharks and dolphins. This pattern of eating is called a food chain.

Use the diagram to answer the following questions on another piece of paper.

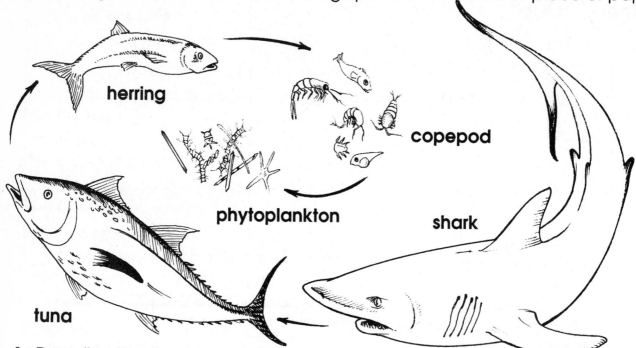

1. Describe the food chain above.

2. If there was a decrease in the copepod population, what would happen to the herring population? Why?

3. What would happen to the phytoplankton population? Why?

4. If the tuna population became endangered, what would the result be?

5. What does it mean when we say, "The death of one species in the food chain upsets the rest of the chain"?

6. An example of a land food chain might be fly-spider-bird-cat. Give an – other example of a land food chain.

7. Draw another sea food chain. Explain and give an example for each step.

Name _____

Polluting Our Seas

The seas provide us with many resources that we need to survive and to keep our industries going. Fish, shellfish, seaweeds, and minerals are just a few of the seas' resources. How long these will last depends on if and how badly we continue to pollute the seas.

For hundreds of years, people have been throwing garbage into the seas. Every day, billions of tons of waste, such as poisonous chemicals, radioactive waste, and plastics, are dumped into the seas. One of the worst sources of pollution is an oil spill. This results when tankers collide with each other or crash into rocks. There are thousands of oil spills every year. Most are small and are not reported, but some are huge. The biggest was in February, 1991, when oil was spilled into the Persian Gulf. It is thought that more than 1.2 million tons of oil spilled into the sea. It was more than 20 times bigger than the *Exxon Valdez* oil spill in 1989 off the coast of Alaska.

The seas cannot continue to be polluted without endangering the sea life. As the world population increases, people will be looking more to the seas to find products and resources.

Pretend you are a reporter. Use the headline below to write an article about pollution of the seas. Research to find interesting facts to back up your story.

SCIENCE

Save Our Seas

Name _____

Animal Comparisons

A Venn diagram is a great way to compare things. Use the one below to compare two animals of the seas. Fill in the circle below the dolphin with characteristics common only to this animal. Fill in the circle below the shark with characteristics common only to the shark. Where the circles overlap, fill in characteristics both animals share. Write a story about your findings on another piece of paper.

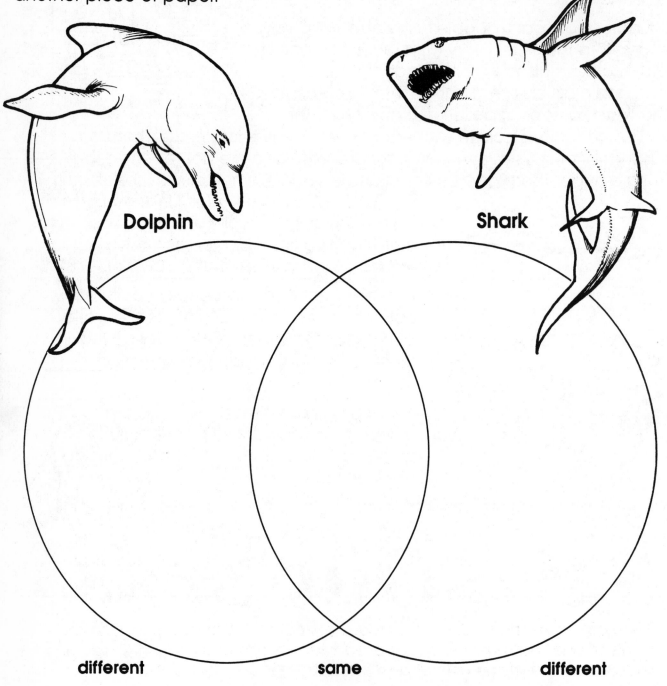

Dolphin   **Shark**

different   **same**   **different**

Name _____

Danger Ahead!

You will never see a dodo bird or a saber-tooth tiger. These animals are gone forever. They are **extinct**.

The animals on this page are not extinct, but they are in danger of becoming extinct. They are **endangered**. There may not be enough of them to reproduce. They are endangered because of the way people live.

There are many reasons why some animals are endangered. The signs on this page give clues to three main reasons.

Look at the signs. What do you think the three reasons are? Write them below.

1. _____

_____

2. _____

_____

3. _____

_____

Unscramble the names of these endangered animals.

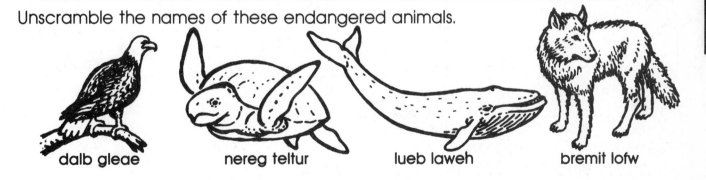

dalb gleae   nereg teltur   lueb laweh   bremit lofw

_____   _____   _____   _____

• There are more than 100 endangered animals in North America. Find the name of one that lives near your area. Make a poster to help people become aware of this animal and the danger it is in.

SCIENCE

Name _____

Threatened and Endangered Animals

Many of the earth's animals are threatened or extinct. Use the names of the animals to build a puzzle. Only use the bold-faced words.
Hint: Build off **rhinoceros**.

Word Box

brown **hyena**	Darwin's **rhea**	red **wolf**	black-footed **ferret**
Spanish **lynx**	Philippine **eagle**	**gavial**	ring-tailed **lemur**
giant **panda**	blue **whale**	**numbat**	resplendent **quetzal**
Arabian **oryx**	Grevy's **zebra**	**kakapo**	Galapagos **penguin**
Indian **python**	wild **yak**	**dugong**	

Use an encyclopedia to answer each question.

1. Which animal above is related to the manatee? _____

2. Which is the cousin of the crocodile? _____

3. Which is related to the ostrich? _____

Name _____

Animal Magic

Read Column A. Choose an answer from Column B. Write the number of the answer in the Magic Square. The first one has been done for you.

Column A	**Column B**
A. grizzly bear	1. large bear of the American grasslands
B. koala	2. lives on dry grasslands of South Africa
C. peregrine falcon	3. the most valuable reptile in the world
D. California condor	4. largest soaring bird of North America
E. black-footed ferret	5. the tallest American bird
F. cheetah	6. the fastest animal on land
G. orangutan	7. the only great ape outside Africa
H. giant panda	8. large aquatic seallike animal
I. Florida manatee	9. large black and white mammal of China
J. kit fox	10. small, fast mammal; nocturnal predator
K. blue whale	11. largest animal in the world
L. whooping crane	12. member of the weasel family
M. red wolf	13. has interbred with coyotes in some areas
N. green sea turtle	14. also called a duck hawk; size of a crow
O. brown hyena	15. eats leaves of the eucalyptus tree
P. jaguar	16. known as *el tigre* in Spanish

A 1	B __	C __	D __
E __	F __	G __	H __
I __	J __	K __	L __
M __	N __	O __	P __

Add the numbers across, down and diagonally. What answer do you get? ____

Why do you think this is called a magic square? _____

Name _____

Bald Eagle Puzzler

Read each statement about the bald eagle. If the statement is false, darken the letter in the circle to the left of that statement. The letters not darkened spell out the name of the chemical that affected the bald eagle's food supply.

(P) Due to federal protection, the bald eagle population is increasing.

(R) It is legal to shoot this bird today.

(E) This bird has keen eyesight and strong wings.

(N) The wingspan of this bird is about 3 feet.

(A) The nest of a bald eagle is made of mud and rocks.

(S) This bird eats mainly fish.

(T) This bird likes to eat only berries and seeds.

(T) The bald eagle is found only in North America.

(B) Only four bald eagles exist today in the United States.

(M) An injured bald eagle may be kept as a pet.

(I) Chemical poisons in the bald eagle's food caused its eggs to crack before incubation could be completed.

(C) The nest of a bald eagle is built high on a cliff or in a tree.

(I) This bird is the national symbol of the United States.

(L) The bald eagle is noted for its bright orange head.

(D) The bald eagle has a hooked beak.

(E) The nest of a bald eagle is called an aerie.

What is the type of chemical? __ __ __ __ __ __ __ __ __

Name _____

Nippers, Rippers, and Grinders

1.

2.

3.

Scientists tell us that some of the dinosaurs were meat-eaters and others were plant-eaters. But how do the scientists know? By looking at the teeth of certain dinosaur fossils, scientists can tell what those dinosaurs ate. Meat-eaters had sharp, saw-edged teeth (figure 1), for cutting and ripping flesh. Plant-eating dinosaurs had either peg-like teeth (figure 2), for nipping plants, or flat grinding teeth (figure 3), to munch tough twigs or leaves.

1. Match the dinosaur to its teeth by writing its name in the space provided.
2. Circle either "M" for meat-eater or "P" for plant-eater.

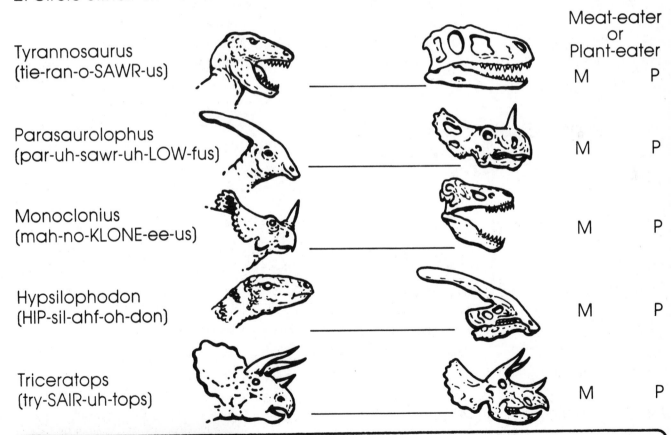

Meat-eater
or
Plant-eater

Tyrannosaurus
(tie-ran-o-SAWR-us)
_____   M   P

Parasaurolophus
(par-uh-sawr-uh-LOW-fus)
_____   M   P

Monoclonius
(mah-no-KLONE-ee-us)
_____   M   P

Hypsilophodon
(HIP-sil-ahf-oh-don)
_____   M   P

Triceratops
(try-SAIR-uh-tops)
_____   M   P

Fantastic Fact

The **Tyrannosaurus**, whose name means "king of the tyrant lizards," was the largest meat-eater. It weighed over 8 tons and was over 15 meters long. Its teeth were over 15 cm long and had edges like a steak knife.

0-7682-3794-7 *Skills & Practice Gr. 4*

SCIENCE

Name _____

Dinosaur Defense

How did the plant-eating dinosaurs protect themselves from the attacks of the fierce meat-eating dinosaurs? One way was to travel in groups. But they also had other ways to defend themselves. For example, some had horns and some could run very fast.

- Look at the plant-eating dinosaurs below. Find the features of their bodies that gave them protection from their enemies. Explain in the space provided.

Stegosaurus
(steg-uh-SAWR-us)

_____
_____
_____
_____

Ankylosaurus
(ang-KILE-uh-sawr-us)

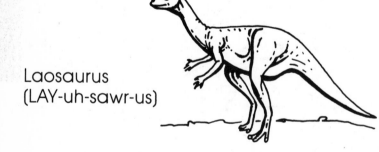

_____
_____
_____
_____
_____

Laosaurus
(LAY-uh-sawr-us)

_____
_____
_____
_____

Triceratops
(try-SAIR-uh-tops)

_____
_____
_____

Name _____

Dino-Find

Find the hidden words in the puzzle below. The words may be written forward, backward, up, down or diagonally. Circle the words. When you have located and circled all the words, write the remaining letters at the bottom of the page to spell out a message.

ALLOSAURUS   **BIRD HIP**   **FOSSIL**   **PLANT-EATER**
APATOSAURUS   **COELURUS**   **JURASSIC**   **PLATED**
ARMORED   **DINOSAUR**   **MEAT-EATER**   **SAUROPOD**
ARCHAEOPTERYX **DIPLODOCUS**   **PALEONTOLOGIST** **STEGOSAURUS**

```
S  D  B  U  R  L  I  S  S  O  F  I  S  M  N
G  U  I  T  H  I  S  P  E  R  I  O  T  E  T
J  D  R  U  A  S  O  N  I  D  S  H  E  A  S
U  A  U  D  U  L  L  O  S  E  W  S  G  T  I
R  E  H  A  A  S  S  R  C  R  O  V  O  A  G
A  E  I  R  E  U  O  P  D  O  M  U  S  U  O
S  C  P  H  O  S  R  F  O  M  N  O  A  R  L
S  R  T  L  U  A  O  T  E  R  R  I  U  E  O
I  C  A  A  N  M  M  E  A  U  U  A  R  M  T
C  R  O  O  D  D  E  A  L  P  A  U  U  A  N
A  C  N  D  R  E  T  I  S  C  A  C  S  S  O
E  X  Y  R  E  A  I  P  E  A  H  U  R  S  E
T  O  T  H  D  T  P  N  A  L  D  C  U  A  L
R  E  T  A  E  T  I  P  N  A  L  P  E  S  A
E  R  A  L  L  O  S  A  U  R  U  S  T  S  P
```

Hidden message: _____

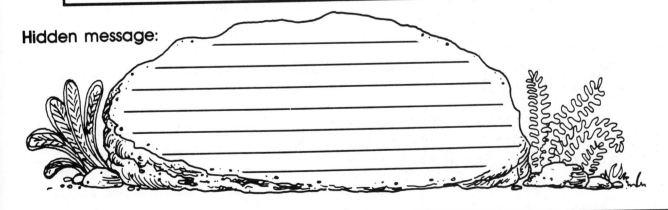

Name _____

Body Building Blocks

Just as some houses are built with bricks, your body is built with cells. Your body is made up of about 500 trillion cells.

Cells differ in **size** and **shape**, but they all have a few things in common. All cells have a nucleus. The **nucleus** is the center of the cell. It controls the cell's activities. Cells can **divide** and become two cells exactly like the original cell.

Your body has many kinds of cells. Each kind has a special job. **Muscle** cells help you move. Nerve cells carry messages between your brain and other parts of your body. Blood cells carry **oxygen** to other cells in your body.

Complete each sentence using the words in bold from above.

The __ __ __ __ __ __ controls the cell's
    3
activities.

Cells differ in __ __ __ __ and __ __ __ __ __.
        2   1

One cell can __ __ __ __ __ __ into two cells.
                 6

__ __ __ __ __ __ cells help you move.
     5

Blood cells carry __ __ __ __ __ __ to other
cells in your body.   4

muscle cell

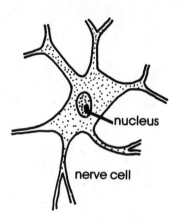

nucleus

nerve cell

Unscramble the numbered letters above to discover this amazing fact.

You began life as a __ __ __ __ __ __ cell!
           1 2 3 4 5 6

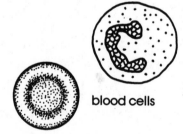

blood cells

Fun Facts

People and most animals are made of billions or even trillions of cells. But some animals are made of only one cell. To find out more about these animals, look up "protozoans" in your library.

Name _____

Bone Up on Your Bones!

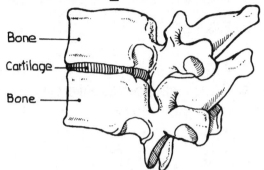

Bone —
Cartilage —
Bone —

When you were born, your skeleton was made of soft bones called cartilage. As you grew, most of that cartilage turned into bone. However, all people still have some cartilage in their bodies. Our noses and our ears are cartilage, and there are pads of cartilage between sections of our backbone that act as cushions.

Besides supporting the body, the bones also serve other important purposes. They are storage houses for important minerals like calcium and phosphorous and the center of the bone, called bone marrow, produces new blood cells for our bodies.

Try the experiment below to discover more about bones.

Materials Needed
soup bones from a butcher
(Shin bones are ideal. Have him/her saw it in half for you.)

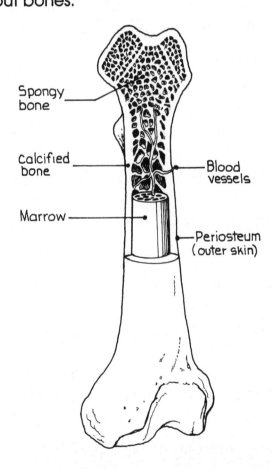

Spongy bone

Calcified bone

Blood vessels

Marrow

Periosteum (outer skin)

1. Look at the end of the whole bone. Find the parts labeled on the diagram to the right.

2. Now, separate the bone. Look inside the cavity which is filled with marrow. Write 5 adjectives to describe the marrow.

_____

_____

3. Pull away the skin covering the bone. What is the name for this outer skin?

_____

If the bone is fresh, you will see small red dots where blood vessels enter the bone. Name two types of blood vessels.

_____

4. Carefully scoop out the bone marrow. Your teacher will now boil the bone to get it really clean. What do you see now? Write three facts about bones.

_____

_____

_____

SCIENCE

Name _____

A Heart-y Puzzle for You

Use the clues to fill in the crossword puzzle about the heart.

Word Box				
aorta	artery	atrium	capillary	cardiovascular
heart	vein	valves	ventricle	heartbeat

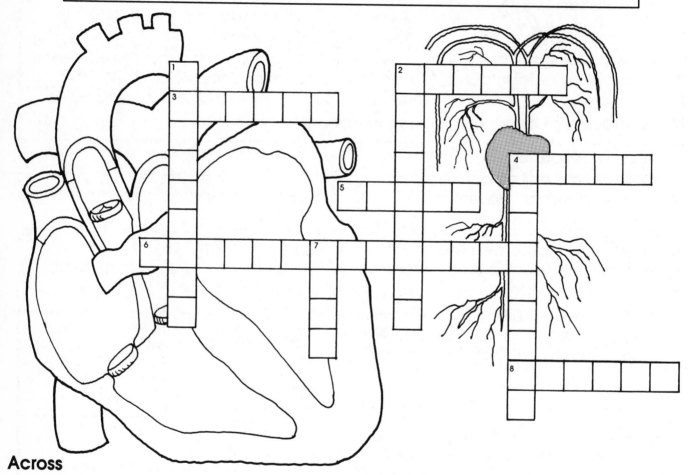

Across

2. control the flow of blood
3. a blood vessel that carries blood away from the heart
4. a muscular organ that circulates blood
5. the main artery
6. pertaining to the heart and blood vessels
8. receives blood into the heart

Down

1. a blood vessel that connects an artery to a vein
2. pumps blood out of the heart
4. a complete pulsation
7. a blood vessel that carries blood into the heart

Name _____

I Can Feel My Heartbeat

Each time your heart pumps the blood through veins and arteries, you can feel it! It's called a pulse. You can feel your pulse in two places where the arteries are close to your skin. Gently, place two fingers on the inside of your wrist or on your neck next to your windpipe. Silently count the pulses and complete the chart below.

*Teacher should time and direct each part. Time for 6 seconds, then multiply by 10.

Pulse Rate	Sitting	Walking Around Room for 1 Minute	Wait 2 Minutes, Then Standing	After 25 Jumping Jacks	Wait 1 Minute, Then Lying Down	After Jogging in Place for 2 Minutes	After Resting for 5 Minutes
in 6 seconds							
in 1 minute							

You should have found that your heart beats faster when you are active. That's because your body uses more oxygen when it exercises, and the blood must circulate faster to get more oxygen! Now, in a group of four, compare pulse rates and find the average for your group (using the 1 minute rate).

Pulse Rate	Sitting	After Walking	After Standing	After Jumping	After Lying Down	After Jogging	After Resting
You							
Person #2							
Person #3							
Person #4							
Total							
÷ 4 to find average							

SCIENCE

0-7682-3794-7 *Skills & Practice Gr. 4*

Name _____

Our Busy Brains

Your body's central nervous system includes your brain, spinal cord, and nerves that transmit information. It is responsible for receiving information from your senses, analyzing this information, and deciding how your body should respond. Once it has decided, it sends instructions triggering the required actions.

The central nervous system makes some simple decisions about your body's actions within the spinal cord. These are called spinal reflexes and include actions like pulling your hand away from a hot object. For the most part, however, the majority of decisions involve the brain.

Your brain, which weighs about three pounds, controls almost all of the activities in your body. It is made up of three major parts—the cerebrum, the cerebellum, and the brain stem. The cerebrum is divided into two hemispheres which are responsible for all thought and learning processes. The cerebellum is also divided into two parts, and they control all voluntary muscle movement. The brain stem, which is about the size of your thumb, takes care of all involuntary functions. Look around your classroom. Everyone's brain is telling him/her to do things. Fill in the jobs of each part of the brain and then answer the questions below.

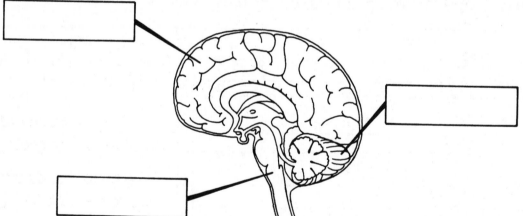

Name someone in your room who is using his/her cerebellum. _____

What is he/she doing? _____

Name someone who is using his/her brain stem. _____

What is he/she doing? _____

Name someone in your room who is using his/her cerebrum. _____

What is he/she doing? _____

Name _____

Find Your Brain Dominance

The two sides of the cerebellum work to control all voluntary movements. These include walking, running, writing and all other movements that we consciously want to do. One side of the cerebellum is usually dominant, or depended upon more heavily. The side that is dominant depends on the person. The left side of the brain controls the right side of your body and vice versa. That means that if a person writes with his/her right hand, he/she is probably left-brain dominant. Answer these questions to find your dominance.

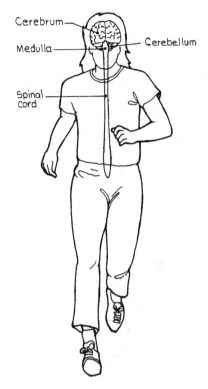

Cerebrum
Medulla
Cerebellum
Spinal Cord

Try This:	Right	Left
Clasp your hands together. Which is on top?		
Pick up a pencil to write. Which hand do you use?		
Take 3 steps. Which foot did your start with?		
Try to do the splits. Which leg is in front?		
Hold your arms. Which arm is on top?		
Blink your eye. Which one did you wink?		
Pick up a fork. Which hand do you eat with?		
Hop 5 times on one foot. Which foot did you use?		
Look through a camera, telescope or microscope. Which eye did you use?		

How many times did you use your right? _____

How many times did you use your left? _____

Which side of your brain is probably more dominant? _____

(Be careful . . . they're opposite.)

*Make a class graph showing dominant sides.

0-7682-3794-7 *Skills & Practice Gr. 4*

Name _____

Your Pizza's Path

The digestive system is the group of organs that work together to gain fuel from the foods we eat and discard the unwanted waste. This system breaks down food into simple substances your body's cells can use. It then absorbs these substances into the bloodstream and any leftover waste matter is eliminated.

When you eat pizza (or any food), each bite you take goes through a path in the human body called the alimentary canal, or the digestive tract. This canal consists of the mouth, esophagus, stomach, and small and large intestines. It is in this path that foods are broken down, vitamins are saved and poisons are discarded. Study the path below.

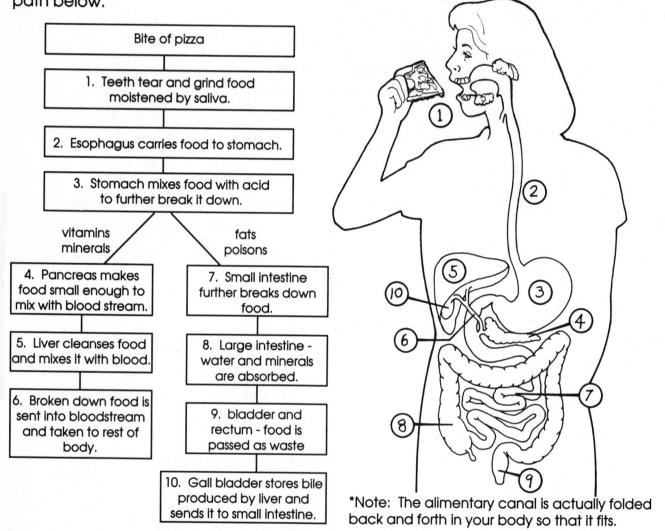

Bite of pizza

1. Teeth tear and grind food moistened by saliva.

2. Esophagus carries food to stomach.

3. Stomach mixes food with acid to further break it down.

vitamins minerals   fats poisons

4. Pancreas makes food small enough to mix with blood stream.

5. Liver cleanses food and mixes it with blood.

6. Broken down food is sent into bloodstream and taken to rest of body.

7. Small intestine further breaks down food.

8. Large intestine - water and minerals are absorbed.

9. bladder and rectum - food is passed as waste

10. Gall bladder stores bile produced by liver and sends it to small intestine.

*Note: The alimentary canal is actually folded back and forth in your body so that it fits.

1. Use a black crayon to trace the path of the healthy parts of the pizza.

2. Use a blue crayon to trace the path of the unhealthy parts of the pizza.

3. Name 3 parts of the pizza that are healthy. _____

4. Name 3 parts of the pizza that are unhealthy. _____

Name _____

Oh, Yes, I See Now!

One of the most sensitive nerves in your body is the optic nerve. It connects your eyes to your brain. The optic nerve receives messages from other nerves that surround your eyes in the retina. As light is caught in the pupils of your eyes, it is sent to the retina, then to the optic nerve, and at last to the brain. Try this experiment to watch your pupils change!

1. Close your eyes and cover them with your hands. Count to 100, open your eyes, and immediately observe them in a mirror. Draw how your eyes look.

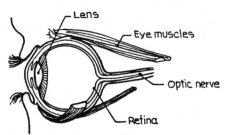

2. Now look at a light in your classroom. Count to 100 and then draw your eyes again.

SCIENCE

3. How did your pupils change from one experiment to another? _____

_____

4. Why do you think they changed? _____

_____

5. Why do people wear sunglasses? _____

_____

0-7682-3794-7 *Skills & Practice Gr. 4*

Name _____

Energy Savers

Fats give you twice as much energy as protein or carbohydrates. Your body uses fats to save energy for future use. The fats we eat come from animals in the form of meat, eggs, milk, and much more. We also get fats from some plants like beans, peanuts, and corn. But not all plants give us fats in our diet.

Look at the pictures.
Circle the foods which are rich in fat.
Then list them on the chart.

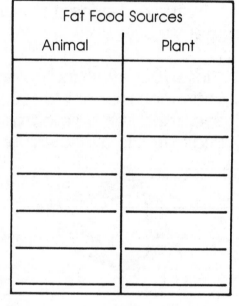

Fat Food Sources	
Animal	Plant

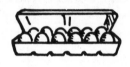

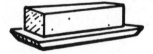

Find Out

Here is a simple test to tell if a food has fat.
1. Cut a brown paper bag into several four-inch squares.
2. Rub a piece of food on a square until it looks wet.
3. Label the paper.
4. Let the paper dry overnight.
5. Hold the paper up to the window the next day. If there is a grease spot, the food contains fat.

Name _____

You Are What You Eat!

Having a nutritious diet helps your body fight diseases. Write the foods from the Word Bank in their correct category(s). Use references if necessary.

<table>
<tr><td colspan="5" align="center">Word Bank</td></tr>
<tr><td>tomatoes</td><td>bread</td><td>eggs</td><td>milk</td><td>potatoes</td></tr>
<tr><td>oranges</td><td>sugar</td><td>fish</td><td>cereal</td><td>green beans</td></tr>
<tr><td>chicken</td><td>margarine</td><td>cheese</td><td>noodles</td><td>rice</td></tr>
<tr><td>butter</td><td>apples</td><td>red meat</td><td></td><td></td></tr>
</table>

Carbohydrates

_____   _____

_____   _____

_____   _____

_____   _____

Proteins

_____   _____

_____   _____

_____   _____

_____   _____

Fats

_____   _____

_____   _____

_____   _____

Minerals

_____   _____

_____   _____

_____   _____

Below is a list of the food groups. Write what you ate yesterday in each group. Did you get enough servings of each?

Milk Group (3 servings a day)

_____

_____

Fruit & Vegetable Group (1 serving a day)

_____

_____

Grain Group (4 servings a day)

_____

_____

Meat-Egg-Nut-Bean Group
(2 servings a day)

_____

_____

SCIENCE

Name _____

What's in a Label?

Labels give us all kinds of information about the foods we eat. The ingredients of a food are listed in a special order. The ingredient with the largest amount is listed first, the one with the next largest amount is listed second, and so on.

Complete the "Breakfast Table Label Survey" using information from the label on this page.

Breakfast Table Label Survey

1. What does R.D.A. mean? _____

2. Calories per serving with milk _____

3. Calories per serving without milk _____

4. Calories per ½ cup serving of milk _____

5. Protein per serving with milk _____

6. Protein per serving without milk _____

7. Protein in ½ cup serving of milk _____

8. Percentage U.S. R.D.A. of Vitamin C _____

9. First ingredient _____

10. Is sugar a listed ingredient? _____

    If yes, in what place is it listed? _____

11. Were any vitamins added? _____

12. What preservative was added? _____

Find Out: What food product has this ingredient label? "Carbonated water, sugar, corn sweetener, natural flavorings, caramel color, phosphoric acid, caffeine."

Nutrition Information Per Serving

Serving Size: 1 OZ. (About 1⅓ Cups) (28.35 g)
Servings Per Package: 14

	1 OZ. (28.35 g) Cereal	with ½ Cup (118mL) Vitamin D Fortified Whole Milk
Calories	110	190
Protein	1 g	5 g
Carbohydrate	25 g	31 g
Fat	1 g	5 g
Sodium	195 mg	255 mg

Percentages Of U.S. Recommended Daily Allowances (U.S. RDA)

Protein	2%	8%
Vitamin A	25%	30%
Vitamin C	*	*
Thiamine	25%	30%
Riboflavin	25%	35%
Niacin	25%	25%
Calcium	*	15%
Iron	10%	10%
Vitamin D	10%	25%
Vitamin B_6	25%	30%
Folic Acid	25%	25%
Vitamin B_{12}	25%	30%
Phosphorus	2%	10%
Magnesium	2%	6%
Zinc	10%	15%
Copper	2%	4%

*Contains less than 2% of the U.S. RDA for these nutrients.

Ingredients: Corn Flour, Sugar, Oat Flour, Salt, Hydrogenated Coconut and/or Palm Kernel Oil, Corn Syrup, Honey and fortified with the following nutrients: Vitamin A Palmitate, Niacinamide, Iron, Zinc Oxide (Source of Zinc), Vitamin B_6, Riboflavin (Vitamin B_2), Thiamine Mononitrate (Vitamin B_1), Vitamin B_{12}, Folic Acid and Vitamin D_2. BHA added to packaging material to preserve freshness.

Carbohydrate Information

	1 OZ. (28.35 g) Cereal	With ½ Cup (118 mL) Whole Milk
Starch and Related Carbohydrates	14 g	14 g
Sucrose and Other Sugars	11 g	17 g
Total Carbohydrates	25 g	31 g

Name _____

I'm Tired

Do you feel tired after raking the lawn? You feel tired then because work takes a lot of energy. **Energy** is the ability to do work.

There are many forms of energy. Food contains **chemical energy**. Your television uses **electrical energy**. The furnace in your house gives you **heat energy**. The moving parts of your bicycle have another form of energy called **mechanical energy**. Anything that moves has mechanical energy.

Energy can be changed from one form to another. Your radio changes electrical energy into sound energy. Your parents' car may change chemical energy into heat energy and the heat energy into mechanical energy.

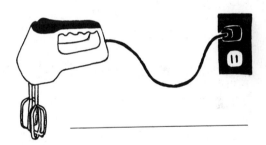

• Complete the puzzle using the clues below.

1. A fire gives us _ _ _ _ energy.

2. Anything that moves has

   _ _ _ _ _ _ _ _ _ _ energy.

3. _ _ _ _ _ _ is the ability to do work.

4. Energy can be _ _ _ _ _ _ _ _ from one form into another form.

5. Food contains _ _ _ _ _ _ _ _ energy.

Name _____

Energy in Motion

"Mom, how can I knock down more pins?" Matt asked. "You are bowling straight enough, Matt. Try rolling the ball faster, or try using a heavier ball," his mom replied.

The bowling ball is doing work by knocking over the pins. The ball has kinetic energy. **Kinetic energy** is the energy of motion.

If the ball had more kinetic energy, it could do more work and knock down more pins. If you increase the mass of the ball or its speed, you would increase its kinetic energy.

Just before Matt rolled the ball, he was standing still and not moving. Matt's body had stored energy that would turn into kinetic energy once he started swinging the ball. This stored energy is called **potential energy.**

• Write **P** next to the pictures that show potential energy and **K** next to the pictures that show kinetic energy.

• Look back at the picture of Matt getting ready to bowl.
  1. At what point will the ball have the most potential energy?_____
  2. At what point will the ball have the most kinetic energy?_____
  3. At what point will the ball have the least kinetic energy?_____
  4. At what point will the ball have the least potential energy?_____

Challenge: A roller-coaster car with people in it will travel much faster than an empty car. Why?

         0-7682-3794-7 *Skills & Practice Gr. 4*

Name _____

Around and Around

A doorknob is a simple machine you use every day. It is a **wheel and axle machine.** The wheel is connected to the axle. The axle is a center post. When the wheel moves, the axle does too.

Opening a door by turning the axle with your fingers is very hard. But by turning the doorknob, which is the "wheel," you use much less force. The doorknob turns the axle for you. The doorknob makes it easy because it is much bigger than the axle. You turn the doorknob a greater distance, but with much less force.

Sometimes the "wheel" of a wheel and axle machine doesn't look like a wheel. But look at the path the doorknob, a wheel, makes when it is turned. The path makes a circle, just like a wheel.

- Color just the wheels of the wheel and axle machines below.

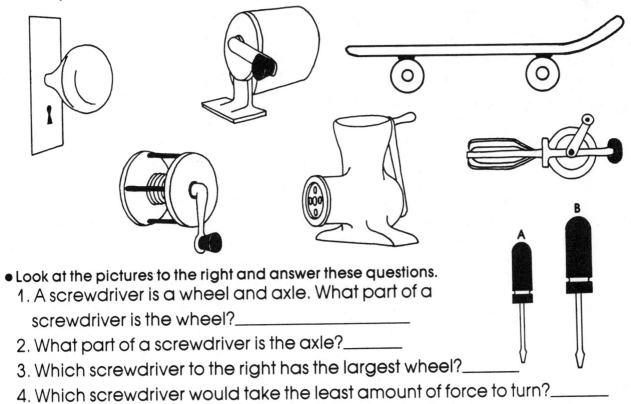

- Look at the pictures to the right and answer these questions.
  1. A screwdriver is a wheel and axle. What part of a screwdriver is the wheel?_____
  2. What part of a screwdriver is the axle?_____
  3. Which screwdriver to the right has the largest wheel?_____
  4. Which screwdriver would take the least amount of force to turn?_____
  5. Which screwdriver must travel the greatest distance?_____

Stumper

Why is the crank on a meat grinder larger than the crank on a pencil sharpener?

Why is the steering wheel on a truck larger than the steering wheel on a car?

SCIENCE

Levers

Name _____

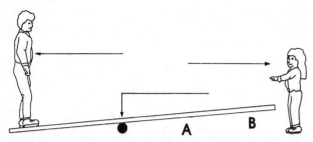

Word Bank

simple	force
easier	load
fulcrum	distance
A	B

• **Use the words from the Word Bank to complete the sentences.**

Mandy wants to try to lift her dad off the ground. Where should Mandy stand on the board? By standing on point __, Mandy can lift her dad.

The board resting on the log is an example of a _ _ _ _ _ _ _ machine called a lever. A **lever** has three parts–the **force**, the **fulcrum**, and the **load.** Mandy is the force. The point on which the lever turns is called the _ _ _ _ _ _ _ _ . And Mandy's dad, the object to be lifted, is called the _ _ _ _. The greater the _ _ _ _ _ _ _ _ between the _ _ _ _ _ and the fulcrum, the _ _ _ _ _ _ _ it is to lift the load. The closer the distance between the **force** and the **fulcrum,** the harder it is to lift the load.

• **Label the picture of Mandy and her father with these words: load, force,** and **fulcrum.**

1   2

Fulcrum far away from load   Fulcrum close to load

The distance between the **load** and the **fulcrum** also affects the force needed to lift a load. The closer the fulcrum is to the load, the easier it is to lift the load.

• **Look at the pictures above to answer these questions.**

1. Matt wants to move a large rock with a lever. Which lever would let him use the least amount of force to move the rock?_____

2. Which lever would have to be moved the greatest distance to move the rock?_____

3. Why is a lever called a simple machine? _____

• **Label the force, fulcrum,** and **load** of the levers below.

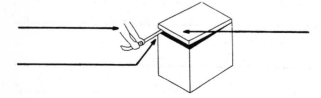

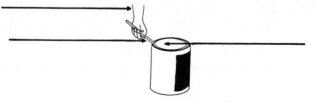

Name _____

Dancing Parsley

Investigate

Run a comb through your hair 30
times. Go only one way. Hold the
comb next to some parsley flakes.
What happened? _____

_____

Run the comb through your hair 30
times again. Hold it next to some
shredded tissue.
What happened? _____

_____

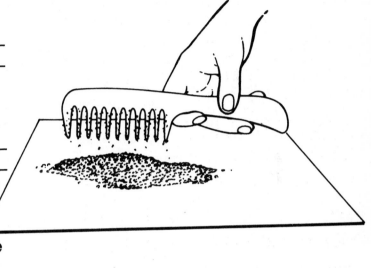

Rub the comb 30 times against the
hairs on your arm, on a woolen
sweater or on a shiny shirt or
blouse. Rub only one way. Hold the
comb next to the parsley flakes.
Did the comb pick them up? _____
Hold the comb next to the shredded tissue.
Did the comb pick up the tissue? _____

Extending the Concept

Tear another tissue into long, thin strips. Run the comb through your hair 30
times. Hold the comb next to one of the strips of tissue.
Did the comb attract the tissue? _____

Dancing Cereal

Arrange two long rows of puffed rice cereal next to each other. Run the
comb through your hair 30 times. Hold the comb between the rows of
cereal.
What happened? _____
Hold the comb with the cereal stuck to it in the air and wait 2 minutes.
What happened? _____

0-7682-3794-7 *Skills & Practice Gr. 4*

Name _____

Charge It!

Have you ever scuffed your feet as you walked across the carpet and then brought your finger close to someone's nose? Zap!! Did the person jump? The spark you made was **static electricity.**

Static electricity is made when objects gain or lose tiny bits of electricity called **electrical charges.** The charges are either positive or negative.

Objects that have electrical charges act like magnets, attracting or repelling each other. If two objects have **like charges** (the same kind of charges), they will repel each other. If two objects have **unlike charges** (different charges), the objects will attract each other.

Find out more about static electricity by unscrambling the word(s) in each sentence.

1. Flashes of (ghtlining) _____ in the sky are caused by static electricity in the clouds.

2. Electrical charges are either (ospivite) _____ or (givnatee) _____.

3. Small units of electricity are called (srgache) _____.

4. Two objects with unlike charges will (arcttat) _____ each other.

5. Sometimes electric charges jump between objects with (unkile) _____ charges. This is what happens when lightning flashes in the sky.

Look at the pictures below to see how static electricity affects objects.

1. Name the two objects that are interacting in each picture.

2. Tell whether the two objects have **like charges** or **unlike charges.**

Objects: _____   _____   _____

_____   _____   _____

Charges: _____   _____   _____

Something Special: Hold this paper against a wall and rub it with 50 quick strokes with the side of your pencil. Take your hand away. Presto! The paper stays on the wall because of the static electricity you have made.

Name _____

Power Paths

A **circuit** is a path along which electricity travels. It travels in a loop around the circuit. In the circuit pictured below, the electricity travels through the wire, battery, switch, and bulb. The electricity must have a source. What is the source in this circuit? You're right if you said the battery.

If the wire in the circuit were cut, there would be a **gap**. The electricity wouldn't be able to flow across the gap. Then the bulb would not light. This is an example of an **open circuit**. If there were no gaps, the bulb would light. This is an example of a **closed circuit**.

switch

1. Draw in the wire to the battery, switch, and bulb to make a closed circuit.

   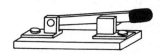

2. Draw in the wire to the battery, switch, and bulb to make an open circuit.

   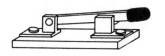

- Unscramble the word at the end of each sentence to fill in the blank.

3. Even the tiniest _____ can stop the electricity from flowing. (apg)

4. A _____ is a path along which electricity flows. (ricituc)

5. If there are no gaps, or openings, a _____ circuit is formed. (sodelc)

6. A battery is a source of _____ in some circuits. (treleciytci)

> **Fun Fact**
>
> If all of the circuits in a small personal computer were made out of wire and metal switches, the computer would fill the average classroom. Today these circuits are found in tiny chips called microchips.

SCIENCE

Name _____

Fill the Gap

The bulb won't light in the circuit above. What's wrong with the circuit? It has a gap. How could you fill the gap to make a closed circuit? The easiest way would be to connect the two wires, but with what?

What would happen if you placed a paper clip across the gap? How about a nail? The bulb would light up. The nail or paper clip would form a bridge across the gap. The nail and paper clip carry, or **conduct,** electricity. They are both **conductors.**

Some materials will not carry the electricity well enough to make the bulb light. Try a rubber band. The bulb won't light. Rubber is a poor conductor of electricity. It is called an **insulator.**

- Find the different materials hidden in the wordsearch. The materials listed "up and down" are conductors. Those written "across" are insulators. List these materials in the correct group.

C O T T O N P	**Insulator**	**Conductor**
O K G T S O R		
P A P E R X K	_____	_____
P L A S T I C	_____	_____
E U D T O R D	_____	_____
R M K E L O S	_____	_____
T I X E R N N	_____	
N N G L A S S		
R U B B E R Z		
K M G R X Z P		

- Now that you know which materials make good conductors and which make good insulators, write **C** under each object that is a conductor and **I** under each object that is an insulator.

_____   _____   _____   _____

Series or Parallel?

A

B

You can light several light bulbs with only one cell. In picture **A,** the bulbs are connected in a **series circuit.** What would happen to the circuit if you unscrewed one bulb? All the lights would go out. In picture **B,** the bulbs are connected in a **parallel circuit.** What would happen if you unscrewed a light bulb in a parallel circuit? The other lights would still burn.

Dry cells can also be connected in series and parallel circuits. However, cells are usually connected in series. A series of cells increases the amount of power that flows in a circuit. A series of cells will make a light bulb burn brighter.

C

D

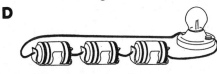

1. In which picture above are the cells connected in a series?_____

2. In which picture above will the bulb light more brightly?_____

3. When one light burned out on Sally's Christmas tree, the rest of the lights went out, too. In what kind of circuit were the bulbs connected?_____

4. Do you think the electric lights in your house are connected in a series circuit or a parallel circuit?_____ Why? _____

_____

5. How are the batteries connected in the flashlight below? In a series or parallel?_____

6. Some flashlights have four or five cells. How would the brightness of the light from this kind of flashlight compare with one that only has one or two cells?

_____

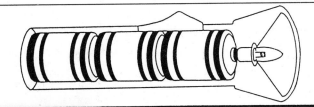

Fun Fact

A single dry cell is often called a battery, but it really isn't a battery. A battery is two or more cells connected together. You can buy batteries that look like a single cell, but they are really two or more cells connected together and put inside one case.

SCIENCE

Name _____

Powered Up

Where does the electricity that is in your house come from? It all begins at a large **power plant.** The power plant has a large **turbine generator.** High pressure steam spins the turbines and the generator that is attached to the turbine shaft. As the generator spins, it produces hundreds of megawatts of electricity.

• Below is a picture of a power plant where electricity is generated. Label each part using the terms found in the Power Bank below.

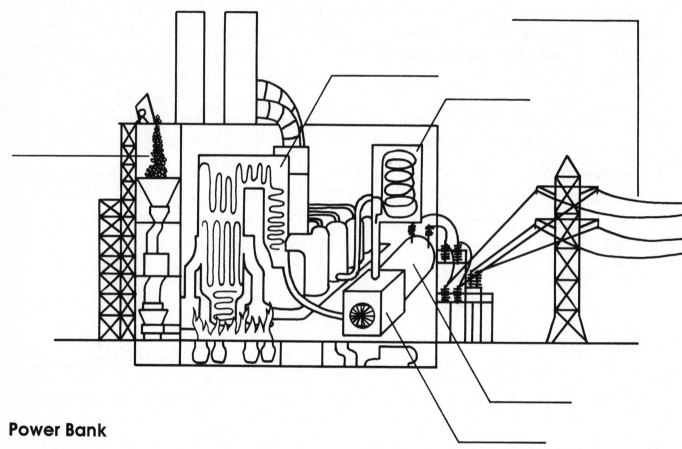

Power Bank

Fuel – Fuel, such as coal, enters the power plant.

Boiler – The burning fuel heats water in the boiler, making high pressure steam.

Turbine – High pressure steam spins the blades of the turbine up to 3,000 times a minute.

Condenser – Steam is cooled in the condenser and is turned back into water. The water is sent back to the boiler.

Generator – The generator attached to the turbine turns, producing hundreds of megawatts of electricity.

Power Lines – Electricity is sent to your home through wires.

Name _____

Portable Power

Steve and Lenny really enjoyed listening to the radio while they fished. Radios need electricity to work. Where did Steve's radio get its power? From a **dry cell battery,** of course. Dry cells are sources of portable power.

Most portable radios use dry cells. A dry cell makes electricity by changing chemical energy into electrical energy. Chemicals in the dry cell act on each other and make **electrons** flow. The flow of electrons is called **electricity.**

• Use the words from the Word Bank to label the parts of the dry cell. You can use your science book to help, but first try to figure out each part by yourself.

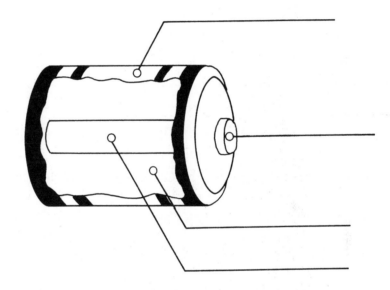

Word Bank

chemical paste
carbon rod
zinc case
terminal

Portable Power Inventory

List the appliances, tools, or toys in your house that are powered with dry cells.

_____ _____

_____ _____

_____ _____

_____ _____

_____ _____

Find Out

Before batteries were invented, scientists did all their experiments with static electricity. Find out who made the first battery and when it was made.

Name _____

Magnetic Attraction

Try to pick up each of these objects with your magnet. Circle the ones which it picks up.

scissors   eraser   ruler   pencil   crayon

paper clip   thumbtack   toothpick   pen

A magnet will only pick up an object made of _____.

Investigate

List all the objects you can find which your magnet picks up or is attracted to.

1. _____   6. _____
2. _____   7. _____
3. _____   8. _____
4. _____   9. _____
5. _____   10. _____

Is the magnet attracted to any non-metal object? _____

Extending the Concept

Hold a piece of tagboard between the magnet and each object you listed in the "Investigate" section. List each one the magnet is still attracted to.

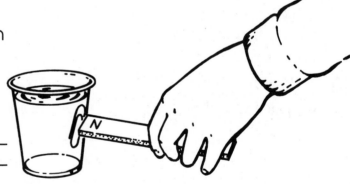

_____
_____

Place each of the objects the magnet is still attracted to in a cup of water.
Hold the magnet against the outside of the cup.

Which items were the magnet still able to attract?_____

_____

What other materials can a magnet attract objects through, besides tagboard and water? _____

Working with Electromagnets

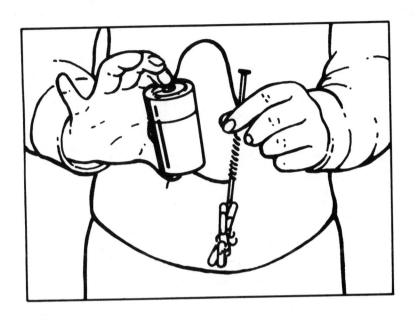

Investigate

1. Strip 1 inch of insulation from each end of a 2-foot-long piece of thin wire.
2. Wrap the wire around a nail 30 times, leaving most of the extra wire dangling at one end.
3. Touch one bare end of the wire to the top of the battery.
4. Touch the other bare end of the wire to the bottom of the battery.
5. Hold the nail near some paper clips.
   How many paper clips did the electromagnet pick up? _____

Making the Electromagnet Stronger

Wrap the wire around the nail 30 more times.
How many paper clips will the electromagnet pick up now? _____
Tape two batteries together with the top of one battery touching the bottom of the other.
How many paper clips will the electromagnet pick up now? _____
Wrap as many coils around the nail as you can.
How many paper clips can you pick up now? _____
Name two ways to make an electromagnet stronger. _____

Name _____

Weight and Gravity

Making a Scale

1. Use a hole punch or scissors to punch two holes at the top of a clear plastic cup. Make the holes exactly opposite each other.

2. Cut a piece of fish line 6 inches long. Tie one end to one hole and the other end to the opposite hole.

3. Tape a ruler to the top of your desk so one end hangs over the edge. Then tape a piece of tagboard to the side of the desk.

4. Wrap a rubber band around the fish line and loop it inside itself. Now hang the rubber band from the ruler. The cup should hang in front of the tagboard.

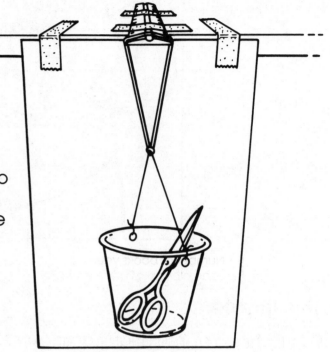

Comparing Weights

To weigh an object, place it in the cup. The heavier the object, the lower the cup will sag. To record its weight, put a mark on the tagboard even with the bottom of the cup and write the name of the object next to the mark.

Weigh these objects. Then number them from lightest to heaviest.

_____scissors   _____water   _____pencil   _____coin
_____stone   _____crayon box   _____eraser   _____magnifying glass

Extending the Concept

Why is gravity important to man? _____

_____

What would happen if there were no gravity? _____

_____

Great Gravity Changes

The gravity that pulls on the moon is ⅙ as strong as the pull on Earth. This means that you could jump up and stay in the air six times longer than you can now! Work with a partner to find the measurements below. Record them and then multiply them by six to see how different life would be on the moon.

Activity/Object	Measurement on Earth	Measurement on Moon (Earth x 6)
Distance you can jump with running start (in inches)		
Height you can jump (in inches)		
Distance you can throw a ball (in feet)		
Distance you can kick a ball (in feet)		
Number of books you can pick up at one time		

The gravitational pull on the sun is 28 times stronger than that on Earth. This means that everything would weigh 28 times more if it were on the sun. Below are several objects. Use a scale to find their approximate weight on the sun by multiplying them by 28. To find their weight on the moon, divide their Earth-weight by 6 because the gravitational pull of the moon is that much less than Earth's.

Object	Weight on Earth	Weight on Sun (Earth x 28)	Weight on Moon (Earth ÷ 6)
your math book			
your book bag (full)			
yourself			
(object of your choice)			
(object of your choice)			
(object of your choice)			

SCIENCE

Name _____

A Lo-o-o-ong Trip

What is the longest trip you have ever taken? Was it 100 km? 500 km? Maybe it was more than 1,000 km. You probably didn't know it, but last year you traveled 1 billion kilometers.

The Earth travels in a path around the sun called its **orbit.** Earth's orbit is almost 1 billion kilometers. It takes 1 year, or 365 days, for the Earth to orbit or **revolve** around the sun.

Look at the picture of
Earth's orbit.
It is not a perfect circle.
It is a special shape
called an **ellipse.**

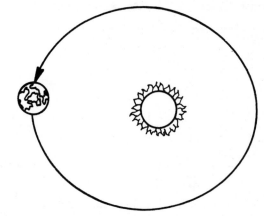

1. How long does it take for the Earth to revolve around the sun? _____

2. How many times has the Earth revolved around the sun since you were born?

_____

3. How many kilometers has the Earth traveled in orbit since you were born?

_____

4. Put an "X" on Earth's orbit to show where it will be in six months.

Experiment

You can draw an ellipse. Place two straight pins about 8 cm apart in a piece of cardboard. Tie the ends of a 25 cm piece of string to the pins. Place your pencil inside the string. Keeping the string tight, draw an ellipse.

Make four different ellipses by changing the length of the string and the distance between the pins. How do the ellipses change?

Fun Fact

Hold on tight. The Earth travels at a speed of 100,000 km per hour in its orbital path around the sun.

Name _____

"Lift-off"

"3-2-1, lift-off!" With a mighty roar, the Saturn V **rocket** leaves the **launch pad**.

Riding high on top of the Saturn V in the **Command Module** are the three Apollo astronauts. Below their Command Module is a Lunar Landing Module that will land two of the astronauts on the moon's surface.

Below this, the Saturn V has three parts, or **stages**. It takes a lot of power to escape the Earth's pull, called **gravity**. The space-craft must reach a speed of almost 40,000 km per hour. The bottom, or first stage, is the largest. After each stage uses up its **fuel**, it drops off and the next stage starts. Each stage has its own fuel and **oxygen**. The fuels need oxygen in order to burn.

The astronauts are now on their 3-day journey to the moon.

Color each Saturn V section a different color. Color the key to match each section.

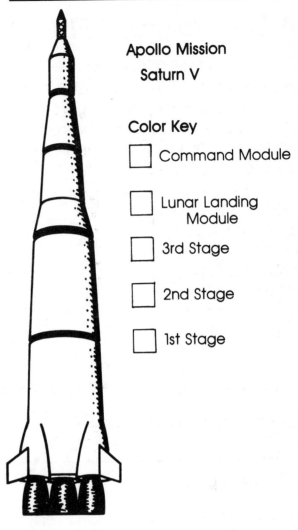

Apollo Mission
Saturn V

Color Key

☐ Command Module

☐ Lunar Landing Module

☐ 3rd Stage

☐ 2nd Stage

☐ 1st Stage

SCIENCE

Fill in the spaces with the words in bold from above. Then use the numbered letters to answer the question.

1. The Saturn V __ __ __ __ __ __ has three main parts, or __ __ __ __ __ __.
                                     13   1   5

2. Rocket engines burn __ __ __ __ and __ __ __ __ __ __.
                            10   8   6   16   7

3. The Earth's pull is called __ __ __ __ __ __ __.
                            16 11   14

4. "Lift-off." The Saturn V leaves the __ __ __ __ __ __ __ __.
                                   9   2   12

5. The Apollo astronauts ride in the __ __ __ __ __ __ __ __ __ __ __ __.
                                           3   15   4

What were the first words spoken from the surface of the moon on July 20, 1969?

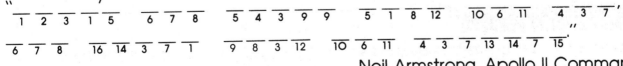

"__ __'
 1 2 3 1 5   6 7 8   5 4 3 9 9   5 1 8 12   10 6 11   4 3 7

__ __"
 6 7 8   16 14 3 7 1   9 8 3 12   10 6 11   4 3 7 13 14 7 15

Neil Armstrong, Apollo II Commander

Name _____

"Live Via Satellite"

"This program is brought to you live via satellite from halfway around the world." Satellites are very helpful in sending TV messages from one side of the world to the other. But this is only one of the special jobs that satellites can do.

Most satellites are placed into orbit around the Earth by riding on top of giant rockets. Only recently have some satellites been carried into orbit by a space shuttle. While orbiting the Earth, the giant doors of the shuttle are opened, and the satellite is pushed into orbit.

This satellite relays TV signals from halfway around the world.

Satellites send information about many things. Use the code to find the different kinds of messages and information satellites send.

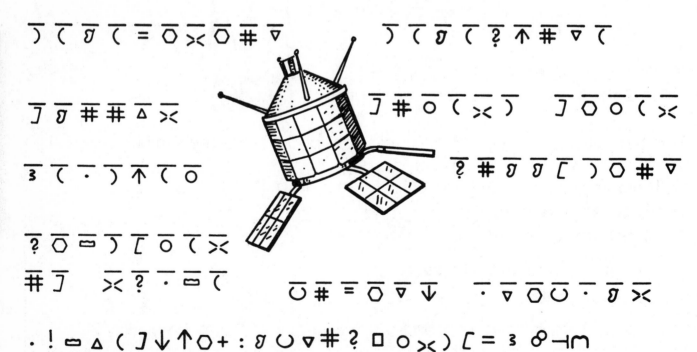

· ! ⊑ △ (⏌ ↓ ↑ ○ + : ʊ ∪ ▽ # ? □ ○ ⤬) [= ³ 𝒪 ┐m
A B C D E F G H I J K L M N O P Q R S T U V W X Y Z

Find Out

Satellites in space need power to send messages. Find out where satellites get their power.

Name _____

Just Imagine . . .

Earth is a very special planet because it is the only planet known to have life. Only Earth has the necessities to support life—water, air, moderate temperatures, and suitable air pressure. Earth is about 92,960,000 miles from the sun and is 7,926 miles in diameter. Its highest recorded temperature was 136° F in Libya and the lowest was -127° F in Antarctica.

Venus is known as Earth's "twin" because the two planets are so similar in size. At about 67,230,000 miles from the sun, Venus is 7,521 miles in diameter. Venus is the brightest planet in the sky, as seen from Earth, and is brighter even than the stars. The temperature on the surface of this planet is about 850° F.

Mercury is the planet closest to the sun. It is about 35,980,000 miles from the sun and is 3,031 miles in diameter. The temperature on this planet ranges from -315° F to 648° F.

Pretend you were going to Venus or Mercury for spring break. Make a list of the things you would bring (you may have to invent them in order to survive) and draw a picture of the vehicle that would take you there. Write about your experiences on another sheet of paper.

SCIENCE

Things I Need to Take

_____
_____
_____
_____
_____
_____
_____
_____
_____
_____
_____
_____

Vehicle

Name _____

The Large Planets

Jupiter is the largest planet in the solar system. The diameter at its equator is about 88,836 miles. It was named after the king of the Roman gods and is the fifth closest planet to the sun at about 483,600,000 miles away. This large planet also spins faster than any other. It makes a complete rotation in about 9 hours and 55 minutes.

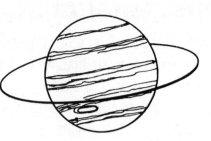

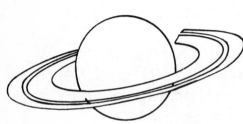

The surface of Jupiter cannot be seen from Earth because of the layers of dense clouds surrounding it. Jupiter has no solid surface but is made of liquid and gases that are held together by gravity.

One characteristic unique to Jupiter is the Great Red Spot that is about 25,000 miles long and about 20,000 miles wide. Astronomers believe the spot to be a swirling, hurricane-like mass of gas.

Saturn, the second largest planet, is well known for its seven thin, flat rings encircling it. Its diameter is about 74,898 miles at the equator. It was named for the Roman god of agriculture. Saturn is the sixth planet closest to the sun and is about 888,200,000 miles away from it. Like Jupiter, Saturn travels around the sun in an oval-shaped (elliptical) orbit, and it takes the planet about 10 hours and 39 minutes to make one rotation.

Scientists believe Saturn is a giant ball of gas that also has no solid surface. Like Jupiter, they believe it too may have an inner core of rocky material.

Fill in the chart below to compare Jupiter and Saturn. Make two of your own categories.

Categories	Jupiter	Saturn
1. diameter		
2. origin of name		
3. distance from sun		
4. rotations		
5. surface		
6. unique characteristics		
7.		
8.		

Name _____

The Twin Planets

1. Uranus and Neptune are similar in size, rotation time, and temperature. Sometimes they are called twin planets. Uranus is about 1,786,400,000 miles from the sun. Neptune is about 2,798,800,000 miles from the sun. What is the difference between these two distances? _____

2. Neptune can complete a rotation in 18 to 20 hours. Uranus can make one in 16 to 28 hours. What is the average time it takes Neptune to complete a rotation? _____ Uranus? _____

3. Can you believe that it is about -353° F on Neptune, and about -357° F on Uranus? Brrr! that's cold! What is the temperature outside today in your town? _____

How much warmer is it in your town than on Neptune? _____ Uranus? _____

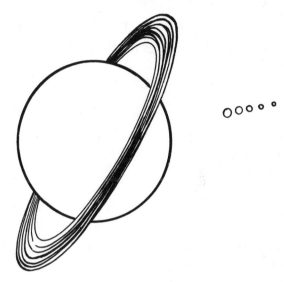

4. Uranus has at least five small satellites moving around it. Their names are Miranda, Ariel, Umbriel, Tatania and Oberon. They are 75, 217, 155, 310 and 280 miles in diameter respectively. What is the average diameter of Uranus' satellites? _____

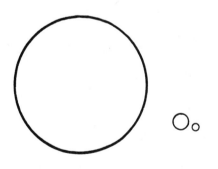

5. Neptune was first seen in 1846 by Johanna G. Galle. Uranus was first discovered by Sir William Herschel in 1781. How many years ago was Neptune discovered? _____ Uranus? _____

About how many years later was Uranus discovered than Neptune? _____

6. Both Uranus and Neptune have names taken from Greek and Roman mythology. Use an encyclopedia to find their names and their origins.

_____

_____

_____

_____

SCIENCE

Name _____

The Moon's Many "Faces"

As the moon orbits Earth, we see different amounts of the moon's lighted part. The moon appears to change its shape. These different shapes are called phases.

1. Use words from the Word Bank below to label each of the moon's phases.
2. In the box next to each phase, draw the shape of the moon's lighted part that is visible from Earth.

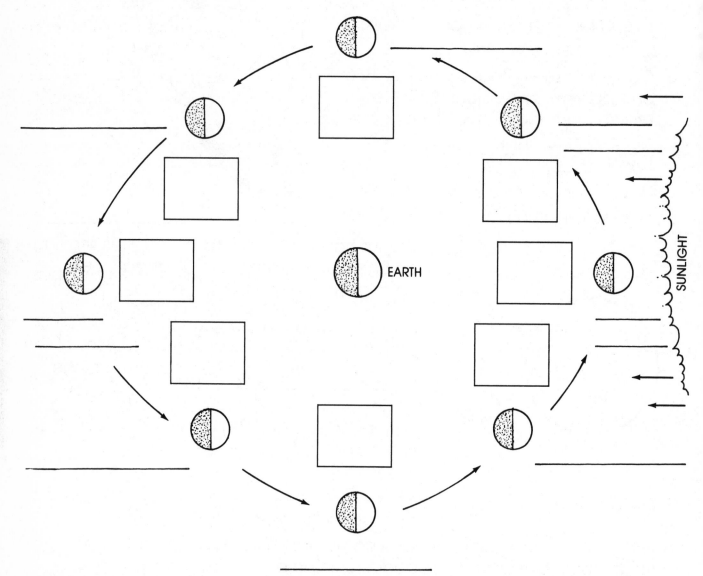

WORD BANK

new moon	waning crescent	waning gibbous	first quarter
waxing gibbous	waxing crescent	last quarter	full moon

Name _____

Comets—Dirty Snowballs

Use words from the Word Bank to label the diagram and complete the following description of a comet.

Word Bank
Sun   nucleus   coma   dust tail   gas tail   rocks   dust   gases   orbits   tail

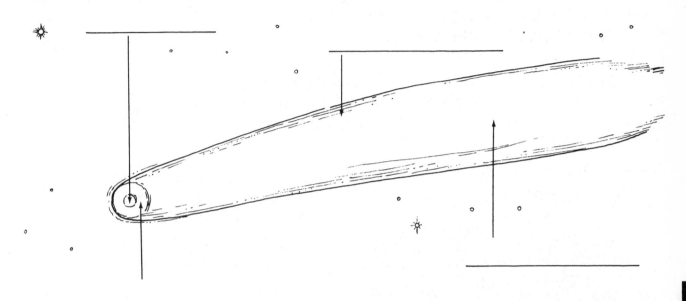

An astronomer once described a comet as a dirty snowball. Its tiny nucleus, measuring less than 10 miles in diameter, is made of _____ and _____ cemented together by frozen _____. Comets travel in long, cigar-shaped _____ that take them from the outermost regions of the solar system toward the _____. As the comet approaches the sun, the ice changes into a huge, hazy gas cloud called a _____. The solar wind pushes on the coma to form a long, thin _____ that is millions of miles long and glows in the sunlight.

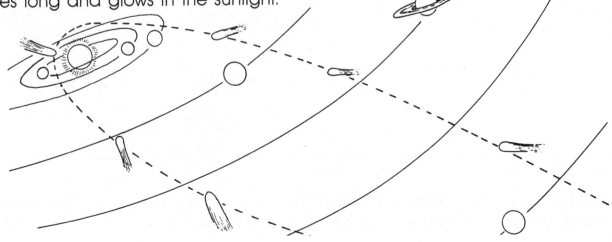

SCIENCE

Name _____

Star Search

On a clear dark night, you can look up in the sky and see about 2,000 stars without the help of a telescope. But unless you know which stars form constellations, all you will be seeing are stars.

Carefully poke holes in the *Constellation Patterns* sheet using a sharp pencil. Then tonight, when it is dark, hold a flashlight behind the paper to make the constellations appear.

Below are star charts to further help you recognize the constellations. To use the charts, turn them until the present month is at the bottom. Depending on your latitude and the time of night, you should be able to see most of the constellations in the middle and upper part of the chart.

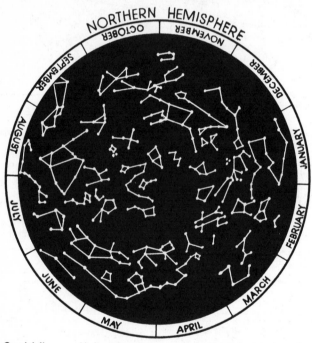

1. Using the *Constellation Patterns* sheet to help you, label as many of the constellations in the chart as you can.

2. Which constellations should you be able to see tonight? _____

_____

_____

3. When it is dark, go outside to look for constellations.

4. Which ones do you actually see?

_____

_____

_____

5. On the back of this paper, draw the night sky you see. Put a small X in the center. This should be the point in the sky directly above you.

Name _____

Constellation Patterns

See pages 226 (*Star Search*) and 228 (*Class Constellation*) for directions.

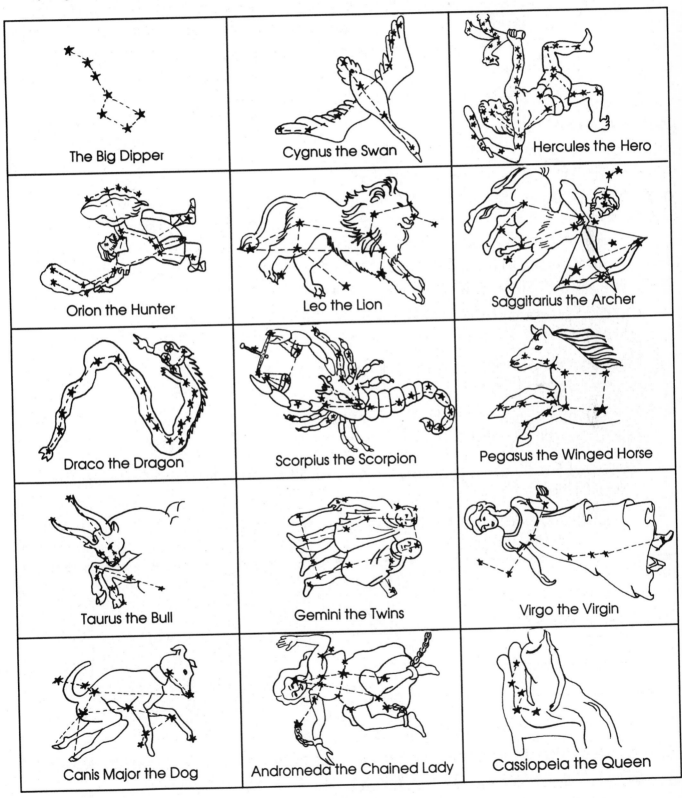

The Big Dipper	Cygnus the Swan	Hercules the Hero
Orion the Hunter	Leo the Lion	Saggitarius the Archer
Draco the Dragon	Scorpius the Scorpion	Pegasus the Winged Horse
Taurus the Bull	Gemini the Twins	Virgo the Virgin
Canis Major the Dog	Andromeda the Chained Lady	Cassiopeia the Queen

SCIENCE

Name _____

Class Constellation

Thousands of years ago, people believed that there were many gods in the heavens above. They believed that the gods made the sun rise, the weather change, the oceans move, and even made people fall in love! The people made up stories (myths) about the gods and their great powers. Many of the characters in these myths can be found in the shapes of the stars. These "star pictures" are called constellations. There are 88 constellations in the sky, but not all of them can be seen from one location. Some are only visible in the Southern Hemisphere while others can only be seen in the Northern Hemisphere. Some are also best observed only in certain seasons. Look at some of the constellations on page 227, *Constellation Patterns*. Pick one or create your own and write a myth about it. Follow the directions below.

1. On a lined sheet of 8 ½"x 11" paper, write your name, the title of your myth, and the myth.

2. Glue the paper on the right side of a 12" x 18" piece of black construction paper.

3. In the box below, design your constellation using star stickers.

4. Connect the stars to show your constellation and add details.

5. Cut out and glue your constellation on the left side of the construction paper.

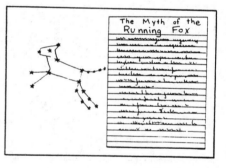

Name _____

Read My Mind

Pretend you have been contacted by NASA to serve as an astronaut on a secret mission. Because of its secrecy, NASA cannot give you your destination. Instead, you must figure it out using the clues below. After each clue, check the possible answers. Your destination will soon be evident.

Destination Clues	Record Answers Here.								
	Mercury	Venus	Earth	Mars	Jupiter	Saturn	Uranus	Neptune	Pluto
It is part of our Solar System.									
It is a bright object in the sky.									
It is less than 2,000,000,000 miles from the sun.									
It orbits the sun.									
It has less than 15 known satellites.									
There is weather here.									
It rotates in the opposite direction of Earth.									
It is the hottest planet.									
Its years are longer than its days.									
It is called "Earth's twin."									
It is closest to Earth.									

Secret Mission Destination is _____

I know this because _____

_____

SCIENCE

Name _____

Space Snowballs

Planets and moons are not the only objects in our solar system that travel in orbits. Comets also orbit the sun.

A **comet** is like a giant dirty snowball from 1 to 5 kilometers wide. It is made of frozen gases, dust, ice, and rocks.

As the comet gets closer to the sun, the frozen gases

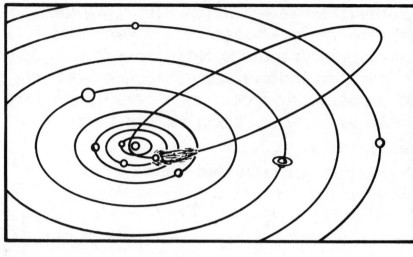

melt and evaporate. Dust particles float in the air. The dust forms a cloud called a **coma**. The "wind" from the sun blows the coma away from the sun. The blowing coma forms the comet's tail.

There are more than 800 known comets. Halley's Comet is the most famous. It appears about every 76 years. The year 1985 was the last scheduled appearance in this century. When will it appear next?

Find the words from the Word Bank in the wordsearch. When you are finished, write down the letters that are not circled. Start at the top of the puzzle and go from left to right.

Word Bank	
dust	orbit
Halley	tail
coma	ice
snowball	sky
melt	shining
solar system	

```
S P M E L T L A N H E
O T S S H A C O M A V
L E N O R D B I T L S
A L O I K U E C I L R
R C W L E S S C O E M
S E B T S T H A V Y E
Y O A R O R B I T B I
S T L S S H A P E D L
T I L K T A I L E A F
E O O T I C E B A L L
M S K Y S H I N I N G
```

_ _ _ _ _ _ _ _ _   _ _ _ _   _ _ _ _ _   _ _ _ _ _   _ _ _ _

_ _ _ _ _ _ _ _,   _ _ _ _ _ _   _ _ _ _   _ _ _ _ _ _

_ _ _ _ _ _   _ _ _ _   _   _ _ _ _ _ _ _ _.

Name _____

Amazing Asteroids

Asteroids are extremely small planets that revolve around the sun. They are also called minor planets or planetoids. These small planets travel mainly between the orbits of Mars and Jupiter. There are thousands of them, and new ones are constantly being discovered.

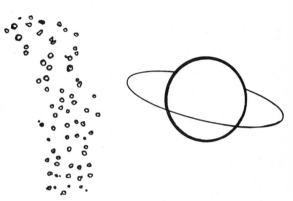

Many asteroids are made of dark, rocky material, have irregular shapes and range widely in size. Ceres, the largest and first-known asteroid, is about 600 miles in diameter. Eros, another asteroid, is only about 6/10 of a mile in diameter.

Because the asteroids' orbits change slowly due to the gravitational attraction of Jupiter and other large planets, asteroids sometimes collide with each other. Fragments from these collisions can cause other collisions. Any resulting small fragments that reach the surface of Earth are called meteorites.

Try your hand at personification. Personification means giving an inanimate (non-living) object human qualities. Draw a cartoon below of two asteroids colliding with each other. Give the asteroids names and write what they might say to each other.

SCIENCE

1	2
3	4

Name _____

Star Light, Star Bright

Lay on your back. Gaze up into the night sky. Which star is the brightest? On a clear night you can see hundreds of stars—some are bright and others are dim.

Why are some stars brighter than others? Let's try to find out by looking at the picture on this page.

1. Look at the two streetlights in the picture. Which streetlight appears the brightest?

   _____

   Why? _____

2. Look at the bicycle and the truck. Which headlights appear the brightest? _____

   Why? _____

3. Some stars appear brighter than others for the same reasons as those stated above. What are the two reasons?

   a. _____

   b. _____

Color Me Hot

Stars differ not only in brightness but also in color. As a star gets hotter, its color changes.

Refer to the chart to color these stars.

Star Color	
Temperature	**Color**
20,000° C	Blue
10,500° C	White
5,500° C	Yellow
3,000° C	Red

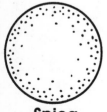

Spica
20,000°C

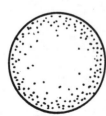

Sirius
10,500°C

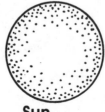

Sun
5,500°C

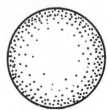

Betelgeuse
3,000°C

0-7682-3794-7 *Skills & Practice Gr. 4*

Name _____

Pass the Profiles

How much do your classmates know about you? Give copies of this sheet to a few other students. Tell them to fill out the information about you. Fill in the blanks that they cannot complete.

Full name: _____

How my name was chosen: _____

Address: _____

Other places I have lived: _____

Parents' names: _____

Parents' occupations: _____

Brothers' and sisters' names: _____

Pets (kinds and names/ present or past): _____

Kinds of clothes I like: _____

Fun things I like to do: _____

Favorite foods: _____

Favorite songs: _____

Favorite videos and TV shows: _____

Someday I'd like to be… _____

I'm really good at… _____

My favorite expression is… _____

States I've visited: _____

My hero or heroine: _____

Some of my closest friends: _____

What I like to do with friends: _____

Someday I'd like to try to… _____

My birthday is… _____

My favorite restaurant is… _____

Things at school I'm good at: _____

0-7682-3794-7 *Skills & Practice Gr. 4*

SOCIAL STUDIES

Name _____

List Bliss!

Making lists helped Harvey cope. Try some lists of your own. Each school day for one month, make a list from one of the titles given below. Keep your lists together in a special notebook or binder. You'll be surprised how well you get to know yourself in one month! Check off each list as you've used it. Make up new list titles if you run out.

1. Big Events in My Life
2. Things That Worry Me
3. Projects I've Liked in School
4. Things I Like about Me
5. Bad Things That Have Happened to Me
6. Things I Like to Make
7. My Favorite Things To Do
8. Jobs I'd Like To Do When I'm Older
9. Gifts I Got That I Didn't Want
10. Sad Moments I Remember
11. Places I've Visited
12. Songs I've Always Liked
13. Important People in My Life
14. Months and Dates Special to Me
15. Foods I Just Don't Like
16. Games That I Play Well
17. Books I've Enjoyed
18. Things I Wish For
19. Animals I'd Like to Have
20. Things That Make Me Happy

Name _____

It's a Shame!

With which children are you most likely to sympathize? Rate these characteristics from the greatest to the least with number **1** drawing the greatest amount of sympathy.

Characteristics	Rating
no father at home	___
teacher's pet	___
poor eating habits	___
overweight	___
cries easily	___
death in the family	___
rich	___
little self-control	___
poor health	___
ignorance	___
bad reputation	___
very thin	___
poor	___
adults have high expectations of	___
uncoordinated	___
little adult guidance	___

Should you be more sympathetic with some people?
Write a contract in which you make a promise you can keep.

Sympathy Contract

I, _____ , do hereby promise to be more understanding and sympathetic to
(your name)
those who _____ . I hope to show consideration by _____

_____

_____

_____   _____
(signature)   (date)
Give this contract to a trustworthy friend or adult who will help you be more caring.

SOCIAL STUDIES

Name _____

Emily Post Says . . .

Emily Post's book *Etiquette,* published in 1922, established behavior guidelines for all sorts of situations. She believed good manners were based on common sense and feelings for others. She kept up with the changing times and wrote ten editions of her book during her lifetime. People still refer to it when they have a question about proper behavior in social situations. Post also gave advice in a newspaper column and on the radio.

Write a column and give advice for the following situations.

1. Jane wants to have a party. There are ten boys and twelve girls in her class. She wants to invite everyone in the class except two of the girls. She also wants to ask her neighbors Emily and Bridgette, but her Mom says she can only have fifteen guests including herself. Who should she ask? How should they be asked? Answer these questions and give reasons for your answers.

   _____

   _____

   _____

   _____

2. Tim is one of the lucky invited guests, but he knows his best friend, Tom, was not asked. What should Tim tell Tom when Tom asks him to spend the night on the night the party is being given? Why?

   _____

   _____

   _____

3. Michael was pleased because he got one of the leading roles in the school play, but Joe was very disappointed because he did not get a part. What can Michael do to not hurt Joe further and perhaps help ease his disappointment?

   _____

   _____

Personality Plus Write a question you have concerning the polite thing to do in a certain situation. Put your question in a box with the questions of your classmates. The questions may be discussed in a small group or as a class.

Name _____

Me and My Shadow

Addie can hardly wait to have a friend. Tilla becomes that friend even though the two are different in many ways. In the chart below, compare yourself to one of your friends. You may wish to compare such things as hair color, eye color, family size, hobbies, favorite songs, and so on.

Myself	My friend	Alike or different?

SOCIAL STUDIES

Name _____

Families

One of the things people all over the world have in common is the need to give and receive love. Love is given when you help, talk, listen and share with another person. Family members are often the ones who do these things to show love for each other.

1. List ways your family cares for you.

   _____
   _____
   _____
   _____

2. What do you do to show your family you care? _____

   _____

   _____

3. Do you have specific chores to do at home daily or weekly? _____
   If yes, what are they? _____

4. Does your parents giving you chores to do show that they care about you?_____
   Why or why not? _____

   _____

5. List things a family member has taught you. _____

   _____

   _____

6. List things you have taught or could teach a member of your family. _____

   _____

   _____

7. List ways a family member helps you deal with a variety of emotions. _____

   _____

8. Members of a family often take on certain roles within the family structure.
   Which member of your family is usually the disciplinarian? _____

9. It is often said that a parent's love for a child is unconditional. What do you think
   unconditional love is? _____

   _____

10. On the back of this page, write two positive statements about each member
    of your family. Share these with the person on a day when he/she needs
    cheering up.

Name _____

It's All in the Family!

Write the names of family members with whom you live. _____

_____

Write the names of the members of your immediate family. _____

_____

Write the names of your extended family on the correct lines in the diagram below. Fill in the names of your immediate family in the box.

great-grandparents

_____   _____   _____   _____

_____   _____   _____   _____

grandparents

_____   _____   _____   _____

mother _____   _____ father

you and your sisters and/or brothers

_____

aunts and uncles   aunts and uncles

_____ _____   _____ _____

_____ _____   _____ _____

_____ _____   _____ _____

cousins   cousins

_____ _____   _____ _____

_____ _____   _____ _____

_____ _____   _____ _____

_____ _____   _____ _____

_____ _____   _____ _____

SOCIAL STUDIES

Name _____

Uniforms

People on all continents wear some type of covering on their bodies. Originally, clothing was used merely to protect a person from climatic conditions. Today, the clothes a person wears tell something about his/her lifestyle or status in society. While many businesses allow people to wear their own clothes to work, others require workers to wear a uniform. Why do you think people in some jobs must wear uniforms? _____

_____

_____

List several jobs that require workers to wear uniforms.

_____

_____

_____

Cut out pictures of people wearing uniforms from old catalogs, magazines, or newspapers. Glue the pictures on a piece of construction paper or posterboard to make a collage of uniforms.

Pretend that you are the president or CEO of your own company. Decide what your company will sell or produce. In the space below, show examples of the uniforms you would require the following workers to wear: 1) clerical; 2) executive officers; 3) assembly line; 4) maintenance.

Should you, as president of the company, have to wear a uniform? _____

Why, or why not? _____

Name _____

Places to Live

Shelters provide a place in which people can live and keep their possessions. Early man took shelter in places provided by nature, such as a cave, hollow or hole in the ground. One of the first shelters devised by humans is still in use today — the tent. As man improved his tools and learned to farm, permanent homes were built. Today, people throughout the world live in a wide variety of homes. List as many different types of shelter as you can think of on the lines below.

_____

_____

_____

Make a list of the different types of shelter the students in your class occupy. Use the information to complete the graph below.

Types of Housing

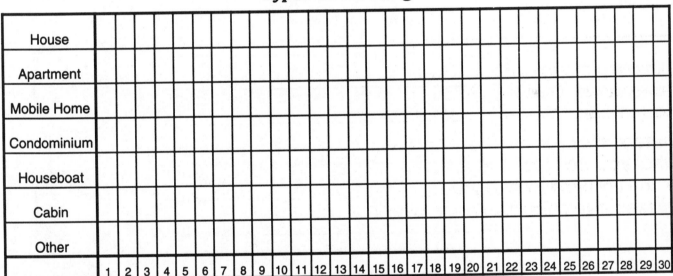

Use the list of homes above to complete this next activity. Some types of shelter are better suited to hot climates. Others are designed for cold climates. Write the name of each type of home under the correct heading. Some may be suitable for both types of climate.

HOT CLIMATES	COLD CLIMATES	BOTH CLIMATES

Name _____

Picture Your Life in Time

Though you have only lived a short time, many significant events have happened in your life and in the world around you. Record some of these events on this page and the next.

Write the year you were born on the first line under **YEAR**. Write every year thereafter up to the current year. Before each year, the age you were during that year is written in parentheses. On the first line after each year, use a blue pen to write something signifcant you did that year. (You may have to ask a family member to help you with this.) On the second and third lines, use a red pen to write an important event that happened in the world during that year. (You may refer to an almanac or another reference.) Try to find a coin minted during each year of your life. Tape it in the circle to the right of the corresponding year.

AGE	YEAR
(0-1)	
(1-2)	
(2-3)	
(3-4)	

Name _____

Picture Your Life in Time (cont.)

(4-5) _____ _____
_____
_____
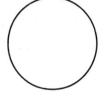

(5-6) _____ _____
_____
_____
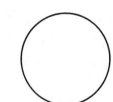

(6-7) _____ _____
_____
_____
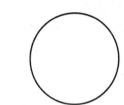

(7-8) _____ _____
_____
_____
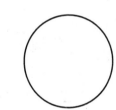

(8-9) _____ _____
_____
_____
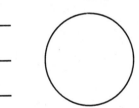

(9-10) _____ _____
_____
_____
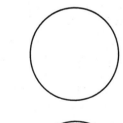

(10-11) _____ _____
_____
_____
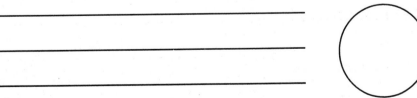

SOCIAL STUDIES

0-7682-3794-7 *Skills & Practice Gr. 4*

Name _____

Customs and Traditions

1. List several special days or occasions you observe, such as holidays or birthdays.

   _____

   _____

2. Pick one of the above that you celebrate with your family. Write a paragraph on the back of this page about what you and your family did to celebrate this special event the last time it occurred.

   Was the celebration the same as it always has been or were there some differences? Write what was the same and what was different.

Same	Different
_____	_____
_____	_____
_____	_____

3. Write the name of a holiday that you observed in the past year. _____

   With whom did you observe it? _____

   What did you do to celebrate? _____

   _____

   Name three things associated with the holiday that are a traditional part of its celebration. _____

   _____

4. List some traditions you and/or your family have. _____

   _____

5. What custom do you carry on today that you would like to see changed or dropped? _____

   Why? _____

6. What custom do you intend to carry on when you have a family? _____

   _____

7. What customs observed by the general population do you no longer see a need for and why? _____

   _____

8. What would you like to see become a custom and why? _____

   _____

Name _____

U.S. Patriotic Holidays

Memorial Day	Flag Day	Columbus Day	Presidents' Day
Bill of Rights Day	Labor Day	Veterans Day	Independence Day

Use the list of holidays above to write each holiday in the appropriate blank in each sentence or paragraph below.

1. _____ , on the third Monday in February, honors two United States Presidents, George Washington and Abraham Lincoln, born in the month.

2. _____ originally was celebrated May 30 and honored the war dead of the Civil War. It now is observed on the last Monday in May and is dedicated to the memory of all war dead. It is also known as Decoration Day because graves of service people are often decorated.

3. _____ , December 15, honors the date in 1791 on which Congress made them law. They are the first ten amendments of the U.S. Constitution.

4. _____ , on the second Monday in October, commemorates the discovery of America by honoring the man who sailed near its shores in 1492.

5. _____ commemorates the act of Congress on June 14, 1777, that adopted America's stars and stripes as the country's official banner.

6. _____ , observed the first Monday in September in all states, honors America's backbone, its workers.

7. _____ , on July 4, perhaps the most patriotic of all America's holidays, is celebrated in all states. It observes the adoption of the Declaration of Independence.

8. _____ was once called Armistice Day. It began in 1926 to commemorate the signing of the armistice that ended World War I in 1918. In 1954, the holiday's name was changed to honor all men and women who have served their country in the armed services.

Select one of the above holidays. Then, on another sheet of paper, do one of the following:
- Design a stamp to honor its observance.
- Write a poem about the holiday.
- Draw a mural of a parade honoring that holiday.

SOCIAL STUDIES

Name _____

An Interview

Person interviewed _____   Date of interview _____

1. Were you my age about 20, 30, 40, 50, 60, 70 or 80 years ago? _____

2. Where did you live when you were my age? _____
   If not here, how long ago did you move here? _____

3. How has the community changed? _____
   _____

4. What time did you get up when you were my age? _____
   What was your morning schedule? _____

5. What did you do after school? _____
   _____

6. What was your bedtime when you were my age? _____

7. What sort of things did you eat when you were my age? _____
   _____

8. What toys did you have? What were your favorites? _____
   _____

9. What chores did you have, if any? _____
   _____

10. Did you get an allowance? _____ How much was it? _____
    Did you earn any money when you were my age? ____ Doing what?
    _____ About what did you make in an hour? _____

11. How did you spend your money? _____
    _____

12. What was your most favorite thing to do during "free time"? _____
    _____ Tell about it. _____
    _____
    _____

13. What games did you play? _____
    _____
    _____

14. What did you study at school? _____
    _____
    _____
    _____

Name _____

An Interview (cont.)

15. How did you get to school? _____
16. What was school like? What did you have that was the same? Different?
    (i.e. physical education, cafeteria, etc.) _____
    _____
    _____
    _____

17. Do you remember any rhymes or songs? _____
    Name one. _____
18. Did you ever get in trouble? _____ Tell about one time. _____

    What happened to you when you got in trouble? _____
    _____

19. What was the best thing that ever happened to you? _____
    _____
    _____

    What was the worst? _____
    _____
    _____

20. What were some of your family customs or traditions (i.e.: birthdays,
    holidays, games, jokes, etc)? _____
    _____

21. What are some of the biggest changes you have seen during your lifetime?
    _____
    _____
    _____

Write additional questions or information given that was not asked for below or
on another sheet of paper.

_____
_____
_____
_____

SOCIAL STUDIES

Name _____

Other Ways to Communicate

For those people who are hearing impaired, vocal communication is not possible. People who cannot hear use sign language. Even those who can hear but do not speak the same language often use a modified form of sign language. You will often see visitors in a foreign land trying to sign to be understood.

Using the alphabet to the right, learn to sign your name, your hometown and the name of your school. Try to have a conversation with a friend using only sign language.

Braille is a system of printing and writing for the blind. It was developed by Louis Braille, a blind Frenchman, in the 1820's. Braille uses raised dots on a page. A blind person reads dots by touching with his/her fingertips. The Braille symbols are large and thick, so they can be felt easily.

Using the alphabet below, write a paragraph about your favorite hobby. After you finish, answer these questions.

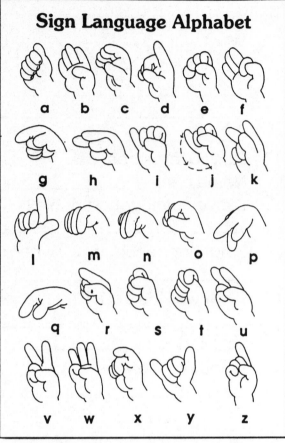

Sign Language Alphabet

1. What is unusual about the symbols used for the numbers? _____

_____

2. The American Printing House for the Blind in Louisville, KY, issues Braille textbooks for free. Why do you think the federal government pays for the publication of these books but does not pay for your textbooks? _____

_____

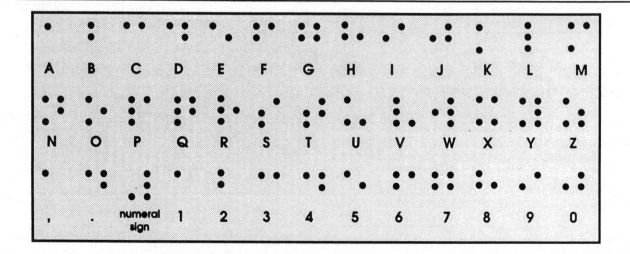

Name _____

Got the Message?

Hieroglyphics is a form of writing used by the ancient Egyptians in which picture symbols represented ideas and sounds. It was the Rosetta Stone, a decree carved on stone with hieroglyphics, that gave the world the key to understanding this writing when it was found in 1799.

Use the hieroglyphics below to write a secret message to your friend. Have him/her decipher your message and write a response to it in hieroglyphics. Then, write your message and his/her response in English. **Note:** There were no vowels in hieroglyphics. Use capital vowels to represent a vowel sound. Note also that there were many variations of this type of writing.

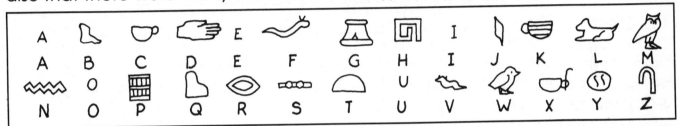

Your message:

Your friend's response:

Translation: _____

_____

In Egyptian archaeology, an oval frame containing the name or symbol of a ruler written in hieroglyphics is called a cartouche. They are often seen on monuments as nameplates of ancient rulers. Use hieroglyphics to make cartouches for the names listed below. Write the name in English on the line under each oval. Again, use capital vowels for vowel sounds.

your first name   **your best friend's name**   **your teacher's name**

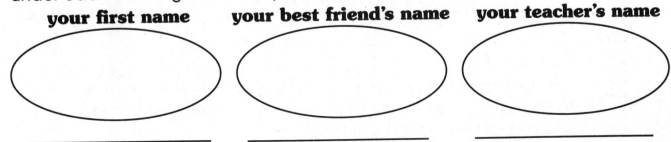

249

0-7682-3794-7 *Skills & Practice Gr. 4*

SOCIAL STUDIES

Name _____

Community Needs

Mother Teresa of Calcutta has dedicated her life to helping "the poorest of the poor." Mother Teresa and the members of her congregation, the Missionaries of Charity, aid poor, sick, and abandoned children and adults around the world.

Think about your community. List three of its social problems or needs.

_____

_____

_____

_____

_____

Tell how you think each problem might be solved. Include what you might do to help in each solution.

_____

_____

_____

_____

_____

_____

_____

_____

_____

_____

_____

_____

Follow the Leader Find out about an organization in your community that works to solve some of the problems you listed above. How do they work to solve the problem? Is there any way you can get involved? Share your information with the class.

Name _____

Community Workers

Ask several men and women in your community what their occupations are (e.g., doctor, farmer, maintenance worker). Record their answers, without names, on another sheet of paper.

When you have completed your survey, plot the two bar graphs below. If you have too many different responses, you may want to group them by categories, such as Medical, Sales, Government, and Service.

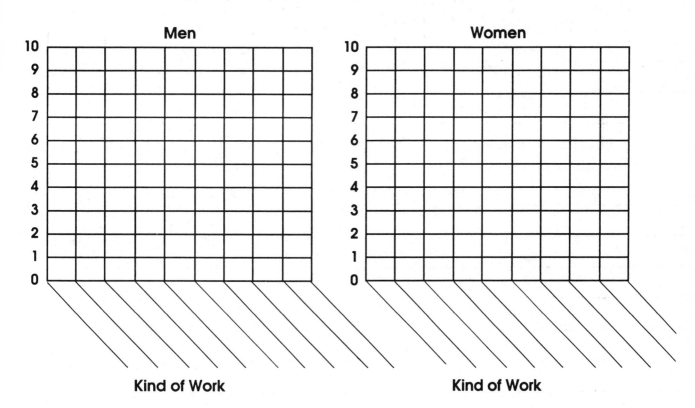

Men

Women

Kind of Work   Kind of Work

Answer these questions to draw some conclusions from your graphs.

What kinds of jobs do most of the community's population have? _____

_____

Are most workers skilled or non-skilled? _____

Are there differences between jobs held by men and women? _____

_____

What types of workers are needed in the community? _____

_____

What else have you observed? _____

_____

Name _____

What Kind of Community?

Read the definitions of three different types of communities below.

Rural Community	**Urban Community**	**Suburban Community**
country; large amount of open space; rustic; agriculture predominates	big city or town; often at least 50,000 people; crowded with buildings and people; business center	largely residential; often near a large city; often incorporated separately

Read the sentences on this page and page 253. Underline only the sentences that describe your community. Then, answer this: In what kind of a community do you live? _____

1. All that can be seen from a rooftop is land criss-crossed by dirt roads and fences.

2. Neighbors may sometimes wake neighbors if they mow their lawns too early in the morning.

3. There is a feeling of open space, and yet there are shopping malls, supermarkets, schools, etc.

4. The sounds of elevated trains and honking horns are heard almost twenty-four hours a day.

5. Many families who work in the city live here because it is quieter, and the commute to the city every day is not too long.

6. During the summer, neighborhood children set up lemonade stands, and families have picnics and barbecues in their back yards.

7. Homes are very close together. Many are stacked one on top of one another in buildings called apartments.

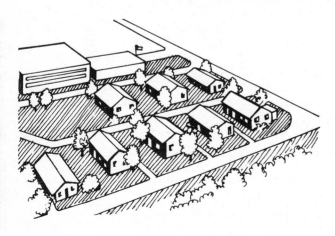

8. Streets and sidewalks are crowded with workers going to and from work and shoppers looking in store front windows.

9. Many people work at farming.

10. Mailboxes are often very far from the houses.

11. Neighbors are often miles apart.

12. It is on the outskirts of a city.

Name _____

What Kind of Community? (cont.)

13. Residents of the community seldom see one another, so a community gathering is a real social event.

14. Hotels provide a place for visitors to stay who come for meetings at the convention center.

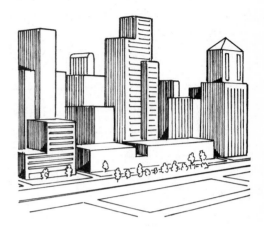

15. The population is over 50,000.

16. The high school's students come from several outlying communities and must ride the bus because distances are great.

17. Nights are quiet except for the occasional sound of an animal.

18. Children play in parks rather than in back yards.

19. There is a feeling of country with the conveniences of a city.

Write two or three paragraphs about your community on the lines below. Ideas to include: its population, contact with neighbors, and availability of services.

_____

_____

_____

_____

_____

_____

_____

_____

_____

_____

_____

_____

_____

_____

SOCIAL STUDIES

Name _____

Waste Materials

Next to each picture on this page and the next, write one or two sentences about what is pictured that is harmful for the environment. Tell why or how it is harmful. Then, write ways to correct the problem.

_____
_____
_____
_____
_____
_____
_____
_____
_____

_____
_____
_____
_____
_____
_____
_____
_____

_____
_____
_____
_____
_____
_____
_____

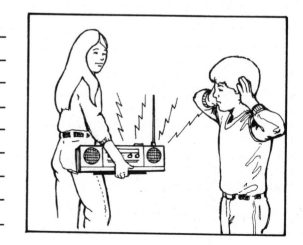

Name _____

Waste Materials (cont.)

_____
_____
_____
_____
_____
_____
_____
_____
_____

_____
_____
_____
_____
_____
_____
_____
_____

_____
_____
_____
_____
_____
_____
_____
_____

_____
_____
_____
_____
_____
_____
_____
_____

Name _____

Money Sources

Ask four people of different ages how they get their money. When they answer yes to a category, check the line in front of it. A person may answer yes to more than one category. Many of the categories may not apply and therefore will not be checked. If the category is "other," write the source.

Ask someone between **8-11** years old: **How do you get your money?**

_____ allowance _____ gifts _____ full-time job _____ part-time job

_____ interest _____ dividends _____ borrowed _____ pension

_____ other: _____

Ask someone between **15-18** years of age: **How do you get your money?**

_____ allowance _____ gifts _____ full-time job _____ part-time job

_____ interest _____ dividends _____ borrowed _____ pension

_____ other: _____

Ask someone between **35-45** years of age: **How do you get your money?**

_____ allowance _____ gifts _____ full-time job _____ part-time job

_____ interest _____ dividends _____ borrowed _____ pension

_____ other: _____

Ask someone over **65** years of age: **How do you get your money?**

_____ allowance _____ gifts _____ full-time job _____ part-time job

_____ interest _____ dividends _____ borrowed _____ pension

_____ other: _____

Compare findings with other class members. Tally where people's money comes from in the different age groups. If desired, make a bar graph for each group.

	8-11	15-18	35-45	65 or over
allowance	_____	_____	_____	_____
gifts	_____	_____	_____	_____
full-time job	_____	_____	_____	_____
part-time job	_____	_____	_____	_____
interest	_____	_____	_____	_____
dividends	_____	_____	_____	_____
borrowed	_____	_____	_____	_____
pension	_____	_____	_____	_____
other	_____	_____	_____	_____

Name _____

Where Money Goes

Ask four people of different ages on what they spend their money. When they answer yes to a category, put a check mark on the line in front of it. A person may answer yes to more than one, or some of the categories may not apply and therefore will not get checked. If the category is "other," write how that money is spent.

Ask someone between **8-11** years old: **On what do you spend your money?**

____ rent/mortgage	____ clothing	____ food	____ utilities
____ transportation	____ vacation	____ taxes	____ savings
____ entertainment	____ insurance	____ dates	____ school
____ investments	____ presents	____ treats	____ supplies
____ medical/doctors	____ eating out	____ sports	____ hobbies

____ other: _____

Ask someone between **15-18** years of age: **On what do you spend your money?**

____ rent/mortgage	____ clothing	____ food	____ utilities
____ transportation	____ vacation	____ taxes	____ savings
____ entertainment	____ insurance	____ dates	____ school
____ investments	____ presents	____ treats	____ supplies
____ medical/doctors	____ eating out	____ sports	____ hobbies

____ other: _____

Ask someone between **35-45** years of age: **On what do you spend your money?**

____ rent/mortgage	____ clothing	____ food	____ utilities
____ transportation	____ vacation	____ taxes	____ savings
____ entertainment	____ insurance	____ dates	____ school
____ investments	____ presents	____ treats	____ supplies
____ medical/doctors	____ eating out	____ sports	____ hobbies

____ other: _____

Ask someone over **65** years of age: **On what do you spend your money?**

____ rent/mortgage	____ clothing	____ food	____ utilities
____ transportation	____ vacation	____ taxes	____ savings
____ entertainment	____ insurance	____ dates	____ school
____ investments	____ presents	____ treats	____ supplies
____ medical/doctors	____ eating out	____ sports	____ hobbies

____ other: _____

Compare class findings. On another page, tally how the age groups spend money.

SOCIAL STUDIES

Name _____

Needs for Your "Full Circle"

We all have **physical**, **intellectual**, **emotional** and **social** needs to live a happy and healthy life. Read each statement from the text and decide which need is being met. Write it on the blank.

1. Mattie finished the test before anyone else and turned her paper over on her desk. She reached inside for a book. _____

2. Matt had dinner started when Mattie got home—salad and leftover spaghetti. _____

3. Mr. Ashby had outdone himself this weekend. His homework assignments included math, spelling, a social studies essay, a book report, and vocabulary words. He was determined to make his fifth graders work.

   _____

4. "But Mattie, I do love you," said Mrs. Benson with tears in her eyes.

   _____

5. When the telephone rang in the living room, Matt called to his sister. It was Toni. _____

6. Humming softly, Mattie sat up, reached in her back pocket and un-wrapped her favorite photograph. She had decided to carry it with her today, and her father's strength seemed to reach out and hold her.

   _____

7. Mattie started dinner—chili, rice, and salad. _____

8. "Oh, Toni, this sounds like a lot of maybes. I'm going to Stern's on Saturday and stopping in to see Mrs. Stamps. I wanted you to come with me."

   _____

Name _____

Do You Speak My Language?

It is estimated that there are about 3,000 spoken languages in use today by the people of the world. This is not a precise figure because linguists disagree as to what constitutes a spoken language and what constitutes a dialect. A dialect is usually considered to be a variation within a language.

Language influences all aspects of a culture, including social behavior. If people can understand each other, human society tends to function smoothly. If people are not able to understand one another, society often grinds to a halt.

To the right are the most widely spoken languages in the world and the percent of the world's population that speaks each one. Use the list to complete the graph below.

Language	
German	1.5
French	1.5
Japanese	2.0
Portuguese	2.0
Arabic	2.0
Spanish	3.0
Russian	3.5
Hindi	4.5
English	6.0
Mandarin	20.0

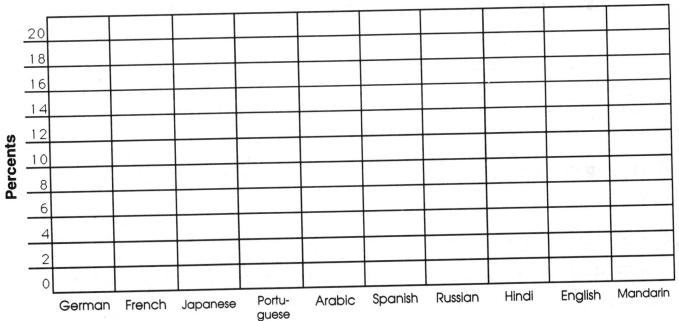

As communication between countries has increased and as companies have increasingly traded with and established branches in other nations, educators have recognized a greater need for students in this country to learn a second language. Most high schools today require students to learn a foreign language. Some elementary schools are also teaching a foreign language.

Survey 15 people who are high school graduates. Ask each person if he/she took a foreign language in school. If the answer is yes, what language did he/she study? Compile your information into a graph similar to the one above.

What career do you plan to pursue when you are an adult? Do you think you will need to know a foreign language for this career? Why, or why not?

SOCIAL STUDIES

Name _____

Where Is Wheat Grown?

Wheat grows best in dry temperate regions. The ideal climate includes a cool, moist spring, a warm dry harvest period and an annual rainfall of 9 to 30 inches. There are nine areas of the world which provide a wheat-growing climate.

I. Locate these wheat-growing areas on the map by writing the number beside each area in the correct blank on the map.

1. Central United States   2. Central Canada   3. Southern Russia
4. Danube River region   5. Northwest India   6. Northcentral China
   of Europe   8. Australia   9. Mediterranean region
7. Argentina

II. Label the seven continents on the map by placing the letter beside each in the correct location.
A. Europe   B. Asia   C. Australia   D. Africa
E. North America   F. South America   G. Antarctica

III. Label each of these bodies of water by writing the name in the correct location on the map: Mediterranean Sea, Pacific Ocean, Atlantic Ocean, Indian Ocean, Arctic Ocean.

IV. On the map, draw a compass rose which shows all cardinal and intermediate directions.

Name _____

The Beginning of Rome

The earliest Roman settlers were mostly shepherds. Their settlements, mainly in the Roman hills, eventually joined to form the city of Rome. It is believed Romulus and Remus were the legendary founders of Rome, but no one knows for sure if they really existed. However, their story exemplifies strength, a quality admired by ancient Romans. There are several versions of the Romulus and Remus legend. Read the one below. Follow the directions after the story.

Romulus and Remus were twin sons of the war god, Mars. They were set adrift in a basket on the Tiber River by a wicked uncle who hoped they would die. But they survived. A she-wolf heard their cries and rescued them. She nursed them until they grew to be young boys. Then, Faustulus, a shepherd, adopted them. Along with his wife, he raised them as if they were his own. When Romulus and Remus became young men, they set out to found a city. The brothers argued about where their city should be located. Then, supposedly, Romulus killed Remus, named Rome after himself, and became Rome's first king.

1. List the things in the story that symbolize or are examples of strength.

   _____

   _____

2. Name places in the story that are real. _____

3. Do you think this is a true story? _____   Give reasons for your opinion. _____

   _____

   _____

   _____

4. Write a pretend story about the founders of your city/town.

   _____

   _____

   _____

   _____

   _____

   _____

   _____

0-7682-3794-7 *Skills & Practice Gr. 4*

SOCIAL STUDIES

Name _____

Two Great Statues

Two of the Seven Wonders of the World are statues. Both of them were in Greece: The Statue of Zeus at Olympia and The Colossus of Rhodes, near the harbor of the island in the Aegean Sea.

The statue of Zeus was made by the Greek sculptor Phidias around 435 B.C. It was dedicated to Zeus, the king of gods. It showed Zeus seated on his throne and was forty feet tall. Zeus' robe and ornaments were made out of gold and his flesh was made of ivory. In his right hand, he held a figure of his messenger, Nike. In his left hand, he held a scepter with an eagle.

Imagine a conversation the statue of Zeus might have had with an athlete at an Olympic Game. Choose an athlete and write the conversation below.

_____

_____

_____

_____

_____

The Colossus of Rhodes, a bronze statue of the sun god, Helios, stood about 120 feet tall. It took the Greek sculptor Chares about twelve years to complete it in the early 200's B.C. The statue did not stand very long as it was destroyed in an earthquake around 224 B.C. It lay in ruins until 653 A.D. when its remains were sold as scrap metal. Imagine what the Colossus of Rhodes would tell you if it could talk. Write about a conversation between you and it below.

_____

_____

_____

_____

Name _____

Comparing Civilizations

A Venn diagram is a great way to compare things. Use the one below to compare two leaders, gods, or civilizations of Ancient Greece or Rome. Write the names of the two things you are comparing on the lines provided. Fill in the unshared portion of each circle with characteristics common only to the subject. In the overlapped portion, write down characteristics the two subjects share. Then write a story about your findings on the lines below.

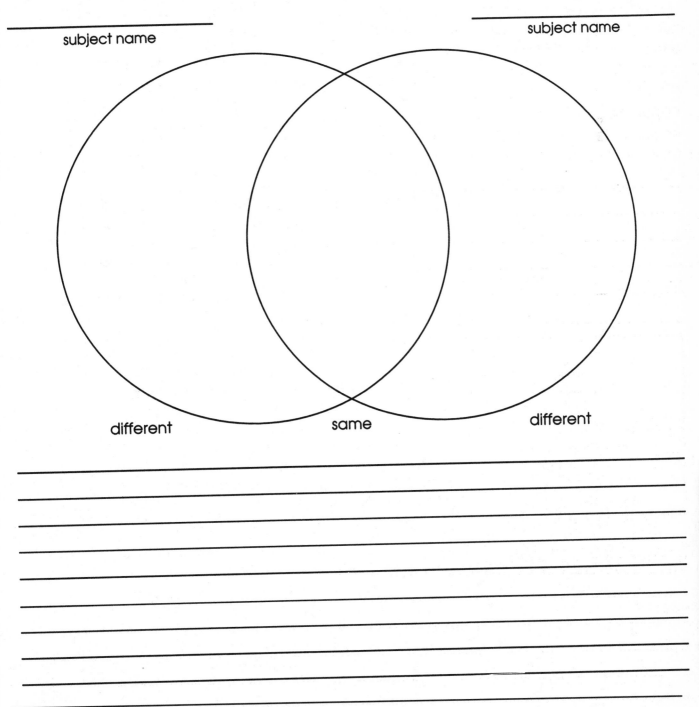

subject name _____

_____ subject name

different   same   different

_____

_____

_____

_____

_____

_____

_____

_____

_____

0-7682-3794-7 *Skills & Practice Gr. 4*

SOCIAL STUDIES

Name _____

How!

How many of these Indian names can you identify as state names? Write the name of the state by each Indian name. Then draw the matching symbol of that state on the United States map where it belongs.

★ Ute _____

◎ Emissourita _____

△ Wishdonsing _____

➷ Mishigamaw _____

☀ Massaadchueset _____

▲ Misisipi _____

▱ Oheo _____

◠ Idaho _____

◇ Dakotas _____

● Alakshak _____

〜 Arizonac _____

🜂 Minisota _____

✕ Iliniwek _____

🌿 Arkansaw _____

🕸 Alibamu _____

Ƴ Tanasi _____

Name _____

Decision-Making Map

As the United States government began
forcing the Sioux off their land, the Sioux
fought to keep it. They took great care of the
land and believed that it belonged to them.
The white settlers believed that they were
smarter and more deserving of the land. The
battles between the two sides resulted in the
death of many men, women, and children.

Was there a better way they could have used to solve the problem? Find the best
solution by working with a partner to complete the chart below.

Problem:		Goal:
	→	

Choices:	1.	2.	3.
Pros for each choice:			
Cons for each choice:			

Decision:	Reason:

SOCIAL STUDIES

Name _____

Welcome to the Union

The fifty United States are listed below alphabetically. The date each one entered the Union is given after it. On the line to the left of each state, write the number that tells in what order the state joined the Union.

____ Alabama	Dec. 14, 1819		____ Montana	Nov. 8, 1889
____ Alaska	Jan. 3, 1959		____ Nebraska	Mar. 1, 1867
____ Arizona	Feb. 14, 1912		____ Nevada	Oct. 31, 1864
____ Arkansas	June 15, 1836		____ New Hampshire	June 21, 1788
____ California	Sept. 9, 1850		____ New Jersey	Dec. 18, 1787
____ Colorado	Aug. 1, 1876		____ New Mexico	Jan. 6, 1912
____ Connecticut	Jan. 9, 1788		____ New York	July 26, 1788
____ Delaware	Dec. 7, 1787		____ North Carolina	Nov. 21, 1789
____ Florida	Mar. 3, 1845		____ North Dakota	Nov. 2, 1889
____ Georgia	Jan. 2, 1788		____ Ohio	Mar. 1, 1803
____ Hawaii	Aug. 21, 1959		____ Oklahoma	Nov. 16, 1907
____ Idaho	July 3, 1890		____ Oregon	Feb. 14, 1859
____ Illinois	Dec. 3, 1818		____ Pennsylvania	Dec. 12, 1787
____ Indiana	Dec. 11, 1816		____ Rhode Island	May 29, 1790
____ Iowa	Dec. 28, 1846		____ South Carolina	May 23, 1788
____ Kansas	Jan. 29, 1861		____ South Dakota	Nov. 2, 1889
____ Kentucky	June 1, 1792		____ Tennessee	June 1, 1796
____ Louisiana	Apr. 30, 1812		____ Texas	Dec. 29, 1845
____ Maine	Mar. 15, 1820		____ Utah	Jan. 4, 1896
____ Maryland	Apr. 28, 1788		____ Vermont	Mar. 4, 1791
____ Massachusetts	Feb. 6, 1788		____ Virginia	June 25, 1788
____ Michigan	Jan. 26, 1837		____ Washington	Nov. 11, 1889
____ Minnesota	May 11, 1858		____ West Virginia	June 20, 1863
____ Mississippi	Dec. 10, 1817		____ Wisconsin	May 29, 1848
____ Missouri	Aug. 10, 1821		____ Wyoming	July 10, 1890

• Draw what comes next.

_____

Name _____

Figure Out Freedom

In 1861, 19 states declared themselves "Free States." People in these states were opposed to slavery. Unscramble each name to find out which states were considered "Free."

EIMNA __ __ __ __ __

EWN SEERJY __ __ __   __ __ __ __ __ __

TREOVMN __ __ __ __ __ __ __

WNE ROYK __ __ __   __ __ __ __

LFIINAAORC __ __ __ __ __ __ __ __ __ __

WIOA __ __ __ __

EGROON __ __ __ __ __ __

NESNOMITA __ __ __ __ __ __ __ __ __

IICHAGMN __ __ __ __ __ __ __ __

DAANIIN __ __ __ __ __ __ __

SILLIONI __ __ __ __ __ __ __ __

SASNKA __ __ __ __ __ __

CHASETSUTSMAS __ __ __ __ __ __ __ __ __ __ __ __ __

NOSSCIIWN __ __ __ __ __ __ __ __ __

HIOO __ __ __ __

CCUTTCIENON __ __ __ __ __ __ __ __ __ __ __

HODER SLANDI __ __ __ __ __   __ __ __ __ __ __

VANPIASENYNL __ __ __ __ __ __ __ __ __ __ __ __

WNE SHEPRAMIH __ __ __   __ __ __ __ __ __ __ __ __

Topical Titles

Name _____

Pick the best title for each paragraph. Be certain to capitalize the first, last and all important words in each title. You will not use all choices listed.

the gregorian calendar	schools in england
george washington's birthday	lieutenant colonel george washington
the french and indian war	mount vernon

1. _____

In 1754, the Governor of Virginia made George Washington a lieutenant colonel and sent him and his troops into the Ohio River Valley to claim the land for Britain. Although the French and their Indian allies fought hard to keep this land, when the war ended in 1763, Britain was the victor.

2. _____

Augustine Washington had three farms. When his son, Lawrence, returned home from school in England, Augustine asked him to manage one of the plantations for him. Lawrence later renamed his plantation "Mount Vernon" in honor of his hero, Admiral Edward Vernon, and both he and George loved living there.

3. _____

George Washington was actually born on February 11. But in 1752, the British adopted a new calendar, and this changed his birthday to February 22. George, however, always considered February 11 to be his date of birth and preferred to celebrate his birthday on that date.

A NOW ... D The picture at the top of this page shows Mount Rushmore, a national memorial that has the largest figures of any statue in the entire world. If you were going to design such a memorial, which four faces would you choose to include? Then draw a picture of what your memorial would look like.

Name _____

Personality Profiles

All the fourth graders are doing reports on famous Americans. Jackie has gathered lots of information on John Adams. Now all she has to do is pull it together. Help her out by numbering the events below in chronological order.

[ ] After teaching school for awhile, Adams studied law. He began practicing in 1758.

[ ] Adams was elected by the people of Braintree to help write what became the Massachusetts Constitution of 1780.

[ ] John Adams was born in Braintree, Massachusetts, on October 30, 1735.

[ ] When Adams was about 20, he was graduated from Harvard College. He was one of the best students in the class.

[ ] In 1778, Congress sent Adams to Paris to help Benjamin Franklin and Arthur Lee strengthen American ties with the French.

[ ] Adams died on July 4, 1826. He lived longer than any other U.S. President.

[ ] In 1789, Adams was named Vice-President under George Washington.

[ ] Adams was chosen as one of the four Massachusetts delegates to the First Continental Congress in 1774.

[ ] In 1764, Adams married Abigail Smith. Their eldest son, John Quincy, became our 6th President.

[ ] John Adams became our 2nd President in 1797. He was the first President to live in the White House.

SOCIAL STUDIES

•SOMETHING EXTRA•

Cut the above facts apart. Glue each of them on a piece of paper. Illustrate each page. Combine the pages to make a book.

Name _____

What a Trip!

Read the paragraphs below about Meriwether Lewis and William Clark's journey to the Pacific Coast. Then, plot their journey on the map below.

Lewis and Clark led the first expedition across our country's vast northwestern wilderness. It began in 1804 and lasted more than two years. The expedition covered almost 7,700 miles.

President Thomas Jefferson chose Lewis to lead the expedition. Then, Jefferson and Lewis selected Clark to be second in command. They, and their group of about 45 people, set out on May 14, 1804, and traveled up the Missouri River. In October, they reached a village of friendly Mandan Indians in what is now North Dakota. They build Fort Mandan near here and spent the winter here.

On April 17, 1805, the journey resumed. By summer, the group made the hardest part of the trip - they crossed the Rocky Mountains. This took them about a month. From here, they reached the Clearwater River in what is now Idaho. They built new canoes and then paddled toward the Columbia River which they reached in October. The expedition continued on in hopes of reaching the Pacific Coast. They succeeded and arrived at the coast in November 1805.

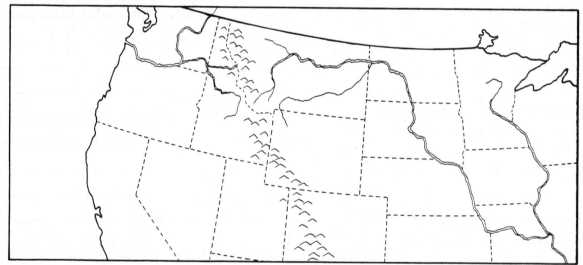

1. Label the areas that are now states through which Lewis and Clark journeyed.
2. Label the rivers on which the expedition traveled.
3. Label the Rocky Mountains.
4. Label the Pacific Ocean.
5. Put a star where the group met the Mandan Indians.

Personality Plus   Pretend you are a news reporter and you get to interview Lewis and Clark about their journey. Write the questions you would ask them and their responses.

Name _____

Down with Slavery

Rewrite the sentences in the paragraph below in the correct order.

John Brown

Brown was tried for and convicted of treason. He rented a farm near Harper's Ferry, Virginia from which he led an armed group of eighteen men. They seized the town and the United States Arsenal there. John Brown spent much of his adult life opposing slavery, but he is best remembered for his final act in 1859. He was hanged in Charleston, South Carolina. Within twenty-four hours the raid was over. Brown's forces were either killed or captured by the United States Marines led by Robert E. Lee.

_____

_____

_____

_____

_____

_____

_____

_____

_____

_____

_____

_____

_____

• Nat Turner is another man who was important in American history. What did he do?

_____

_____

_____

_____

Published by Frank Schaffer Publications. Copyright protected. 0-7682-3794-7 *Skills & Practice Gr. 4*

Name _____

Nuts About Nuts!

A famous American was responsible for the recognition of the peanut as a crop. This brilliant and creative person was George Washington Carver. Carver's research lead to the development of over 300 products made with peanuts!

To find out the influence of peanuts on our lives, complete the activities below.

1. Find 10 food products that contain a form of peanuts.
   Example: Tortilla chips contain peanut oil.

   _____ _____
   _____ _____
   _____ _____
   _____ _____
   _____ _____

2. List 4 non-edible items that contain a form of peanuts. **Example:** A derivative of peanuts is used to make plastic.

   _____
   _____
   _____
   _____

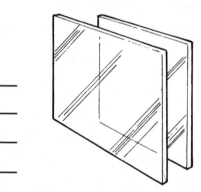

3. Write your favorite recipe below that contains a form of peanuts. Share it with the class.

   _____
   _____
   _____
   _____
   _____
   _____

Personality Plus   Find another person who you think contributed something important to our society. Write what he/she contributed and why you think it was important. Share it with your class.

Name _____

A Point of View

W.E.B. Du Bois and Booker T. Washington were influential black leaders. Though both men were against racial discrimination, their approaches to improving black civil rights were different. Du Bois criticized Washington for his compromising ways. Du Bois believed blacks must speak out against discrimination by demanding voting rights and desegregation of schools, and that educated blacks should lead the civil rights fight. Washington, on the other hand, urged blacks not to make demands but to develop skills and to get along with whites. He believed they would earn equal rights with the economic prosperity hard work would bring them.

Whose approach to promoting civil rights would you take and why?

_____
_____
_____
_____
_____

Taking this approach, write a newspaper editorial calling for civil rights.

Editorial	by _____

SOCIAL STUDIES

Name _____

One Great Inventor

Rewrite the set of sentences in the correct order.
Use the proper paragraph form.

Thomas Edison

1. By the time he was twelve years old, he was selling newspapers to finance his experiments.
2. He sold the firm his patents and used the money from this sale to set himself up as a freelance inventor.
3. Thomas Edison was taught at home by his mother.
4. At the age of twenty-one, while working for a stock-ticker firm, Thomas patented various improvements on the stock ticker.

_____

_____

_____

_____

_____

_____

_____

_____

_____

_____

• What other inventions are Thomas Edison noted for?

_____

_____

• Name one other inventor. Tell what he invented and when.

_____

_____

_____

• Draw what comes next. 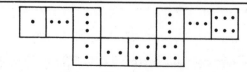 _____

Name _____

Inventions in Time

Use the time line to help decide whether each statement is **true** or **false**.

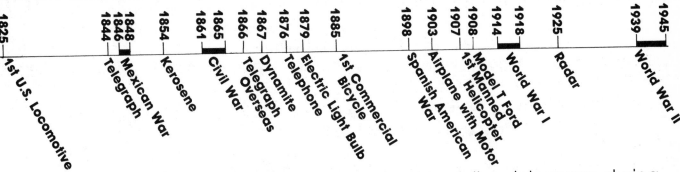

_____ The bicycle as we know it today was used to deliver telegrams during the Civil War.

_____ The helicopter was used during the Spanish American War.

_____ People in New York could talk to people in California on the telephone during the first World War.

_____ Dynamite could have been used during the Civil War by the Union Army.

_____ Kerosene was used before the Civil War.

_____ In 1865 Andrew Johnson was notified by telephone that Lincoln had been shot.

_____ The Spanish American War was the second major war that the United States was involved in since 1840.

_____ When Lincoln studied law in the 1830's he sat by the fire at night in order to have light to read by.

_____ Planes were used in combat during World War II.

_____ Trains were not used until 1878.

_____ America fought in five wars in ninety-nine of the years shown above.

_____ A telegram could be sent between New York and England after the Civil War.

_____ World War I ended four years after it began.

_____ The airplane was invented before the helicopter.

_____ The Model T was used before World War I.

SOCIAL STUDIES

• Draw what comes next.

   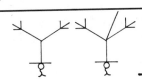 _____

Name _____

Visiting Chile

Chile is a long, narrow country on the west coast of South America. It is more than 10 times as long as it is wide. In fact, it is the longest country in the world, stretching 2,650 miles from north to south, yet it averages only about 265 miles from east to west at its widest section. The world's longest mountain range, the Andes Mountains, forms Chile's eastern border. Its name probably comes from the Indian word *chilli* meaning "where the land ends."

Pretend that you are on a trip from the top to the bottom of Chile. You will need your ruler and the map scale shown to figure the distances that you travel.

1. Your trip begins at Arica at the top of the Atacama Desert, one of the driest areas in the world. You travel by Land Rover to Calama near the location of the world's largest open-pit copper mine. You traveled _____ miles.

2. From Calama, you again travel southward to Antofagasta. From there you fly directly to Santiago, the capital. You traveled a total of _____ miles.

3. More than a third of the Chileans live in Santiago. If it has a population of about 4,500,000 people, what is the approximate population of Chile? _____

4. On the outskirts of Santiago, you were surprised to see many grape arbors. You learned that nearly three-fourths of the grapes imported to the U.S. (40 million boxes) come from Chile. How many grapes does the U.S. import altogether? _____

5. While visiting a school in Santiago, you learned that 90 percent of all Chileans 15 years of age and older can read and write. Children must attend school for 8 years. From Santiago you flew to Puerto Montt, a distance of _____ miles.

6. At Puerto Montt, you were surprised to see the German influence. This area was settled largely by Germans in the mid-1800s. From there, you flew into the rugged Archipelago, landing at Punta Arenas. You flew a distance of _____ miles.

7. Northwest of Punta Arenas is Torres del Paine National Park. Since it was only _____ miles away, you traveled by land rover. The park is named after three sheer granite towers. The tallest tower rises 8,530 feet into the sky.

8. This was the end of your journey in Chile. As a final challenge, figure this out: Punta Arenas is 3,800 kilometers west of Chile's most distant spot, Easter Island. About how many miles away is Easter Island? _____

Name _____

Rich Coast

Costa Rica is located between Nicaragua and Panama in Central America. Christopher Columbus was the first European to see and explore the region on his second voyage in 1502. He and the Spaniards who came after him called it *Costa Rica*, "rich coast." Costa Rica's fertile soil is its chief natural resource. Coffee, bananas, sugar, chocolate, and meat are its leading exports.

Costa Rica is a small, mountainous region. Its coasts have some of the best beaches north of the equator. San José, established in 1737, is the capital and the country's environmental, artistic, educational, and cultural center.

Significant sights include Barva Volcano in Braulio Carrilo National Park, Barra de Matina Beach, site of a leatherback turtle sanctuary, and Bosque Eterno de los Niños, the Children's Eternal Forest. This rain forest has been preserved due to the efforts of school-children around the world who donated time and money.

Choose 10 words from the information above. Write the words on the lines below and then incorporate them into a wordsearch on the Costa Rican flag. Then, lightly color the flag as follows: the top and bottom stripe blue, the center stripe red. Leave the other two stripes white.

_____
_____
_____
_____
_____
_____
_____
_____
_____

SOCIAL STUDIES

The Great Sphinx

Name _____

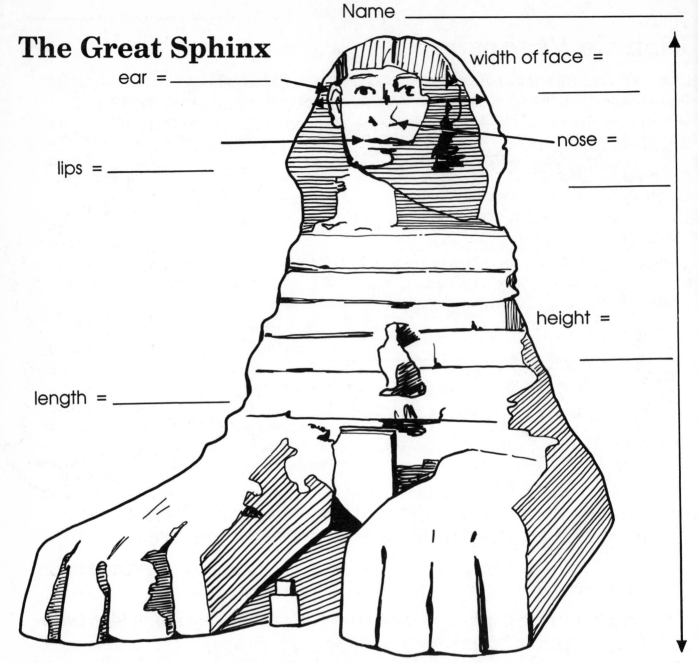

ear = _____

width of face = _____

nose = _____

lips = _____

height = _____

length = _____

Probably the most incredible sight a visitor would see in Egypt is the Great Sphinx. The Great Sphinx has the head of a man and the body of a lion. No one knows for sure which king built the Great Sphinx. Most historians say that this sphinx has the facial features of the Egyptian king, Khafre, and that he had it built.

Convert these measurements from inches to feet. Label the Great Sphinx with the new measurements.

height = 792 inches
width of face = 164 inches
length = 2,880 inches

ear = 54 inches
nose = 67 inches
lips = 91 inches

Name _____

Tour de France

The Tour de France is a 2,000-mile bicycle race that winds around France for over three weeks in July. The route changes from year to year. The map of France below shows the principal cities through which more than 100 professional bicyclists might travel. Pretend you are a rider striving for the yellow jersey. Follow the directions below.

1. You live in Luxembourg. You and your bicycle fly from Luxembourg across Belgium to Lille on July 1st. Draw a solid red line from Luxembourg to Lille. You begin the race here.

2. Next travel to St. Malo. Draw a solid blue line from Lille to St. Malo.

3. Continue on to Tours. Draw a red line from St. Malo to Tours.

4. From Tours, you travel to Bordeaux. Draw a solid red line from Tours to Bordeaux.

5. Draw a blue dotted line from Bordeaux to Agen. This takes you about halfway through the race. What a relief!

6. From Agen, you ride your bicycle down to the border of Spain and back up to Toulouse. Continue your blue dotted line.

7. From Toulouse, you go east to Marseille on the Mediterranean Sea. Draw your route in red and label the sea.

8. Draw a wiggly red line from Marseille through the French Alps to Alpe d'Huez.

9. Your climb to Alpe d'Huez is nine miles long and has 21 hairpin turns. Thousands of spectators are watching you. On the back of your paper, draw what you look like when you reach the top.

10. From there you cycle to just a few miles outside of Paris. Draw a blue dotted line to that point.

11. You are first to cross the finish line! Draw and decorate your yellow T-shirt on construction paper.

279

0-7682-3794-7 *Skills & Practice Gr. 4*

SOCIAL STUDIES

Name _____

A Tale of Two Families

A September, 1991, issue of *National Geographic* told a story of the lives of two families who live only 30 miles apart, yet whose lives are worlds apart. The Hapide family, in what was West Germany, live a modest, but comfortable life. The article pictured Eva celebrating her eleventh birthday with friends in the finished basement of their house. Her mother has time for sewing, batik, and a class in jazz dancing. Sometimes Eva's father will pick up chicken, butter, milk, and vegetables as he returns from work at a printing company.

In contrast, the Rabe family in East Germany has few frills in life though Gunther, the father, has his own electrical business. The teenaged son of the family was depicted cutting kindling for the coal furnace that heats their home. For them, raising pigs and chickens and growing a garden is a necessity. Under Communism, they had their jobs, a home and food but they could not speak or travel freely. Time will tell if democracy serves to lessen the gap between these two families.

Let's learn to write a diamante poem. There are seven lines in this type of poem.

- Line 1 is made up of one noun that tells the subject of the poem.
- Line 2 has 2 adjectives describing that noun.
- Line 3 has 3 verbs ending in "ing" that tell what the subject does.
- Next, think of a word that is opposite of or contrasts to line 1. This is line 7.
- Line 6 has 2 adjectives that describe line 7.
- Line 5 usually has 3 verbs ending in "ing" that tell what the word in line 7 does.
- Line 4 has 4 words relating to lines 1 and 7. These are usually nouns.

1	Farms
2	Quiet, Spacious
3	Plowing, Planting, Pruning
4	Tractors, Barns, Cars, Planes
5	Waiting, Walking, Working
6	Noisy, Crowded
7	Cities

In the box to the left, practice writing a diamante poem about Germany. Think of the two nouns first. You could use East and West, Communism and Democracy, or Germany and the U.S. Or, you could be creative and come up with your own pair of nouns! After refining your poem, copy and illustrate it on another sheet of paper.

Name _____

Journey to Japan

Use colored pencils to label the map
according to the instructions below.

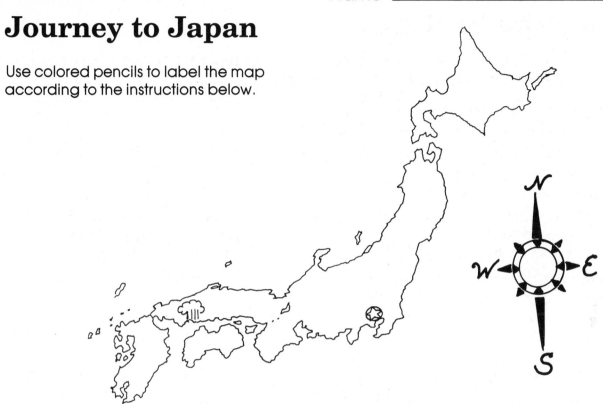

1. Label the islands of Japan from north to south in this order.
   Hokkaido   Honshu   Shikoku   Kyushu
2. Draw brown mountains on all the islands, but not on the east coast of Honshu.
3. Trace the ⬠ red and label Tokyo as the capital of Japan.
4. Color the mushroom atom bomb cloud black. Label the city Hiroshima.
5. Label the water to the northwest of Japan "Sea of Japan" in blue.
6. Label the water to the east of the islands "North Pacific Ocean" in green letters.
7. Place a golden crane in the northwest corner of the map.
8. Draw two orange lines under the Japanese island that has the most vowels.
9. Japan's flag is a white rectangle with a large red circle in the center. Draw it in the
   northeast corner of the map.
10. Japan's highest mountain, an inactive volcano, is Mount Fuji. Label and draw it on
    Honshu.
11. Japan is one of the world's greatest fishing countries. Draw and color six different kinds of
    fish surrounding the islands.
12. Draw 日本, the symbol for Japan, in the southeast corner of the map.
13. Light a candle for Sadako. Draw a lit candle anywhere on the map. Write the date of
    Japan's Peace Day, August 6, by the candle.

SOCIAL STUDIES

Name _____

Visiting New Zealand

Laura took a trip to a location deep in the South Pacific—New Zealand. Nearly a thousand miles away from its neighbors, Australia and New Caldonia, New Zealand is a land of incredible beauty. Long ago, Rudyard Kipling sang of it as "loneliest, loveliest, exquisite, apart . . . the Happy Isles!" North Island is the site of the largest city, Auckland. It is a modern, cosmopolitan area with hints of the emerald isles in its subtropical climate. South Island, with its snowy, glacier-hung alps and remote deer, sheep and cattle stations, is the site of Wellington, the nation's capital.

Thousands of Pacific Islanders have been coming to Auckland in recent years—Samoans, Tongans and Fijians to name a few. Combined with the native Maori, the first inhabitants of the area, they are making Auckland into one of the largest Polynesian cities in the world. By the year 2000, every third or fourth New Zealander will have a Polynesian ancestor.

About the size of Colorado, New Zealand is nearly equidistant from the South Pole and the equator. Nowhere are you ever more than 80 miles from the sea. The fishermen harvest and export rock lobsters, blue cod, abalone and grouper. Salmon farming is a new, growing industry. The farms are actually out in the open sea with pens on either sides of causeways.

New Zealand offers a free education to all students up to the age of 19. If students live too far away to ride the bus, they receive instruction from the Correspondence School in Wellington. The school mails lessons to the students who then send their homework back.

Fill in the blanks below.

A. Write the names of New Zealand's nearest neighbors. _____

B. From the above paragraph, copy words or group of words meaning the same as the following:
   1. snow-covered mountains (paragraph 1) _____
   2. ranches (paragraph 1) _____
   3. urban (paragraph 1) _____
   4. people who occupy a land (paragraph 2) _____
   5. older relative (paragraph 2) _____
   6. same distance (paragraph 3) _____
   7. schooling (paragraph 4) _____

C. From the list on the right, choose the correct meanings of the words on the left which are in the story.

   1. incredible _____   green

   2. emerald _____   raised roads

   3. location _____   unbelievable

   4. causeways _____   site

D. Find the words in the story that are the opposite of the words below.

   1. sow _____   3. ugliest _____

   2. import _____   4. teachers _____

Name _____

The South American Rainforests

Pretend you just spent a great summer vacation visiting the rainforest in South America. You know you covered a lot of ground and you want to find out just how many miles you traveled. Chart your trip and the miles you covered using a ruler and the map below. Hint: Pretend each centimeter equals 250 miles.

1. You started off your South American rainforest adventure at the basin of the Amazon River. There you saw a jaguar taking a drink. Up in the trees, you see a three-toed sloth casually munching on green leaves. It was hard to leave, but you had to fly westward to Ecuador east of the Andes Mountains. You traveled about _____ miles.

2. The Andes Mountains were beautiful! From there, you flew into Guyana and were surrounded to the west, east, and north by rainforests filled with sound and color. A noisy red-green macaw and a spider monkey watched you from their perches in the canopy. Off in the bush, you were sure you heard a hunting coati. What a great place Guyana was! You traveled about _____ miles.

3. Leaving this part of South America, you flew to the smaller strips of rainforest to the west of the Andes, in Colombia. As you continued observing and photographing the animals, you realized that any animal caught unaware on the forest floor by another animal could become this animal's next meal. While you were thinking about this, you saw butterflies searching for blossoms and a red-eyed tree frog waiting for insects. Your next stop took you back to

   _____ .

4. Add three more stops in your trip. You could even venture to one of the rainforests in another land. Use maps to help you!

SOCIAL STUDIES

Name _____

Americans All!

People from many different countries have come to live in the United States. They have brought with them the rich heritage and culture of their native lands.

Build a puzzle with the names of twenty-one countries from which people have emigrated to America. The letters given in the puzzle will help you.

Word Box

China	Egypt	Haiti	India	Italy
Japan	Korea	Spain	France	Mexico
Norway	Poland	Russia	Denmark	England
Ireland	Nigeria	Romania	Vietnam	Tanzania
Hungary				

0-7682-3794-7 *Skills & Practice Gr. 4*

Name _____

What Happened?

Below you will learn what was happening during the lives of some famous Americans. Shade in the boxes following the events that occurred during the lifetime of each person listed at the bottom of the chart.

1972	Gloria Steinem founded *Ms.* magazine.
1966	Betty Friedan helped found NOW.
1957	Dr. Tom Dooley helped found MEDICO.
1955	Rosa Parks helped start Civil Rights Movement.
1936	Jesse Owens won 4 gold medals at Summer Olympics.
1896	George W. Carver received a master's degree.
1889	Jane Addams helped found Hull House.
1881	Clara Barton established American Red Cross.
1879	Edison invented the electric light.
1872	Buffalo Bill first appeared in "Wild West" show.
1857	Dred Scott Decision
1839	Horace Mann founded first state normal school in U.S.
1814	Francis Scott Key wrote "The Star-Spangled Banner."
1794	Dolley Todd married President Madison.
1776	Nathan Hale was hung by British as a spy.
1621	Massasoit made treaty with Plymouth Colony.

Column headers (names):
Betsy Ross (1752–1836), Emily Post (1872–1960), John C. Frémont (1813–1890), Noah Webster (1758–1843), Orville Wright (1871–1948), Eliot Ness (1902–1957), Pocahontas (1595–1617), Joseph Pulitzer (1847–1911), Sacagawea (1786–1812), Ann S. Macy (1866–1936), Walter Cronkite (1916–), Edward R. Murrow (1908–1965), Norman Thomas (1884–1968), Sitting Bull (1837–1890)

1. Who did not live during any of the events listed above? _____

2. During which event were none of the personalities alive? _____

3. What is NOW? _____

4. Of which of the events listed above would you have liked to have been a part? Why?

_____

Personality Plus   Make a list of 10 important events that have occurred during your lifetime. Share them with the class.

_____

SOCIAL STUDIES

Name _____

Where Did They Come From?

Our country has been shaped by great minds from many states. Use the clues and the Word Bank to discover from which states many American personalities came. Label the map with the appropriate states' names or abbreviations.

Word Bank
Massachusetts
Pennsylvania
New York
Texas
Illinois
California
South Dakota
Tennessee
Ohio
Georgia
Virginia
Alabama

1. Samuel Adams, Susan B. Anthony, W.E.B. Du Bois, Ben Franklin and John Hancock once lived in this state which is now home to Harvard, Martha's Vineyard and the Freedom Trail. _____

2. This Land of Infinite Variety is mainly a farm state and was once home to Hubert Humphrey. _____

3. One of four states officially known as a commonwealth, this Keystone State is where Daniel Boone and George Marshall were born. _____

4. William Tecumseh Sherman and Ulysses S. Grant once called this Buckeye State home. _____

5. Niagara Falls graces this Empire State in which John Jay, John Rockefeller, Elizabeth Cady Stanton and Geraldine Ferraro were born. _____

6. Martin Luther King, Jr. once called this Goober State home. _____

7. The second largest state in the U.S., it was the birthplace of Sandra Day O'Connor, Chester Nimitz and Dwight D. Eisenhower. _____

8. Known as the Mother of Presidents, this state was also home at one time to Booker T. Washington, Robert E. Lee, Henry Clay, Patrick Henry, Sam Houston, Thomas "Stonewall" Jackson and John Marshall. _____

9. President Abraham Lincoln lived much of his life in this state as did William Jennings Bryan. _____

10. Jesse Owens and George Wallace were born in this Heart of Dixie. _____

11. The site of the famous gold rush, George S. Patton, Jr., and Earl Warren were both born in this Golden State. _____

12. Indians once roamed this Volunteer State where Sam Rayburn and Dave Farragut were born. _____

Personality Plus   Make a list of some people from your state who you think are famous Americans in history. Tell what they have done.

     0-7682-3794-7 *Skills & Practice Gr. 4*

Name _____

Treasure Hunt in the Rainforest

Tribes living in the rainforest use as many of its treasures as they can for meals, shelter, clothes, medicines, tools and cosmetics. Your home is filled with rainforest products too. Many fruits and nuts and even the domestic chicken originated from the rainforest. And scientists believe that there is much more to learn from the rainforest. To learn more about some of the rainforest's treasures, follow the directions below. You will need another sheet of paper on which to draw your discoveries.

1. Title the top of your map, Rainforest Treasure Hunt.

2. Draw a compass rose in the top left corner.

3. In the southwest corner of your paper, draw an orange and black frog. This is an arrow-poison frog. These tiny rainforest frogs produce a strong poison. This poison is extracted and used on the tips of blowpipe darts when hunting big game.

4. Travel northeast to the center of your paper. There is an Amazonian tree that produces a sap very similar to diesel. It can be used as fuel by trucks. Draw a tree with a gas hose coming from it.

5. Heading southeast, you discover plants and animals from which medicines originate. Draw a picture of medicine bottles in this corner.

6. Move up to the northeast corner to see the insects that provide an alternative to expensive pesticides. Three types of wasps were successfully introduced in Florida to control pests that were damaging citrus tree crops. Draw three wasps in this corner.

7. Traveling west, you stop to listen to a scientist estimating that there are at least 1,500 potential new fruits and vegetables growing in the rainforest. Draw a picture of a fruit or vegetable you discovered. Be sure to name it.

8. Return home and discuss with your parents the interesting facts you learned on your treasure hunt.

Name _____

Problems in the Rainforest

In many countries, slash-and-burn agriculture is one of the leading causes of tropical deforestation. Slash-and-burn farmers clear rainforest land to grow their crops. During the first few years, the crops do well, but after the land has been cultivated for a while, the soil becomes worn out and the plot is abandoned. The rains wash away the topsoil and the land becomes difficult to cultivate. What can you do to help the rainforests?

Before solving a problem, it is often helpful to go through it in steps. For example, read the steps below to learn how you can try to help solve the slash-and-burn problem.

1. Restate the problem into a question.
2. State the facts you know about the problem.
3. Brainstorm possible ways to help solve the problem. Remember, in brainstorming, all the ideas you have are written down, even if you aren't sure they will work.

| How can we stop slash-and-burn agriculture? |

| |
| 1. Many trees are cut down. |
| 2. The soil is only fertile for a short while. |
| 3. The land is abandoned. |

| |
| 1. Remove the trees with aerial cables instead of heavy logging equipment. |
| 2. Allow only certain areas to be cut down one at a time. |
| 3. Research to learn more about how rainforests can regenerate. |

Read the following problem and fill in your ideas in the graphic organizer to the left. Share your ideas with the class.

Deforestation has a direct impact on tribes native to the rainforest. In many cases, these people are forced to move or relocate through government programs. The people also suffer from diseases brought by "outsiders."

1. Restate the problem into a question.

2. State the facts you know about the problem.

3. Brainstorm possible ways to help solve the problem.

Answer Key

The National Pastime

Print the names of the National League Baseball Teams in ABC order on the lines below. Then write the letters in the circles on the lines at the bottom of the page to decode the message.

1. A s t r a s
2. B r a v e s
3. C a r d i n a l s
4. C u b s
5. D o d g e r s
6. E x p o s
7. G i a n t s
8. M a r l i n s
9. M e t s
10. P a d r e s
11. P h i l l i e s
12. P i r a t e s
13. R e d s
14. R o c k i e s

These teams belong to the:

N a t i o n a l   L e a g u e

8² 10 12 14   5 3 1   11 13 2   7   4 6

8¹ = 1st circled letter   8² = 2nd circled letter

Teams
- Marlins
- Padres
- Phillies
- Giants
- Rockies
- Cardinals
- Reds
- Dodgers
- Braves
- Mets
- Astros
- Expos
- Pirates
- Cubs

Page 1

Are You Alphabetically Inclined?

Below are several groups of words. If the group is in the correct alphabetical order, draw a star around it. If it is incorrect, write it correctly in the blanks provided at the bottom of the page.

slithering	dialect	tomahawk	mingle
Seminole	doleful	thatch	metallic
sorrowful	deafen	tourniquet	mythical
salvage	defiance	turban	muslin

platform	abrupt	strewn	capable
pompadour	askew	superintendent	college
prominent	accordion	suspend	comprehend
protrude	arthritis	swamp	cymbal

gig	hammock	awaken	bloodhound
garfish	hoist	astonishment	bellow
gawk	horde	adz	bespeak
glum	inaudible	atmospheric	bewilder

salvage	deafen	thatch	metallic
Seminole	defiance	tomahawk	mingle
slithering	dialect	tourniquet	muslin
sorrowful	doleful	turban	mythical

abrupt	garfish	adz	bellow
accordion	gawk	astonishment	bespeak
arthritis	gig	atmospheric	bewilder
askew	glum	awaken	bloodhound

Page 2

Compound Checkup

Write the compound word from the Word Box that matches each definition.

1. physical examination – checkup
2. a giant Pacific coast evergreen – redwood
3. difficult thing to bear – hardship
4. an outdoor advertising sign – billboard
5. small metal pot for cooking – saucepan
6. on a lower floor – downstairs
7. a glass container used for measuring time – hourglass
8. a movable ramp to a ship – gangplank
9. to betray – double-cross
10. a person with a quick temper – hothead
11. to intimidate – browbeat
12. delighted – overjoyed
13. a logger – lumberjack
14. lower half of a chicken leg – drumstick
15. a very clever person – mastermind
16. a robbery – holdup
17. a limited-access highway – freeway
18. an insect with brightly-colored wings – butterfly
19. a large area for dancing – ballroom
20. a path in the street marked for pedestrians – crosswalk

Word Box					
ballroom	billboard	browbeat	butterfly		checkup
crosswalk	double-cross	downstairs	drumstick		freeway
gangplank	hardship	holdup	hothead		hourglass
lumberjack	mastermind	overjoyed	redwood		saucepan

Page 3

Compound It!

Help Rufus find as many compound words as you can by using the grid. First give the location and then write the word. Use the back of this sheet if you run out of room.

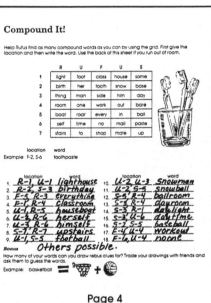

	R	U	F	U	S
1	light	foot	class	house	some
2	birth	her	tooth	snow	base
3	thing	man	side	him	day
4	room	one	work	out	bare
5	boat	roar	every	in	ball
6	self	time	no	mail	paste
7	stairs	to	shop	mate	up

location   word
Example: F-2, S-6   toothpaste

location	word		location	word
1. R-1, U-1	lighthouse	10.	U-2, U-3	snowman
2. R-2, S-3	birthday	11.	U-2, S-5	snowball
3. F-5, R-3	everything	12.	S-5, R-4	ballroom
4. F-1, R-4	classroom	13.	S-3, R-4	dayroom
5. U-1, R-5	houseboat	14.	S-3, U-6	daylight
6. U-2, R-6	herself	15.	S-3, U-6	daytime
7. U-3, R-6	himself	16.	S-2, S-5	baseball
8. S-7, R-7	upstairs	17.	F-4, U-4	workout
9. U-1, S-5	football	18.	F-6, U-4	noone

Bonus
Others possible.

How many of your words can you draw rebus clues for? Trade your drawings with friends and ask them to guess the words.

Example: basketball

Page 4

Words That Break

Divide each word into two words with a slash (/). Then choose one of the two words and combine it with a word from the Word Bank to form a different word.

Example: side/walk—boardwalk

Others possible.

1. afternoon — afterthought
2. junkyard — backyard
3. handkerchief — handsome
4. football — baseball
5. downstairs — downtown
6. eggshell — seashell
7. understand — underwear
8. heartbreak — daybreak
9. outgrow — outboard
10. without — within
11. everybody — everywhere
12. inside — backside
13. overdue — overheat
14. teapot — teaspoon
15. lighthouse — daylight
16. cowboy — cowbell

Word Bank			
back	day	in	town
base	heat	off	wear
bell	flash	sea	where
board	thought	spoon	some

Take two unrelated words to create a whole new compound word. Then tell what it means and use it in a sentence.

Example: junktea – a blend of tea made from garbage. We bought our junktea at a reduced price.

1. Sentences will vary.
2. _____
3. _____
4. _____

Page 5

Comma Quandary

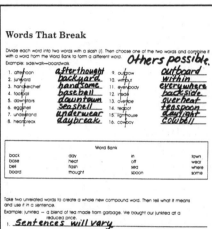

Oh, now I get it!

Look at the underlined parts in each sentence. If each is a complete thought, place a comma in the box. If it is not a complete thought, place an X in the box.

1. Squanto crawled up a sand hill ☒ and looked over the top.
2. He was not afraid ⊡ and he remembered what his mother had said.
3. It was good to see the sky again ☒ and to breathe the fresh air.
4. They sailed along the shore ☒ and into the port of Malaga.
5. The Brothers took Squanto to their home ⊡ and soon he was well enough to work in the gardens.
6. The captain said that Squanto could sail with him ⊡ but the ship was going to London, not America.
7. The Indian was hungry ⊡ but he had no money to buy food.
8. That night Squanto ate ☒ and slept in the home of John Slanie.

Copy these sentences adding capitals and punctuation as needed.

9. squanto liked living in london at mistress robbins' house but he still wanted to go back to america to see his family
Squanto liked living in London at Mistress Robbin's house, but he still wanted to go back to America to see his family.

10. squanto wanted to help the people from england but some of them were not very kind to him
Squanto wanted to help the people from England, but some of them were not very kind to him.

Page 6

The Prisoner's Sentence Is Imperative!

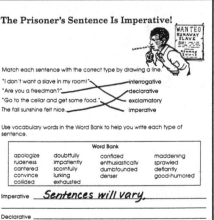

WANTED RUNAWAY SLAVE

Match each sentence with the correct type by drawing a line.

"I don't want a slave in my room!" — interrogative
"Are you a freedman?" — declarative
"Go to the cellar and get some food." — exclamatory
The fall sunshine felt nice. — imperative

Use vocabulary words in the Word Bank to help you write each type of sentence.

Word Bank			
apologize	doubtfully	confided	maddening
rudeness	impatiently	enthusiastically	sprawled
cantered	scornfully	dumbfounded	defiantly
convince	lurking	denser	good-humored
collided	exhausted		

Imperative   Sentences will vary.

Declarative _____

Exclamatory _____

Interrogative _____

Page 7

Makin' Room

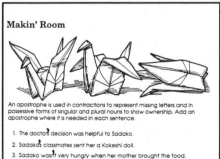

An apostrophe is used in contractions to represent missing letters and in possessive forms of singular and plural nouns to show ownership. Add an apostrophe where it is needed in each sentence.

1. The doctor's decision was helpful to Sadako.
2. Sadako's classmates sent her a Kokeshi doll.
3. Sadako wasn't very hungry when her mother brought the food.
4. The golden cranes' wings blew in the wind. (or crane's)
5. Eiji's paper donation smelled of candy.
6. Sadako's good luck cranes became a symbol for peace and hope.
7. "I'll get better," said Sadako over and over.
8. There wasn't enough room on the table for all of the paper cranes so Masahiro hung Sadako's cranes from the ceiling.
9. Chizuko really didn't believe in superstitions like Sadako did.
10. Sadako couldn't sleep very well after she was told she could go home for a visit.
11. Mrs. Sasaki's slippers slapped softly on the floor.
12. "Here's your first crane," said Chizuko.

Page 8

Keep It Simple

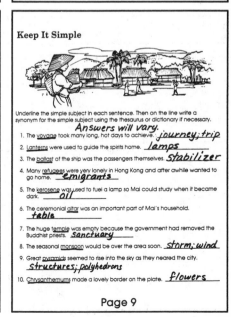

Underline the simple subject in each sentence. Then on the line write a synonym for the simple subject using the thesaurus or dictionary if necessary.

Answers will vary.

1. The voyage took many long, hot days to achieve. journey; trip
2. Lanterns were used to guide the spirits home. lamps
3. The ballast of the ship was the passengers themselves. stabilizer
4. Many refugees grew very lonely in Hong Kong and after awhile wanted to go home. emigrants
5. The kerosene was used to fuel a lamp so Mai could study when it became dark. oil
6. The ceremonial altar was an important part of Mai's household. table
7. The huge temple was empty because the government had removed the Buddhist priests. sanctuary
8. The seasonal monsoon would be over the area soon. storm; wind
9. Great pyramids seemed to rise into the sky as they neared the city. structures; polyhedrons
10. Chrysanthemums made a lovely border on the plate. flowers

Page 9

That's Mine!

dog's bones   dogs' bones

Change the underlined word to show possession by adding an apostrophe or apostrophe and s. Write the possessive form on the line.

	Possessive
1. Mother took me to <u>Tony</u> house.	Tony's
2. The <u>chickens</u> eggs were large.	chickens'
3. <u>Jonathan</u> bicycle needs new brakes.	Jonathan's
4. Follow the <u>team</u> rules.	team's
5. The <u>shoes</u> soles need repair.	shoes'
6. Mrs. <u>Thomas</u> car was in the driveway.	Thomas's
7. My <u>brother</u> story won first prize.	brother's
8. Our <u>neighbors</u> lawns need cutting.	neighbors'
9. <u>Ellen</u> paintings were on display.	Ellen's
10. The truck <u>drivers</u> routes were long.	drivers'
11. The <u>babies</u> toys are put away.	babies'
12. The <u>principal</u> office is small.	principal's
13. The <u>bird</u> nest is completed.	bird's
14. The <u>doctors</u> hours were long.	doctors'
15. The <u>painter</u> brushes were clean.	painter's
16. The <u>skunk</u> scent was not pleasant.	skunk's
17. The <u>aliens</u> spaceship had landed.	aliens'

Page 10

Know Your Nouns

Find and circle the proper nouns in each sentence. Then write them correctly.

1. Miss brophy grew up in lake champlain new york.
   Miss Brophy Lake Champlain, New York
2. The children really enjoyed the stories mr. fency told them when he visited.
   Mr. Fency
3. Addie had to visit the settlement of ree heights to see tilla.
   Ree Heights Tilla
4. Addie carried her doll ruby lillian everywhere she went.
   Ruby Lillian
5. Addie and her family were living in hutchinson county.
   Hutchinson County
6. The mills had moved from sabula to oak hollow.
   Mills Sabula Oak Hollow
7. Malcolm and daniel connolly were very mischievous boys.
   Daniel Connolly
8. Addie wrote a poem titled "the wild prairie rose."
   "The Wild Prairie Rose"
9. Miss brophy often recited poetry written by henry wadsworth longfellow.
   Brophy Henry Wadsworth Longfellow
10. Tilla, katya, addie, and nellie all went on a picnic down by the creek.
    Tilla, Katya, Addie, and Nellie

Page 11

A View of the Past?

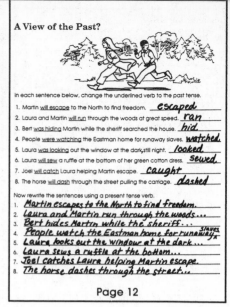

In each sentence below, change the underlined verb to the past tense.

1. Martin <u>will escape</u> to the North to find freedom. *escaped*
2. Laura and Martin <u>will run</u> through the woods at great speed. *ran*
3. Bert <u>was hiding</u> Martin while the sheriff searched the house. *hid*
4. People <u>were watching</u> the Eastman home for runaway slaves. *watched*
5. Laura <u>was looking</u> out the window at the dark, still night. *looked*
6. Laura <u>will sew</u> a ruffle at the bottom of her green cotton dress. *sewed*
7. Joel <u>will catch</u> Laura helping Martin escape. *caught*
8. The horse <u>will dash</u> through the street pulling the carriage. *dashed*

Now rewrite the sentences using a present tense verb.

1. *Martin escapes to the North to find freedom.*
2. *Laura and Martin run through the woods...*
3. *Bert hides Martin while the sheriff...*
4. *People watch the Eastman home for runaway slaves.*
5. *Laura looks out the window at the dark...*
6. *Laura sews a ruffle at the bottom...*
7. *Joel catches Laura helping Martin escape.*
8. *The horse dashes through the street...*

Page 12

Are You in the Past or Present?

Underline the verb in each sentence. On the line after each sentence write if the verb is past or present tense.

1. Sadako <u>ran</u> home from school every day. *past*
2. The wind almost <u>blew</u> the light out of the ceremonial lantern on Peace Day. *past*
3. Sadako <u>dreamed</u> of good health. *past*
4. The wind <u>caught</u> the paper cranes. *past*
5. Sadako's gums <u>were swollen</u>. *past*
6. Sadako <u>read</u> all of the letters. *past*
7. The sun <u>shines</u> brightly on the balcony of the hospital. *present*
8. Sadako <u>slept</u> very soundly after the shot of medication. *past*
9. Sadako <u>runs</u> faster than almost anyone. *present*
10. Kenji <u>knew</u> about leukemia. *past*

Page 13

Three Playful Kittens

Rule An adjective is a word that describes a noun or a pronoun. It tells what kind, how many, or which one.

Example All of these adjectives can be used to describe kittens: black, several, these, playful, furry, three, many, young.

Exercise Place an X in the blanks in front of the adjectives. Then complete the sentence with those adjectives.

1. X striped / __ one / __ carefully / __ soon
   One striped zebra ran through the jungle.
2. X powerful / __ ahead / X two / __ cautiously
   Two powerful elephants trudged along the path.
3. __ yesterday / __ quickly / X scaly / X spotted
   A *scaly spotted* snake darted through the grass.
4. X colorful / X graceful / __ happily / __ however
   The *colorful graceful* birds soared through the air.

- Underline the nouns in the sentences below. Circle the adjectives.
1. The huge gray elephant lumbered through the hot jungle.
2. Three swift lions raced through the long green grass.
3. The playful monkeys swung from the high tree branches.
4. The lazy green turtle slept under the hot tropical sun.
5. The large horned rhinoceros slipped into the muddy river.
6. The scaly old crocodile blinked its large dark eyes.

Page 14

The Fragrant Flowers

Rule Adjectives answer these specific questions about the nouns they modify.

Which one?	What kind?	How many?

Example

these, those, that, this	tall, colorful, red, majestic	three, many, several, few, one

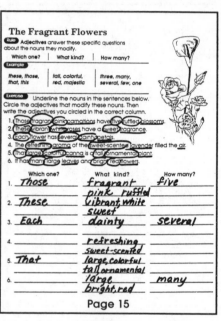

Exercise Underline the nouns in the sentences below. Circle the adjectives that modify these nouns. Then write the adjectives you circled in the correct column.

1. Those fragrant pink carnations have five ruffled blossoms.
2. These vibrant white roses have a sweet fragrance.
3. Each flower has several dainty petals.
4. The refreshing aroma of the sweet-scented lavender filled the air.
5. That large colorful canna is a tall ornamental plant.
6. It has many large leaves and bright red flowers.

Which one?	What kind?	How many?
1. Those	fragrant pink ruffled	five
2. These	vibrant white sweet	
3. Each	dainty	several
4.	refreshing sweet-scented	
5. That	large, colorful tall ornamental	
6.	large bright, red	many

Page 15

Adverbs Answer

Adverbs modify verbs or adjectives and tell how, when, or where.

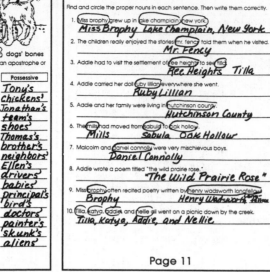
(How when where ??)

How—I read slowly.
Where—I read inside.
When—I was reading today.

Write either how, when, or where after each adverb.

Example	Example	Example
easily — *how*	today — *when*	below — *where*
carefully — *how*	busily — *how*	fast — *how*
here — *where*	far — *where*	uphill — *where*
slowly — *how*	lately — *when*	away — *where*
inside — *where*	noisily — *how*	yearly — *when*
neatly — *how*	after — *when*	early — *when*
perfectly — *how*	under — *where*	annually — *when*

Page 16

That's How It's Done!

Adverbs answer the questions when, where, and how. The adverbs in the sentences below answer how. Underline the adverb(s) in each sentence. Then circle the verb it describes. The first one is done for you.

1. The two boys <u>solemnly</u> shook hands.
2. Chip looked down <u>incredulously</u> at the fallen shingle which landed <u>softly</u> at his feet.
3. "I don't salvage," remarked Rudy <u>calmly</u> when his counselor glared at him.
4. "Rudy," whispered Mike <u>warningly</u>. Chip was glaring in their direction.
5. The door opened and Mr. Warden emerged, <u>smartly</u> dressed in a white tennis outfit.
6. "Harold, you have no soul," explained Rudy <u>pleasantly</u>.
7. "Why do you <u>immediately</u> assume that I'm guilty?" asked Rudy in a hurt tone.
8. "I'd <u>rather</u> go back to arts and crafts," nodded Mike <u>sheepishly</u>.
9. "Tomorrow," Rudy said <u>thoughtfully</u> as they <u>carefully</u> daubed pale blue paint onto their creation, "we'll go earlier."
10. Arms flailing <u>wildly</u>, Chip rushed <u>anxiously</u> toward his cabin.
11. "Let's just walk <u>directly</u> away from the lake," decided Rudy.

Write four sentences of your own containing adverbs. Underline the adverbs and circle the verbs that are described.

1. *Sentences will vary.*
2. _____
3. _____
4. _____

Page 17

They're Coming!

Circle the 24 pronouns in the following story.

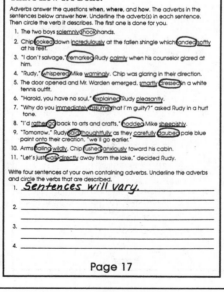

A Scary Dream

"They are coming after us," Rhonda said to her brother, Scott. Believe me, Scott. I saw them with their funny-looking faces. The two of them had long, orange hair, and they had gigantic feet. I thought they could be from Mars because they spoke a funny language.

One of them glared at me with his strange-looking face. The other one looked like she had on her clothes from outer space.

Scott, you can't imagine my thoughts as I saw them coming after me with their weird looks and their weird clothes.

Finish this story. Use at least six different pronouns. Circle the pronouns you use.

Story endings will vary

Page 18

Page 19

Listen to the Music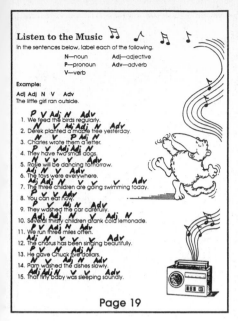

In the sentences below, label each of the following.

N—noun   Adj—adjective
P—pronoun   Adv—adverb
V—verb

Example:
Adj Adj N V   Adv
The little girl ran outside.

1. P V Adj N   Adv
   We feed the birds regularly.
2. N V Adj N N   Adv
   Derek planted a maple tree yesterday.
3. N V P N
   Charles wrote them a letter.
4. P V Adj Adj N
   They have two small dogs.
5. N V V   Adv
   Rosie will be dancing tomorrow.
6. Adj N V Adv
   The toys were everywhere.
7. Adj Adj N V V   Adv
   The three children are going swimming today.
8. P V V   Adv
   You can eat now.
9. P V Adj N   Adv
   They washed the car carefully.
10. Adj Adj N V Adj N
   Several thirsty children drank cold lemonade.
11. P V Adj N   Adv
   We run three miles often.
12. Adj N V V   Adv
   The chorus has been singing beautifully.
13. P V N Adj N
   He gave Chuck five dollars.
14. N V Adj N   Adv
   Pam washed the dishes slowly.
15. Adj Adj N V V   Adv
   That tiny baby was sleeping soundly.

Page 20

Break It Up!

For each word given below, give the base word and the prefix and/or suffix. Remember, some base words' spellings have been changed before adding suffixes. Not all words will have a prefix and a suffix.

Word	Prefix	Base Word	Suffix
resourceful	re	source	ful
accomplishment		accomplish	ment
numbness		numb	ness
convincing		convince	ing
merciless		mercy	less
sturdiest		sturdy	est
disobeying	dis	obey	ing
unmistakable	un	mistake	able
disinfecting	dis	infect	ing
disclaimed	dis	claim	ed
reopening	re	open	ing
inventive		invent	ive
restless		rest	less
precaution	pre	caution	
imitating		imitate	ing

Page 21

Fore and Aft

Fill in the blanks with the appropriate affixes. Some will be used more than once.

Prefixes: dis- im- mis- re- un-   Suffixes: -ful -ish -ist -less -ly -ness -ward

	Meaning	Root Word + Affix	New Word
1.	having no fear	fear **less**	fearless
2.	to vanish	**dis** appear	disappear
3.	toward a lower level	down **ward**	downward
4.	having no friends	friend **less**	friendless
5.	an error in action	**mis** take	mistake
6.	to enter again	**re** enter	reenter
7.	too many to count	count **less**	countless
8.	not happy	**un** happy	unhappy
9.	perfection seeker	perfection **ist**	perfectionist
10.	quality of being dark	dark **ness**	darkness
11.	not possible	**im** possible	impossible
12.	having doubts	doubt **ful**	doubtful
13.	without a care	care **less**	careless
14.	sad from being alone	lone **ly**	lonely
15.	not thinking	**un** thinking	unthinking
16.	without shoes	shoe **less**	shoeless
17.	in a mysterious way	mysterious **ly**	mysteriously
18.	appear again	**re** appear	reappear
19.	in a quiet manner	quiet **ly**	quietly
20.	call by wrong name	**mis** call	miscall
21.	somewhat yellow	yellow **ish**	yellowish
22.	cautious	care **ful**	careful
23.	to release	**dis** engage	disengage

Page 22

Don't Miss This!

The prefix **mis –** means wrong or wrongly, bad or badly, no or not. Underline the base word in the following list. Then circle the base words in the wordsearch. Words may go → ← ↑ ↓ ↘ ↙.

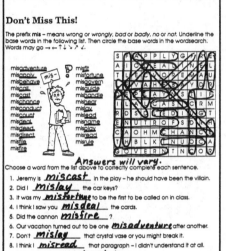

misadventure   misfit
misapply   misfortune
misbehave   misgovern
miscall   misguide
miscast   mishandle
mischance   mishear
misconduct   mislay
miscount   mislead
misdeal   misname
misdeeds   misplay
misdirect   misread
misfile   misrule
misfire

Answers will vary.

Choose a word from the list above to correctly complete each sentence.

1. Jeremy is **miscast** in the play – he should have been the villain.
2. Did I **mislay** the car keys?
3. It was my **misfortune** to be the first to be called on in class.
4. I think I saw you **misdeal** the cards.
5. Did the cannon **misfire**?
6. Our vacation turned out to be one **misadventure** after another.
7. Don't **mislay** that crystal vase or you might break it.
8. I think I **misread** that paragraph – I didn't understand it at all.
9. Robbing a bank is a **misconduct**.
10. The drawings of the beautiful vacation resort **mislead** us – it wasn't even half finished.

Page 23

Similar in Some Way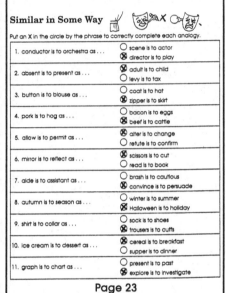

Put an X in the circle by the phrase to correctly complete each analogy.

1. conductor is to orchestra as . . .
   ○ scene is to actor
   ⊗ director is to play
2. absent is to present as . . .
   ⊗ adult is to child
   ○ levy is to tax
3. button is to blouse as . . .
   ○ coat is to hat
   ⊗ zipper is to skirt
4. pork is to hog as . . .
   ○ bacon is to eggs
   ⊗ beef is to cattle
5. allow is to permit as . . .
   ⊗ alter is to change
   ○ refute is to confirm
6. mirror is to reflect as . . .
   ⊗ scissors is to cut
   ○ read is to book
7. aide is to assistant as . . .
   ○ brash is to cautious
   ⊗ convince is to persuade
8. autumn is to season as . . .
   ○ winter is to summer
   ⊗ Halloween is to holiday
9. shirt is to collar as . . .
   ○ sock is to shoes
   ⊗ trousers is to cuffs
10. ice cream is to dessert as . . .
   ⊗ cereal is to breakfast
   ○ supper is to dinner
11. graph is to chart as . . .
   ○ present is to past
   ⊗ explore is to investigate

Page 24

Daffy Definitions!

If you know baseball, then you probably know what a *grand slam* is. It's a home run with the bases loaded. But if you like word play, you can come up with a daffy definition: A *grand slam* is someone who slaps $1,000 onto a table. A thousand dollars is sometimes called a *grand*. By using that meaning of *grand*, you can get the daffy definition of *grand slam*.

How daffy are you? See if you can match the expressions below with their crazy definitions. Write your answers on the lines.

   rock garden   capital punishment   New Jersey
   diamond cutter   net profit   bank balance

1. The person who mows the grass on a baseball field
   diamond cutter
2. A place where outdoor music concerts are held
   rock garden
3. Having to stay after school in Washington, D.C.
   capital punishment
4. What is left after the fishing boat owner pays all expenses
   net profit
5. A replacement for a worn-out turtleneck sweater
   New Jersey
6. What keeps a building full of money from tipping over **bank balance**

Now try the same thing with single words. Think about the sound of each word, as well as its meaning.

   bamboo   cartoon   pharmacy   watchdog   footnotes

7. A school where you learn to be a farmer
   pharmacy
8. An animal that knows how to tell time **watchdog**
9. Music that is written and played for dancing
   footnotes
10. A song you might hum while you're driving
   cartoon

Page 25

Let's Change Laura's Disposition

Antonyms are words that mean almost the opposite. Replace the underlined word in each sentence with an antonym from the Word Bank.

1. Laura stood by the door with a mournful look on her face. **happy**
2. Laura retreated at the sound of voices outside the springhouse.
   advanced
3. Laura scornfully accepted the fact that they would be hiding a runaway slave. **respectfully**
4. When Joel asked Laura to read a book of his, she was very resentful.
   cheerful
5. Bert asked Laura to look in the wardrobe for Martin. She was very impatient in her search. **tolerant**
6. Laura swiftly went to her room and firmly closed the door. **sluggishly**
7. Martin quickly descended the stairs when they heard a wagon out front.
   climbed
8. Laura was very indignant about the idea of having Martin hiding in her room. **gratified**

Word Bank		
respectfully	tolerant	cheerful	gratified
sluggishly	happy	climbed	advanced

Choose three of the vocabulary words underlined above and use each one in a sentence.

1. **Answers will vary.**
2. _____
3. _____

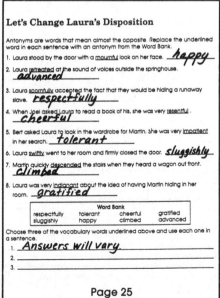

Page 26

Antonym Action

Using the words from the Word Box, write a word that means the opposite of each numbered word. Then circle each word from the Word Box in the wordsearch. Words may go → ← ↑ ↓ ↘ ↙.

Word Box			
hero	deny	clean	bright	ancient
exit	stale	rebel	compel	divulge
raze	solid	greedy	corrupt	educated

1. approve – **deny**
2. coax – **compel**
3. conform – **rebel**
4. construct – **raze**
5. coward – **hero**
6. dreary – **bright**
7. enter – **exit**
8. fresh – **stale**
9. generous – **greedy**
10. hide – **divulge**
11. honest – **corrupt**
12. ignorant – **educated**
13. modern – **solid**
14. modern – **ancient**
15. soiled – **clean**

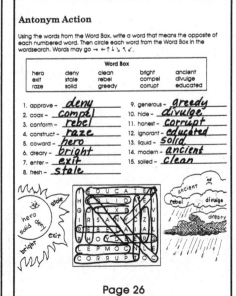

Page 27

Code Names

Use the code to write a synonym for each word.

a	c	e	g	h	o	p	r	t	y
1	2	3	4	5	6	7	8	9	10

1. enclose – **cage** 2 1 4 3
2. inexpensive – **cheap** 2 5 3 1 7
3. right – **correct** 2 6 8 8 3 2 9
4. transport – **carry** 2 1 8 8 10
5. center – **core** 2 6 8 3
6. duplicate – **copy** 2 6 7 10
7. pen – **coop** 2 6 6 7
8. table – **chart** 2 5 1 8 9
9. conversation – **chat** 2 5 1 9
10. applaud – **cheer** 2 5 3 3 8
11. harvest – **crop** 2 8 6 7
12. crawl – **creep** 2 8 3 3 7
13. concern – **care** 2 1 8 3
14. capture – **catch** 2 1 9 2 5
15. class – **category** 2 1 9 3 4 6 8 10
16. price – **charge** 2 5 1 8 4 3
17. stick – **cohere** 2 6 5 3 8 3
18. force – **coerce** 2 6 3 8 2 3
19. task – **chore** 2 5 6 8 3
20. swindle – **cheat** 2 5 3 1 9

Write ten new words. Then use the code to write the numbers to spell synonyms for each word. Trade your paper with a classmate to see if he or she can decipher your code.

Example: deed – **act** 1 2 9

1. **Words will vary** 6. _____
2. _____ 7. _____
3. _____ 8. _____
4. _____ 9. _____
5. _____ 10. _____

Published by Frank Schaffer Publications. Copyright protected.

0-7682-3794-7   *Skills & Practice Gr. 4*

The Synonymous Sleuth

Write the synonym for the backwards word in each sentence. Decode and use the backwards synonyms at the bottom.

1. Miss Whitehead's feet look regral this year. **bigger**
2. I kniht Miss Elson is one of those people you don't bother to think about twice. **believe**
3. It's just what Ole Golly says, hcir people are boring. **wealthy**
4. When I look at him, I could tae 1,000 tomato sandwiches. **devour**
5. He looks yppah except I wouldn't like all those cats. **content**
6. Is he a tnereffid person when he's with someone else? **distinct**
7. She snwort when she looks at things close. **scowls**
8. I just feel ynnuf all over. **strange**
9. Spies should not get thguac. **captured**
10. It was just too suoregnad to go there. **risky**
11. Every time I have a dab dream, I feel like leaving town. **terrible**
12. Sometimes Sport is like a little old namow. **lady**
13. I have deman him the boy with the purple socks. **labeled**
14. Maybe they think I'm a gnilkaew, but I'm trained for this kind of fight. **wimp**
15. There is no rest for the yraew. **tired**
16. This cook certainly makes a lot of esion. **racket**
17. Ole Golly is thgir, sometimes you have to lie. **correct**
18. They're trying to lortnoc me and make me give up. **rule**
19. I will never give up this notebook, but it is raelc that they are going to be as mean as they can. **plain**
20. I will be the tseb spy there ever was and I will know everything. **greatest**

Clues

egnarts	ydal	reggib	slwocs	derit	tekcar
yksir	ruoved	eveileb	yhtlaew	pmiw	rue	tcerroc
tnetnoc	tcnitsid	derutpac	nialp	tsetaerg	elbirret

Page 28

Super Synonyms

Read each sentence below. Write a synonym for each underlined word. You may want to use a thesaurus. **Words will vary.**

1. Mattie and Toni find a beautiful pin for Mattie's mother. _____
2. Matt is thrilled to be on the basketball team. _____
3. Mrs. Benson works very hard to keep everything done around the apartment building. _____
4. Mrs. Stamps is a friendly person to visit. _____
5. Mr. Ashby tries to be a fair teacher. _____
6. Angel is wicked toward everyone around her. _____
7. The Bacon family really enjoyed Mattie's babysitting service. _____
8. Charlene took the bracelet from Angel because she was envious of Angel. _____
9. Mr. Phillips was amazed by Mattie's story. _____
10. Mattie had been very helpful to her mother. _____

Now use the thesaurus to find an antonym for each synonym you wrote above.

1. _____   6. _____
2. _____   7. _____
3. _____   8. _____
4. _____   9. _____
5. _____   10. _____

Page 29

You Can Count on the Count

Homographs are words that are spelled the same but have different meanings. Write the correct homograph for the underlined word(s) in each sentence.

Word Bank

bank	spruce	pupil
flag	hide	stake
brush	arms	bay

1. She hid the gold by the evergreen tree. **spruce**
2. The soldiers carried weapons. **arms**
3. I have a dark center in my eye. **pupil**
4. The children had a lot at risk if they were caught with the gold. **stake**
5. The kids could signal for help if needed. **flag**
6. The skin on the alligator was thick and dark. **hide**
7. The ship docked in the inlet. **bay**
8. The tentacles on the octopus moved constantly. **arms**
9. The dog suddenly began to howl. **bay**
10. The children could conceal the gold in the snow. **hide**
11. Uncle Victor had a banner hanging in his ship. **flag**
12. Someone was hiding in the bushes by the Snake River. **brush**
13. The land along the river was covered with brush. **bank**
14. She had a close encounter with danger. **brush**
15. The snow pile was as tall as a tree. **bank**
16. She was a quiet student. **pupil**
17. I will help you fix up things around here. **spruce**
18. They drove a post in the ground to mark the spot. **stake**

Page 30

Help with Homophones

Circle the correct homophones in each sentence.

1. I'd like to (halve, **have**) a piece when you (**halve**, have) that apple.
2. Please give me the (**real**, reel) fishing rod (real, **reel**).
3. Our (**guessed**, guest) (**guessed**, guest) the correct answer.
4. I heard (**him**, hymn) sing the (him, **hymn**).
5. The robber was (scene, **seen**) at the (**scene**, seen) of the crime.
6. The (**band**, banned) could not play the (band, **banned**) song.
7. I heard Alex (**moan**, mown) when he was reminded he had not yet (moan, **mown**) the grass.
8. The weather forecaster said the (missed, **mist**) had (**missed**, mist) our area.
9. When the knight hurled his (soared, **sword**), it (**soared**, sword) into the air.
10. It's so (chill, **chilly**) today, let's have (**chili**, chilly) for supper.

On the lines below, write a sentence for each pair of homophones.

ate, eight **Sentences will vary.**

dear, deer _____

we'd, weed _____

hoarse, horse _____

scent, sent _____

Page 31

Homophone Hype

For each word given below find and circle the homophone(s) in the wordsearch. List the homophones in the spaces provided. Then write a sentence using the given word and at least one homophone.

1. Main **Maine   mane**
Sentence: **sentences will vary.**
2. Liar **lyre**
Sentence: _____
3. Farrow **pharaoh   faro**
Sentence: _____
4. Bridle **bridal**
Sentence: _____
5. I'll **aisle   isle**
Sentence: _____
6. Graze (Hint: plural form of a color) **grays**
Sentence: _____
7. Here **hear**
Sentence: _____
8. Way **weigh   whey**
Sentence: _____
9. Do **due   dew**
Sentence: _____
10. Sent **scent   cent**
Sentence: _____

Page 32

Indefatigable Idioms

Use the code to find idioms for each phrase.

1. wasting time — **killing time**
XVYJVVAJ GVZR
2. start to think — **wheels begin to turn**
JURBYJ ORTVA GB GHEA
3. became weak and weary — **run down**
EHA QBJA
4. self-evident — **it goes without saying**
VG TBRF JVGUBHG FNVVAT
5. take back what he said — **eat his words**
RNG UVF JBEQF
6. what a person deserves — **just desserts**
WHFG QRFFREGF
7. she attempts to do too much — **bites off more than she can chew**
OVGRF BSS ZBER GUNA FUR PNA PURJ
8. poorly planning — **half baked**
UNYS — ONXRQ

Code

A	N
B	O
C	P
D	Q
E	R
F	S
G	T
H	U
I	V
J	W
K	X
L	Y
M	Z

Challenge: Write a story using as many idioms as possible. You might want to include: play it by ear, child's play, eyes peeled, double cross, ham it up, see red, over a barrel, wound up, down in the dumps, time flies, make ends meet, on the tip of my tongue.

Page 33

Watch for Grandpa's Watch

Each "watch" in the title of this worksheet has a different meaning. One means "to look for," and the other means "time piece." Write two meanings for the words below. **Words will vary.**

	Meaning 1	Meaning 2
1. spring		
2. run		
3. ruler		
4. duck		
5. suit		
6. cold		
7. fail		
8. tire		
9. rose		
10. face		
11. train		
12. play		
13. foot		
14. pen		
15. box		
16. dice		
17. fly		
18. seal		
19. bowl		
20. ride		
21. line		

Challenge: Choose some of the above words and illustrate their two meanings on another piece of paper.

Page 34

Double Trouble

Fill in the blanks with the correct definition number for each underlined word.

Example: **3** I was covered with pitch after climbing the pine tree.

winding	1. having bends or curves
	2. the act of turning something around a central core
wolf	1. to gulp down
	2. a large carnivorous member of the dog family
pitch	1. to sell or persuade
	2. to throw a ball from the mound to the batter
	3. a resin that comes from the sap of pine trees

1 1. Do girl scouts pitch cookies?
2 2. We are winding the top's string tightly.
2 3. The adult wolf returned to her lair.
2 4. Red didn't pitch after the fourth inning.
1 5. The Mather family had a winding driveway.
1 6. The young ball player wolfed down his lunch.

choke	1. to strangle
	2. to bring the hands up on the bat
hitch	1. obstacle
	2. to fasten or tie temporarily
wind-up	1. the swing of the pitcher's arm just before the pitch
	2. to close or conclude

2 1. We hitched the mule to the cart.
2 2. Tip would not choke up on his bat.
1 3. Paul wished to play, but there was just one hitch.
2 4. We wish to wind-up our program with more music.
1 5. Mom was afraid the dog would choke itself on its leash.
1 6. He has a great wind-up and curve ball.

Page 35

Words We Can Hear . . . Onomatopoeia

Words that imitate the sounds that they are associated with are onomatopoeic. Use words from the Word Bank to write a poem or short story.

Word Bank

whack	buzz	hiss	creak	squeal	honk
twang	cuckoo	grind	clink	ping	crack
thump	crash	bow wow	chug	moo	blip
flip flop	squish	beep	smack	chug	chirp
ding dong	rustle	clomp			

_____

Stories will vary.

Page 36

Describe It Please!

Decide in which category each word from the Word Bank belongs.

Word Bank

robust	slimy	sour	energetic	forgiving
aggravated	devoted	enormous	outraged	prickly
affectionate	delighted	tart	spiteful	silky
enraged	happy	gooey	well	depressed
miserable	adorable	fit	ecstatic	
gloomy	gigantic			

Anger
aggravated
enraged
outraged
spiteful

Some answers may vary.

Sadness
miserable
gloomy
depressed

Joy
delighted
happy
ecstatic

Love
affectionate
devoted
delighted
forgiving

Feel (Touch)
slimy
gooey
prickly
silky

Taste
sour
tart

Size
gigantic
enormous

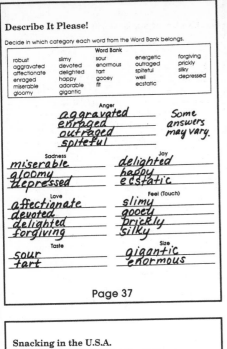

Page 37

As Sharp As a Tack

Similes use **like** or **as** to compare two unlike things that share a characteristic. Draw a red line under the two things being compared in each sentence.

1. The snow reached high into the sky like a mountain peak.
2. The barn door felt like a lost friend.
3. The Connolly brothers are as mean as skunks.
4. The huge hill climbed into the sky like a giant's belly as he lay on his back.
5. The wood stovepipe was as red as a fire engine.
6. Tilla's eyes were as blue as a cornflower.
7. The barn was dark like a cave.
8. The warm cow was like a comfortable blanket.
9. George looked like a coyote peering into a henhouse.
10. Tilla's brother was as strong as an ox.

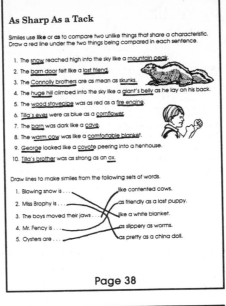

Draw lines to make similes from the following sets of words.

1. Blowing snow is . . . — like a white blanket.
2. Miss Brophy is . . . — as pretty as a china doll.
3. The boys moved their jaws . . . — like contented cows.
4. Mr. Fency is . . . — as slippery as worms.
5. Oysters are . . . — as friendly as a lost puppy.

Page 38

Like . . . a Simile!

In the sentences below, underline the two objects, persons, etc... being compared. In the blank, write if the comparison is a simile or a metaphor. Remember, a simile uses **like** or **as**; metaphors do not.

1. Angel was as mean as a wild bull. — **simile**
2. Toni and Mattie were like toast and jam. — **simile**
3. Mr. Ashby expected the students to be as busy as beavers. — **simile**
4. The pin was a masterpiece in Mattie's mind. — **metaphor**
5. The park's peacefulness was a friend to Mattie. — **metaphor**
6. The words came as slow as molasses into Mattie's mind. — **simile**
7. Mrs. Stamps' apartment was like a museum. — **simile**
8. Mrs. Benson was as happy as a lark when Mattie won the contest. — **simile**
9. Mr. Phillip's smile was a glowing beam to Mattie and Mrs. Benson. — **metaphor**
10. Mattie ran as fast as the wind to get her money. — **simile**
11. Angel's mean words cut through Charlene like glass. — **simile**
12. Mr. Bacon was a fairy godmother to Mattie. — **metaphor**
13. The gingko tree's leaves were like fans. — **simile**

Complete the following sentences using similes.

1. Matt was as artistic as — *Sentences will vary.*
2. Hannibal's teeth were like _____
3. Toni's mind worked fast like _____
4. Mattie was as sad as _____
5. Mrs. Stamps was like _____

Page 39

Snacking in the U.S.A.

Ned's award for losing weight was a trip to Disney World. Travel to these vacation spots in the U.S.A. and list the foods you could eat there that begin with the same first letter as the place. For example, Disney World = doughnuts, dill pickles.

Words will vary.

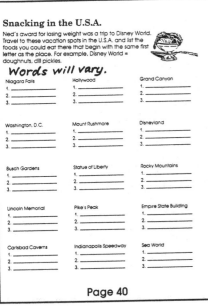

Niagara Falls
1.
2.
3.

Hollywood
1.
2.
3.

Grand Canyon
1.
2.
3.

Washington, D.C.
1.
2.
3.

Mount Rushmore
1.
2.
3.

Disneyland
1.
2.
3.

Busch Gardens
1.
2.
3.

Statue of Liberty
1.
2.
3.

Rocky Mountains
1.
2.
3.

Lincoln Memorial
1.
2.
3.

Pike's Peak
1.
2.
3.

Empire State Building
1.
2.
3.

Carlsbad Caverns
1.
2.
3.

Indianapolis Speedway
1.
2.
3.

Sea World
1.
2.
3.

Page 40

Abracadabra Magical Sentences

Make magical sentences by using words that begin with each of the letters in the animal names given below.

For example: FROG = Foxes Run Over Grasslands.
BEAR = Blue Elephants Are Rare!

1. SNAKE = *Sentences will vary.*
2. LION =
3. GORILLA =
4. CROW =
5. SHEEP =
6. PIG =
7. PYTHON =
8. RABBIT =
9. HORSE =
10. WOLF =
11. CAMEL =
12. MOUSE =
13. HAMSTER =

Challenge: Illustrate your best abracadabra sentences on drawing paper.

Page 41

R.I.P.

Not all epitaphs are serious or sentimental. Some are humorous. Below are two examples.

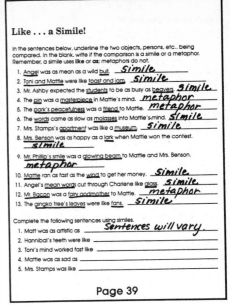

Epitaph for a Dachshund
The bone he fetched
Was still attached
. . . To a bulldog

Epitaph for a School Crossing Guard
Oh, Mrs. Toots, our crossing guard
Why didn't you use your head?
We wish you hadn't o'er stepped the curb
But looked both ways instead

Try your hand at writing an epitaph. Here are some ideas of characters for whom you might write:

a sports announcer	a bank teller
a waiter or waitress	an aerial performer
a carpenter	a pet boa constrictor
a professional wrestler	a lawyer
a talkative parrot	a minister, rabbi or priest

Here lies _____
name

born _____ died _____
(month, day, year)   (month, day, year)

epitaph

will vary

Page 42

Publishing House

Theodor Seuss Geisel was best known by his pen name, Dr. Seuss. His children's books are usually written in verse and combine nonsense with humor. Draw a picture of a nonsensical being in the box below. Give it a name. Then, write a poem about it on the lines to the right.

Poems will vary.

Norman Rockwell was an illustrator of everyday people involved in everyday situations. His pictures told stories. They were filled with actions, feeling and details. Think of something you just did with your family, or a feeling you just experienced. Draw a detailed account of the situation in the box to the right.

Pictures will vary.

Page 43

Dear . . .

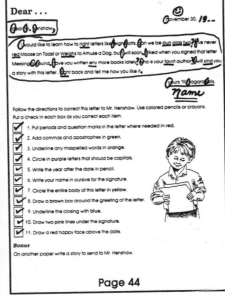

November 30, 19--

Dear Mr. Henshaw,

I would like to learn how to right letters like you do. Can we be pen pals? I've never red Moose on Toast or Ways to Amuse a Dog, but I will soon. I liked when you signed that letter Messing around. Have you written any more books lately? Who is your favrit author? I will send you a story with this letter. Right back and tell me how you like it.

Yours 'till Niagara Falls,
Name

Follow the directions to correct this letter to Mr. Henshaw. Use colored pencils or crayons. Put a check in each box as you correct each item.

- ☑ 1. Put periods and question marks in the letter where needed in red.
- ☑ 2. Add commas and apostrophes in green.
- ☑ 3. Underline any misspelled words in orange.
- ☑ 4. Circle in purple letters that should be capitals.
- ☑ 5. Write the year after the date in pencil.
- ☑ 6. Write your name in cursive for the signature.
- ☑ 7. Circle the entire body of this letter in yellow.
- ☑ 8. Draw a brown box around the greeting of the letter.
- ☑ 9. Underline the closing with blue.
- ☑ 10. Draw two pink lines under the signature.
- ☑ 11. Draw a red happy face above the date.

Bonus
On another paper write a story to send to Mr. Henshaw.

Page 44

Mistake'n Letter

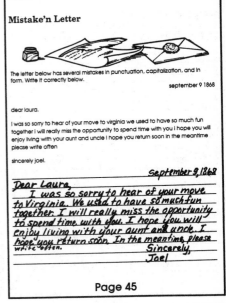

The letter below has several mistakes in punctuation, capitalization, and in form. Write it correctly below.

september 9 1868

dear laura.

I was so sorry to hear of your move to virginia we used to have so much fun together i will really miss the opportunity to spend time with you i hope you will enjoy living with your aunt and uncle i hope you return soon in the meantime please write often

sincerely joel

September 9, 1868

Dear Laura,
　I was so sorry to hear of your move to Virginia. We used to have so much fun together. I will really miss the opportunity to spend time with you. I hope you will enjoy living with your aunt and uncle. I hope you return soon. In the meantime, please write often.
　　　　Sincerely,
　　　　Joel

Page 45

0-7682-3794-7 *Skills & Practice Gr. 4*

Matching Before and After

Match the first part of each sentence with its last part. Write the matching parts on the lines below the boxes.

First Part — Before — Second Part

First Part	Second Part
Call the store to see if they have turkey	you need it.
It's better to have insurance	hot weather set in.
I had my hair cut	you could count to three.
My room was cleaned	we drive there to get it.
Refill the water jar.	you put it back in the refrigerator.

Call the store to see if... before you need it.
It's better to have insurance before hot weather set in.
I had my hair cut before you could count to three.
My room was cleaned before we drive there to get it.
Refill the water jar before you put it back in the refrigerator.

First Part — After — Second Part

First Part	Second Part
We had plenty of hot water	he took some hitting lessons.
Let's have a party.	we finish our tests.
My mom and dad ordered new carpet	we bought a larger water heater.
We were suntanned	we came back from a long vacation.
Sam's golf game improved by several points	the puppy was trained.

We had plenty of hot water after we bought a larger water heater.
Let's have a party after we finish our tests.
My mom and dad ordered... after the puppy was trained.
We were suntanned after we came back from...
Sam's golf game... after he took some hitting lessons.

• Write what comes next.
at bat cat eat fat hat **mat**

Page 46

When Do You Do It?

Write the listed activities that you do under the appropriate heading. If you do any activities more than once a day, write them more than once. Cross out the ones you don't do.

Activities

make my bed	take care of a pet	turn off alarm clock
go to school	carry out trash	organized sports
go to scouts	go to dentist	go to lunchroom
eat brunch	watch cartoons	play with friend after school
homework	take bath or shower	sleep a long time
do the dishes	go to Sunday school	go home from school
go to bed	have pleasant dreams	go to dance lessons
have lunch recess	play after school	kiss mom and/or dad goodnight

Between Dinner and Breakfast
Answers will vary.

Between Breakfast and Lunch

Between Lunch and Dinner

• Write what comes next.
△ ▲ ▲ ▽ ▼ ▼

Page 47

If – Then

Match the sentence parts that go together best. Write the number of the first sentence part on the line in front of the last sentence part for each one.

1. If you baby-sit for me Saturday night
2. If you are nice
3. If we leave work by 4:30
4. If you leave a note on your door
5. If you don't have enough money for the movie
6. If my father isn't too tired
7. If the wind keeps up
8. If you want to get a seat at the concert
9. If our neighbor cuts the grass early Sunday morning
10. If the plant doesn't feel damp
11. If my house were painted white
12. If everyone talked at the same time
13. If you don't get a haircut
14. If the tea kettle whistles
15. If no one answers the door
16. If the little boy crosses the street
17. If the horse is tired
18. If you have a long fork
19. If you don't want any dessert
20. If a king comes into a room
21. If it snows a lot tomorrow

4 the delivery man will leave the package.
10 it needs to be watered.
18 you could roast marshmallows.
15 probably no one is at home.
20 everyone will rise.
1 I'll pay you double.
14 the water is boiling.
7 tomorrow will be a great kite-flying day.
17 let him rest.
12 no one could hear directions.
3 we will avoid rush hour.
19 say "No thank you."
9 the noise will wake me up.
21 we can build an igloo.
6 he said he would show me how to shoot baskets.
11 it would look like a miniature White House.
16 he must hold onto his mother's hand.
2 you will have many friends.
8 you will have to be at the auditorium early.
13 you will have long hair.

• Write what comes next.
A ∞ ℂ ⊃ E **ℼ**

Page 48

Putting It in Perspective

Cut along the dotted lines to divide the events related to the life of Michelangelo listed below. Then rearrange them in chronological order to put the events in historical perspective. Glue the ordered events to your own paper.

1508–1512 Michelangelo works on the Sistine Chapel Ceiling project. — 10

1564 Having worked on projects until his very last days, Michelangelo dies at the age of 89. His contemporaries describe his death as the passing of a "divine angel." — 15

c.1515 Michelangelo completes one of his most famous sculptures, Moses. — 11

1386 Donatello is born. His techniques will influence Michelangelo, and one of his former students will serve as Michelangelo's teacher at art school. — 2

1475 Michelangelo Buonarroti is born to a distinguished Florentine family. — 4

1488–1489 Michelangelo apprentices with Domenico Ghirlandaio. — 5

1501–1504 Michelangelo works on the marble figure of David. — 8

1452 Leonardo da Vinci is born. His work and Michelangelo's work will be displayed side by side at least once in their lifetimes. — 3

1350 The Renaissance era in art, music, literature, and religion is born. Michelangelo will contribute substantially to the High Renaissance period within this era. — 1

1517 The Reformation is initiated when Martin Luther nails his 95 Theses to the door of a German cathedral, criticizing practices of the Catholic church. The resulting split in the church and beginning of the Protestant faith affects the religious Michelangelo, whose works display more sorrow and disillusionment. — 12

1498–1500 Michelangelo works on the Pietà. — 7

1541 Michelangelo completes the Last Judgment mural. — 13

1492 Michelangelo's first patron, Lorenzo de Medici, dies, his family falls out of favor in Florence, and Michelangelo finds himself in exile in Bologna two years later. — 6

1505–1516 The Vatican is the primary patron of Michelangelo's work. — 9

1550 Michelangelo begins work on a sculpture many believe he wished to be placed at his own burial site. Out of depression or disappointment in the quality of the work, he destroys his own work, which is later repaired. — 14

Page 49

Time for Titles

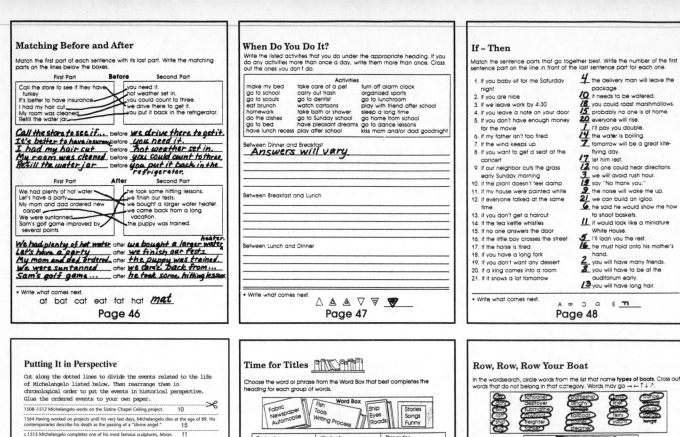

Choose the word or phrase from the Word Box that best completes the heading for each group of words.

Word Box: Fabric, Newspaper, Automobile, Fish, Tools, Writing Process, Ship, Eyes, Roads, Stories, Songs, Funny

Parts of a . . . **ship**
helm
rudder
gunwale

Kinds of . . . **roads**
boulevard
freeway
avenue

Things for . . . **eyes**
goggles
spectacles
contacts

Other words for . . . **funny**
witty
hilarious
humorous

Parts of an . . . **automobile**
headlight
windshield
seatbelt

Kinds of . . . **fabric**
satin
velvet
flannel

Kinds of . . . **stories**
legend
myth
parable

Kinds of . . . **tools**
pliers
chisel
crowbar

Parts of a . . . **newspaper**
headline
column
article

Kinds of . . . **songs**
lullaby
anthem
hymn

Part of the . . . **writing process**
edit
proofread
revise

Kinds of . . . **fish**
flounder
sardine
salmon

Page 50

Row, Row, Row Your Boat

In the wordsearch, circle words from the list that name types of boats. Cross out words that do not belong in that category. Words may go → ← ↑ ↓ ↗.

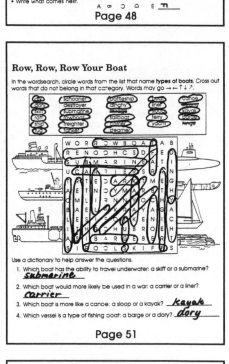

Use a dictionary to help answer the questions.

1. Which boat has the ability to travel underwater: a skiff or a submarine? **submarine**

2. Which boat would more likely be used in a war: a carrier or a liner? **carrier**

3. Which boat is more like a canoe: a sloop or a kayak? **kayak**

4. Which vessel is a type of fishing boat: a barge or a dory? **dory**

Page 51

Classification

Read the paragraph. Write each sentence in the correct category.

The civilians of the town had a strange disease. The disease was somewhat like scarlet fever, and it spread through the town like a plague. However, the disease only affected small children. All of the small children who had the disease had to be quarantined. The children did not lose their appetite and did not have a temperature. The Commandant ordered that they keep a careful quarantine. The German army had ammunition, but none to fight this type of war. The lieutenant did not want his sentries around the diseased children, so they did not go into town. The witty doctor created a disease for the children and it was a success! The children moved the gold safely.

Sentences relating to the townspeople
The civilians of the town had a strange disease.
The disease was somewhat like scarlet fever...
However, the disease only affected small children.
All the small children who had the disease...
The children did not lose their appetite and...
The witty doctor created a disease for...
The children moved the gold safely.

Sentences relating to the German army
The Commandant ordered that they keep...
He was afraid the infantrymen might...
The German army had ammunition, but...
The lieutenant did not want his sentries...

Page 52

Scaredy-Cat!

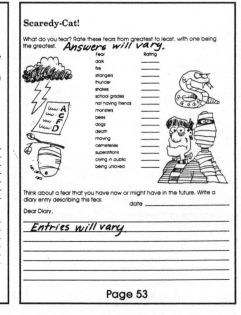

What do you fear? Rate these fears from greatest to least, with one being the greatest. _Answers will vary._

Fear	Rating
dark	
fire	
strangers	
thunder	
snakes	
school grades	
not having friends	
monsters	
bees	
dogs	
death	
moving	
cemeteries	
superstitions	
crying in public	
being unloved	

Think about a fear that you have now or might have in the future. Write a diary entry describing this fear.

date _____

Dear Diary,

Entries will vary.

Page 53

In Other Words . . .

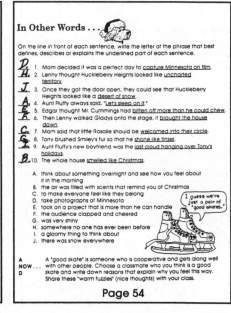

On the line in front of each sentence, write the letter of the phrase that best defines, describes or explains the underlined part of each sentence.

D 1. Mom decided it was a perfect day to capture Minnesota on film.
H 2. Lenny thought Huckleberry Heights looked like uncharted territory.
J 3. Once they got the door open, they could see that Huckleberry Heights looked like a desert of snow.
A 4. Aunt Fluffy always said, "Let's sleep on it."
E 5. Edgar decided Mr. Cummings had bitten off more than he could chew.
F 6. Then Lenny walked Gladys onto the stage, it brought the house down.
C 7. Mom said that little Rosalie should be welcomed into their circle.
G 8. Tony brushed Smiley's fur so that he shone like tinsel.
I 9. Aunt Fluffy's new boyfriend was the last cloud hanging over Tony's holidays.
B 10. The whole house smelled like Christmas.

A. think about something overnight and see how you feel about it in the morning
B. the air was filled with scents that remind you of Christmas
C. to make everyone feel like they belong
D. take photographs of Minnesota
E. took on a project that is more than he can handle
F. the audience clapped and cheered
G. was very shiny
H. somewhere no one has ever been before
I. a gloomy thing to think about
J. there was snow everywhere

A "good skate" is someone who is cooperative and gets along well with other people. Choose a classmate who you think is a good skate and write down reasons that explain why you feel this way. Share these "warm fuzzies" (nice thoughts) with your class.

A NOW D . . .

Page 54

What a Tragedy!

Drama is a play performed by actors. A drama tells a story. Drama can be serious, or funny, or sometimes both. There are three basic kinds of drama: tragedy, comedy and melodrama.

A tragedy is a drama about a serious subject. Tragedies often deal with the meaning of life, and how people treat each other.

A comedy is a drama that uses feelings of joy. Comedy can also show very exaggerated and ridiculous behavior.

A melodrama is a drama which tells a story of good against evil. A melodrama features an evil villain who tries to destroy the good characters.

Drama is believed to have begun in ancient Greece. The

Greeks performed their plays in outdoor theaters. Many of the Greek tragedies were about myths. Drama was later popular in many countries: Italy, England, Spain, France, India, China and Japan. Today, drama is popular in practically every country in the world.

Circle and check.

Drama . . . is a costume **play** performed by actors.

. . . tells a: ☐ joke ☐ part ☑ story

. . . can be serious, or funny, or both. ☑ T ☐ F

Write.

Drama is believed to have begun in ancient _Greece_. The Greeks performed their dramas in _outdoor_ theaters. Many of the Greek tragedies were about _myths_.

• Write a plot or story for each of the three kinds of drama.

Page 55

Scrambled Words

Unscramble the letters in parentheses to spell a word that makes sense in each sentence.

1. Cookies don't _appeal_ to me; I prefer candy. (paaple)
2. The desert is a good place to see a _cactus_. (saccut)
3. When is Halley's _comet_ supposed to appear again? (tomec)
4. Take a deep breath and then _exhale_. (elahxe)
5. Place the _funnel_ in the can before pouring the gasoline. (nenuf)
6. I am learning how to do _magic_ tricks. (gicam)
7. "I don't have a _single_ thing to wear!" complained Jill. (glens)
8. An _adobe_ home is made of sun-dried bricks. (bedaa)
9. _vanilla_ ice cream your favorite? (alavin)
10. This word scramble is _simply_ too difficult for me. (splmiy)
11. Mother set the china on the _linen_ tablecloth. (enni)
12. I am _hungry_ for chocolate chip cookies. (gumyn)
13. I wish you much _success_ on your new job. (usseccs)
14. How many people are employed at that _factory_? (ytorcaf)
15. Hold your breath to help get rid of the _hiccups_. (spuhic)

Page 56

Perfect Pairs

Some words just seem to belong together. See how many word pairs you can make by using words from Column B to complete the phrases in Column A.
Example: salt and _pepper_

Column A		Column B
1. Rocky and	_Bullwinkle_	brush
2. cup and	_saucer_	Bullwinkle
3. pencil and	_paper_	butter
4. cookies and	_milk_	chairs
5. cats and	_dogs_	cheese
6. rock and	_roll_	coat
7. hammer and	_nails_	dance
8. Batman and	_Robin_	day
9. mustard and	_ketchup_	dogs
10. song and	_dance_	eggs
11. shoes and	_socks_	vegetables
12. hat and	_coat_	groom
13. ham and	_cheese_	jelly
14. peanut butter and	_jelly_	Jill
15. bacon and	_eggs_	ketchup
16. Jack and	_Jill_	milk
17. night and	_day_	nails
18. table and	_chairs_	oranges
19. comb and	_brush_	paper
20. bread and	_butter_	Robin
21. apples and	_oranges_	roll
22. fruits and	_vegetables_	saucer
23. bride and	_groom_	socks

Page 57

Babes in Arms

Situation: It's five o'clock p.m. and you are babysitting for a family with three young children. Before the adults leave, what questions should you ask?

Number these questions in importance, listing 1 as the most important. Cross out any questions you feel are inappropriate.

Answers will vary.

___ Does your stereo system work well?
___ How much does the job pay?
___ How long do you expect to be out?
___ Where is your telephone?
___ Are you expecting any phone calls?
___ Do you have a VCR?
___ Do I have to wash the dishes?
___ What is an appropriate bedtime for the children?
___ Where do you keep snacks?
___ May I invite a friend over to stay with me?
___ How much money do you make?
___ How might I reach you in an emergency?
___ When was the last time you vacuumed your carpet?
___ What shall I feed the children?
___ Has your dog been tested for rabies?
___ May I share some candy with the children?

Comment on either a question you crossed out as inappropriate or a question you rated very high.

On another sheet of paper, provide a list of ten tips for prospective babysitters.

Page 58

Ride with the Wind

Size: 22-inch frame   Tire Pressure: 65 lbs
Weight: 37 lbs.   Gears: 3
Tire Size: 26" x 1 3/8"

The tires provide good grip on both wet and dry road surfaces. The narrow tires decrease friction and allow for greater speed.

When these caliper brake levers are depressed, 'shoes' or pads on both sides of the wheel rim press in to bring the wheel to a halt.

The side basket is useful for carrying a wide variety of items from newspapers to groceries.

The frame is lighter than most bikes of this time. It is painted maroon or "icky brick."

With the bike's three gears, the rider can easily adjust pedal speed to match the road conditions.

The streamers and raccoon tail are just two ways for a rider to give her or his individual touch.

Use the diagram above to answer these questions about Addie's bike.

1. Why does Addie's bike go faster than other children's bikes? _The narrow tires decrease friction and allow for greater speed._
2. Where can Addie carry her flowers? _the side basket_
3. How many gears does Addie's bike have? _three_
4. Where does the raccoon tail hang? _On the back fender_
5. What is the color of the bike? _maroon or "icky brick"_
6. How do the brakes work? _when they're pressed, "shoes" or pads press in to bring the wheel to a halt._
7. How heavy is this bike? _37 lbs._
8. How many more pounds of pressure are in Addie's bike tires than are in Carla Mae's which has 41 pounds of pressure? _24 lbs._
9. Does this bike have a chain guard? _yes_ Why does this help? _keeps feet and clothes from getting caught._
10. How is this bike different from many bikes today? _Answers will vary. Lighter, more gears now._

Page 59

Jumping to Conclusions

Write your own conclusion to each situation in the space provided.

Situations	Conclusions
1. Your brother just turned five. He has chocolate all over his face and he looks sheepish.	_Answers will vary._

2. Your parents are gone. It's 9:00 p.m. and you hear a thump and a cry.

3. You are making a cake. You hear the sound of beating wings and a thin, shrill squeal.

4. You are outdoors after dark during summer vacation. You see a sudden flash of light and smell a smoky odor.

5. One morning at school you see your friend looking dreamy-eyed. On her paper, she writes SW + SD.

6. A large column of clouds appears in the western sky, and a strong wind starts blowing.

7. You hear a noise in your parents' bedroom. Then you see a broken window and a baseball rolling across the floor.

8. In the classroom next door you see a desk tipped over, text books scattered, and one boy crying.

Challenge: Describe a new situation on another paper. Include four important details and make up a conclusion in your head. Then let a friend read what you've written and guess your conclusion. Does your friend draw the same conclusion?

Page 60

It's Greek to Me

Anti – is a prefix from the Greek word **anti** which means *against*. Look up each word in the dictionary and write its definition.

Definitions may vary.

1. antibiotic _another a substance able when diluted to kill_
2. antidote _a remedy to counteract the effects of poison_
3. antiknock _a substance used to prevent knocking in internal combustion engine_
4. antipathy _dislike_
5. antiperspirant _preparation used to check excessive perspiration_
6. antiseptic _germicide_

Answer the questions in complete sentences. _Sentences may vary._

1. If a person was accidentally poisoned, would he or she be given an antidote or an antiseptic? _He or she would be given an antidote._
2. If you strongly disliked fish, would you have an antibiotic or an antipathy toward it? _You would have an antipathy toward it._
3. Which would a person more likely use on his or her body: an antiperspirant or an antipathy? _A person would use an antiperspirant on his or her body._
4. To prevent infection from a cut, would you use an antiperspirant or an antiseptic? _You use an antiseptic to keep cuts from becoming infected._
5. Is penicillin an example of an antibiotic or an antiseptic? _Penicillin is an example of an antibiotic._

Page 61

Borrowed from Abroad

Many words in the English language have come from other languages. For example, **garage** comes from a French word meaning *protect*.

Use a dictionary to find the language from which each of the following words was taken. Write the name of the language and a short meaning for each word. _Meanings may vary._

1. gimlet: _French; a small tool with a screw point, used for boring holes_
2. hacienda: _Spanish; a large estate, plantation_
3. javelin: _Celt; a slender shaft thrown for distance in a field event_
4. jerky: _Spanish; preserved meat_
5. morgue: _French; a place where bodies of dead persons are kept until identified by relatives_
6. terrazzo: _Italian; a mosaic flooring_

Answer the following questions in complete sentences. _May vary._

1. Which two words above are from Spanish? _Hacienda and jerky are from Spanish._
2. Which two words are French in origin? _Gimlet and morgue are French in origin._
3. Which word is the name of something to eat? _Jerky is the name of something to eat._
4. Where would you likely find terrazzo – in a morgue or a hacienda? _Terrazzo would likely be found in a hacienda._
5. Which might an athlete use: a javelin or a gimlet? _An athlete might use a javelin._

Page 62

My Own Secret Kingdom

Create your own kingdom by following these directions. Use a large sheet of drawing paper. _Kingdoms will vary._

1. Draw a directional compass in the southeast corner of the paper.
2. Draw your castle in the northeast corner of the kingdom. Add plenty of details.
3. There is a river that runs north and south through your kingdom. Color the river blue and write its name beside it.
4. Two bridges cross the river. One crosses the northern section and one crosses the southern section. Draw them.
5. Draw a moat around your castle.
6. Add a large forest south of the castle.
7. Horses and chariots are stabled in a barn surrounded by a corral. The corral is between the forest and the river.
8. There are four lookout towers protecting your land. Place one in each of the corners of the kingdom. Add different colored flags at the top of each.
9. A pond lies in the southeast part of the kingdom, west of the river and east of the tower and directional compass.
10. Your guardian dog, _____ (name), is napping by the pond. He is a _____ (breed).
11. Secret evergreen groves are north of the pond. In the center of the grove is a meeting place built with rocks.
12. In the northwest corner by the tower, draw your kingdom's crest or symbol.
13. Now add four more features to your kingdom. List them here.

_____
_____
_____

14. Name your kingdom.

Page 63

Pictures from the Palace

Fold a piece of drawing paper into four parts and draw a picture for each descriptive paragraph below. Number the pictures to match the paragraphs.

Pictures will vary.

1. The Emperor sat on a golden throne. The huge chair was taller than any man and carved with dragons and snakes. Multicolored jewels were embedded in the gold. The Emperor wore a royal blue and gold robe. His hat resembled a blue graduation cap with several strands of multicolored beads hanging from the brim. His shoes were black. He held a paper scroll in both hands.

2. The Princess was beautiful. Her long black hair was knotted into several sections. A pink butterfly hair clip was fastened off to one side. She had black, almond-shaped eyes and rosy cheeks. Her flowered pink, green, and yellow silk gown was tied with a green sash. Pink slippers adorned her feet. She carried a pink fan decorated with Chinese nature scenes.

3. The palace kitchen had a long wooden table in the middle of the room, filled with steaming pots of food. The back wall was made of brick. Long-handled copper and silver pans and skillets hung near the top of this brick wall. Huge ovens covered the left wall. On the right, several cooks chopped and diced fresh vegetables. Vegetable baskets lined the floor.

4. The summer palace was small, built high up on bamboo poles. The roof was made of straw and bamboo with upward curving edges. Its long, vertical windows were covered with paper and colorful Chinese murals. A balcony was built around the outside.

Page 64

Hamsterology

Carefully read the following paragraph about golden hamsters. Then follow the directions.

Native to Central Asia and Europe, the golden hamster is a nocturnal animal that makes its home in complex tunnels under the ground. It is a rodent, related to mice and rats. It eats mostly vegetables, grains and seeds which it stores in its cheek pouches to take back to its tunnel. In the wild, the hamster will also prey upon small animals and bugs. It grows to be about 5 inches long and has a short tail. It weighs 4 to 5 ounces and has golden brown fur. The female breeds when she is seven to eight weeks old, producing litters of six to seven babies. Golden hamsters make good pets. Their life span is two to three years.

Directions:
1. Circle in yellow every "hamster" in the paragraph.
2. Make blue boxes around the places where golden hamsters originated.
3. Underline in red the plant foods that gold hamsters eat.
4. Draw an orange X over the animals a hamster will eat.
5. Draw a purple, wiggly line under the word that means hamsters sleep during the day and are awake at night.
6. Put a green R over the word that tells what type of animal the hamster is.
7. Draw a brown star over the place where hamsters store their food.
8. Make a pink line below the hamster's habitat.
9. Draw a red line on top of the word that describes their tails.
10. Circle in red the number of babies most female hamsters have.
11. Underline in black how long hamsters live.
12. Draw an orange box around how long hamsters grow to be.
13. Put a green heart around the verb that as a noun means an animal eaten by a meat-eating animal.
14. Draw a brown, wiggly line under the color of the hamster's fur.

Challenge: Use the encyclopedia to write a report on field mice, gerbils, kangaroo rats or guinea pigs, comparing them to golden hamsters. Share your findings with the rest of the class.

Page 65

Answering Questions

Within each group draw a line from each question on the left to the answer that matches it best on the right.

Where will you stay if the hotel can't take you? — Whenever is best for you.
Who has the lead part in the play? — had to go to my grandmother's birthday dinner.
Why didn't you complete your homework last night? — I'll make that decision then.
When was the last time you saw your gerbil? — If it's raining, there will be very few.
What time do you want to meet? — They are posting the roles after lunch.
How many people will be at the game? — Last Friday when he climbed into the wastebasket.

Are there any holes in that sieve? — I was too tired.
Why are the dishes still in the sink? — He has lived next to me for two years.
Would you show me how to play? — It's a secret.
How well do you know him? — It's in perfect condition.
What did you tell her? — I will when there is time.
Why didn't you go to the concert? — Dad said he'd do them.

Why aren't you eating dinner? — I mailed it to her yesterday.
What is the boy saying? — It is supposed to be available now.
Why isn't the new boy playing kickball? — We had a late lunch.
When will it be ready? — He's giving the score.
Did anyone send a thank-you note to our room mother? — It's the best I've seen.
Does she have good handwriting? — He doesn't know how.

Has anyone heard anything about the new play? — They need water.
How are the flowers? — The teacher wanted to see him.
Why did Tom stay after school? — Jean said it was very long.
How old is the antique dresser? — Barbara finished the crumbs.
Is there any cake left? — It was caught in the fence.
Where did you find the ball? — It was my great grandmother's.

Page 66

What's the Point?

Locate and underline the main idea in each group of sentences.

1. Bert returned with half a baked ham, butter, and a jug of milk. <u>Martin had not eaten since the night before last.</u> Laura set the table for their late night snack.

2. When Laura woke up, <u>Martin looked like a different boy.</u> He was wearing a pair of Bert's pants and one of his old shirts. He looked as though he had taken a bath.

3. Humming, Laura began to scrape and stack the dishes. She put water on the stove to heat. <u>Laura enjoyed working in the kitchen.</u>

4. The sheriff and slave hunters stormed through the house. Laura heard the crash of a chair. They searched every room and closet. <u>The men were looking for a fugitive slave.</u>

5. The field behind the vegetable garden was aglow with goldenrod and wild flowers. The autumn sun shone brightly in the yard. Laura looked out the window. <u>She longed to go outside on this beautiful autumn day.</u>

Now write one detail sentence from each group on the lines below.

1. *Answers will vary.*
2. _____
3. _____
4. _____
5. _____

Page 67

Camp Rules

Donald, Arnold and Jack are all at Camp Explore-It-All this week. They think camp is a lot of fun, but they have also learned from their instructors that there are some very important rules all campers must obey so that everyone has a good time.

All campers had to take swimming tests to see what depth of water they will be allowed to swim in. Donald and Jack passed the advanced test and can swim in the deep water. Arnold, however, only passed the intermediate test. He is supposed to stay in the area where the water is waist deep. When it is time to swim, Arnold decides to sneak into deep water with Donald and Jack. After all, he has been swimming in deep water for three years. No way is he going to stay in the shallow water with the sissies.

Donald and Jack don't think Arnold should come into the deep water, but they can't tell him anything. So the boys jump into the water and start swimming and playing. Fifteen minutes later, Arnold is yelling, "Help!" He swam out too far and is too tired to make it back in. The lifeguard jumps in and pulls him out. Everyone stops to see what is happening. Arnold feels very foolish.

Check.
The main idea of this story is . . .
☐ Arnold ends up feeling foolish. ☐ Camp is fun.
☐ All campers take swimming tests. ☑ Rules are made for good reasons.
☐ You can learn a lot from instructors. ☐ Rules are made to be broken.

Underline.
Arnold got himself into a(n) _____ situation.
amusing   funny   <u>dangerous</u>   ambiguous

Circle.
Arnold thought the guys in the shallow area were (bullies/sissies). However, he should have (stayed with them/gone to the advanced area).

Write.
What lesson do you think Arnold learned? *Answers will vary.*

What do you think the other campers learned? _____

Page 68

From Whose Point of View?

Read each sentence below. Decide if it is the first or third person's point of view. If it is a first person's point of view, rewrite the sentence to make it a third person's point of view. If it is a third person's point of view, rewrite it to make it a first person's point of view. *Sentences may vary.*

1. I wanted to tell Anh and Thant the secret of our leaving, but I had given my word.
   He wanted to tell Anh and Thant the secret of their leaving, but he had given his word.
2. The grandmother did not want to go aboard the boat.
   I did not want to go aboard the boat.
3. The people on shore were pushing to get on the deck of the boat.
   We were pushing to get on the deck of the boat.
4. Though I had worked many days in the rice paddies watching planes fly over, I never thought I'd be on one.
   Though she had worked many days in the rice paddies watching planes fly over, she had never thought she'd...
5. Loi made a net from pieces of string and caught a turtle with his new device.
   I made a net from pieces of string and caught a turtle with my new device.
6. I know of a place where we can wash our clothes.
   She knew of a place where they could wash their clothes.
7. The officer looked at them with great interest.
   I looked at them with great interest.
8. When I looked into the harbor, I could see the shape of the sampan boats.
   When he looked into the harbor, he could see the shape of the sampan boats.
9. This is my duck and I choose to share it with everyone on the boat for the celebration of Tet.
   This is her duck and she chose to share it with everyone on the boat for the celebration of Tet.

Page 69

Make Your Mark Here

Use the proofreader marks shown to the right to correct the sentences below.

apostrophe ∨   end marks ⊙ ⑦ ⑦
quotation marks ⌄⌄   comma ∧
capitalize ≡

1. Lucy walked. cant go to the party I told everyone what a great costume I was going to have.
2. carla said okay meet me at my place the basement apartment of the eucalyptus tree do you know where that is?
3. are you a real vampire? Lucy demanded.
4. hold it Lucy I dropped my fangs down your neck mumbled the embarrassed knievel.
5. knievel howled dont you have more thats the best chocolate cupcake I ever ate! why did I eat everything?
6. stay right there squeaked the rabbit I'll get you something dont move.
7. where's the tv questioned susannah looking around I'm sure I heard one before we came in.
8. mordecai rubbed his hands and smiled shyly I'll be back he whispered then he vanished.
9. I'm pretty sure knievel got the poisoned candy when he was with us susannah said. I don't think he had any trick-or-treating before he met us.
10. I forgot my key shouted aunt louise how are you going where's that niece of mine?

Draw a picture to go with one of the quotes above. Write the quote next to it.

Quote: *Quotes will vary*

Page 70

Fish Facts

All of the fourth graders in Miss Freed's class did reports on animals. Jackie did hers on fish. She learned so much about these fascinating animals. She can't wait to share her information with her class.

Jackie didn't know much about fish when she started. She has since learned that fish are vertebrates because they have backbones. She was also amazed to learn that there are more kinds of fish than all other kinds of water and land vertebrates put together. The kinds of fish differ so greatly in shape, color and size that Jackie can hardly believe they all belong to the same group of animals.

Some fish, Jackie found out, look like lumpy rocks. Others look like wriggly worms. Some can blow themselves up like balloons, and others are as flat as pancakes. Fish can be all the colors of the rainbow, and also striped and polka-dotted. The one fish Jackie definitely never wants to run into is the stonefish. Though it is small, it can kill a person in a few minutes. The subject of fish turned out to be a lot more interesting than Jackie ever imagined.

Circle.
Fish are (invertebrates/vertebrates) because they (do not have/have) backbones.

Underline.
Fish differ greatly in . . .
taste.   <u>size</u>.   <u>shape</u>.   <u>color</u>.   <u>length</u>.

Check.
Fish can be . . .
☑ lumpy.   ☐ depressed.   ☑ colorful.   ☑ striped.
☐ smart.   ☑ flat.   ☑ polka-dotted.   ☐ sad.

Write.
Describe the kinds of fish found in aquariums. Use adjectives relating to size, shape and color.
Answers will vary.

What kinds of fish have you eaten? _____

Page 71

Mixed-Up Recipe

In a story, Laura decides to make a batch of homemade applesauce. Below is a recipe she may have followed. However, by looking at the directions, it is easy to see that something is mixed-up.

> **Applesauce**
>
> 12 to 16 medium pears
> 3 cups vinegar
> 1 to 1 1/2 cups of flour
>
> **Directions:**
> Add water to pan. Peel and slice the apples into quarters. Simmer over low heat for 20 to 30 minutes or until soft. Stir occasionally. Stir in sugar and heat through. Add 1 teaspoon cinnamon if you wish.
>
> Makes 12 servings.

Correct Directions:

12 to 16 medium apples

3 cups water

1 to 1 1/2 cups of sugar

Add water to pan. Peel and slice the apples into quarters. Simmer over low heat for 20 to 30 minutes or until soft. Stir occasionally. Stir in sugar and heat through. Add 1 teaspoon cinnamon if you wish.

Page 72

Weekend Fun

Number each group of sentences in the correct order.

3 I had a hamburger, but everyone else had a salad.
6 My parents picked us up after the movie.
1 A horse drawn carriage took us for a ride through the park to the zoo.
5 I didn't buy any popcorn during the movie.
2 We spent a couple of hours at the zoo before we took a bus to meet our friends for lunch.
4 We walked to the movie after lunch.

6 A wind lifted the kite high in the air.
5 Father let out the string while I ran with the kite.
2 The park was crowded with people flying kites when we got there.
3 We found a spot to fly the kite away from the other people.
1 Father and I took a kite to the park.
4 We had to tie a tail on the kite before it was ready to be flown.

2 I took an atlas home with me on Friday.
4 I wrote down important facts about each country.
6 I turned in my report on Monday morning.
3 After I watched cartoons Saturday morning, I looked up England and Germany in the atlas.
5 I wrote a report about England and Germany from my notes.
1 Friday morning the teacher said our reports on different countries were due on Monday.

3 We decided what kind of cones we wanted while standing in line.
5 Larry fell down and the cone flew into the air.
4 While walking down the street with our cones, a large dog charged Larry.
1 There was a long line at the ice-cream shop when Larry and I got there.
6 The dog caught the cone and ran away with it.
2 We stood behind the last person in line.

Page 73

Putting Them in Order

Rewrite the sentences in each paragraph below in the correct order.

There was a loud crack and the ice Elizabeth was on began to sink. Her mother warned her not to go too far out on the ice, but she forgot. Elizabeth asked her mother if she could go skating on the pond. Elizabeth's cries for help were answered, and some other skaters pulled her to safety.

Elizabeth asked her mother if she could go skating on the pond. Her mother warned her not to go too far out on the ice, but she forgot. There was a loud crack and the ice Elizabeth was on began to sink. Elizabeth's cries for help were answered, and some other skaters pulled her to safety.

When Marcy and Tony were walking home from school he suggested they go a different way. The stream twisted and turned, and it eventually led them back to school. They followed the stream in the direction they thought would take them home. They cut across a farmer's field and down a hill to a stream.

When Marcy and Tony were walking home from school he suggested they go a different way. They cut across a farmer's field and down a hill to a stream. They followed the stream in the direction they thought would take them home. The stream twisted and turned, and it eventually led them back to school.

• Write what comes next.

VI VOI VOIVI VOIVOI

Page 74

Moving Time

David's family is buying a new house. Their old house is just too small. However, there are two houses that they like equally as much. The first one is in the neighborhood in which they live now. David's family would still be around all their same friends, and David could still ride to school with his best friend. The only problem is that this house doesn't have a playroom where David and his friends could go, which was one of the reasons for moving. It also needs a lot of painting, which David's dad is not happy about. But, it's a good buy.

The second house is across town. David could still go to the same school, but he wouldn't be close to his old friends. This house is really big with a huge playroom, and it has just been freshly painted. Even though it costs more than the other one, it's still a good deal.

So now David's family has to decide if they want less room, more work and the same neighborhood, or more room and less work. Both houses have 3 bedrooms and big family rooms, so his parents are happy about that. What a decision!

Underline.

David and his family have found two houses that they like . . .

equally as well. almost as much as their old one. in his neighborhood. a little.

Circle.

David would want to buy the second house except that it . . .

has a big playroom. needs to be painted. (isn't close to his friends.)

Check.

The first house is different from the second one because it . . .

- ☐ has three bedrooms.
- ☑ is in David's same neighborhood.
- ☑ doesn't have a play room.
- ☐ has a family room.
- ☑ needs to be painted.
- ☐ is a good buy.

Write.

List at least 3 reasons David's family is having a hard time deciding which house to buy.

Answers will vary.

1. They like both houses.
2. Both houses are good buys.
3. Both houses have 3 bedrooms.

If you ever had to move, how would you feel about it? List five positive things and five negative things about moving.

Page 75

Yesterday and Today

Read each sentence. If it tells about a past event, write THEN on the line. If it tells about an event that is happening in the present, write NOW on the line.

Now The forest fire is burning out of control.
Then We sent money to help feed and clothe the flood victims.
Now The river rushing past my window keeps me up at night.
Now I am taking a series of tennis lessons on Wednesdays.
Then Glaciers covered over one-fifth of the world.
Now The student council sets rules for the student body to follow.
Then I bought enough glue to last a lifetime.
Then The third grade had the best attendance record.
Then The picnic was cancelled because of the heavy downpour.
Now I belong to the scouts.
Now The forest floor is covered with ferns and moss.
Now The Hopi Indians live within the Navajo Indian nation.
Then My aunt and uncle stayed with us for a week.
Then The day started out sunny.
Now My grade in penmanship indicates great improvement.
Then I baked banana bread for the room mother's tea.
Now I watch television every night for an hour before going to bed.
Now Melissa is the fastest runner in the class.
Then I made a deposit in my savings account.
Then I cut my birthday cake after I blew out all the candles.
Now The patrol boys and girls help younger children cross the street.
Now The snow is continuing to fall.
Now I save my pennies for rainy days.
Then The chandelier swayed during the earthquake.
Then We fastened our seat belts before father started the car.
Then The native dancers' clothes were colorful.

• Write what comes next.

BA ED IH ON VU

Page 76

Keeping in Touch

On the lines next to the letter, write the correct category **(who, what, when, where or why)** for each underlined word or phrase in Genevieve's letter.

Dear Mom and Dad,

I have been very busy (1) here in the United States taking care of Lucas and the twins. (2) A few weeks ago (3) Lucas and his friends (4) climbed up onto the roof of the Cotts' home (5) to get a better view of the neighborhood. (6) He has spent a lot of time with me (7) since then.

(8) Today, I (9) taught him how to dance (10) so he can have a girlfriend (11) when he gets older. (12) Julio danced with us (13) in the living room, too. (14) I miss you both.

Love,
Genevieve

1. where
2. when
3. who
4. what
5. why
6. who
7. when
8. when
9. what
10. why
11. when
12. who
13. where
14. who

A
NOW . . . Write an essay titled, "The Importance of Being Trustworthy." Share it with your classmates and discuss what each of you thinks about *being* trustworthy and *expecting* trust from others.
D

Page 77

Are You Mixed Up?

Unscramble the letters on the left to create words which match the meanings on the right.

	Word	Word Meaning
1. degtti	fidget	To move restlessly or nervously
2. spygy	gypsy	A member of a wandering people believed to have come out of India
3. pureto	troupe	A group of actors or dancers
4. tayjun	jaunty	Having a self-confident manner
5. nastioyrta	stationary	Not capable of being moved
6. caottitep	petticoat	A woman's slip or underskirt
7. ever	veer	To swerve
8. rylub	burly	Heavy, strong and muscular
9. merba	amber	A brownish-yellow color
10. laiggni	galling	Very annoying

Write sentences using four of the words you unscrambled.

1. Sentences will vary.
2.
3.
4.

Page 78

Say It Again

Add a letter to each word to make a new word. Use letters from the Letter Bank and the clues to help. The letter may be added anywhere to the word.

Example:

word		letter		new word	clue
hove	+	l	=	hovel	a hut

Word	Letter	New Word	Clue
gain	r	grain	Small seed
rate	g	grate	Used in fireplaces
par	e	pear	A fruit
rip	e	ripe	Ready for harvest
sing	e	singe	To burn at the edges
tick	h	thick	Slow witted
pear	s	spear	Weapon that can be thrown
ad	o	ado	Fuss or bother
mat	s	mast	Important to sailing ships
boar	d	board	Two-by-four
die	r	dire	Urgent
men	o	omen	Sign of a future event
yarn	e	yearn	To want
tool	s	stool	Place to sit
toe	t	tote	To carry
single	h	shingle	Roofing material

Letter Bank

d e e e e g h h o o r r s s s t

Page 79

Guide-Worthy Words

Use a pencil to write ten vocabulary words from the Word Bank under each of the guide words. Remember to put them in alphabetical order.

Reflection	Syllable
reindeer	scowl
resolute	stance
retort	stealth
salute	subside
schoolmaster	surpass

Abrupt	Authority
accidentally	ammunition
accustom	ancient
additional	appoint
allow	ashamed
almanac	assign

Babyhood	Crest
barometer	commerce
barracks	commotion
beneficial	consternation
burrow	cordial
calamity	corporal

Defense	Exult
defiant	earthenware
demoralize	enormous
discard	entirely
disposition	epidemic
disturbance	explosive

Word Bank

burrow	commence	cordial	corporal	accustom
accidentally	barracks	barometer	explosive	schoolmaster
stealth	allow	calamity	stance	defiant
epidemic	ancient	scowl	discard	ammunition
disturbance	subside	salute	reindeer	consternation
assign	demoralize	disposition	appoint	beneficial
resolute	enormous	ashamed	retort	entirely
earthenware	additional	commotion	almanac	surpass

Page 80

Hey, Look Me Over

Use the dictionary pronunciations to answer the questions below.

concoction (kən kok′ shən) *noun.* something prepared by mixing ingredients.

1. Which syllable is accented? 2nd
2. How many syllables have a "schwa" sound? 2
3. How many syllables are in "concoction?" 3

hover (huv′ ər) *verb. hovered hovering.* to flutter over or about.

1. How many syllables are in *hover*? 2
2. Which syllable is accented? 1st
3. How many syllables are found in *hovering*? 3

eternity (i tur′ nə tē) *noun.* an endless length of time.

1. Which syllable has a long "e" sound? 4th
2. Which syllable is accented? 2nd
3. How many syllables are in *eternity*? 4

honeysuckle (hun′ ē suk′ əl) *noun.* a climbing shrub with pleasant-smelling flowers.

1. How many syllables are in "honeysuckle?" 4
2. Which syllable has a primary accent? 1st
3. Which syllable has a secondary accent? 3rd
4. Which syllable has a "schwa" sound? 4th
5. Which two syllables have the same vowel sound? 1st, 3rd

Challenge: Write the phonetic spellings of these words. May vary.

audible ô′ də bəl camouflage kam′ ə fläzh
pneumonia nōō mōn′ yə municipal myōō nis′ ə pəl
supernatural sōō pər nach′ ər əl

Page 81

Weird Words

Use a dictionary to help you answer the questions using complete sentences. *Sentences will vary.*

1. Which would you use to treat a sore throat: a gargoyle or a gargle?
   A gargle helps treat a sore throat.

2. Which might be used on a gravestone: an epiphyte or an epitaph?
   An epitaph might be used on a gravestone.

3. Which is an instrument: calligraphy or a calliope?
   A calliope is an instrument.

4. Would a building have a gargoyle or an argyle on it?
   A building would have a gargoyle on it.

5. If you trick someone, do you bamboozle him or barcarole him?
   When you trick someone, you bamboozle him.

6. If you studied handwriting, would you learn calligraphy or cajolery?
   If you studied handwriting, you would learn calligraphy.

7. What would a gondolier sing: a barcarole or an argyle?
   A gondolier sings a barcarole.

8. If you tried to coax someone, would you be using cajolery or calamity?
   You use cajolery to try to coax someone.

9. Which might you wear: argyles or calliopes?
   You might wear argyles.

10. In Venice, Italy, would you travel in a gondola or a calamity?
    In Venice, Italy, you would travel in a gondola.

Page 82

From the Diary of Milo

Use a dictionary to help you circle the correct definition for each underlined word. In the space, write the dictionary page number. *Page numbers vary.*

1. We saw debris scattered everywhere after the fortress fell.
   smoke   (rubble)   vegetation

2. The beautiful island beckoned us to its rich bounty.
   warned   darkened   (lured)

3. The strange creature doffed his hat and welcomed us to Digitopolis.
   pounded   washed   (tipped)

4. We ducked our heads to avoid the cave's stalactites.
   pitfalls   (icicle-shaped mineral deposits)   dripping water

5. The soup's pot loosed a savory steam into the air.
   boiling   safe   (appetizing)

6. If I continue to add ones, I could count into infinity.
   (endlessness)   a secret chamber   wee hours of the night

7. The sheer mountain walls made climbing difficult for our traveling band.
   icy   (very steep)   sharply spiked

8. The giant whined peevishly when we asked him to assist us.
   (crossly)   weakly   foolishly

9. As the demons drew near, we noted their loathsome odors.
   powerful   angry   (disgusting)

10. The ugly demon, whose bulbous nose honked constantly, fell from his perch.
    reddened   wart-covered   (bulb-shaped)

Page 83

Hang Tough, Student

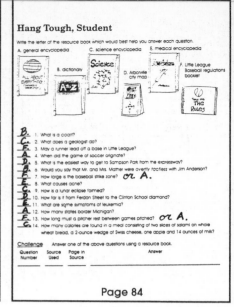

Write the letter of the resource book which would best help you answer each question.

A. general encyclopedia   C. science encyclopedia   E. medical encyclopedia
B. dictionary   D. Arborville city map   F. Little League Baseball regulations booklet

B. 1. What is a coati?
C. 2. What does a geologist do?
E. 3. May a runner lead off a base in Little League?
A. 4. When did the game of soccer originate?
D. 5. What is the easiest way to get to Sampson Park from the expressway?
A. 6. Would you say that Mr. and Mrs. Mather were overtly tactless with Jim Anderson?
F. 7. How large is the baseball strike zone? *or A.*
E. 8. What causes acne?
C. 9. How is a lunar eclipse formed?
D. 10. How far is it from Ferdon Street to the Clinton School diamond?
E. 11. What are some symptoms of leukemia?
A. 12. How many states border Michigan?
F. 13. How long must a pitcher rest between games pitched? *or A.*
C. 14. How many calories are found in a meal consisting of two slices of salami on whole wheat bread, a 2-ounce wedge of Swiss cheese, one apple and 14 ounces of milk?

Challenge Answer one of the above questions using a resource book.

Question Number	Source Used	Page in Source	Answer

Page 84

Jimminy Cricket!

Underline the key word in each question. Then write the encyclopedia volume number you would use to find information to answer each question.

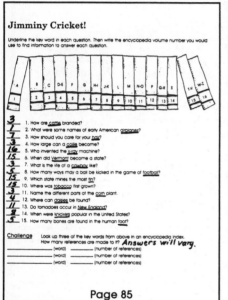

3. 1. How are cattle branded?
1. 2. What were some names of early American airplanes?
7. 3. How should you care for your hair?
10. 4. How large can a coua become?
16. 5. Who invented the x-ray machine?
15. 6. When did Vermont become a state?
3. 7. What is the life of a cowpox like?
5. 8. How many ways may a ball be kicked in the game of football?
15. 9. Which state mines the most tin?
13. 10. Where was tobacco first grown?
3. 11. Name the different parts of the corn plant.
7. 12. Where can daisies be found?
11. 13. Do tornadoes occur in New England?
8. 14. When were knickers popular in the United States?
5. 15. How many bones are found in the human foot?

Challenge Look up three of the key words from above in an encyclopedia index. How many references are made to it? *Answers will vary.*

_____ (word) _____ (number of references)
_____ (word) _____ (number of references)
_____ (word) _____ (number of references)

Page 85

Furoshiki Bundle

Sadako's mother wrapped all of Sadako's favorite foods in a *furoshiki* bundle. The bundle contained an egg roll, rice, chicken, plums, and bean cakes. List the heading under which you might find information on these foods in a recipe book.

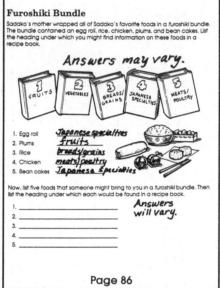

Answers may vary.

1. Egg roll — *Japanese specialties*
2. Plums — *Fruits*
3. Rice — *breads/grains*
4. Chicken — *meats/poultry*
5. Bean cakes — *Japanese Specialties*

Now, list five foods that someone might bring to you in a *furoshiki* bundle. Then list the heading under which each would be found in a recipe book.

1. _____
2. _____   *Answers will vary.*
3. _____
4. _____
5. _____

Page 86

Mumps, Measles, and Other Diseases

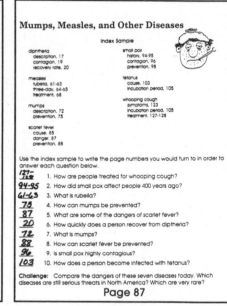

Index Sample

diphtheria
  description, 17
  contagion, 19
  recovery rate, 20

measles
  rubella, 61-63
  three-day, 64-65
  treatment, 68

mumps
  description, 72
  prevention, 75

scarlet fever
  cause, 85
  danger, 87
  prevention, 88

small pox
  history, 94-95
  contagion, 96
  prevention, 98

tetanus
  cause, 103
  incubation period, 105

whooping cough
  symptoms, 123
  incubation period, 105
  treatment, 127-128

Use the index sample to write the page numbers you would turn to in order to answer each question below.

127-128   1. How are people treated for whooping cough?
94-95   2. How did small pox affect people 400 years ago?
61-63   3. What is rubella?
75   4. How can mumps be prevented?
87   5. What are some of the dangers of scarlet fever?
20   6. How quickly does a person recover from diptheria?
72   7. What is mumps?
88   8. How can scarlet fever be prevented?
96   9. Is small pox highly contagious?
103   10. How does a person become infected with tetanus?

Challenge: Compare the dangers of these seven diseases today. Which diseases are still serious threats in North America? Which are very rare?

Page 87

Place Value

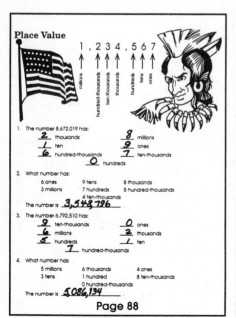

1,234,567
millions, hundred-thousands, ten-thousands, thousands, hundreds, tens, ones

1. The number 8,672,019 has:
   2 thousands   8 millions
   1 ten   9 ones
   6 hundred-thousands   0 ten-thousands
   0 hundreds

2. What number has:
   6 ones   9 tens   8 thousands
   3 millions   7 hundreds   5 hundred-thousands
   The number is 3,548,796

3. The number 6,792,510 has:
   9 ten-thousands   0 ones
   6 millions   2 thousands
   5 hundreds   7 ten
   7 hundred-thousands

4. What number has:
   5 millions   6 thousands   4 ones
   3 tens   1 hundred   8 ten-thousands
   0 hundred-thousands
   The number is 5,086,134

Page 88

The First State

What state is known as the first state? Follow the directions below to find out.

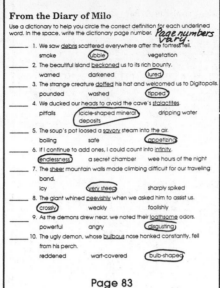

1. Put an A above number 2 if 31,842 rounded to the nearest thousand is 31,000.
2. Put an E above number 2 if 62 rounded to the nearest ten is 60.
3. Put an R above number 7 if 4,234 rounded to the nearest hundred is 4,200.
4. Put an L above number 3 if 677 rounded to the nearest hundred is 600.
5. Put an E above number 5 if 344 rounded to the nearest ten is 350.
6. Put an A above number 4 if 5,599 rounded to the nearest thousand is 6,000.
7. Put an A above number 6 if 1,549 rounded to the nearest hundred is 1,500.
8. Put a W above number 2 if 885 rounded to the nearest hundred is 800.
9. Put an E above number 8 if 521 rounded to the nearest ten is 520.
10. Put an R above number 6 if 74 rounded to the nearest ten is 80.
11. Put an L above number 3 if 3,291 rounded to the nearest thousand is 3,000.
12. Put an R above number 4 if 248 rounded to the nearest hundred is 300.
13. Put a D above number 1 if 615 rounded to the nearest ten is 620.
14. Put a W above number 1 if 188 rounded to the nearest ten is 200.
15. Put a W above number 5 if 6,817 rounded to the nearest thousand is 7,000.

D E L A W A R E
1 2 3 4 5 6 7 8

Page 89

Underwater Addition

446 + 489 = 935

476 + 527 = 1003   509 + 375 = 884

708 + 507 = 1215   438 + 419 = 857   334 + 278 = 612

251 + 368 = 619

464 + 456 = 920   589 + 322 = 911   288 + 377 = 665

811 + 386 = 1197

810 + 428 = 1238   831 + 483 = 1314   445 + 476 = 921

531 + 249 = 780   714 + 185 = 899

319 + 287 = 606

609 + 475 = 1084   230 + 284 = 514   767 + 246 = 1013

211 + 396 = 607   911 + 427 = 1338

Page 90

0-7682-3794-7 *Skills & Practice Gr. 4*

Grand Prix Addition

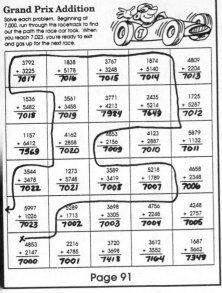

Solve each problem. Beginning at 7,000, run through this racetrack to find out the path the race car took. When you reach 7,023, you're ready to exit and gas up for the next race.

3792 + 3225 = 7017	1838 + 5178 = 7016	3767 + 3248 = 7015	1874 + 5140 = 7014	4809 + 2204 = 7013
1536 + 5482 = 7018	3561 + 3458 = 7019	3771 + 4213 = 7984	2435 + 5214 = 7649	1725 + 5287 = 7012
1157 + 6412 = 7569	4162 + 2858 = 7020	4853 + 2156 = 7009	4123 + 2887 = 7010	5879 + 1132 = 7011
3544 + 3478 = 7022	1273 + 5748 = 7021	3589 + 3419 = 7008	5218 + 1789 = 7007	4658 + 2348 = 7006
5997 + 1026 = 7023	5289 + 1713 = 7002	3698 + 3305 = 7003	4756 + 2248 = 7004	4248 + 2757 = 7005
4853 + 2147 = 7000	2216 + 4785 = 7001	3720 + 3698 = 7418	3612 + 3552 = 7164	1687 + 5662 = 7349

Page 91

Fishy Problems

Solve each problem. Locate the fish in the aquarium that has the sum for each problem floating around in its stomach. Write the letter to match each answer in the box above each problem.

G	L	M	O	A
1. 31,604 + 29,217 = 60,821	2. 47,215 + 23,094 = 70,309	3. 92,185 + 18,293 = 110,478	4. 20,815 + 19,903 = 40,718	5. 49,248 + 27,181 = 76,429

F	E	D	C	J
6. 53,614 + 29,193 = 82,807	7. 21,385 + 23,492 = 44,877	8. 45,218 + 12,649 = 57,867	9. 64,218 + 13,924 = 78,142	10. 81,346 + 13,497 = 94,843

H	I	N	B	K
11. 30,249 + 28,926 = 59,175	12. 42,618 + 34,193 = 76,811	13. 50,006 + 29,999 = 80,005	14. 26,149 + 81,224 = 107,373	15. 76,415 + 21,248 = 97,663

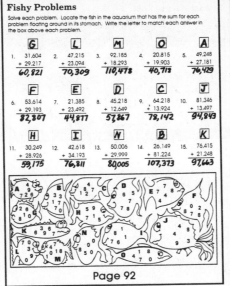

Page 92

Batter Up!

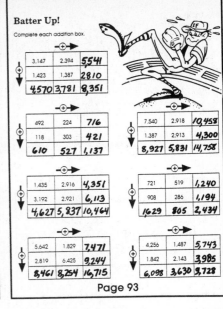

Complete each addition box.

⊕→		
3,147	2,394	5,541
1,423	1,387	2,810
4,570	3,781	8,351

492	224	716
118	303	421
610	527	1,137

7,540	2,918	10,458
1,387	2,913	4,300
8,927	5,831	14,758

1,435	2,916	4,351
3,192	2,921	6,113
4,627	5,837	10,464

721	519	1,240
908	286	1,194
1,629	805	2,434

5,642	1,829	7,471
2,819	6,425	9,244
8,461	8,254	16,715

4,256	1,487	5,743
1,842	2,143	3,985
6,098	3,630	9,728

Page 93

Addition Slides

213 + 825 + 132 + 691 = 1,648	206 413 641 + 823 + 227 = 1,677 / 846
462 + 381 + 253 = 1,096	603 247 + 314 = 1,164
	485 232 + 126 = 843	420 382 + 156 = 958	321 643 + 284 = 1,248
629 312 + 438 = 1,379	523 146 + 384 = 1,053	462 310 + 293 = 1,065
426 559 + 675 = 1,660	569 243 + 284 = 1,096	803 261 + 342 = 1,406	540 262 + 351 = 1,153
549 261 + 341 = 1,151	542 681 + 346 = 1,569	326 243 + 814 = 1,383	643 251 + 382 = 1,276

Page 94

Pinball Mathematics

Solve the problems in the pinball machine.

7,215 62 141 + 2,015 = 9,433	4,621 35 1,318 + 1,423 = 5,983 / 8,143 60 235 1,423 = 9,861
435 242 6 + 1,203 = 1,486	7,006 242 31 + ... = 7,283	521 3,134 64 + 243 = 3,962
496 8,172 83 + 199 = 8,950	6,201 325 41 + 51 = ... 8,703	5,242 342 8 + 503 = 5,643	4,162 328 41 + ... = 5,034	6,425 41 324 + 3 = 6,793
6,117 24 315 + 2,136 = 8,592	4,205 81 310 + ... = 4,703	2,516 310 82 + 3 = 2,911	5,426 310 512 + 4 = 6,252	2,481 2,514 2 + 43 = 5,040	3,204 182 23 + 5 = 3,414

Page 95

Knowing When to Add

Circle the key addition words and solve the problems.

1. The choir at Madison School is made up of 26 girls and 18 boys. What is the total choir membership?
$26 + 18 = 44$

2. The band at Madison School is composed of 19 girls and 22 boys. How many band members are there in all?
$19 + 22 = 41$

3. There are 214 girls and 263 boys attending Madison School. How many students altogether attend Madison School?
$214 + 263 = 477$

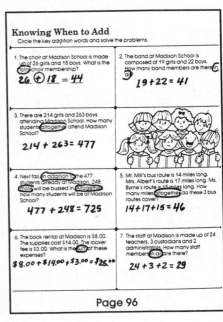

4. Next fall, in addition to the 477 students already at Madison, 248 more will be bussed in. Altogether, how many students will be at Madison School?
$477 + 248 = 725$

5. Mr. Mill's bus route is 14 miles long. Mrs. Albert's route is 17 miles long. Ms. Byrne's route is 15 miles long. How many miles altogether do these 3 bus routes cover?
$14 + 17 + 15 = 46$

6. The book rental at Madison is $8.00. The supplies cost $14.00. The locker fee is $3.00. What is the sum of these expenses?
$\$8.00 + \$14.00 + \$3.00 = \$25.00$

7. The staff at Madison is made up of 24 teachers, 3 custodians and 2 administrators. How many staff members in all are there?
$24 + 3 + 2 = 29$

Page 96

Math Cranes

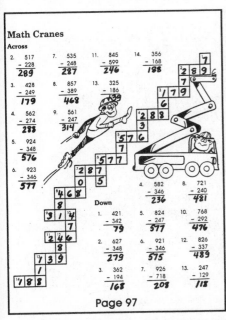

Across

2. 517 − 228 = 289
3. 428 − 249 = 179
4. 562 − 274 = 288
5. 924 − 348 = 576
6. 923 − 346 = 577
7. 535 − 248 = 287
8. 857 − 389 = 468
9. 561 − 247 = 314
11. 845 − 599 = 246
14. 356 − 168 = 188

Down

1. 421 − 342 = 79
3. 627 − 348 = 279
5. 824 − 247 = 577
6. 921 − 346 = 575
10. 768 − 292 = 476
12. 826 − 337 = 489
13. 247 − 129 = 118
3. 362 − 194 = 168
7. 926 − 718 = 208

Page 97

Timely Zeros

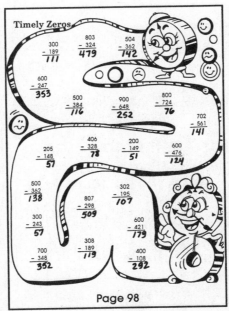

300 − 189 = 111	803 − 324 = 479	504 − 362 = 742
600 − 247 = 353		
500 − 384 = 116	900 − 648 = 252	800 − 724 = 76
		702 − 561 = 141
205 − 148 = 57	406 − 328 = 78	200 − 149 = 51	600 − 476 = 124
500 − 362 = 138	302 − 195 = 107		
300 − 243 = 57	807 − 298 = 509	600 − 421 = 179	
700 − 348 = 352	308 − 189 = 119	400 − 108 = 292	

Page 98

Subtraction Maze

Work problems.

4172 − 1536 = 2636	6723 − 2586 = 4137	547 − 259 = 288	834 − 463 = 371	562 − 325 = 237	7146 − 3498 = 3648
9427 − 6648 = 2779	8149 − 5372 = 2777	5389 − 1652 = 3737	421 − 275 = 146	7456 − 3724 = 3732	818 − 639 = 179
772 − 586 = 186	6529 − 4538 = 1991	5379 − 2835 = 2544	6275 − 3761 = 2514	5612 − 1505 = 4107	8355 − 5366 = 2989

Shade in answers to find path.

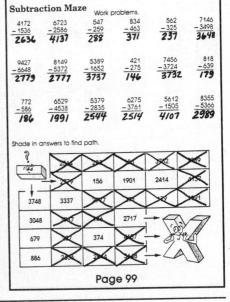

		156	1901	2414	
3748	3337				
3048			2717		
679		374			
886					

Page 99

High Class Math

MATH BLIMPS OF AMERICA, INC.

8,248 − 1,513 = 6,735
3,270 − 1,529 = 1,741
7,648 − 3,291 = 4,357
4,321 − 1,809 = 2,512
8,241 − 3,516 = 4,725
3,002 − 1,231 = 1,771
9,200 − 3,146 = 6,054
5,017 − 2,408 = 2,609
8,254 − 3,187 = 5,067
7,265 − 2,134 = 5,131
3,846 − 1,359 = 2,487
8,006 − 3,084 = 4,922
3,084 − 1,926 = 1,158
6,265 − 4,189 = 2,076
4,824 − 1,913 = 2,911
6,205 − 1,054 = 5,151
5,253 − 4,428 = 825
9,205 − 3,187 = 6,018
5,809 − 3,913 = 1,896
5,642 − 2,408 = 3,234

Page 100

Under the Big Top!

43 × 4 = 172
2 × 58 = 116
86 × 7 = 602
406
65 × 4 = 260
5 × 77 = 385
325   308

Page 101

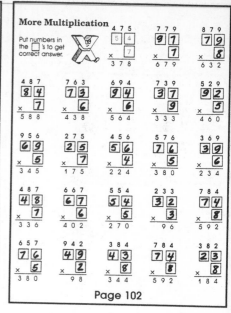

More Multiplication

Put numbers in the ☐'s to get correct answer.

475 × 4 = 378 (54 × 7)
779 × 7 = 679 (91)
879 × 9 = 632 (79 × 8)

487 × 7 = 588 (84)
763 × 6 = 438 (73)
694 × 6 = 564 (94)
739 × 9 = 333 (37)
529 × 5 = 460 (92)

956 × 5 = 345 (69)
275 × 7 = 175 (25)
456 × 4 = 224 (56)
576 × 5 = 380 (76)
369 × 6 = 234 (39)

487 × 7 = 336 (48)
667 × 6 = 402 (67)
554 × 5 = 270 (54)
233 × 3 = 96 (32)
784 × 8 = 592 (74)

657 × 6 = 380 (76)
942 × 2 = 98 (49)
384 × 8 = 344 (43)
784 × 4 = 592 (74)
382 × 8 = 184 (23)

Page 102

Solve It!

What set of ridges, loops and whirls are different on every person? To find out, solve the following problems and put the corresponding letter above the answer at the bottom of the page.

I. 303 × 3 = 909
R. 214 × 2 = 428
N. 413 × 2 = 826
N. 142 × 2 = 284
R. 211 × 4 = 844
F. 104 × 2 = 208
T. 131 × 2 = 262
E. 301 × 2 = 602
I. 134 × 1 = 134
G. 244 × 2 = 488
S. 334 × 2 = 668
P. 232 × 3 = 696

F i n g e r p r i n t s
208 909 826 488 602 844 696 428 134 284 262 668

Page 103

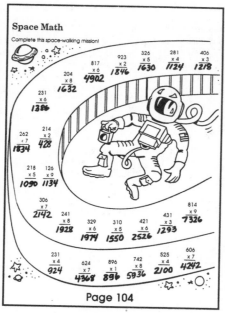

Space Math

Complete this space-walking mission!

817 × 6 = 4902
923 × 2 = 1846
326 × 5 = 1630
281 × 4 = 1124
406 × 3 = 1218
204 × 8 = 1632
231 × 6 = 1386
262 × 7 = 1834
214 × 2 = 428
218 × 5 = 1090
126 × 9 = 1134
306 × 7 = 2142
241 × 8 = 1928
329 × 6 = 1974
310 × 5 = 1550
421 × 6 = 2526
431 × 3 = 1293
814 × 9 = 7326
231 × 4 = 924
624 × 7 = 4368
896 × 1 = 896
742 × 8 = 5936
525 × 4 = 2100
606 × 7 = 4242

Page 104

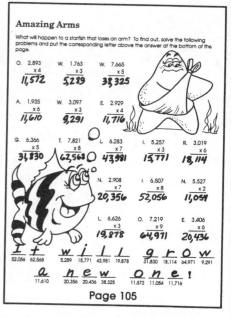

Amazing Arms

What will happen to a starfish that loses an arm? To find out, solve the following problems and put the corresponding letter above the answer at the bottom of the page.

O. 2,893 × 4 = 11,572
W. 1,763 × 3 = 5,289
W. 7,665 × 5 = 38,325
A. 1,935 × 6 = 11,610
W. 3,097 × 3 = 9,291
E. 2,929 × 4 = 11,716
G. 6,366 × 5 = 31,830
T. 7,821 × 8 = 62,568
L. 6,283 × 7 = 43,981
L. 5,257 × 3 = 15,771
R. 3,019 × 6 = 18,114
N. 2,908 × 7 = 20,356
I. 6,507 × 8 = 52,056
N. 5,527 × 2 = 11,054
L. 6,626 × 3 = 19,878
O. 7,219 × 9 = 64,971
E. 3,406 × 6 = 20,436

I t   w i l l   g r o w
52,056 62,568   5,289 15,771 43,981 19,878   31,830 18,114 64,971 9,291

a   n e w   o n e !
11,610   20,356 20,436 38,325   11,572 11,054 11,716

Page 105

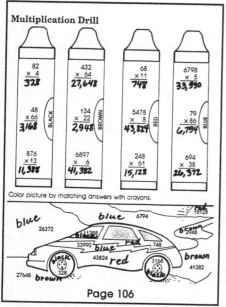

Multiplication Drill

82 × 4 = 328
432 × 64 = 27,648
68 × 11 = 748
6798 × 5 = 33,990
48 × 66 = 3,168 (BLACK)
134 × 22 = 2,948 (BROWN)
5478 × 8 = 43,824 (RED)
79 × 86 = 6,794 (BLUE)
876 × 13 = 11,388
6897 × 6 = 41,382
248 × 61 = 15,128
694 × 38 = 26,372

Color picture by matching answers with crayons.

blue   blue   6794
26372   51,388
33990   red   748
blue   red
43824   red
27648   brown   3168   41382   brown

Page 106

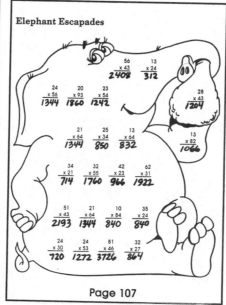

Elephant Escapades

56 × 43 = 2408
13 × 24 = 312
24 × 56 = 1344
20 × 93 = 1860
23 × 54 = 1242
28 × 43 = 1204
21 × 64 = 1344
25 × 34 = 850
13 × 64 = 832
13 × 82 = 1066
34 × 21 = 714
32 × 55 = 1760
42 × 23 = 966
62 × 31 = 1922
51 × 43 = 2193
21 × 64 = 1344
10 × 84 = 840
35 × 24 = 840
24 × 30 = 720
24 × 53 = 1272
81 × 46 = 3726
32 × 27 = 864

Page 107

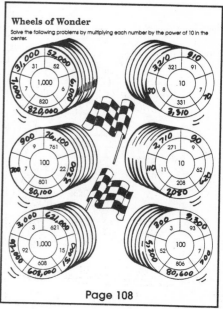

Wheels of Wonder

Solve the following problems by multiplying each number by the power of 10 in the center.

31 → 31,000 / 52 → 52,000 / 1,000 / 820 → 820,000 / 7,000

321 → 3,210 / 91 → 910 / 10 / 331 → 3,310

761 → 7,610 / 100 / 22 → 2,200 / 801 → 80,100 / 700

271 → 2,710 / 9 → 90 / 10 / 208 → 2,080 / 62

3 → 3,000 / 621 → 621,000 / 1,000 / 608 → 608,000 / 15

3 → 300 / 93 → 9,300 / 100 / 806 → 80,600 / 52 → 5,200

Page 108

Published by Frank Schaffer Publications. Copyright protected.

300

0-7682-3794-7   Skills & Practice Gr. 4

Page 109 — Step by Step

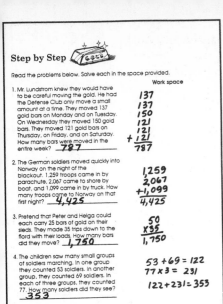

Read the problems below. Solve each in the space provided.

Work space

1. Mr. Lundstrom knew they would have to be careful moving the gold. He had the Defense Club only move a small amount at a time. They moved 137 gold bars on Monday and on Tuesday. On Wednesday they moved 150 gold bars. On Thursday, on Friday, and on Saturday, they moved 121 gold bars. How many bars were moved in the entire week? **787**

```
  137
  137
  150
  121
  121
+ 121
  787
```

2. The German soldiers moved quickly into Norway on the night of the blackout. 1,259 troops came in by parachute, 2,067 came to shore by boat, and 1,099 came in by truck. How many troops came to Norway on that first night? **4,425**

```
  1,259
  2,067
+ 1,099
  4,425
```

3. Pretend that Peter and Helga could each carry 25 bars of gold on their sleds. They made 35 trips down to the fiord with their loads. How many bars did they move? **1,750**

```
    50
  x 35
  1,750
```

4. The children saw many small groups of soldiers marching. In one group they counted 53 soldiers. In another group, they counted 69 soldiers. In each of three groups, they counted 77. How many soldiers did they see? **353**

53 + 69 = 122
77 x 3 = 231
122 + 231 = 353

Page 110 — Whacky Waldo's Snow Show

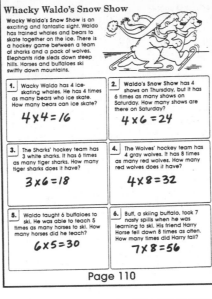

Wacky Waldo's Snow Show is an exciting and fantastic sight. Waldo has trained whales and bears to skate together on the ice. There is a hockey game between a team of sharks and a pack of wolves. Elephants ride sleds down steep hills. Horses and buffaloes ski swiftly down mountains.

1. Wacky Waldo has 4 ice-skating whales. He has 4 times as many bears who ice skate. How many bears can ice skate?
$4 \times 4 = 16$

2. Waldo's Snow Show has 4 shows on Thursday, but it has 6 times as many shows on Saturday. How many shows are there on Saturday?
$4 \times 6 = 24$

3. The Sharks' hockey team has 3 white sharks. It has 6 times as many tiger sharks. How many tiger sharks does it have?
$3 \times 6 = 18$

4. The Wolves' hockey team has 4 gray wolves. It has 8 times as many red wolves. How many red wolves does it have?
$4 \times 8 = 32$

5. Waldo taught 6 buffaloes to ski. He was able to teach 5 times as many horses to ski. How many horses did he teach?
$6 \times 5 = 30$

6. Buff, a skiing buffalo, took 7 nasty spills when he was learning to ski. His friend Harry Horse fell down 8 times as often. How many times did Harry fall?
$7 \times 8 = 56$

Page 111 — Molly Mugwumps

Molly Mugwumps is the toughest kid in school. She picks fights with kindergarteners and spends more time in the office than the principal does.

1. Molly is the toughest football player in her school. She ran for 23 yards on one play and went 3 times as far on the next play. How far did she run the second time?
$23 \times 3 = 69$

2. Molly keeps a rock collection. She has 31 rocks in one sack. She has 7 times as many under her bed. How many rocks are under her bed?
$31 \times 7 = 217$

3. Molly had 42 marbles when she came to school. She went home with 4 times as many. How many did she go home with?
$42 \times 4 = 168$

4. Molly stuffed 21 sticks of gum in her mouth in the morning. In the afternoon, she crammed 9 times as many sticks into her mouth. How many sticks did she have in the afternoon?
$21 \times 9 = 189$

5. Molly got 51 problems wrong in math last week. This week, she missed 8 times as many. How many did she miss this week?
$51 \times 8 = 408$

6. Molly was sent to the office 21 days last year. This year, she was sent 7 times as often. How many days did she go to the office this year?
$21 \times 7 = 147$

Page 112 — Snowball Bash

Help Pete climb down this mound of giant snowballs!

12 — $7\overline{)84}$	15 — $5\overline{)75}$

15 — $3\overline{)45}$ 11 — $9\overline{)99}$ 22 — $4\overline{)88}$ 16 — $5\overline{)80}$

16 — $4\overline{)64}$ 19 — $3\overline{)57}$ 26 — $3\overline{)78}$ 24 — $3\overline{)72}$ 12 — $8\overline{)96}$

43 — $2\overline{)86}$ 19 — $2\overline{)38}$ 11 — $6\overline{)66}$ 13 — $5\overline{)65}$ 13 — $4\overline{)52}$

17 — $4\overline{)68}$ 13 — $6\overline{)78}$ 13 — $7\overline{)91}$ 21 — $2\overline{)42}$ 12 — $6\overline{)72}$

Page 113 — Scaling the Heights

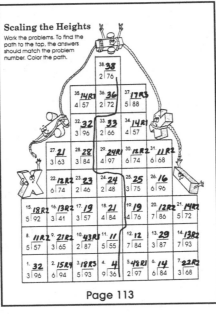

Work the problems. To find the path to the top, the answers should match the problem number. Color the path.

38. 38 — $2\overline{)76}$

35. $14 R1$ — $4\overline{)57}$ 36. 36 — $2\overline{)72}$ 37. $17 R3$ — $5\overline{)88}$

32. 32 — $3\overline{)96}$ 33. 33 — $2\overline{)66}$ 34. $14 R1$ — $4\overline{)57}$

27. 21 — $3\overline{)63}$ 28. 28 — $3\overline{)84}$ 29. $24 R1$ — $4\overline{)97}$ 30. $11 R2$ — $6\overline{)74}$ 31. 11 — $6\overline{)68}$

22. $12 R2$ — $6\overline{)74}$ 23. 23 — $2\overline{)46}$ 24. 24 — $2\overline{)48}$ 25. 25 — $3\overline{)75}$ 26. 16 — $6\overline{)96}$

15. $18 R2$ — $5\overline{)92}$ 16. $13 R2$ — $3\overline{)41}$ 17. 19 — $2\overline{)84}$ 18. 21 — $4\overline{)84}$ 19. 19 — $7\overline{)86}$ 20. $12 R2$ — $7\overline{)86}$ 21. $14 R2$ — $5\overline{)72}$

8. $11 R2$ — $5\overline{)57}$ 9. $21 R2$ — $3\overline{)65}$ 10. $43 R1$ — $2\overline{)87}$ 11. 11 — $5\overline{)55}$ 12. 12 — $7\overline{)84}$ 13. 29 — $3\overline{)87}$ 14. $13 R2$ — $7\overline{)93}$

1. 32 — $3\overline{)96}$ 2. $15 R4$ — $6\overline{)94}$ 3. $18 R3$ — $5\overline{)93}$ 4. 4 — $9\overline{)36}$ 5. $48 R1$ — $2\overline{)97}$ 6. 14 — $6\overline{)84}$ 7. $22 R2$ — $3\overline{)68}$

Page 114 — Geometric Division!

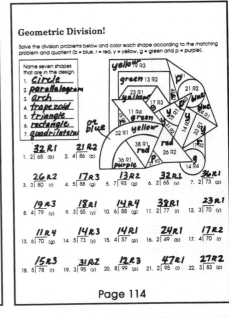

Solve the division problems below and color each shape according to the matching problem and quotient (b = blue, r = red, y = yellow, g = green and p = purple).

Name seven shapes that are in the design.
1. circle
2. parallelogram
3. arch
4. trapezoid
5. triangle
6. rectangle
7. quadrilateral

1. 32 — $2\overline{)65}$ (b) 2. 21 — $4\overline{)86}$ (b)

3. $26 R2$ — $3\overline{)80}$ (r) 4. $17 R3$ — $5\overline{)88}$ (r) 5. $13 R2$ — $7\overline{)93}$ (g) 6. 32 — $2\overline{)65}$ (y) 7. $36 R1$ — $2\overline{)73}$ (p)

8. $19 R3$ — $4\overline{)79}$ (y) 9. $18 R1$ — $3\overline{)55}$ (y) 10. $14 R4$ — $6\overline{)88}$ (g) 11. $38 R1$ — $2\overline{)77}$ (r) 12. $23 R1$ — $3\overline{)70}$ (y)

13. $11 R4$ — $6\overline{)70}$ (g) 14. $14 R3$ — $5\overline{)73}$ (y) 15. $14 R1$ — $4\overline{)57}$ (p) 16. $24 R1$ — $2\overline{)49}$ (b) 17. $17 R2$ — $4\overline{)70}$ (r)

18. $15 R3$ — $5\overline{)78}$ (y) 19. $31 R2$ — $3\overline{)95}$ (y) 20. $12 R3$ — $8\overline{)99}$ (p) 21. $47 R1$ — $2\overline{)95}$ (p) 22. $27 R2$ — $3\overline{)83}$ (p)

Page 115 — On-Stage Division

148 — $6\overline{)888}$ 478 — $2\overline{)956}$ 356 — $2\overline{)712}$

215 — $4\overline{)860}$ 125 — $6\overline{)750}$ 111 — $9\overline{)999}$

121 — $8\overline{)968}$ 258 — $3\overline{)774}$ 147 — $5\overline{)735}$ 115 — $8\overline{)920}$ 169 — $5\overline{)845}$

115 — $7\overline{)805}$ 123 — $8\overline{)984}$ 125 — $4\overline{)500}$ 423 — $2\overline{)846}$ 178 — $4\overline{)712}$

135 — $6\overline{)810}$ 126 — $7\overline{)882}$

214 — $3\overline{)642}$ 159 — $3\overline{)477}$

Page 116 — Puzzling Problems

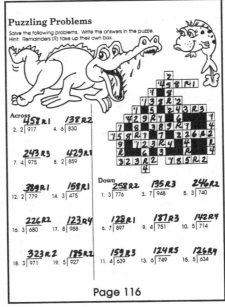

Solve the following problems. Write the answers in the puzzle.
Hint: Remainders (R) take up their own box.

Across
2. $458 R1$ — $2\overline{)917}$ 4. $138 R2$ — $6\overline{)830}$

7. $243 R3$ — $4\overline{)975}$ 8. $429 R1$ — $2\overline{)859}$

12. $389 R1$ — $2\overline{)779}$ 14. $158 R1$ — $3\overline{)475}$

16. $226 R2$ — $3\overline{)680}$ 17. $123 R4$ — $8\overline{)988}$

18. $323 R2$ — $3\overline{)971}$ 19. $185 R2$ — $5\overline{)927}$

Down
1. $258 R2$ — $3\overline{)776}$ 3. $135 R3$ — $7\overline{)948}$ 5. $246 R2$ — $3\overline{)740}$

6. $128 R1$ — $7\overline{)897}$ 9. $187 R3$ — $4\overline{)751}$ 10. $142 R4$ — $5\overline{)714}$

11. $159 R3$ — $4\overline{)639}$ 13. $124 R5$ — $6\overline{)749}$ 15. $126 R4$ — $5\overline{)634}$

Page 117 — Division Checklist

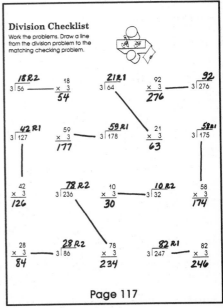

Work the problems. Draw a line from the division problem to the matching checking problem.

$18 R2$ — $3\overline{)56}$ — $\begin{array}{r}18\\ \times\ 3\\ \hline 54\end{array}$

$21 R1$ — $3\overline{)64}$ — $\begin{array}{r}92\\ \times\ 3\\ \hline 276\end{array}$ — 92 — $3\overline{)276}$

$42 R1$ — $3\overline{)127}$ — $\begin{array}{r}59\\ \times\ 3\\ \hline 177\end{array}$

$59 R1$ — $3\overline{)178}$ — $\begin{array}{r}21\\ \times\ 3\\ \hline 63\end{array}$ — $58 R1$ — $3\overline{)175}$

$\begin{array}{r}42\\ \times\ 3\\ \hline 126\end{array}$ — $78 R2$ — $3\overline{)236}$ — $\begin{array}{r}10\\ \times\ 3\\ \hline 30\end{array}$ — $10 R2$ — $3\overline{)32}$ — $\begin{array}{r}58\\ \times\ 3\\ \hline 174\end{array}$

$\begin{array}{r}28\\ \times\ 3\\ \hline 84\end{array}$ — $28 R2$ — $3\overline{)86}$ — $\begin{array}{r}78\\ \times\ 3\\ \hline 234\end{array}$ — $82 R1$ — $3\overline{)247}$ — $\begin{array}{r}82\\ \times\ 3\\ \hline 246\end{array}$

0-7682-3794-7 Skills & Practice Gr. 4

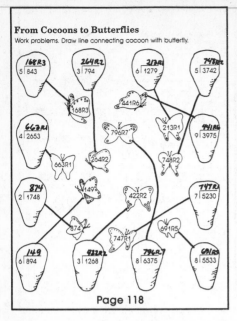

From Cocoons to Butterflies
Work problems. Draw line connecting cocoon with butterfly.

168 R3 / 5) 843 264 R2 / 3) 794 213 R1 / 6) 1279 748 R2 / 5) 3742
663 R1 / 4) 2653 441 R6 / 9) 3975
874 / 2) 1748 747 R / 7) 5230
149 / 6) 894 422 R / 3) 1268 796 R / 8) 6375 691 R5 / 8) 5533

Page 118

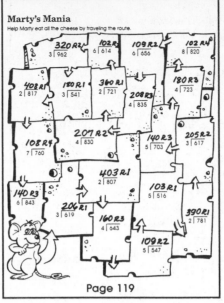

Marty's Mania
Help Marty eat all the cheese by traveling the route.

320 R2 / 3) 962 102 / 6) 614 109 R2 / 6) 656 102 R4 / 8) 820
408 R / 2) 817 180 R1 / 3) 541 360 R1 / 2) 721 180 R3 / 4) 723
208 R3 / 4) 835
108 R4 / 7) 760 207 R2 / 4) 830 140 R3 / 5) 703 205 R2 / 3) 617
403 R1 / 2) 807
140 R3 / 6) 843 103 R1 / 5) 516
206 R1 / 3) 619 160 R3 / 4) 643 390 R1 / 2) 781
109 R2 / 5) 547

Page 119

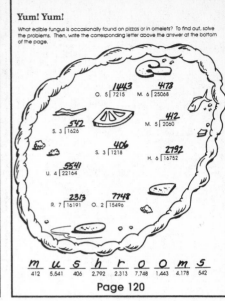

Yum! Yum!
What edible fungus is occasionally found on pizzas or in omelets? To find out, solve the problems. Then, write the corresponding letter above the answer at the bottom of the page.

O. 5) 7215 1443   M. 6) 25068 4178
S. 3) 1626 542   M. 5) 2060 412
S. 3) 1218 406   H. 6) 16752 2792
U. 4) 22164 5541
R. 7) 16191 2313   O. 2) 15496 7748

m u s h r o o m s
412 5,541 406 2,792 2,313 7,748 1,443 4,178 542

Page 120

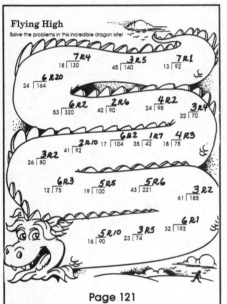

Flying High
Solve the problems in this incredible dragon kite!

7 R4 / 18) 130 3 R5 / 45) 140 7 R1 / 13) 92
6 R20 / 24) 164
6 R2 / 53) 320 2 R6 / 42) 90 4 R2 / 24) 98 3 R4 / 22) 70
2 R10 / 41) 92 6 R2 / 17) 104 1 R7 / 35) 42 4 R3 / 18) 75
3 R2 / 26) 80
6 R3 / 12) 75 5 R5 / 19) 100 5 R6 / 43) 221 3 R2 / 61) 185
5 R10 / 16) 90 3 R5 / 23) 74 6 R1 / 32) 193

Page 121

Lizzy the Lizard Bags Her Bugs
Lizzy the Lizard is a great hunter of insects. She separates her bugs into separate bags so that her lunch is ready for the week. Help her decide how to divide the bugs.

1. Lizzy bagged 45 cockroaches. She put 5 into each bag. How many bags did she use? **9**
$45 \div 5$

2. Lizzy found 32 termites. She put 4 into each bag. How many bags did she need? **8**
$32 \div 4$

3. Lizzy captured 49 stinkbugs. She put them into 7 bags. How many stinkbugs were in each bag? **7**
$49 \div 7$

4. Lizzy captured 27 horn beetles. She used 3 bags. How many beetles went into each bag? **9**
$27 \div 3$

5. Lizzy lassoed 36 butterflies. She put 9 into each bag. How many bags did she need? **4**
$36 \div 9$

6. Lizzy went fishing and caught 48 water beetles. She used 6 bags for her catch. How many beetles went into each bag? **8**
$48 \div 6$

Page 122

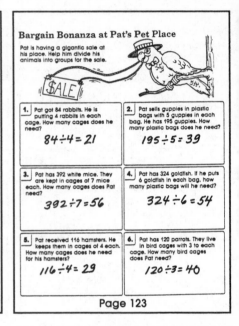

Bargain Bonanza at Pat's Pet Place
Pat is having a gigantic sale at his place. Help him divide his animals into groups for the sale.

1. Pat got 84 rabbits. He is putting 4 rabbits in each cage. How many cages does he need?
$84 \div 4 = 21$

2. Pat sells guppies in plastic bags with 5 guppies in each bag. He has 195 guppies. How many plastic bags does he need?
$195 \div 5 = 39$

3. Pat has 392 white mice. They are kept in cages of 7 mice each. How many cages does Pat need?
$392 \div 7 = 56$

4. Pat has 324 goldfish. If he puts 6 goldfish in each bag, how many plastic bags will he need?
$324 \div 6 = 54$

5. Pat received 116 hamsters. He keeps them in cages of 4 each. How many cages does he need for his hamsters?
$116 \div 4 = 29$

6. Pat has 120 parrots. They live in bird cages with 3 to each cage. How many bird cages does Pat need?
$120 \div 3 = 40$

Page 123

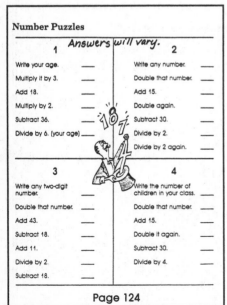

Number Puzzles

Answers will vary.

1
Write your age. ____
Multiply it by 3. ____
Add 18. ____
Multiply by 2. ____
Subtract 36. ____
Divide by 6. (your age) ____

2
Write any number. ____
Double that number. ____
Add 15. ____
Double again. ____
Subtract 30. ____
Divide by 2. ____
Divide by 2 again. ____

3
Write any two-digit number. ____
Double that number. ____
Add 43. ____
Subtract 18. ____
Add 11. ____
Divide by 2. ____
Subtract 18. ____

4
Write the number of children in your class. ____
Double that number. ____
Add 15. ____
Double it again. ____
Subtract 30. ____
Divide by 4. ____

Page 124

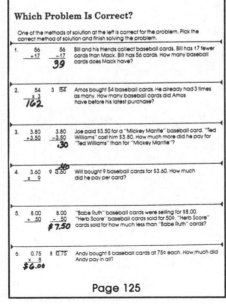

Which Problem Is Correct?
One of the methods of solution at the left is correct for the problem. Pick the correct method of solution and finish solving the problem.

1. 56 +17 / 56 -17 = **39**   Bill and his friends collect baseball cards. Bill has 17 fewer cards than Mack. Bill has 56 cards. How many baseball cards does Mack have?

2. 54 x3 / 3) 54 = **162**   Amos bought 54 baseball cards. He already had 3 times as many. How many baseball cards did Amos have before his latest purchase?

3. 3.80 +3.50 / 3.80 -3.50 = **.30**   Joe paid $3.50 for a "Mickey Mantle" baseball card. "Ted Williams" cost him $3.80. How much more did he pay for "Ted Williams" than for "Mickey Mantle"?

4. 3.60 x9 / 9) 3.60 = **.40**   Will bought 9 baseball cards for $3.60. How much did he pay per card?

5. 8.00 +.50 / 8.00 -.50 = **$7.50**   "Babe Ruth" baseball cards were selling for $8.00. "Herb Score" baseball cards sold for 50¢. "Herb Score" cards sold for how much less than "Babe Ruth" cards?

6. 0.75 x8 / 8) 0.75 = **$6.00**   Andy bought 8 baseball cards at 75¢ each. How much did Andy pay in all?

Page 125

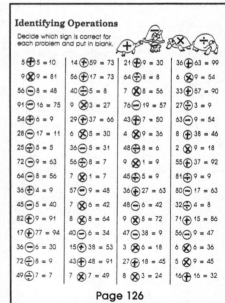

Identifying Operations
Decide which sign is correct for each problem and put in blank.

5 + 5 = 10	14 + 59 = 73	21 + 9 = 30	36 + 63 = 99
9 × 9 = 81	56 + 17 = 73	64 ÷ 8 = 8	6 × 9 = 54
56 − 8 = 48	40 ÷ 5 = 8	7 × 8 = 56	33 + 57 = 90
91 − 16 = 75	9 × 3 = 27	76 − 19 = 57	27 ÷ 3 = 9
54 ÷ 6 = 9	29 + 37 = 66	43 + 7 = 50	63 − 9 = 54
28 − 17 = 11	6 × 5 = 30	4 × 9 = 36	8 + 38 = 46
25 ÷ 5 = 5	36 − 5 = 31	48 ÷ 8 = 6	2 × 9 = 18
72 − 9 = 63	56 ÷ 8 = 7	9 × 1 = 9	55 + 37 = 92
64 − 8 = 56	7 × 1 = 7	45 ÷ 5 = 9	81 ÷ 9 = 9
36 + 4 = 9	57 − 9 = 48	36 + 27 = 63	80 − 17 = 63
45 − 5 = 40	7 × 6 = 42	48 ÷ 6 = 42	32 ÷ 4 = 8
82 + 9 = 91	8 × 8 = 64	9 × 8 = 72	71 + 15 = 86
17 + 77 = 94	40 − 6 = 34	47 − 38 = 9	56 − 9 = 47
36 − 6 = 30	15 + 38 = 53	3 × 6 = 18	6 × 6 = 36
72 ÷ 8 = 9	43 + 48 = 91	27 + 18 = 45	5 × 9 = 45
49 ÷ 7 = 7	7 × 7 = 49	8 × 3 = 24	16 + 16 = 32

Page 126

Published by Frank Schaffer Publications. Copyright protected.   0-7682-3794-7 *Skills & Practice Gr. 4*

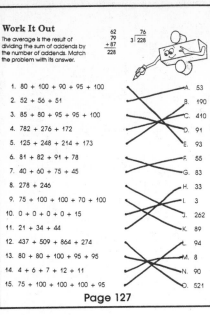

Work It Out

The average is the result of dividing the sum of addends by the number of addends. Match the problem with its answer.

62	76
79	3⟌228
+87	
228	

1. 80 + 100 + 90 + 95 + 100   A. 53
2. 52 + 56 + 51   B. 190
3. 85 + 80 + 95 + 95 + 100   C. 410
4. 782 + 276 + 172   D. 91
5. 125 + 248 + 214 + 173   E. 93
6. 81 + 82 + 91 + 78   F. 55
7. 40 + 60 + 75 + 45   G. 83
8. 278 + 246   H. 33
9. 75 + 100 + 100 + 70 + 100   I. 3
10. 0 + 0 + 0 + 0 + 15   J. 262
11. 21 + 34 + 44   K. 89
12. 437 + 509 + 864 + 274   L. 94
13. 80 + 80 + 100 + 95 + 95   M. 8
14. 4 + 6 + 7 + 12 + 11   N. 90
15. 75 + 100 + 100 + 100 + 95   O. 521

Page 127

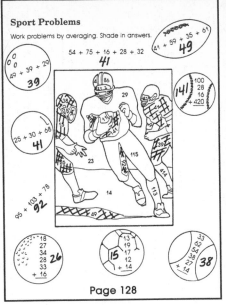

Sport Problems

Work problems by averaging. Shade in answers.

41 + 59 + 35 + 61 = **49**

54 + 75 + 16 + 28 + 32 = **41**

49 + 39 + 29 = **39**

100 + 28 + 16 + 420 = **141**

25 + 30 + 68 = **41**

95 + 103 + 78 = **92**

18 + 27 + 34 + 28 + 33 + 16 = **26**

13 + 19 + 17 + 14 = **15**

33 + 52 + 54 + 38 + 27 + 14 = **38**

Page 128

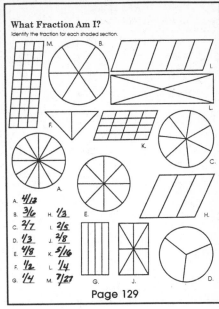

What Fraction Am I?

Identify the fraction for each shaded section.

A. 4/12
B. 3/6   H. 1/3
C. 2/7   I. 2/7
D. 1/3   J. 3/8
E. 4/8   K. 5/16
F. 1/2   L. 1/4
G. 1/4   M. 7/27

Page 129

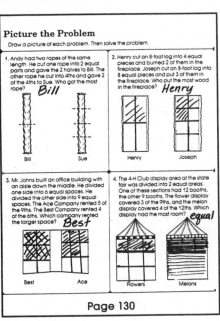

Picture the Problem

Draw a picture of each problem. Then solve the problem.

1. Andy had two ropes of the same length. He cut one rope into 2 equal parts and gave the 2 halves to Bill. The other rope he cut into 4ths and gave 2 of the 4ths to Sue. Who got the most rope? **Bill**

2. Henry cut an 8-foot log into 4 equal pieces and burned 2 of them in the fireplace. Joseph cut an 8-foot log into 8 equal pieces and put 3 of them in the fireplace. Who put the most wood in the fireplace? **Henry**

3. Mr. Johns built an office building with an aisle down the middle. He divided one side into 6 equal spaces. He divided the other side into 9 equal spaces. The Ace Company rented 5 of the 9ths. The Best Company rented 4 of the 6ths. Which company rented the larger space? **Best**

4. The 4-H Club display area at the state fair was divided into 2 equal areas. One of these sections had 12 booths, the other 9 booths. The flower display covered 3 of the 9ths, and the melon display covered 4 of the 12ths. Which display had the most room? **equal**

Page 130

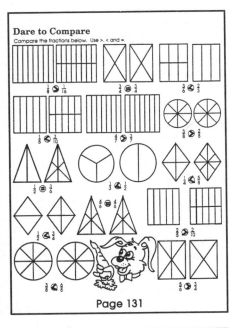

Dare to Compare

Compare the fractions below. Use >, < and =.

Page 131

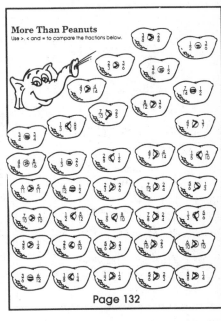

More Than Peanuts

Use >, < and = to compare the fractions below.

Page 132

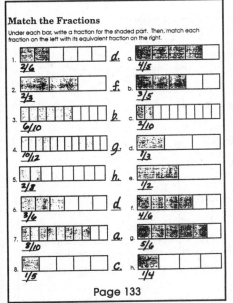

Match the Fractions

Under each bar, write a fraction for the shaded part. Then, match each fraction on the left with its equivalent fraction on the right.

1. 2/6   d.   a. 4/5
2. 2/3   f.   b. 3/5
3. 6/10   b.   c. 3/10
4. 10/12   g.   d. 1/3
5. 2/8   h.   e. 4/2
6. 3/6   d.   f. 4/6
7. 8/10   a.   g. 5/6
8. 1/5   c.   h. 1/4

Page 133

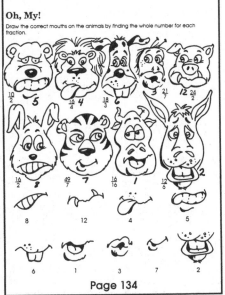

Oh, My!

Draw the correct mouths on the animals by finding the whole number for each fraction.

10/2 = **5**   16/4 = **4**   18/3 = **6**   21/7 = **3**   12, 24/2 = **12**

16/2 = **8**   49/7 = **7**   16/16 = **1**   12/6 = **2**

8   12   4   7   5

6   1   3   7   2

Page 134

Reduce the Fat Grams

Help this reducing machine function properly! Reduce each fraction.

5/25 = 1/5   8/16 = 1/2   12/18 = 2/3   10/25 = 2/5   12/30 = 2/5   3/30 = 1/10

6/30 = 1/5   12/20 = 3/5   3/18 = 1/6   3/9 = 1/3   4/26 = 2/13   4/28 = 1/7

7/21 = 1/3   16/20 = 4/5   2/10 = 1/5   3/27 = 1/9   5/60 = 1/12

21/35 = 3/5   3/12 = 1/4   24/40 = 3/5   5/24 = 1/3

16/40 = 2/5   9/36 = 1/4   15/25 = 3/5   7/35 = 1/5

NO GAL

Page 135

0-7682-3794-7 *Skills & Practice Gr. 4*

"Gator Aid"
Climb these obstacle ledges to the top.

$\frac{3}{7} = \frac{9}{21}$

$\frac{4}{5} = \frac{16}{20}$

$\frac{4}{6} = \frac{12}{18}$ $\frac{1}{3} = \frac{8}{24}$

$\frac{2}{3} = \frac{10}{15}$ $\frac{2}{3} = \frac{4}{6}$ $\frac{7}{9} = \frac{14}{18}$

$\frac{1}{2} = \frac{6}{12}$ $\frac{5}{7} = \frac{35}{49}$ $\frac{1}{4} = \frac{6}{24}$

$\frac{2}{3} = \frac{8}{12}$ $\frac{4}{7} = \frac{16}{28}$

$\frac{1}{2} = \frac{4}{8}$ $\frac{1}{6} = \frac{6}{36}$

$\frac{1}{8} = \frac{2}{16}$ $\frac{1}{3} = \frac{4}{12}$

$\frac{2}{3} = \frac{4}{6}$ $\frac{4}{9} = \frac{12}{27}$

$\frac{2}{3} = \frac{6}{9}$ $\frac{3}{8} = \frac{9}{24}$

$\frac{1}{2} = \frac{8}{16}$

$\frac{2}{5} = \frac{10}{25}$

$\frac{2}{7} = \frac{4}{14}$ $\frac{3}{6} = \frac{6}{12}$

Page 136

Figure It Out
Work problems. Connect the dots in order of answers.

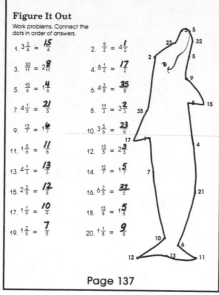

1. $3\frac{3}{4} = \frac{15}{4}$
2. $\frac{9}{2} = 4\frac{1}{2}$
3. $\frac{30}{11} = 2\frac{8}{11}$
4. $8\frac{1}{2} = \frac{17}{2}$
5. $\frac{10}{2} = 1\frac{4}{?}$
6. $4\frac{3}{8} = \frac{35}{8}$
7. $4\frac{1}{5} = \frac{21}{5}$
8. $\frac{11}{3} = 3\frac{2}{3}$
9. $\frac{13}{7} = 1\frac{6}{7}$
10. $3\frac{5}{6} = \frac{23}{6}$
11. $1\frac{5}{6} = \frac{11}{6}$
12. $2\frac{3}{?} = ?$
13. $4\frac{1}{3} = \frac{13}{3}$
14. $\frac{7}{5} = 1\frac{2}{5}$
15. $2\frac{2}{5} = \frac{12}{5}$
16. $6\frac{2}{5} = \frac{32}{5}$
17. $1\frac{1}{9} = \frac{10}{9}$
18. $\frac{13}{8} = 1\frac{5}{8}$
19. $1\frac{2}{5} = \frac{7}{5}$
20. $1\frac{1}{8} = \frac{9}{8}$

Page 137

Make the Move
Lighten the load by solving the puzzle.

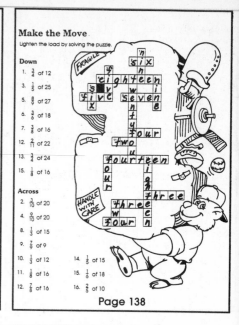

Crossword answers: six, eighteen, five, seven, four, two, fourteen, four, three, four

Down
1. $\frac{3}{4}$ of 12
3. $\frac{3}{5}$ of 25
5. $\frac{5}{9}$ of 27
6. $\frac{3}{9}$ of 18
7. $\frac{3}{8}$ of 16
12. $\frac{2}{11}$ of 22
13. $\frac{3}{4}$ of 24
15. $\frac{3}{8}$ of 16

Across
2. $\frac{3}{10}$ of 20
4. $\frac{9}{10}$ of 20
8. $\frac{1}{3}$ of 15
9. $\frac{7}{9}$ of 9
10. $\frac{1}{3}$ of 12
11. $\frac{1}{8}$ of 16
12. $\frac{7}{16}$ of 16
14. $\frac{1}{5}$ of 15
15. $\frac{1}{9}$ of 18
16. $\frac{2}{5}$ of 10

Page 138

Make a Wish
Begin this acrobatic challenge of mathematics and skill. Work your way to the top and make a little magic for Marty the mouse.

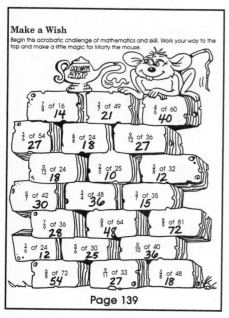

$\frac{7}{8}$ of 16 = **14**	$\frac{3}{7}$ of 49 = **21**	$\frac{4}{6}$ of 60 = **40**
$\frac{3}{6}$ of 54 = **27**	$\frac{3}{4}$ of 24 = **18**	$\frac{9}{12}$ of 36 = **27**
$\frac{9}{12}$ of 24 = **18**	$\frac{2}{5}$ of 25 = **10**	$\frac{3}{8}$ of 32 = **12**
$\frac{5}{7}$ of 42 = **30**	$\frac{3}{4}$ of 48 = **36**	$\frac{7}{9}$ of 35 = **?**
$\frac{7}{9}$ of 36 = **28**	$\frac{6}{8}$ of 64 = **48**	$\frac{8}{9}$ of 81 = **72**
$\frac{3}{6}$ of 24 = **12**	$\frac{5}{6}$ of 30 = **25**	$\frac{9}{10}$ of 40 = **36**
$\frac{6}{8}$ of 72 = **54**	$\frac{9}{11}$ of 33 = **27**	$\frac{3}{8}$ of 48 = **18**

Page 139

The Ultimate Adding Machine
Find the sum for each problem. Reduce to lowest terms.

$\frac{7}{9} + \frac{1}{9} = \frac{8}{9}$ $\frac{4}{12} + \frac{3}{12} = \frac{7}{12}$ $\frac{3}{6} + \frac{2}{6} = \frac{5}{6}$

$\frac{1}{9} + \frac{3}{9} = \frac{4}{9}$

$\frac{4}{10} + \frac{2}{10} = \frac{3}{5}$ $\frac{3}{6} + \frac{2}{6} = \frac{5}{6}$ $\frac{5}{9} + \frac{3}{9} = \frac{8}{9}$ $\frac{2}{5} + \frac{1}{5} = \frac{3}{5}$

$\frac{5}{11} + \frac{5}{11} = \frac{10}{11}$ $\frac{3}{7} + \frac{2}{7} = \frac{5}{7}$ $\frac{4}{8} + \frac{1}{8} = \frac{5}{8}$ $\frac{4}{12} + \frac{5}{12} = \frac{9}{12}$

$\frac{5}{8} + \frac{2}{8} = \frac{7}{8}$ $\frac{1}{12} + \frac{4}{12} = \frac{5}{6}$ $\frac{4}{11} + \frac{4}{11} = \frac{8}{11}$

$\frac{2}{5} + \frac{2}{5} = \frac{4}{5}$ $\frac{5}{8} + \frac{1}{8} = \frac{3}{4}$

$\frac{1}{9} + \frac{2}{9} = \frac{1}{3}$

$\frac{7}{10} + \frac{2}{10} = \frac{9}{10}$ $\frac{4}{6} + \frac{1}{6} = \frac{5}{6}$

WOW!

Page 140

Bubble Math
Reduce each sum to a whole number or a mixed number in lowest terms.

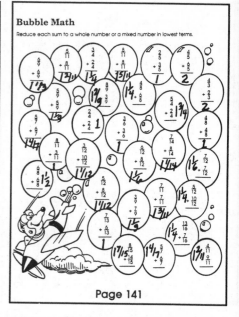

Page 141

Bug Me!
Solve the puzzle.

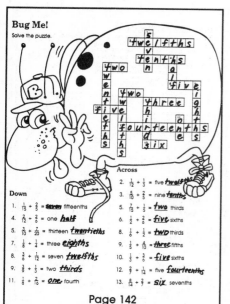

Crossword answers: twelfths, tenths, two, five, twenty, two, three, five, eighths, twelfths, fourteenths, six

Down
1. $\frac{1}{15} + \frac{2}{3} =$ **seven** fifteenths
4. $\frac{1}{3} + \frac{1}{6} =$ one **half**
5. $\frac{3}{10} + \frac{7}{20} =$ thirteen **twentieths**
7. $\frac{1}{8} + \frac{1}{4} =$ three **eighths**
8. $\frac{3}{4} + \frac{7}{12} =$ seven **twelfths**
9. $\frac{3}{9} + \frac{1}{3} =$ two **thirds**
11. $\frac{1}{8} + \frac{1}{8} =$ **one** fourth

Across
2. $\frac{1}{12} + \frac{1}{3} =$ five **twelfths**
3. $\frac{1}{10} + \frac{1}{2} =$ nine **tenths**
5. $\frac{7}{15} + \frac{1}{5} =$ **two** thirds
6. $\frac{1}{3} + \frac{1}{2} =$ **five** sixths
8. $\frac{1}{6} + \frac{1}{2} =$ **two** thirds
9. $\frac{1}{5} + \frac{2}{10} =$ **three** fifths
10. $\frac{1}{3} + \frac{3}{6} =$ **five** sixths
12. $\frac{2}{7} + \frac{3}{14} =$ five **fourteenths**
13. $\frac{3}{14} + \frac{4}{7} =$ **six** sevenths

Page 142

Soaring Subtraction
Solve each subtraction problem. Reduce each difference to lowest terms.

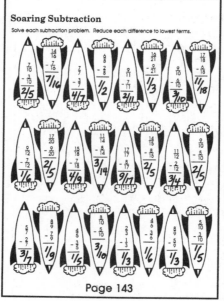

Page 143

Take a Closer Look
What is a stamp collector called?

To find out, solve the following subtraction problems, reduce to lowest terms, and then put the letter above its corresponding answer at the bottom of the page.

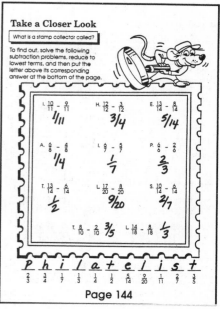

L. $\frac{10}{11} - \frac{9}{11} = \frac{1}{11}$ H. $\frac{12}{12} - \frac{3}{12} = \frac{3}{4}$ E. $\frac{13}{14} - \frac{8}{14} = \frac{5}{14}$

A. $\frac{6}{8} - \frac{4}{8} = \frac{1}{4}$ I. $\frac{9}{7} - \frac{4}{7} = \frac{1}{7}$ P. $\frac{6}{6} - \frac{2}{6} = \frac{2}{3}$

T. $\frac{13}{14} - \frac{6}{14} = \frac{1}{2}$ L. $\frac{17}{20} - \frac{8}{20} = \frac{9}{20}$ S. $\frac{10}{14} - \frac{4}{14} = \frac{2}{7}$

T. $\frac{8}{10} - \frac{2}{10} = \frac{3}{5}$ L. $\frac{14}{18} - \frac{8}{18} = \frac{1}{3}$

P h i l a t e l i s t

$\frac{2}{3}$ $\frac{3}{4}$ $\frac{1}{7}$ $\frac{9}{20}$ $\frac{1}{4}$ $\frac{1}{2}$ $\frac{5}{14}$ $\frac{1}{3}$ $\frac{1}{11}$ $\frac{2}{7}$ $\frac{3}{5}$

Page 144

Numeral Nibblers

Finish these number sentences.

$\frac{15}{16}$	−	$\frac{1}{2}$	=	$\frac{7}{16}$
$\frac{3}{4}$	−	$\frac{10}{16}$	=	$\frac{1}{8}$
$\frac{3}{16}$	−	$\frac{1}{8}$	=	$\frac{1}{16}$
$\frac{2}{3}$	−	$\frac{2}{12}$	=	$\frac{1}{2}$	−	$\frac{1}{48}$
$\frac{2}{9}$	−	$\frac{21}{24}$	−	$\frac{5}{6}$	=	$\frac{1}{24}$
$\frac{4}{9}$		$\frac{3}{4}$	−	$\frac{7}{12}$	=	$\frac{1}{6}$
$\frac{1}{8}$	$\frac{1}{4}$

Page 145

Figuring Distance

Find the perimeter of each figure.

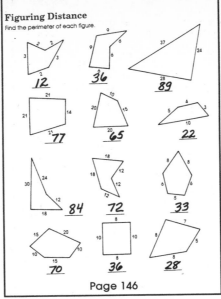

12   *36*   *89*

77   *65*   *22*

84   *72*   *33*

70   *36*   *28*

Page 146

Quilt Math

Find the perimeter and area of each quilt.

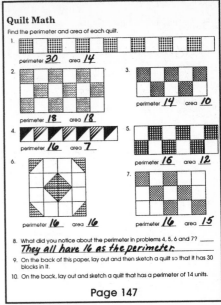

1. perimeter **30** area **14**

2. perimeter **18** area **18**

3. perimeter **14** area **10**

4. perimeter **16** area **7**

5. perimeter **16** area **12**

6. perimeter **16** area **16**

7. perimeter **16** area **15**

8. What did you notice about the perimeter in problems 4, 5, 6 and 7? _____
   They all have 16 as the perimeter.

9. On the back of this paper, lay out and then sketch a quilt so that it has 30 blocks in it.

10. On the back, lay out and sketch a quilt that has a perimeter of 14 units.

Page 147

Suzy Spider, Interior Decorator

Suzy Spider is decorating her house. She is a very clever decorator, but she needs your help figuring out the area and perimeter.

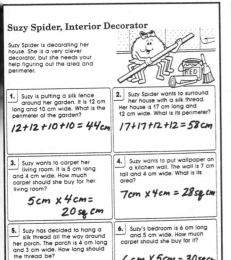

1. Suzy is putting a silk fence around her garden. It is 12 cm long and 10 cm wide. What is the perimeter of the garden?
   $12+12+10+10=44cm$

2. Suzy Spider wants to surround her house with a silk thread. Her house is 17 cm long and 12 cm wide. What is its perimeter?
   $17+17+12+12=58cm$

3. Suzy wants to carpet her living room. It is 5 cm long and 4 cm wide. How much carpet should she buy for her living room?
   $5cm \times 4cm = 20 sq. cm$

4. Suzy wants to put wallpaper on a kitchen wall. The wall is 7 cm tall and 4 cm wide. What is its area?
   $7cm \times 4cm = 28 sq. cm$

5. Suzy has decided to hang a silk thread all the way around her porch. The porch is 4 cm long and 3 cm wide. How long should the thread be?
   $4+4+3+3=14cm$

6. Suzy's bedroom is 6 cm long and 5 cm wide. How much carpet should she buy for it?
   $6cm \times 5cm = 30 sq cm$

Page 148

Turn Up the Volume

The **volume** is the measure of the inside of a space figure. Find the volume. Count the boxes.

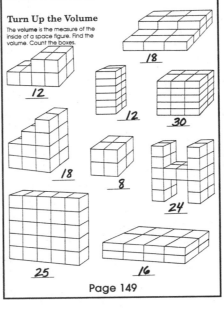

12   *18*

18   *12*   *30*

8   *24*

25   *16*

Page 149

Krab E. Krabby

Krab E. Krabby carries a yardstick with him everywhere he goes, and he measures everything that he can.

Key Facts:
12 inches = 1 foot
36 inches = 3 feet = 1 yard

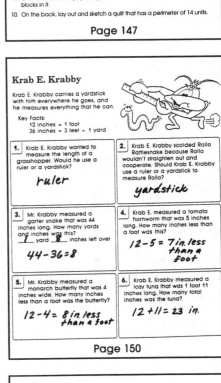

1. Krab E. Krabby wanted to measure the length of a grasshopper. Would he use a ruler or a yardstick?
   ruler

2. Krab E. Krabby scolded Rollo Rattlesnake because Rollo wouldn't straighten out and cooperate. Should Krab E. Krabby use a ruler or a yardstick to measure Rollo?
   yardstick

3. Mr. Krabby measured a garter snake that was 44 inches long. How many yards and inches was this?
   1 yard **8** inches left over
   $44-36=8$

4. Krab E. measured a tomato hornworm that was 5 inches long. How many inches less than a foot was this?
   $12-5=7in.$ less than a foot

5. Mr. Krabby measured a monarch butterfly that was 4 inches long. How many inches less than a foot was the butterfly?
   $12-4=8 in.$ less than a foot

6. Krab E. Krabby measured a lazy tuna that was 1 foot 11 inches long. How many total inches was the tuna?
   $12+11=23$ in.

Page 150

Animal Math

The chart below lists some of the body statistics of 15 endangered animals. Use these measurements to solve the problems below the chart.

Animal	Height	Weight	Length
Mountain gorilla	6 feet	450 pounds	
Brown hyena	25 inches	70 pounds	3 feet
Black rhinoceros	5.5 feet	4000 pounds	12 feet
Cheetah	2.5 feet	100 pounds	5 feet
Leopard	2 feet	150 pounds	4.5 feet
Spectacled bear	2.5 feet	300 pounds	5 feet
Giant armadillo		100 pounds	4 feet
Vicuna	2.5 feet	100 pounds	
Central American tapir	3.5 feet	500 pounds	8 feet
Black-footed ferret		1.5 pounds	20 inches
Siberian tiger	38 inches	600 pounds	6 feet
Orangutan	4.5 feet	200 pounds	
Giant panda		300 pounds	6 feet
Polar Bear		1600 pounds	8 feet
Yak	5.5 feet	1200 pounds	

Problems to solve:
1. What is the total height of a mountain gorilla, a vicuna and a yak? **14 ft**
2. What is the total weight of a leopard, a cheetah and a polar bear? **1850 lb**
3. What is the total weight of a giant panda and a giant armadillo? **400 lb**
4. Add the lengths of a black rhinoceros, a spectacled bear and a Siberian tiger. **23 ft**
5. Add the heights of two leopards, three yaks and four orangutans. **38.5 ft**
6. Subtract the height of a vicuna from the height of a cheetah. **0**
7. Multiply the height of a Central American tapir by the height of a mountain gorilla. **21'**
8. Add the heights of a brown hyena and a Siberian tiger. **5'3"**
9. Add the weights of all the animals. **9671½ lbs**
10. For the animals whose lengths are given, arrange the lengths of the animals from longest to shortest on another sheet of paper. **See above.**

Page 151

It Suits Me to a Tee!

How many centimeters from the tee to the flag? Stay on "course"!

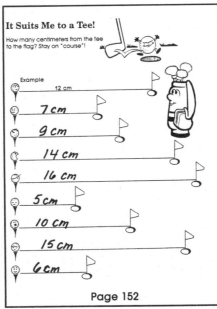

Example   12 cm

7 cm

9 cm

14 cm

16 cm

5 cm

10 cm

15 cm

6 cm

Page 152

Digging for Lost Treasure

While vacationing on Octopus Island in the Caribbean Sea, you discover an old treasure map in a bottle on the beach. Using a metric ruler, follow the directions below by plotting your movements to the location of the buried treasure using vertical and horizontal lines. Mark the spot on the map where you locate the treasure. You will be rewarded if you are correct!

1. From the starting point, go 8 centimeters east.
2. Go 6 centimeters north.
3. Go 9 centimeters east.
4. Go 3 centimeters south.
5. Go 7 centimeters west.
6. Go 5 centimeters north.
7. Go 7.5 centimeters west.
8. Go 2 centimeters north.
9. Go 9.5 centimeters east.
10. Go 10 centimeters south. Dig for treasure!

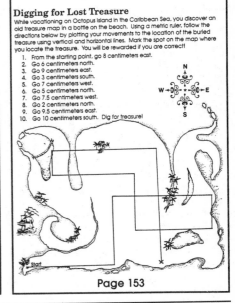

Page 153

Page 154 — Discovering Metric Equivalents

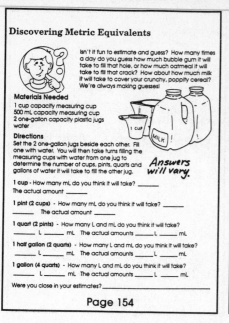

Isn't it fun to estimate and guess? How many times a day do you guess how much bubble gum it will take to fill that hole, or how much oatmeal it will take to fill that crack? How about how much milk it will take to cover your crunchy, poppity cereal? We're always making guesses!

Materials Needed
1 cup capacity measuring cup
500 mL capacity measuring cup
2 one-gallon capacity plastic jugs
water

Directions
Set the 2 one-gallon jugs beside each other. Fill one with water. You will then take turns filling the measuring cups with water from one jug to determine the number of cups, pints, quarts and gallons of water it will take to fill the other jug.

Answers will vary.

1 cup - How many mL do you think it will take? _____
The actual amount _____

1 pint (2 cups) - How many mL do you think it will take? _____
The actual amount _____

1 quart (2 pints) - How many L and mL do you think it will take?
_____ L _____ mL The actual amount _____ mL

1 half gallon (2 quarts) - How many L and mL do you think it will take?
_____ L _____ mL The actual amounts _____ L _____ mL

1 gallon (4 quarts) - How many L and mL do you think it will take?
_____ L _____ mL The actual amounts _____ L _____ mL

Were you close in your estimates? _____

Page 154

Gliding Graphics

Draw the lines as directed from point to point for each graph.

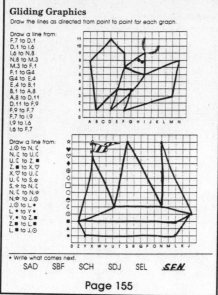

Draw a line from:
F.7 to D.1
D.1 to I.6
I.6 to N.8
N.8 to M.3
M.3 to F.1
F.1 to G4
G.4 to E.4
E.4 to B.1
B.1 to A.8
A.8 to D.11
D.11 to F.9
F.9 to F.7
F.7 to I.9
I.9 to I.6
I.6 to F.7

Draw a line from:
J.☉ to N.☾
N.☾ to U.☾
U.☾ to Z.■
Z.■ to X.♡
X.♡ to U.☾
U.☾ to S.☆
S.☆ to N.☾
N.☾ to N.☆
N.☆ to J.☉
J.☉ to L.◆
L.◆ to L.☾
Y.★ to U.☾
Z.■ to L.☾
L.■ to L.☉

• Write what comes next.
SAD SBF SCH SDJ SEL **SFN**

Page 155

School Statistics

Read each graph and do as directed.

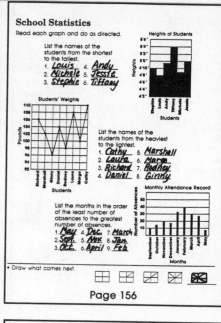

List the names of the students from the shortest to the tallest.
1. Louis   4. Andy
2. Michele 5. Jessie
3. Stephie 6. Tiffany

List the names of the students from the heaviest to the lightest.
1. Cathy   5. Marshall
2. Laura   6. Marge
3. Richard 7. Rodney
4. Daniel 8. Ginny

List the months in the order of the least number of absences to the greatest number of absences.
1. May   4. Dec. 7. March
2. Sept. 5. Nov. 8. Jan.
3. Oct. 6. April 9. Feb.

• Draw what comes next.

Page 156

It's About Time!

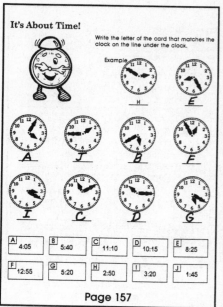

Write the letter of the card that matches the clock on the line under the clock.

Example: H   E

A   B   F

I   C   D   G

| A | 4:05 | B | 5:40 | C | 11:10 | D | 10:15 | E | 8:25 |
| F | 12:55 | G | 5:20 | H | 2:50 | I | 3:20 | J | 1:45 |

Page 157

Father Time Teasers

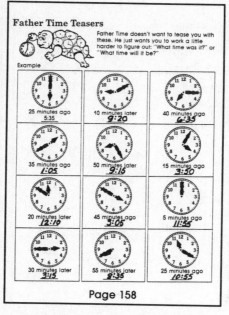

Father Time doesn't want to tease you with these. He just wants you to work a little harder to figure out: "What time was it?" or "What time will it be?"

Example

25 minutes ago **5:35**

10 minutes later **9:20**

40 minutes ago **6:35**

35 minutes ago **1:05**

50 minutes later **9:15**

15 minutes ago **3:50**

20 minutes later **12:10**

45 minutes ago **3:05**

5 minutes ago **11:55**

30 minutes later **3:15**

55 minutes later **9:35**

25 minutes ago **10:55**

Page 158

Time "Tables"

"Set" these tables by drawing the hands on these clocks.

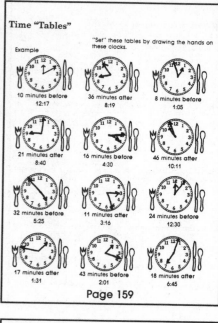

Example

10 minutes before 12:17

36 minutes after 8:19

8 minutes before 1:05

21 minutes after 8:40

16 minutes before 4:30

46 minutes after 10:11

32 minutes before 5:25

11 minutes after 3:16

24 minutes before 12:30

17 minutes after 1:31

43 minutes before 2:01

18 minutes after 6:45

Page 159

Time Problems

Draw the hands on the clocks to show the starting time and the ending time. Then write the answer to the problem.

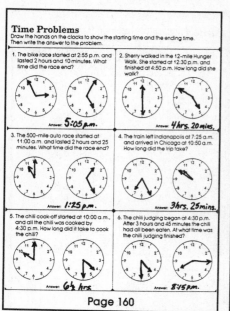

1. The bike race started at 2:55 p.m. and lasted 2 hours and 10 minutes. What time did the race end?
Answer: **5:05 p.m.**

2. Sherry walked in the 12-mile Hunger Walk. She started at 12:30 p.m. and finished at 4:50 p.m. How long did she walk?
Answer: **4 hrs. 20 mins.**

3. The 500-mile auto race started at 11:00 a.m. and lasted 2 hours and 25 minutes. What time did the race end?
Answer: **1:25 p.m.**

4. The train left Indianapolis at 7:25 a.m. and arrived in Chicago at 10:50 a.m. How long did the trip take?
Answer: **3 hrs. 25 mins.**

5. The chili cook-off started at 10:00 a.m. and all the chili was cooked by 4:30 p.m. How long did it take to cook the chili?
Answer: **6½ hrs**

6. The chili judging began at 4:30 p.m. After 3 hours and 45 minutes the chili had all been eaten. At what time was the chili judging finished?
Answer: **8:15 p.m.**

Page 160

Super Savers!

Adding money means you're saving money! Keep saving. It adds up. Here are a few success stories. Add 'em up!

Sam's Account
$8.03
.84
+ 5.47
$14.34

Debbie's Account
$45.32
2.41
+ 34.28
82.01

Sarah's Account
$85.42
12.58
+ 2.21
100.21

Roberto's Account
$41.46
8.89
+ .00
50.35

Cheryl's Account
$54.26
3.04
+ .25
57.55

Alex's Account
$ 4.06
81.23
+ 2.84
88.13

Eva's Account
$89.42
3.06
+ .94
93.42

Bill's Account
$62.41
3.84
+ 64.21
130.46

Monica's Account
$20.04
3.42
+ 25.81
49.27

David's Account
$56.04
2.81
+ .94
59.79

Tom's Account
$ 8.05
21.21
+ .98
30.24

Andy's Account
$ .47
31.24
+ 2.38
34.09

Earl's Account
$50.42
3.84
+ .98
55.24

Mark's Account
$21.46
20.00
+ 5.58
47.04

Michele's Account
$ .55
30.24
+ 3.49
34.28

Katelyn's Account
$ .42
.59
+ 3.42
4.43

Kimberly's Account
$ 5.42
40.64
+ 3.89
49.95

Gwen's Account
$60.42
3.84
+ 21.25
85.51

Whose account is the largest? **Bill's**
Whose is the smallest? **Katelyn's**
Whose is closest to $50? **Kimberly's**

Page 161

Match the $ale

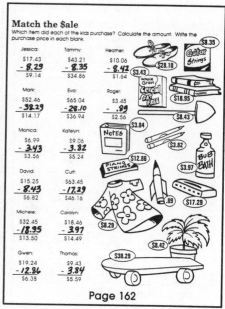

Which item did each of the kids purchase? Calculate the amount. Write the purchase price in each blank.

Jessica:
$17.43
- 8.29
$9.14

Tammy:
$43.21
- 8.35
$34.86

Heather:
$10.06
- 8.42
$1.64

Mark:
$52.46
- 38.29
$14.17

Eva:
$65.04
- 28.10
$36.94

Roger:
$3.45
- .99
$2.56

Monica:
$6.99
- 3.43
$3.56

Katelyn:
$9.06
- 3.32
$5.24

David:
$15.25
- 8.43
$6.82

Curt:
$63.45
- 17.29
$46.16

Michele:
$32.45
- 18.95
$13.50

Carolyn:
$18.46
- 3.97
$14.49

Gwen:
$19.24
- 12.86
$6.38

Thomas:
$9.43
- 3.84
$5.59

Price tags: $8.35, $28.10, $3.43, $18.95, $8.43, $3.84, $3.82, $12.86, $3.97, $.89, $17.29, $8.29, $8.42, $38.29

Page 162

McMealworm

McMealworm's is the latest restaurant of that famous fast food creator, Buggs I. Lyke. His McMealworm Burger costs $1.69. An order of Roasted Roaches costs $.59 for the regular size and $.79 for the large size. A Cricket Cola is $.89.

1. You buy a McMealworm Burger and a regular order of Roasted Roaches. What is the total?

$1.69 + .59 = 2.28

2. Your best friend in class orders a McMealworm Burger, a large order of Roasted Roaches and a Cricket Cola. How much will it cost?

$.79 + .89 + $1.69 = 3.37

3. Your teacher buys a Cricket Cola and a regular order of Roasted Roaches. What does it cost?

$.89 + .59 = 1.48

4. The principal is very hungry, so his bill comes to $14.37. How much change will he get from $20.00?

$20 - 14.37 = 5.63

5. Your mom goes to McMealworm's to buy your dinner. She spends $3.37. How much change does she get from a $5.00 bill?

$5 - 3.37 = 1.63

6. You have $1.17 in your bank. How much more do you need to pay for a McMealworm Burger?

$1.69 - 1.17 = .52$

Page 163

One-Stop Shopping

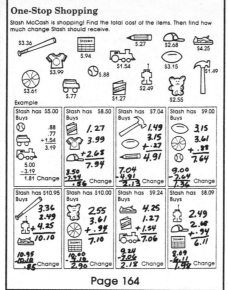

Stash McCash is shopping! Find the total cost of the items. Then find how much change Stash should receive.

$3.36 $.94 $.27 $2.68 $4.25
$3.99 $.88 $1.54 $3.15
$3.61 $.77 $2.49 $1.27 $2.55 $1.49

Example
Stash has $5.00 Buys
.88
.77
+ 1.54
3.19
5.00
- 3.19
1.81 Change

Stash has $8.50 Buys
1.27
3.99
+ 2.68
7.94
8.50
- 7.94
.56 Change

Stash has $7.04 Buys
1.49
3.15
+ .27
4.91
7.04
- 4.91
2.13 Change

Stash has $9.00 Buys
3.15
3.61
+ .88
7.64
9.00
- 7.64
1.36 Change

Stash has $10.95 Buys
3.36
2.49
+ 4.25
10.10
10.95
- 10.10
.85 Change

Stash has $10.00 Buys
2.55
3.61
+ .94
7.10
10.00
- 7.10
2.90 Change

Stash has $9.24 Buys
4.25
1.27
+ 1.54
7.06
9.24
- 7.06
2.18 Change

Stash has $8.09 Buys
2.49
2.68
+ .94
6.11
8.09
- 6.11
1.98 Change

Page 164

Shifty Sam's Shop

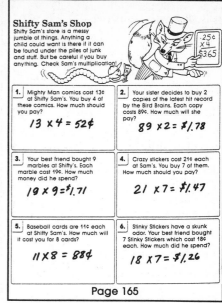

Shifty Sam's store is a messy jumble of things. Anything a child wants it can be found under the piles of junk and stuff. But be careful if you buy anything. Check Sam's multiplication!

.25¢
× 4
$3.65

1. Mighty Man comics cost 13¢ at Shifty Sam's. You buy 4 of these comics. How much should you pay?

$13 \times 4 = 52¢$

2. Your sister decides to buy 2 copies of the latest hit record by the Bird Brains. Each copy costs 89¢. How much will she pay?

$89 \times 2 = 1.78

3. Your best friend bought 9 marbles at Shifty's. Each marble costs 19¢. How much money did he spend?

$19 \times 9 = 1.71

4. Crazy stickers cost 21¢ each at Sam's. You buy 7 of them. How much should you pay?

$21 \times 7 = 1.47

5. Baseball cards are 11¢ each at Shifty Sam's. How much will it cost you for 8 cards?

$11 \times 8 = 88¢$

6. Stinky Stickers have a skunk odor. Your best friend bought 7 Stinky Stickers which cost 18¢ each. How much did he spend?

$18 \times 7 = 1.26

Page 165

What a Great Catch!

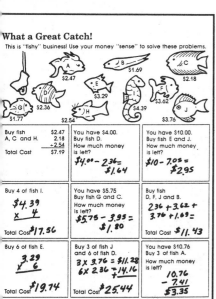

This is "fishy" business! Use your money "sense" to solve these problems.

A $2.47 B $1.69 C $2.18
D $3.29 E ? F $3.62
G $2.36 H $2.54 I $4.39 J $3.76

Buy fish A, C and H.
$2.47
2.18
+ 2.54
Total Cost $7.19

You have $4.00. Buy fish D. How much money is left?
$4.00 - 2.36 = $1.64

You have $10.00. Buy fish E and J. How much money is left?
$10 - 7.05 = $2.95

Buy 4 of fish I.
$4.39
× 4
Total Cost $17.56

You have $5.75. Buy fish G and C. How much money is left?
$5.75 - 3.95 = $1.80

Buy fish D, F, J and B.
2.36 + 3.62 + 3.76 + 1.69 = Total Cost $11.43

Buy 6 of fish E.
3.29
× 6
Total Cost $19.74

Buy 3 of fish J and 6 of fish D.
3 × 3.76 = $11.28
6 × 2.36 = 14.16
Total Cost $25.44

You have $10.76. Buy 3 of fish A. How much money is left?
10.76 - 7.41 = $3.35

Page 166

Money Math

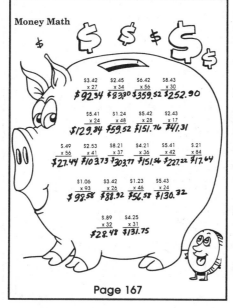

$3.42 $2.45 $6.42 $8.43
× 27 × 34 × 56 × 30
$92.34 $83.30 $359.52 $252.90

$5.41 $1.24 $5.42 $2.43
× 24 × 48 × 28 × 17
$129.84 $59.52 $151.76 $41.31

$.49 $2.53 $8.21 $5.41 $2.10
× 56 × 41 × 37 × 42 × 84
$27.44 $103.73 $303.77 $151.56 $227.22 $17.64

$1.06 $3.42 $1.23 $5.43
× 93 × 26 × 46 × 24
$98.58 $88.92 $56.58 $130.32

$.89 $4.25
× 32 × 31
$28.48 $131.75

Page 167

Sam Sillicook's Doughnut Shoppe

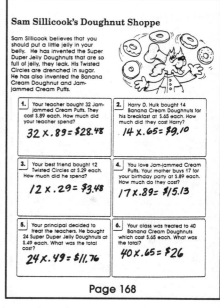

Sam Sillicook believes that you should put a little jelly in your belly. He has invented the Super Duper Jelly Doughnuts that are so full of jelly, they leak. His Twisted Circles are drenched in sugar. He has also invented the Banana Cream Doughnut and Jam-jammed Cream Puffs.

1. Your teacher bought 32 Jam-jammed Cream Puffs. They cost $.89 each. How much did your teacher spend?

$32 \times .89 = 28.48

2. Harry D. Hulk bought 14 Banana Cream Doughnuts for his breakfast at $.65 each. How much did they cost Harry?

$14 \times .65 = 9.10

3. Your best friend bought 12 Twisted Circles at $.29 each. How much did he spend?

$12 \times .29 = 3.48

4. You love Jam-jammed Cream Puffs. Your mother buys 17 for your birthday party at $.89 each. How much did she spend?

$17 \times .89 = 15.13

5. Your principal decided to treat the teachers. He bought 24 Super Duper Jelly Doughnuts at $.49 each. What was the total cost?

$24 \times .49 = 11.76

6. Your class was treated to 40 Banana Cream Doughnuts which cost $.65 each. What was the total?

$40 \times .65 = 26

Page 168

Perplexing Problems

Heather and Gwen went to the water park. How much did each of them pay?
Total: $9.68
$4.84

On Saturday, James, Gary, Ted and Raul went to the zoo. What was their individual cost to get in?
Total: $8.72
$2.18

Mark, David, Curt and Sam rented a motorized skateboard for 1 hour. How much was the cost for each of them — split equally 4 ways?
Total: $7.36
$1.84

Five students pitched in to buy Mr. Jokestopper a birthday gift. How much did each of them contribute?
Total: $9.60
$1.92

All 6 members of the volleyball team received a special shirt for being in the final game. What was the amount of each shirt?
Total: $8.16
$1.36

Mary, Cheryl and Betty went to the skating rink. What was their individual cost?
Total: $7.44
$2.48

Carol, Katelyn and Kimberly bought lunch at their favorite salad shop. What did each of them pay for lunch?
Total: $8.52
$2.84

Debbie, Sarah, Michele and Kelly earned $6.56 altogether for collecting cans. How much did each of them earn individually?
Total: $6.56
$1.64

Five friends went to the Hamburger Hot Spot Cafe for lunch. They all ordered the special. What did it cost?
Total: $7.45
$1.49

Lee and Ricardo purchased an awesome model rocket together. What was the cost for each of them?
Total: $9.52
$4.76

The total fee for Erik, Bill and Steve to enter the science museum was $8.76. What amount did each of them pay?
Total: $8.76
$2.92

Page 169

Too Much Information

Underline the distractor and solve the problems.

1. All 20 of the students from Sandy's class went to the movies. Tickets cost $1.50 each. Drinks cost 55¢ each. How much altogether did the students spend on tickets?

$20 \times $1.50 = 30

2. Of the students, 11 were girls and 9 were boys. At $1.50 per ticket, how much did the boys' tickets cost altogether?

$9 \times $1.50 = 13.50

3. While 5 students had ice cream, 12 others had candy. Ice cream cost 75¢ per cup. How much did the students spend on ice cream?

$5 \times 75¢ = 3.75

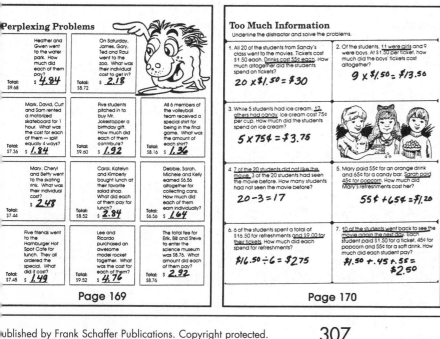

4. 7 of the 20 students did not like the movie. 3 of the 20 students had seen the movie before. How many students had not seen the movie before?

$20 - 3 = 17$

5. Mary paid 55¢ for an orange drink and 65¢ for a candy bar. Sarah paid 45¢ for popcorn. How much did Mary's refreshments cost her?

$55¢ + 65¢ = 1.20

6. 6 of the students spent a total of $16.50 for refreshments and $9.00 for their tickets. How much did each spend for refreshments?

$16.50 \div 6 = 2.75

7. 10 of the students went back to see the movie again the next day. Each student paid $1.50 for a ticket, 45¢ for popcorn and 55¢ for a soft drink. How much did each student pay?

$1.50 + .45 + .55 = 2.50

Page 170

Get the Point

When you add or subtract decimals, remember to "include the point."

Add
3.6
+ 3.3
6.9

Subtract
6.8
- 2.6
4.2

4.2	6.4	3.1	4.7	4.9	3.4
+ 5.2	+ 1.4	+ 7.8	+ 3.2	+ 2.0	+ 1.2
9.4	7.8	10.9	7.9	6.9	4.6
5.9	6.7	7.8	5.8	3.9	5.8
- 3.2	- 5.6	- 2.5	- 3.3	- 1.5	- 2.2
2.7	1.1	5.3	2.5	2.4	3.6
.23	.43	.26	.64	.68	.26
+ .25	+ .16	+ .42	+ .15	+ .31	+ .31
.48	.59	.68	.79	.99	.57
.87	.98	.79	.87	.83	.96
- .42	- .35	- .15	- .67	- .12	- .12
.45	.63	.64	.20	.71	.84
3.13	4.72	6.87	4.98	5.97	5.89
+ 2.26	+ 1.15	+ 2.11	- 2.32	- 2.54	- 1.35
5.39	5.87	8.98	2.66	3.43	4.54
4.86	5.86	6.98	6.73	4.27	3.46
- 1.76	- 3.83	- 1.45	+ 1.15	+ 5.52	+ 2.31
3.10	2.03	5.53	7.88	9.79	5.77

Page 171

0-7682-3794-7 Skills & Practice Gr. 4

Doing Decimals

DECIMAL POINT—A dot placed between the ones place and the tenths place

.2 is read as two tenths.　　.4 four tenths.

Write answer as decimal for shaded parts.

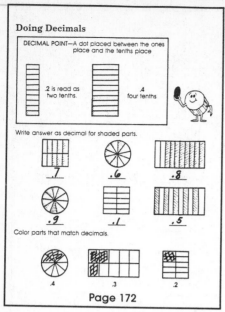

.7　.6　.8

.9　.1　.5

Color parts that match decimals.

.4　.3　.2

Page 172

Animal Trivia

Name _____

1. A wood rat has a tail which is 23.6 cm long. A deer mouse has a tail 12.2 cm long. What is the difference?

$23.6 - 12.2 = 11.4$ cm

2. A rock mouse is 26.1 cm long. His tail adds another 14.4 cm. What is his total length from his nose to the tip of his tail?

$26.1 + 14.4 = 40.5$ cm

3. A spotted bat has a tail 4.9 cm long. An evening bat has a tail 3.7 cm long. What is the difference?

$4.9 - 3.7 = 1.2$ cm

4. A pocket gopher has a hind foot 3.5 cm long. A ground squirrel's hind foot is 6.4 cm long. How much longer is the ground squirrel's foot?

$6.4 - 3.5 = 2.9$ cm

5. A cottontail rabbit has ears which are 6.8 cm long. A jackrabbit has ears 12.9 cm long. How much shorter is the cottontail's ear?

$12.9 - 6.8 = 6.1$ cm

6. A porcupine has a tail 30.0 cm long. A possum has a tail 53.5 cm long. How much longer is the possum's tail?

$53.5 - 30.0 = 23.5$ cm

7. The hind foot of a river otter is 14.6 cm long. The hind foot of a hog-nosed skunk is 9.0 cm long. What is the difference?

$14.6 - 9.0 = 5.6$ cm

Page 173

Living History Books

You can learn a lot about a tree by reading its special calendar of rings. Every year a tree grows a new layer of wood. This makes the tree trunk get fatter and fatter. The new layer makes a ring.

You can see the rings on a freshly cut tree stump. When the growing season is wet, the tree grows a lot and the rings are wide. When the season is dry, the tree grows very little. Then the rings are narrow.

This tree was planted in 1973. Use the picture clues to color the rings of the tree stump. Where will the very first ring be?

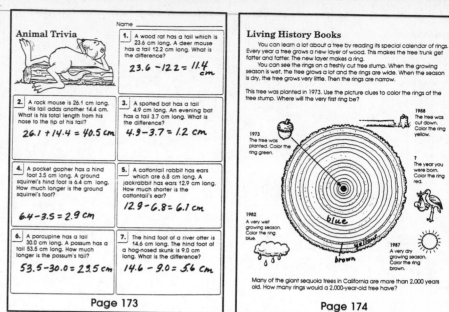

1988 The tree was cut down. Color the ring yellow.

1973 The tree was planted. Color the ring green.

? The year you were born. Color the ring red.

1982 A very wet growing season. Color the ring blue.

1987 A very dry growing season. Color the ring brown.

blue
yellow
brown

Many of the giant sequoia trees in California are more than 2,000 years old. How many rings would a 2,000-year-old tree have?

Page 174

Jogging Geraniums

You will probably never see a flower running down the sidewalk, but you might see one climbing a fence. Most plants are rooted in one place, but they still move. Roots, stems, leaves, and even flowers move in different ways. The leaves grow toward the light. Roots will grow toward water. Even gravity will make a plant grow straight up in the air, away from the center of the earth.

Look at the three plants below. Tell what made the plants "move" or grow the way they did.

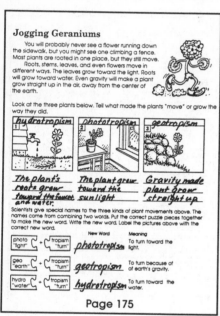

hydrotropism | phototropism | geotropism

The plant's roots grew toward the water. | The plant grew toward the sunlight. | Gravity made plant grow straight up.

Scientists give special names to the three kinds of plant movements above. The names come from combining two words. Put the correct puzzle pieces together to make the new word. Write the new word. Label the pictures above with the correct new word.

	New Word	Meaning
photo "light" + tropism "turn"	phototropism	To turn toward the light.
geo "earth" + tropism "turn"	geotropism	To turn because of earth's gravity.
hydro "water" + tropism "turn"	hydrotropism	To turn toward the water.

Page 175

Cruising Coconuts

"Look at this coconut!" Amy called to Matt as they walked along the beach. Safe inside its thick husk, the coconut had floated across the water. Once it washed up on shore, the green leaves sprouted from this large seed.

Seeds travel in many ways. Below are five ways that seeds travel. Tell how each seed travels.

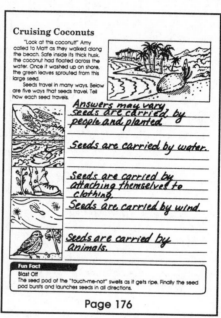

Answers may vary

Seeds are carried by people and planted

Seeds are carried by water.

Seeds are carried by attaching themselves to clothing.

Seeds are carried by wind.

Seeds are carried by animals.

Fun Fact
Blast Off
The seed pod of the "touch-me-not" swells as it gets ripe. Finally the seed pod bursts and launches seeds in all directions.

Page 176

Corny Medicine

Use the words from the Word Bank to complete the puzzle. Cross out each word in the Word Bank as you use it. The remaining words in the Word Bank will help you answer the "Corny Medicine" riddle.

Across
4. Deep growing type of root
6. Beautiful, seed-making part of plant
7. Brightly colored "leafy" parts of the flower
9. Large part of seed that supplies food
10. Sweet food made by the leaves

Down
1. Making food with the help of light
2. Green food-making material in a leaf
3. Plant's "food factory"
5. Plant's anchor
8. Plants get their energy from the

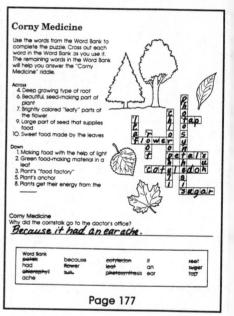

photosynthesis, chlorophyll, tap, leaf, flower, petals, cotyledon, sugar

Corny Medicine
Why did the cornstalk go to the doctor's office?

Because it had an earache.

Word Bank				
petals	because	cotyledon	it	root
had	flower	leaf	an	sugar
chlorophyll	sun	photosynthesis	ear	tap
ache				

Page 177

Guess What?

Use the following hints and the Word Bank to decide what insect each riddle describes.

1. I have stout, spiny forelegs.
I eat insects, including some of my own kind.
I camouflage well in my surroundings.
My forelegs make me appear to be praying.
What am I? **praying mantis**

2. I have clear wings.
My body is quite round.
The males of my species make long, shrill sounds in summer.
Some of us take 17 years to develop.
What am I? **cicada**

3. I have two pairs of long, thin wings.
I eat mosquitoes and other small insects.
I live near lakes, ponds, streams and rivers.
My abdomen is very long . . . as long as a darning needle.
What am I? **dragonfly**

4. I am a type of beetle.
My young are often called glowworms.
My abdomen produces light.
What am I? **lightning bug**

5. I like warm, damp and dark places and come out at night.
Humans hate me.
I am a destructive household pest.
I am closely related to grasshoppers and crickets.
What am I? **cockroach**

Word Bank			
lightning bug	cicada	dragonfly	termite
mosquito	ladybug	aphid	praying mantis
bumblebee	cockroach		

Challenge: Research an insect. Draw a detailed picture and write a report about it.

Page 178

Going Places

Looking at a bird's feet can tell you a lot about how they are used. Look at the bird's feet below. Unscramble the bird's name. Write the bird's name by the best sentence. Can you match the pictures with the names?

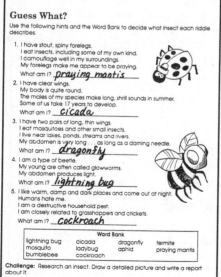

duck "My webbed feet are great for swimming."

woodpecker "My feet are great for walking up trees."

heron "I use my feet with long toes to wade in the water and mud."

hawk "I use my strong, powerful feet to catch small animals."

kawh **hawk** / noreh **heron**
ckud **duck** / reckwoodeep **woodpecker**

Can the shape of a bird's bill tell you anything about what it eats? Look closely at the bills below. Unscramble the bird's name. Write the bird's name by the best sentence. Can you match the pictures with the names?

woodpecker "I pound holes in wood to find insects."

hummingbird "I use my long bill to get nectar from flowers."

cardinal "I use my strong bill to crack open seeds."

hawk "I use my sharp bill to tear the flesh of animals."

heron "I stab at small fish with my sharp bill."

pelican "I scoop up large mouthfuls of water and fish."

noreh **heron** / reckwoodep **woodpecker**
bumminghird **hummingbird** / kawh **hawk**
panicel **pelican** / dinalcar **cardinal**

Page 179

Family Ties

Unscramble the names of the mom, pop, and baby of these animal families. The coordinates in front of each scrambled name tell where to write it on the chart.

(J-2) nhe	(B-2) woc	(A-1) obc	(C-1) roba
(E-2) ckdu	(G-3) ignolgs	(B-3) plewh	(I-1) arm
(F-2) exrvin	(D-3) wfna	(I-3)baim	(G-1) greadn
(I-2) wee	(C-2) ows	(A-3)gentyc	(E-1) kared
(H-2) ream	(D-1) bcku	(H-1) mot	(J-1) mot
(H-3) loaf	(B-1) luib	(G-2) sogeo	(A-2) nep
(D-2) eod	(C-3) buc	(J-3) tupoi	(H-1) lastonil
(E-3) gludcink	(F-1) odg		

	Male (1)	Female (2)	Baby (3)
A swan	cob	pen	cygnet
B seal	bull	cow	whelp
C bear	boar	sow	cub
D deer	buck	doe	fawn
E duck	drake	duck	duckling
F fox	dog	vixen	cub
G goose	gander	goose	gosling
H horse	stallion	mare	foal
I sheep	ram	ewe	lamb
J turkey	tom	hen	poult

Challenge: Find the group names of these animals and write them on another sheet of paper.

Page 180

Adopt an Animal

The seas of the world are filled with an amazing variety of life. Starfish, crabs, flying fish, angelfish, worms, turtles, sharks and whales all make their home underwater. The shape, color and size of most sea animals depend on their lifestyle and where they live in the seas. Select a sea animal and become an expert on it. Research your animal and complete the profile below. *Answers will vary.*

Common Name _____
Scientific Name _____

Description	
weight:	**Picture**
length:	
body shape:	
tail shape:	
color:	
unusual characteristics:	

Behaviors

Description of Habitat: _____

Food and Feeding Habits: _____

Migration (if applicable): _____

Page 181

Food Chains

All living things in the seas depend on each other for food. The food chain begins with sea plants called phytoplankton. These plants make their own food using energy from the sun. Tiny sea animals, called zooplankton, feed on the phytoplankton. These animals include shrimp, copepods, and jellyfish. Some of the most common fish—herring, anchovies, and sprats—feed on zooplankton. These fish are eaten by others, such as tuna and mackerel, which in turn are eaten by the superpredators, such as sharks and dolphins. This pattern of eating is called a food chain.

Use the diagram to answer the following questions on another piece of paper.

Answers will vary.

herring copepod phytoplankton shark tuna

1. Describe the food chain above.
2. If there was a decrease in the copepod population, what would happen to the herring population? Why? *It would decrease. Not enough food.*
3. What would happen to the phytoplankton population? Why? *Increase. Less predators.*
4. If the tuna population became endangered, what would the result be? *Chain would be disrupted.*
5. What does it mean when we say, "The death of one species in the food chain upsets the rest of the chain"? *All are dependent on each other.*
6. An example of a land food chain might be fly-spider-bird-cat. Give an other example of a land food chain.
7. Draw another sea food chain. Explain and give an example for each step.

Page 182

Polluting Our Seas

The seas provide us with many resources that we need to survive and to keep our industries going. Fish, shellfish, seaweeds, and minerals are just a few of the seas' resources. How long these will last depends on if and how badly we continue to pollute the seas.

For hundreds of years, people have been throwing garbage into the seas. Every day, billions of tons of waste, such as poisonous chemicals, radioactive waste, and plastics, are dumped into the seas. One of the worst sources of pollution is an oil spill. This results when tankers collide with each other or crash into rocks. There are thousands of oil spills every year. Most are small and are not reported, but some are huge. The biggest was in February, 1991, when oil was spilled into the Persian Gulf. It is thought that more than 1.2 million tons of oil spilled into the sea. It was more than 20 times bigger than the *Exxon Valdez* oil spill in 1989 off the coast of Alaska.

The seas cannot continue to be polluted without endangering the sea life. As the world population increases, people will be looking more to the seas to find products and resources.

Pretend you are a reporter. Use the headline below to write an article about pollution of the seas. Research to find interesting facts to back up your story. *Articles will vary.*

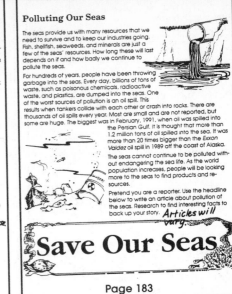

Save Our Seas

Page 183

Animal Comparisons

A Venn diagram is a great way to compare things. Use the one below to compare two animals of the seas. Fill in the circle below the dolphin with characteristics common only to this animal. Fill in the circle below the shark with characteristics common only to the shark. Where the circles overlap, fill in characteristics both animals share. Write a story about your findings on another piece of paper.

Answers will vary.

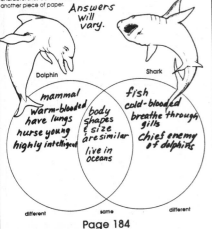

Dolphin Shark

mammal, warm-blooded, have lungs, nurse young, highly intelligent

body shapes & size are similar, live in oceans

fish, cold-blooded, breathe through gills, chief enemy of dolphins

different same different

Page 184

Danger Ahead!

You will never see a dodo bird or a saber-tooth tiger. These animals are gone forever. They are extinct.

The animals on this page are not extinct, but they are in danger of becoming extinct. They are endangered. There may not be enough of them to reproduce. They are endangered because of the way people live.

There are many reasons why some animals are endangered. The signs on this page give clues to three main reasons.

Look at the signs. What do you think the three reasons are? Write them below.

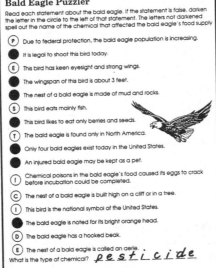

1. *Loss of habitat - trees cut down.*
2. *Hunting. Animals are killed by man, though hunting of some animals is sometimes necessary.*
3. *Pollution destroys habitats and also introduces poisons.*

Unscramble the names of these endangered animals.

dalb glece → *bald eagle*
nereg teltur → *green turtle*
lueb lawen → *blue whale*
bremit lotw → *timber wolf*

• There are more than 100 endangered animals in North America. Find the name of one that lives near your area. Make a poster to help people become aware of this animal and the danger it is in.

Page 185

Threatened and Endangered Animals

Many of the earth's animals are threatened or extinct. Use the names of the animals to build a puzzle. Only use the bold-faced words.
Hint: Build off **rhinoceros**.

Word Box			
brown **hyena**	**Darwin's rhea**	red **wolf**	black-footed **ferret**
Spanish **lynx**	Philippine **eagle**	**gavial**	ring-tailed **lemur**
giant **panda**	blue **whale**	**numbat**	resplendent **quetzal**
Arabian **oryx**	Grevy's **zebra**	**kakapo**	Galapagos **penguin**
Indian **python**	wild **yak**	**dugong**	

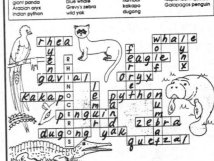

Use an encyclopedia to answer each question.
1. Which animal above is related to the manatee? *the dugong*
2. Which is the cousin of the crocodile? *the gavial*
3. Which is related to the ostrich? *Darwin's rhea*

Page 186

Animal Magic

Read Column A. Choose an answer from Column B. Write the number of the answer in the Magic Square. The first one has been done for you.

Column A	Column B
A. grizzly bear	1. large bear of the American grasslands
B. koala	2. lives on dry grasslands of South Africa
C. peregrine falcon	3. the most valuable reptile in the world
D. California condor	4. largest soaring bird of North America
E. black-footed ferret	5. the tallest American bird
F. cheetah	6. the fastest animal on land
G. orangutan	7. the only great ape outside Africa
H. giant panda	8. large aquatic sealike animal
I. Florida manatee	9. large black and white mammal of China
J. kit fox	10. small, fast mammal; nocturnal predator
K. blue whale	11. largest mammal in the world
L. whooping crane	12. member of the weasel family
M. red wolf	13. has interbred with coyotes in some areas
N. green sea turtle	14. also called a duck hawk; size of a crow
O. brown hyena	15. eats leaves of the eucalyptus tree
P. jaguar	16. known as *el tigre* in Spanish

A 1	B 15	C 14	D 4
E 12	F 6	G 7	H 9
I 8	J 10	K 11	L 5
M 13	N 3	O 2	P 16

Add the numbers across, down and diagonally. What answer do you get? *34*
Why do you think this is called a magic square? _____

Page 187

Bald Eagle Puzzler

Read each statement about the bald eagle. If the statement is false, darken the letter in the circle to the left of that statement. The letters not darkened spell out the name of the chemical that affected the bald eagle's food supply.

(P) Due to federal protection, the bald eagle population is increasing.
● It is legal to shoot this bird today.
(E) This bird has keen eyesight and strong wings.
● The wingspan of this bird is about 3 feet.
● The nest of a bald eagle is made of mud and rocks.
(S) This bird eats mainly fish.
● This bird likes to eat only berries and seeds.
(T) The bald eagle is found only in North America.
● Only four bald eagles exist today in the United States.
● An injured bald eagle may be kept as a pet.
(I) Chemical poisons in the bald eagle's food caused its eggs to crack before incubation could be completed.
(C) The nest of a bald eagle is built high on a cliff or in a tree.
(I) This bird is the national symbol of the United States.
● The bald eagle is noted for its bright orange head.
(D) The bald eagle has a hooked beak.
(E) The nest of a bald eagle is called an aerie.

What is the type of chemical? *pesticide*

Page 188

Nippers, Rippers, and Grinders

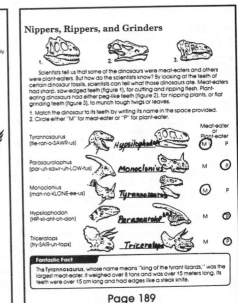

1. 2. 3.

Scientists tell us that some of the dinosaurs were meat-eaters and others were plant-eaters. But how do the scientists know? By looking at the teeth of certain dinosaur fossils, scientists can tell what those dinosaurs ate. Meat-eaters had sharp, saw-edged teeth (figure 1), for cutting and ripping flesh. Plant-eating dinosaurs had either peg-like teeth (figure 2), for nipping plants, or flat grinding teeth (figure 3), to munch tough twigs or leaves.

1. Match the dinosaur to its teeth by writing its name in the space provided.
2. Circle either "M" for meat-eater or "P" for plant-eater.

		Meat-eater or Plant-eater
Tyrannosaurus (tie-ran-o-SAWR-us)	*Hypsilophodon*	Ⓜ P
Parasaurolophus (par-uh-sawr-uh-LOW-fus)	*Monoclonius*	M Ⓟ
Monoclonius (mah-no-KLONE-ee-us)	*Tyrannosaurus*	Ⓜ P
Hypsilophodon (HIP-sil-ahf-oh-don)	*Parasaurolophus*	Ⓟ
Triceratops (try-SAIR-uh-tops)	*Triceratops*	M Ⓟ

Fantastic Fact
The Tyrannosaurus, whose name means "king of the tyrant lizards," was the largest meat-eater. It weighed over 8 tons and was over 15 meters long. Its teeth were over 15 cm long and had edges like a steak knife.

Page 189

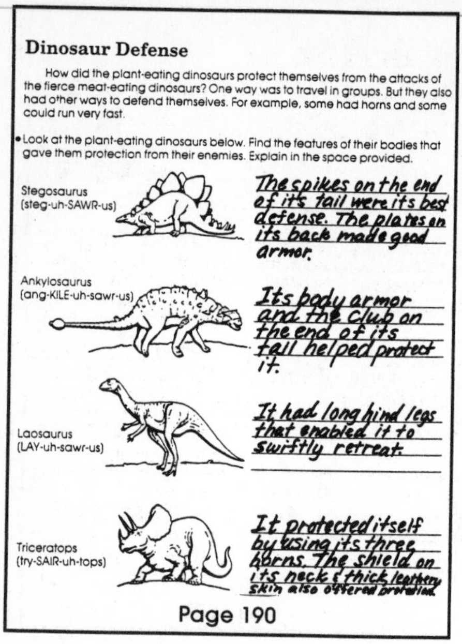

Dinosaur Defense

How did the plant-eating dinosaurs protect themselves from the attacks of the fierce meat-eating dinosaurs? One way was to travel in groups. But they also had other ways to defend themselves. For example, some had horns and some could run very fast.

- Look at the plant-eating dinosaurs below. Find the features of their bodies that gave them protection from their enemies. Explain in the space provided.

Stegosaurus (steg-uh-SAWR-us) — The spikes on the end of its tail were its best defense. The plates on its back made good armor.

Ankylosaurus (ang-KILE-uh-sawr-us) — Its body armor and the club on the end of its tail helped protect it.

Laosaurus (LAY-uh-sawr-us) — It had long hind legs that enabled it to swiftly retreat.

Triceratops (try-SAIR-uh-tops) — It protected itself by using its three horns. The shield on its neck & thick leathery skin also offered protection.

Page 190

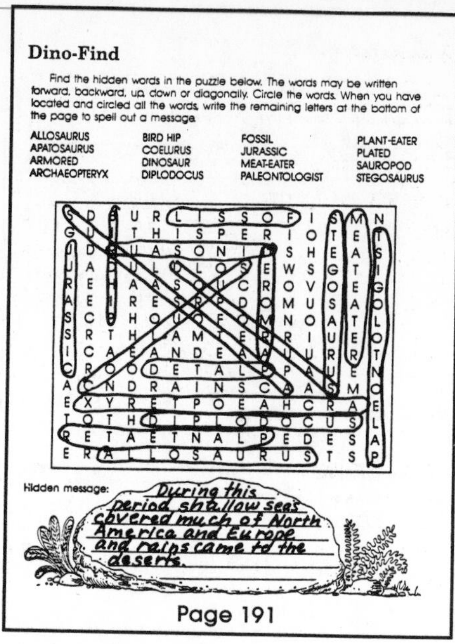

Dino-Find

Find the hidden words in the puzzle below. The words may be written forward, backward, up, down or diagonally. Circle the words. When you have located and circled all the words, write the remaining letters at the bottom of the page to spell out a message.

ALLOSAURUS	BIRD HIP	FOSSIL	PLANT-EATER
APATOSAURUS	COELURUS	JURASSIC	PLATED
ARMORED	DINOSAUR	MEAT-EATER	SAUROPOD
ARCHAEOPTERYX	DIPLODOCUS	PALEONTOLOGIST	STEGOSAURUS

Hidden message: During this period shallow seas covered much of North America and Europe and rains came to the deserts.

Page 191

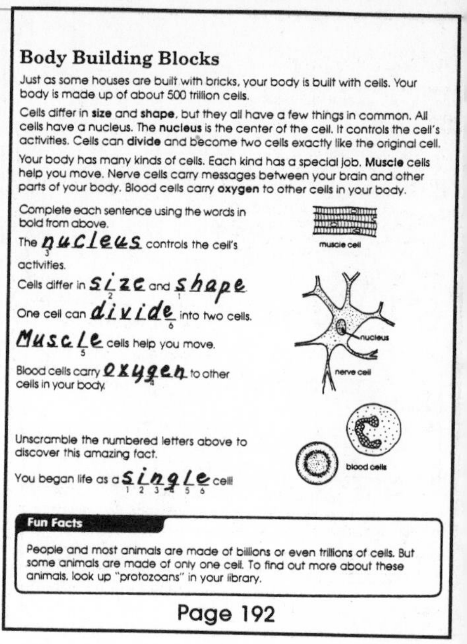

Body Building Blocks

Just as some houses are built with bricks, your body is built with cells. Your body is made up of about 500 trillion cells.

Cells differ in **size** and **shape**, but they all have a few things in common. All cells have a nucleus. The **nucleus** is the center of the cell. It controls the cell's activities. Cells can **divide** and become two cells exactly like the original cell.

Your body has many kinds of cells. Each kind has a special job. **Muscle** cells help you move. Nerve cells carry messages between your brain and other parts of your body. Blood cells carry **oxygen** to other cells in your body.

Complete each sentence using the words in bold from above.

The nucleus controls the cell's activities.

Cells differ in size and shape.

One cell can divide into two cells.

Muscle cells help you move.

Blood cells carry oxygen to other cells in your body.

Unscramble the numbered letters above to discover this amazing fact.

You began life as a single cell.

muscle cell — nucleus — nerve cell — blood cells

Fun Facts

People and most animals are made of billions or even trillions of cells. But some animals are made of only one cell. To find out more about these animals, look up "protozoans" in your library.

Page 192

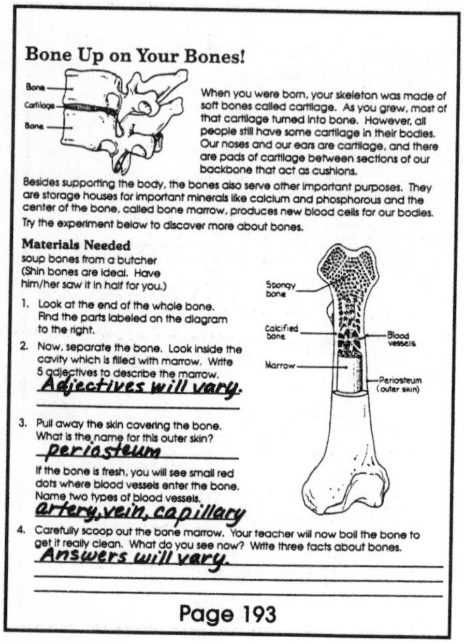

Bone Up on Your Bones!

Bone — Cartilage — Bone

When you were born, your skeleton was made of soft bones called cartilage. As you grew, most of that cartilage turned into bone. However, all people still have some cartilage in their bodies. Our noses and our ears are cartilage, and there are pads of cartilage between sections of our backbone that act as cushions.

Besides supporting the body, the bones also serve other important purposes. They are storage houses for important minerals like calcium and phosphorous and the center of the bone, called bone marrow, produces new blood cells for our bodies. Try the experiment below to discover more about bones.

Materials Needed

soup bones from a butcher (Shin bones are ideal. Have him/her saw it in half for you.)

1. Look at the end of the whole bone. Find the parts labeled on the diagram to the right.
2. Now, separate the bone. Look inside the cavity which is filled with marrow. Write 5 adjectives to describe the marrow. Adjectives will vary.
3. Pull away the skin covering the bone. What is the name for this outer skin? periosteum

   If the bone is fresh, you will see small red dots where blood vessels enter the bone. Name two types of blood vessels. artery, vein, capillary
4. Carefully scoop out the bone marrow. Your teacher will now boil the bone to get it really clean. What do you see now? Write three facts about bones. Answers will vary.

Spongy bone — Calcified bone — Marrow — Blood vessels — Periosteum (outer skin)

Page 193

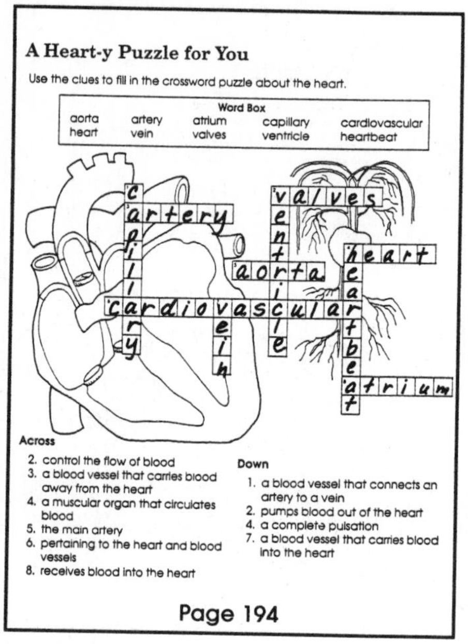

A Heart-y Puzzle for You

Use the clues to fill in the crossword puzzle about the heart.

Word Box				
aorta	artery	atrium	capillary	cardiovascular
heart	vein	valves	ventricle	heartbeat

Across

2. control the flow of blood
3. a blood vessel that carries blood away from the heart
4. a muscular organ that circulates blood
5. the main artery
6. pertaining to the heart and blood vessels
8. receives blood into the heart

Down

1. a blood vessel that connects an artery to a vein
2. pumps blood out of the heart
4. a complete pulsation
7. a blood vessel that carries blood into the heart

Page 194

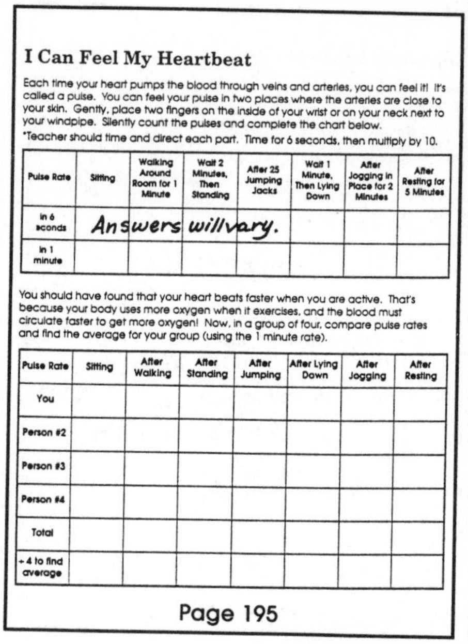

I Can Feel My Heartbeat

Each time your heart pumps the blood through veins and arteries, you can feel it! It's called a pulse. You can feel your pulse in two places where the arteries are close to your skin. Gently, place two fingers on the inside of your wrist or on your neck next to your windpipe. Silently count the pulses and complete the chart below.

*Teacher should time and direct each part. Time for 6 seconds, then multiply by 10.

Pulse Rate	Sitting	Walking Around Room for 1 Minute	Wait 2 Minutes, Then Standing	After 25 Jumping Jacks	Wait 1 Minute, Then Lying Down	After Jogging in Place for 2 Minutes	After Resting for 5 Minutes
in 6 seconds	Answers will vary.						
in 1 minute							

You should have found that your heart beats faster when you are active. That's because your body uses more oxygen when it exercises, and the blood must circulate faster to get more oxygen! Now, in a group of four, compare pulse rates and find the average for your group (using the 1 minute rate).

Pulse Rate	Sitting	After Walking	After Standing	After Jumping	After Lying Down	After Jogging	After Resting
You							
Person #2							
Person #3							
Person #4							
Total							
÷ 4 to find average							

Page 195

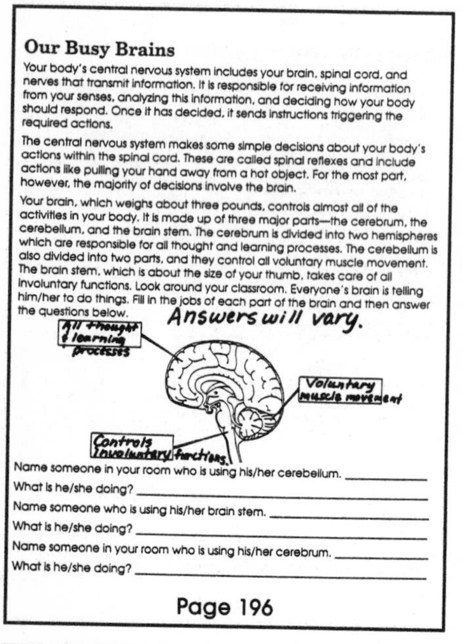

Our Busy Brains

Your body's central nervous system includes your brain, spinal cord, and nerves that transmit information. It is responsible for receiving information from your senses, analyzing this information, and deciding how your body should respond. Once it has decided, it sends instructions triggering the required actions.

The central nervous system makes some simple decisions about your body's actions within the spinal cord. These are called spinal reflexes and include actions like pulling your hand away from a hot object. For the most part, however, the majority of decisions involve the brain.

Your brain, which weighs about three pounds, controls almost all of the activities in your body. It is made up of three major parts—the cerebrum, the cerebellum, and the brain stem. The cerebrum is divided into two hemispheres which are responsible for all thought and learning processes. The cerebellum is also divided into two parts, and they control all voluntary muscle movement. The brain stem, which is about the size of your thumb, takes care of all involuntary functions. Look around your classroom. Everyone's brain is telling him/her to do things. Fill in the jobs of each part of the brain and then answer the questions below. Answers will vary.

All thought & learning processes — Voluntary muscle movement — Controls involuntary functions

Name someone in your room who is using his/her cerebellum. ______

What is he/she doing? ______

Name someone who is using his/her brain stem. ______

What is he/she doing? ______

Name someone in your room who is using his/her cerebrum. ______

What is he/she doing? ______

Page 196

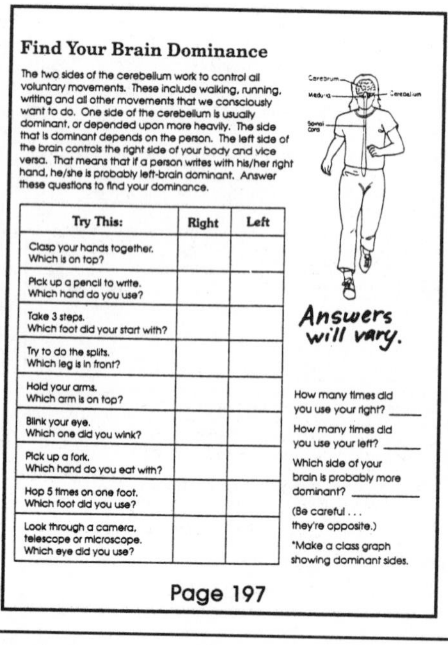

Find Your Brain Dominance

The two sides of the cerebellum work to control all voluntary movements. These include walking, running, writing and all other movements that we consciously want to do. One side of the cerebellum is usually dominant, or depended upon more heavily. The side that is dominant depends on the person. The left side of the brain controls the right side of your body and vice versa. That means that if a person writes with his/her right hand, he/she is probably left-brain dominant. Answer these questions to find your dominance.

Cerebrum — Medulla — Cerebellum — Spinal Cord

Try This:	Right	Left
Clasp your hands together. Which is on top?		
Pick up a pencil to write. Which hand do you use?		
Take 3 steps. Which foot did your start with?		
Try to do the splits. Which leg is in front?		
Hold your arms. Which arm is on top?		
Blink your eye. Which one did you wink?		
Pick up a fork. Which hand do you eat with?		
Hop 5 times on one foot. Which foot did you use?		
Look through a camera, telescope or microscope. Which eye did you use?		

Answers will vary.

How many times did you use your right? ______

How many times did you use your left? ______

Which side of your brain is probably more dominant? ______

(Be careful . . . they're opposite.)

*Make a class graph showing dominant sides.

Page 197

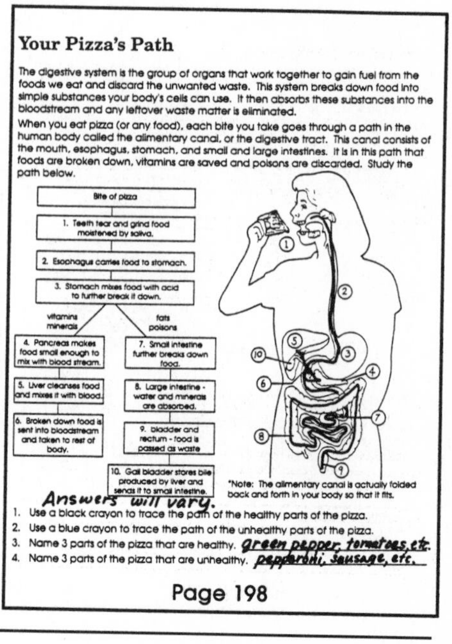

Your Pizza's Path

The digestive system is the group of organs that work together to gain fuel from the foods we eat and discard the unwanted waste. This system breaks down food into simple substances your body's cells can use. It then absorbs these substances into the bloodstream and any leftover waste matter is eliminated.

When you eat pizza (or any food), each bite you take goes through a path in the human body called the alimentary canal, or the digestive tract. This canal consists of the mouth, esophagus, stomach, and small and large intestines. It is in this path that foods are broken down, vitamins are saved and poisons are discarded. Study the path below.

Bite of pizza

1. Teeth tear and grind food moistened by saliva.
2. Esophagus carries food to stomach.
3. Stomach mixes food with acid to further break it down.

vitamins minerals — fats poisons

4. Pancreas makes food small enough to mix with blood stream.
5. Liver cleanses food and mixes it with blood.
6. Broken down food is sent into bloodstream and taken to rest of body.
7. Small intestine further breaks down food.
8. Large intestine - water and minerals are absorbed.
9. bladder and rectum - food is passed as waste
10. Gall bladder stores bile produced by liver and sends it to small intestine.

*Note: The alimentary canal is actually folded back and forth in your body so that it fits.

Answers will vary.

1. Use a black crayon to trace the path of the healthy parts of the pizza.
2. Use a blue crayon to trace the path of the unhealthy parts of the pizza.
3. Name 3 parts of the pizza that are healthy. green pepper, tomatoes, etc.
4. Name 3 parts of the pizza that are unhealthy. pepperoni, sausage, etc.

Page 198

Oh, Yes, I See Now!

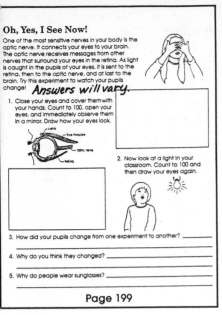

One of the most sensitive nerves in your body is the optic nerve. It connects your eyes to your brain. The optic nerve receives messages from other nerves that surround your eyes in the retina. As light is caught in the pupils of your eyes, it is sent to the retina, then to the optic nerve, and at last to the brain. Try this experiment to watch your pupils change! **Answers will vary.**

1. Close your eyes and cover them with your hands. Count to 100, open your eyes, and immediately observe them in a mirror. Draw how your eyes look.

2. Now look at a light in your classroom. Count to 100 and then draw your eyes again.

3. How did your pupils change from one experiment to another? _____

4. Why do you think they changed? _____

5. Why do people wear sunglasses? _____

Page 199

Energy Savers

Fats give you twice as much energy as protein or carbohydrates. Your body uses fats to save energy for future use. The fats we eat come from animals in the form of meat, eggs, milk, and much more. We also get fats from some plants like beans, peanuts, and corn. But not all plants give us fats in our diet.

Look at the pictures.
Circle the foods which are rich in fat.
Then list them on the chart.

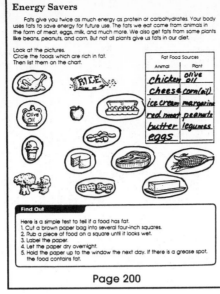

Fat Food Sources	
Animal	Plant
chicken	olive oil
cheese	corn (oil)
ice cream	margarine
red meat	peanuts
butter	legumes
eggs	

Find Out
Here is a simple test to tell if a food has fat.
1. Cut a brown paper bag into several four-inch squares.
2. Rub a piece of food on a square until it looks wet.
3. Label the paper.
4. Let the paper dry overnight.
5. Hold the paper up to the window the next day. If there is a grease spot, the food contains fat.

Page 200

You Are What You Eat!

Having a nutritious diet helps your body fight diseases. Write the foods from the Word Bank in their correct category(s). Use references if necessary.

Word Bank				
tomatoes	bread	eggs	milk	potatoes
oranges	sugar	fish	cereal	green beans
chicken	margarine	cheese	noodles	rice
butter	apples	red meat		

Carbohydrates
bread, green beans, sugar, potatoes, oranges, cereal, noodles, apples, tomatoes, rice

Proteins
red meat, cheese, fish, milk, eggs, bread, chicken, rice, noodles, cereal

Fats
butter, milk, margarine, cheese, eggs

Minerals
red meat, milk, chicken, fish, potatoes, oranges

Below is a list of the food groups. Write what you ate yesterday in each group. Did you get enough servings of each? **Answers will vary.**

Milk Group (3 servings a day) _____

Fruit & Vegetable Group (1 serving a day) _____

Grain Group (4 servings a day) _____

Meat-Egg-Nut-Bean Group (2 servings a day) _____

Page 201

What's in a Label?

Labels give us all kinds of information about the foods we eat. The ingredients of a food are listed in a special order. The ingredient with the largest amount is listed first, the one with the next largest amount is listed second, and so on.

Complete the "Breakfast Table Label Survey" using information from the label on this page.

Nutrition Information Per Serving
Serving Size: 1 OZ. (About 1¼ Cups) (28.35 g)
Servings Per Package: 14

	1 OZ (28.35 g) Cereal	with ½ Cup Vitamins A&D Milk
Calories	110	190
Protein	1 g	5 g
Carbohydrate	25 g	31 g
Fat	1 g	5 g
Sodium	195 mg	255 mg

Breakfast Table Label Survey

1. What does R.D.A. mean? **Recommended Daily Allowances**
2. Calories per serving with milk **190**
3. Calories per serving without milk **110**
4. Calories per ½ cup serving of milk **80**
5. Protein per serving with milk **8%**
6. Protein per serving without milk **2%**
7. Protein in ½ cup serving of milk **6%**
8. Percentage U.S. R.D.A. of Vitamin C **less than 2%**
9. First ingredient **Corn flour**
10. Is sugar a listed ingredient? **yes**

   If yes, in what place is it listed? **second**
11. Were any vitamins added? **yes**
12. What preservative was added? **BHA**

Find Out: What food product has this ingredient label? "Carbonated water, sugar, corn sweetener, natural flavorings, caramel color, phosphoric acid, caffeine."

Page 202

I'm Tired

Do you feel tired after raking the lawn? You feel tired then because work takes a lot of energy. **Energy** is the ability to do work.

There are many forms of energy. Food contains **chemical energy**. Your television uses **electrical energy**. The furnace in your house gives you **heat energy**. The moving parts of your bicycle have another form of energy called **mechanical energy**. Anything that moves has mechanical energy.

Energy can be changed from one form to another. Your radio changes electrical energy into sound energy. Your parents' car may change chemical energy into heat energy and the heat energy into mechanical energy.

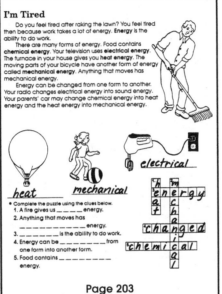

heat   mechanical   electrical

• Complete the puzzle using the clues below.
1. A fire gives us _ _ _ _ energy.
2. Anything that moves has _ _ _ _ _ _ _ _ _ _ energy.
3. _ _ _ _ _ _ is the ability to do work.
4. Energy can be _ _ _ _ _ _ _ from one form into another form.
5. Food contains _ _ _ _ _ _ _ _ energy.

Page 203

Energy in Motion

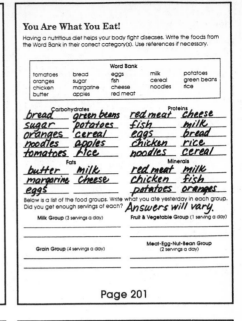

"Mom, how can I knock down more pins?" Matt asked. "You are bowling straight enough, Matt. Try rolling the ball faster, or try using a heavier ball," his mom replied.

The bowling ball is doing work by knocking over the pins. The ball has kinetic energy. **Kinetic energy** is the energy of motion.

If the ball had more kinetic energy, it could do more work and knock down more pins. If you increase the mass of the ball or its speed, you would increase its kinetic energy.

Just before Matt rolled the ball, he was standing still and not moving. Matt's body had stored energy that would turn into kinetic energy once he started swinging the ball. This stored energy is called **potential energy**.

• Write P next to the pictures that show potential energy and K next to the pictures that show kinetic energy.

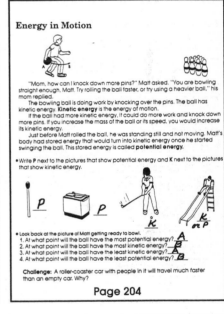

• Look back at the picture of Matt getting ready to bowl.
1. At what point will the ball have the most potential energy? **A**
2. At what point will the ball have the most kinetic energy? **B**
3. At what point will the ball have the least kinetic energy? **A**
4. At what point will the ball have the least potential energy? **B**

Challenge: A roller-coaster car with people in it will travel much faster than an empty car. Why?

Page 204

Around and Around

A doorknob is a simple machine you use every day. It is a **wheel and axle machine**. The wheel is connected to the axle. The axle is a center post. When the wheel moves, the axle does too.

Opening a door by turning the axle with your fingers is very hard. But by turning the doorknob, which is the "wheel," you use much less force. The doorknob turns the axle for you. The doorknob makes it easy because it is much bigger than the axle. You turn the doorknob a greater distance, but with much less force.

Sometimes the "wheel" of a wheel and axle machine doesn't look like a wheel. But look at the path the doorknob, a wheel, makes when it is turned. The path makes a circle, just like a wheel.

• Color just the wheels of the wheel and axle machines below.

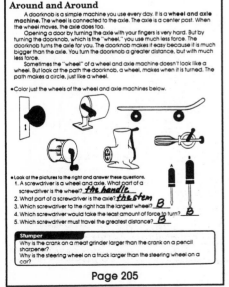

• Look at the pictures to the right and answer these questions.
1. A screwdriver is a wheel and axle. What part of a screwdriver is the wheel? **the handle**
2. What part of a screwdriver is the axle? **the stem**
3. Which screwdriver to the right has the largest wheel? **B**
4. Which screwdriver would take the least amount of force to turn? **B**
5. Which screwdriver must travel the greatest distance? **B**

Stumper
Why is the crank on a meat grinder larger than the crank on a pencil sharpener?
Why is the steering wheel on a truck larger than the steering wheel on a car?

Page 205

Levers

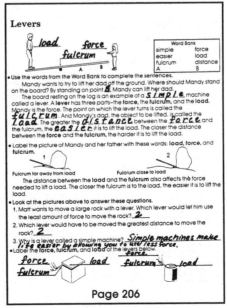

load   force   fulcrum

Word Bank	
simple	force
easier	load
fulcrum	distance
A	B

• Use the words from the Word Bank to complete the sentences.
Mandy wants to try to lift her dad off the ground. Where should Mandy stand on the board? By standing on point **B** Mandy can lift her dad.

The board resting on the log is an example of a **simple** machine called a lever. A **lever** has three parts–the **force**, the **fulcrum**, and the **load**. Mandy is the force. The point on which the lever turns is called the **fulcrum**. And Mandy's dad, the object to be lifted, is called the **load**. The greater the **distance** between the **force** and the fulcrum, the **easier** it is to lift the load. The closer the distance between the **force** and the **fulcrum**, the harder it is to lift the load.

• Label the picture of Mandy and her father with these words: **load, force,** and **fulcrum.**

Fulcrum far away from load   Fulcrum close to load

The distance between the **load** and the **fulcrum** also affects the force needed to lift a load. The closer the fulcrum is to the load, the easier it is to lift the load.

• Look at the pictures above to answer these questions.
1. Matt wants to move a large rock with a lever. Which lever would let him use the least amount of force to move the rock? **2**
2. Which lever would have to be moved the greatest distance to move the rock? **2**
3. Why is a lever called a simple machine? **Simple machines make it're easier by allowing you to use less force.**
• Label the force, fulcrum, and load of the levers below.

force   load   fulcrum   load
fulcrum   force

Page 206

Dancing Parsley

Results may vary.

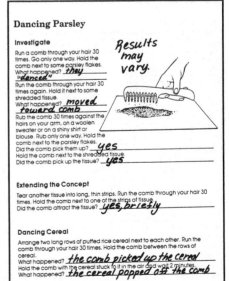

Investigate
Run a comb through your hair 30 times. Go only one way. Hold the comb next to some parsley flakes. What happened? **they "danced"**

Run the comb through your hair 30 times again. Hold it next to some shredded tissue. What happened? **moved toward comb**

Rub the comb against the hairs on your arm, on a woolen sweater or on a shiny shirt or blouse. Rub only one way. Hold the comb next to the parsley flakes. Did the comb pick them up? **yes**
Hold the comb next to the shredded tissue. Did the comb pick up the tissue? **yes**

Extending the Concept
Tear another tissue into long, thin strips. Run the comb through your hair 30 times. Hold the comb next to one of the strips of tissue. Did the comb attract the tissue? **yes, briefly**

Dancing Cereal
Arrange two long rows of puffed rice cereal next to each other. Run the comb through your hair 30 times. Hold the comb between the rows of cereal. What happened? **the comb picked up the cereal**
Hold the comb with the cereal stuck to it in the air and wait 2 minutes. What happened? **the cereal popped off the comb**

Page 207

0-7682-3794-7 Skills & Practice Gr. 4

Charge It!

Have you ever scuffed your feet as you walked across the carpet and then brought your finger close to someone's nose? Zap!! Did the person jump? The spark you made was **static electricity.**

Static electricity is made when objects gain or lose tiny bits of electricity called **electrical charges.** The charges are either positive or negative.

Objects that have electrical charges act like magnets, attracting or repelling each other. If two objects have **like charges** (the same kind of charges), they will repel each other. If two objects have **unlike charges** (different charges), the objects will attract each other.

Find out more about static electricity by unscrambling the word(s) in each sentence.

1. Flashes of (ghtlining) *lightning* in the sky are caused by static electricity in the clouds.
2. Electrical charges are either (ospivite) *positive* or (givnatee) *negative*
3. Small units of electricity are called (srgache) *charges*.
4. Two objects with unlike charges will (arcttat) *attract* each other.
5. Sometimes electric charges jump between objects with (unkile) *unlike* charges. This is what happens when lightning flashes in the sky.

Look at the pictures below to see how static electricity affects objects.
1. Name the two objects that are interacting in each picture.
2. Tell whether the two objects have **like charges** or **unlike charges.**

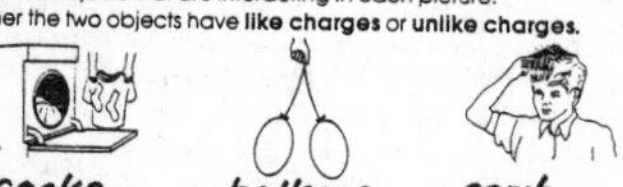

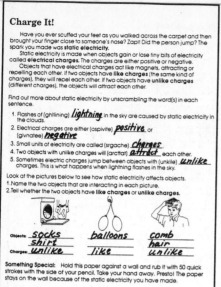

Objects:	*socks shirt*	*balloons*	*comb hair*
Charges:	*unlike*	*like*	*unlike*

Something Special: Hold this paper against a wall and rub it with 50 quick strokes with the side of your pencil. Take your hand away. Presto! The paper stays on the wall because of the static electricity you have made.

Page 208

Power Paths

A **circuit** is a path along which electricity travels. It travels in a loop around the circuit. In the circuit pictured below, the electricity travels through the wire, battery, switch, and bulb. The electricity must have a source. What is the source in this circuit? You're right if you said the battery.

If the wire in the circuit were cut, there would be a **gap**. The electricity wouldn't be able to flow across the gap. Then the bulb would not light. This is an example of an **open circuit**. If there were no gaps, the bulb would light. This is an example of a **closed circuit**.

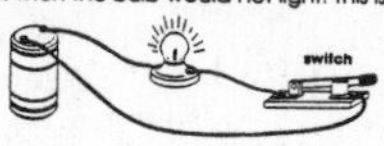

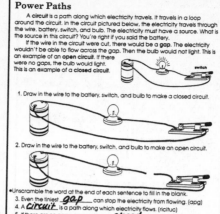

1. Draw in the wire to the battery, switch, and bulb to make a closed circuit.

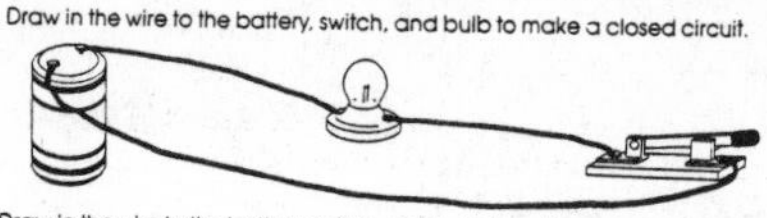

2. Draw in the wire to the battery, switch, and bulb to make an open circuit.

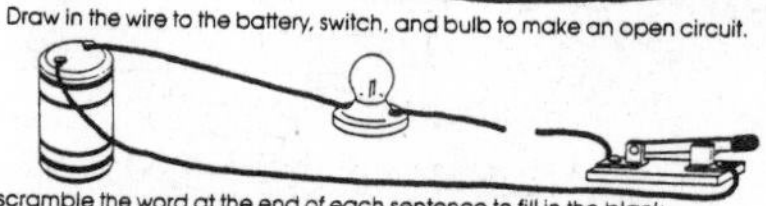

• Unscramble the word at the end of each sentence to fill in the blank.

3. Even the tiniest *gap* can stop the electricity from flowing. (apg)
4. A *circuit* is a path along which electricity flows. (ricituc)
5. If there are no gaps, or openings, a *closed* circuit is formed. (sodelc)
6. A battery is a source of *electricity* in some circuits. (treleciytci)

Fun Fact

If all of the circuits in a small personal computer were made out of wire and metal switches, the computer would fill the average classroom. Today these circuits are found in tiny chips called microchips.

Page 209

Fill the Gap

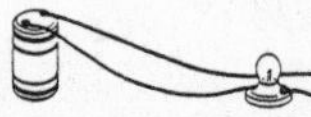

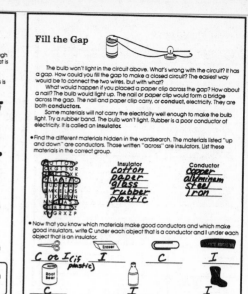

The bulb won't light in the circuit above. What's wrong with the circuit? It has a gap. How could you fill the gap to make a closed circuit? The easiest way would be to connect the two wires, but with what?

What would happen if you placed a paper clip across the gap? How about a nail? The bulb would light up. The nail or paper clip would form a bridge across the gap. The nail and paper clip carry, or **conduct**, electricity. They are both **conductors**.

Some materials will not carry the electricity well enough to make the bulb light. Try a rubber band. The bulb won't light. Rubber is a poor conductor of electricity. It is called an **insulator**.

• Find the different materials hidden in the wordsearch. The materials listed "up and down" are conductors. Those written "across" are insulators. List these materials in the correct group.

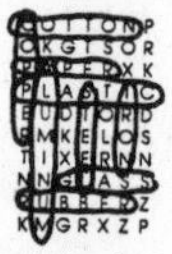

Insulator	Conductor
cotton	*copper*
paper	*aluminum*
glass	*steel*
rubber	*iron*
plastic	

• Now that you know which materials make good conductors and which make good insulators, write **C** under each object that is a conductor and **I** under each object that is an insulator.

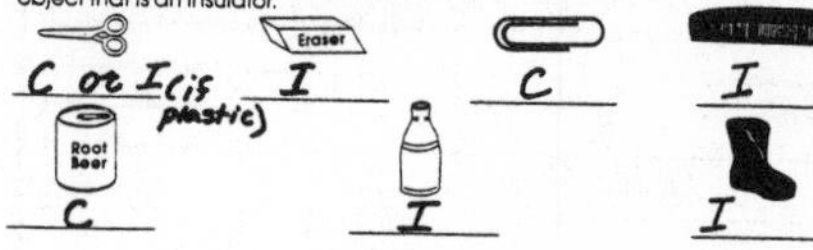

C or I (is plastic) *I* *C* *I*
C *I* *I*

Page 210

Series or Parallel?

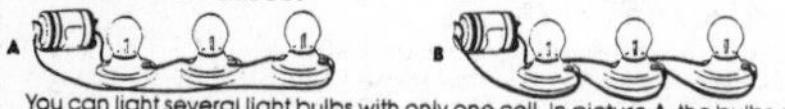

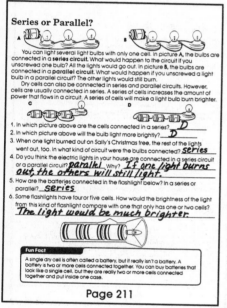

You can light several light bulbs with only one cell. In picture **A**, the bulbs are connected in a **series circuit.** What would happen to the circuit if you unscrewed one bulb? All the lights would go out. In picture **B**, the bulbs are connected in a **parallel circuit.** What would happen if you unscrewed a light bulb in a parallel circuit? The other lights would still burn.

Dry cells can also be connected in series and parallel circuits. However, cells are usually connected in series. A series of cells increases the amount of power that flows in a circuit. A series of cells will make a light bulb burn brighter.

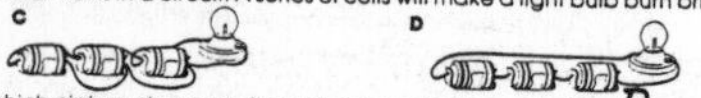

1. In which picture above are the cells connected in a series? *D*
2. In which picture above will the bulb light more brightly? *D*
3. When one light burned out on Sally's Christmas tree, the rest of the lights went out, too. In what kind of circuit were the bulbs connected? *series*
4. Do you think the electric lights in your house are connected in a series circuit or a parallel circuit? *parallel* Why? *If one light burns out, the others will still light.*
5. How are the batteries connected in the flashlight below? In a series or parallel? *series*
6. Some flashlights have four or five cells. How would the brightness of the light from this kind of flashlight compare with one that only has one or two cells? *The light would be much brighter.*

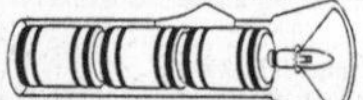

Fun Fact

A single dry cell is often called a battery, but it really isn't a battery. A battery is two or more cells connected together. You can buy batteries that look like a single cell, but they are really two or more cells connected together and put inside one case.

Page 211

Powered Up

Where does the electricity that is in your house come from? It all begins at a large **power plant.** The power plant has a large **turbine generator.** High pressure steam spins the turbines and the generator that is attached to the turbine shaft. As the generator spins, it produces hundreds of megawatts of electricity.

• Below is a picture of a power plant where electricity is generated. Label each part using the terms found in the Power Bank below.

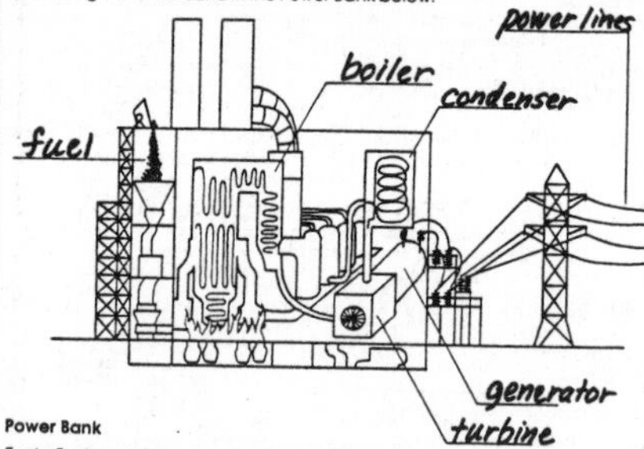

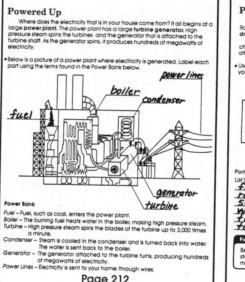

Power Bank

Fuel – Fuel, such as coal, enters the power plant.
Boiler – The burning fuel heats water in the boiler, making high pressure steam.
Turbine – High pressure steam spins the blades of the turbine up to 3,000 times a minute.
Condenser – Steam is cooled in the condenser and is turned back into water. The water is sent back to the boiler.
Generator – The generator attached to the turbine turns, producing hundreds of megawatts of electricity.
Power Lines – Electricity is sent to your home through wires.

Page 212

Portable Power

Steve and Lenny really enjoyed listening to the radio while they fished. Radios need electricity to work. Where did Steve's radio get its power? From a **dry cell battery,** of course. Dry cells are sources of portable power.

Most portable radios use dry cells. A dry cell makes electricity by changing chemical energy into electrical energy. Chemicals in the dry cell act on each other and make **electrons** flow. The flow of electrons is called **electricity.**

• Use the words from the Word Bank to label the parts of the dry cell. You can use your science book to help, but first try to figure out each part by yourself.

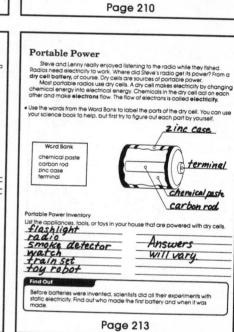

Word Bank
chemical paste
carbon rod
zinc case
terminal

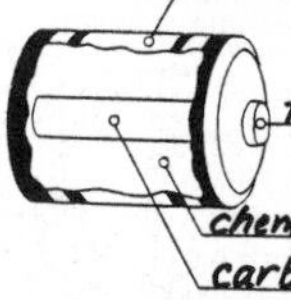

Portable Power Inventory

List the appliances, tools, or toys in your house that are powered with dry cells.

flashlight
radio
smoke detector
watch
train set
toy robot

Answers will vary.

Find Out

Before batteries were invented, scientists did all their experiments with static electricity. Find out who made the first battery and when it was made.

Page 213

Magnetic Attraction

Try to pick up each of these objects with your magnet. Circle the ones which it picks up. *If metal.*

scissors eraser ruler pencil crayon
paper clip thumbtack toothpick pen

A magnet will only pick up an object made of *metal*.

Investigate

List all the objects you can find which your magnet picks up or is attracted to.

1. *Answers will*
2. *vary.*
3.
4.
5.
6.
7.
8.
9.
10.

Is the magnet attracted to any non-metal object? *no*

Extending the Concept

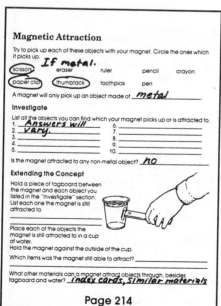

Hold a piece of tagboard between the magnet and each object you listed in the "Investigate" section. List each one the magnet is still attracted to.

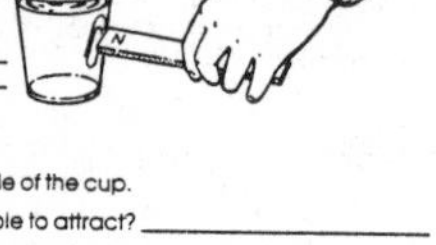

Place each of the objects the magnet is still attracted to in a cup of water.

Hold the magnet against the outside of the cup.

Which items was the magnet still able to attract?

What other materials can a magnet attract objects through, besides tagboard and water? *index cards, similar materials*

Page 214

Working with Electromagnets

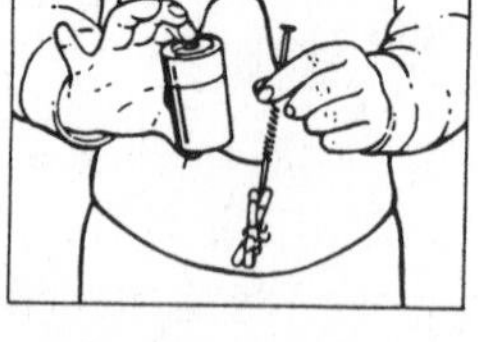

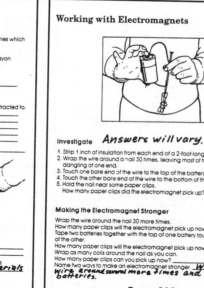

Investigate *Answers will vary.*

1. Strip 1 inch of insulation from each end of a 2-foot-long piece of thin wire.
2. Wrap the wire around a nail 30 times, leaving most of the extra wire dangling at one end.
3. Touch one bare end of the wire to the top of the battery.
4. Touch the other bare end of the wire to the bottom of the battery.
5. Hold the nail near some paper clips.

How many paper clips did the electromagnet pick up?

Making the Electromagnet Stronger

Wrap the wire around the nail 30 more times.
How many paper clips will the electromagnet pick up now?
Tape two batteries together with the top of one battery touching the bottom of the other.
How many paper clips will the electromagnet pick up now?
Wrap as many coils around the nail as you can.
How many paper clips can you pick up now?
Name two ways to make an electromagnet stronger. *Wrap the wire around several more times and use extra batteries.*

Page 215

Weight and Gravity

Making a Scale

1. Use a hole punch or scissors to punch two holes at the top of a clear plastic cup. Make the holes exactly opposite each other.
2. Cut a piece of fish line 6 inches long. Tie one end to one hole and the other end to the opposite hole.
3. Tape a ruler to the top of your desk so one end hangs over the edge. Then tape a piece of tagboard to the side of the desk.
4. Wrap a rubber band around the fish line and loop it inside itself. Now hang the rubber band from the ruler. The cup should hang in front of the tagboard.

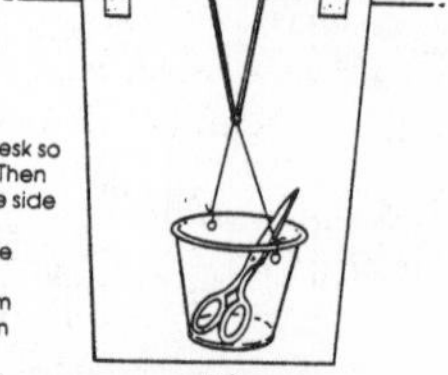

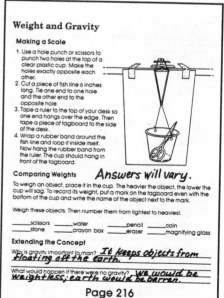

Comparing Weights *Answers will vary.*

To weigh an object, place it in the cup. The heavier the object, the lower the cup will sag. To record its weight, put a mark on the tagboard even with the bottom of the cup and write the name of the object next to the mark.

Weigh these objects. Then number them from lightest to heaviest.

____scissors ____water ____pencil ____coin
____stone ____crayon box ____eraser ____magnifying glass

Extending the Concept

Why is gravity important to man? *It keeps objects from floating off the earth.*

What would happen if there were no gravity? *We would be weightless; earth would be barren.*

Page 216

Great Gravity Changes

The gravity that pulls on the moon is ⅙ as strong as the pull on Earth. This means that you could jump up and stay in the air six times longer than you can now! Work with a partner to find the measurements below. Record them and then multiply them by six to see how different life would be on the moon.

Activity/Object	Measurement on Earth	Measurement on Moon (Earth x 6)
Distance you can jump with running start (in inches)	Answers will	
Height you can jump (in inches)	vary.	
Distance you can throw a ball (in feet)		
Distance you can kick a ball (in feet)		
Number of books you can pick up at one time		

The gravitational pull on the sun is 28 times stronger than that on Earth. This means that everything would weigh 28 times more if it were on the sun. Below are several objects. Use a scale to find their approximate weight on the sun by multiplying them by 28. To find their weight on the moon, divide their Earth-weight by 6 because the gravitational pull of the moon is that much less than Earth's.

Object	Weight on Earth	Weight on Sun (Earth x 28)	Weight on Moon (Earth ÷ 6)
your math book			
your book bag (full)			
yourself			
(object of your choice)			
(object of your choice)			
(object of your choice)			

Page 217

A Lo-o-o-ong Trip

What is the longest trip you have ever taken? Was it 100 km? 500 km? Maybe it was more than 1,000 km. You probably didn't know it, but last year you traveled 1 billion kilometers.

The Earth travels in a path around the sun called its **orbit**. Earth's orbit is almost 1 billion kilometers. It takes 1 year, or 365 days, for the Earth to orbit or **revolve** around the sun.

Look at the picture of Earth's orbit. It is not a perfect circle. It is a special shape called an **ellipse**.

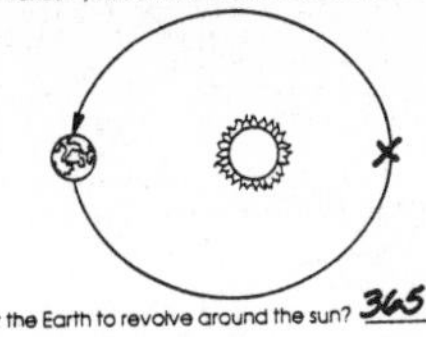

1. How long does it take for the Earth to revolve around the sun? 365 days
2. How many times has the Earth revolved around the sun since you were born? Answers will vary.
3. How many kilometers has the Earth traveled in orbit since you were born? Age x 1 billion km
4. Put an "X" on Earth's orbit to show where it will be in six months.

Experiment

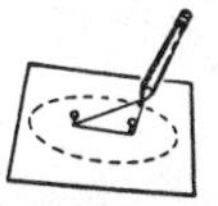

You can draw an ellipse. Place two straight pins about 8 cm apart in a piece of cardboard. Tie the ends of a 25 cm piece of string to the pins. Place your pencil inside the string. Keeping the string tight, draw an ellipse.

Make four different ellipses by changing the length of the string and the distance between the pins. How do the ellipses change?

Fun Fact

Hold on tight. The Earth travels at a speed of 100,000 km per hour in its orbital path around the sun.

Page 218

"Lift-off"

"3-2-1, lift-off!" With a mighty roar, the Saturn V **rocket** leaves the **launch pad**.

Riding high on top of the Saturn V in the **Command Module** are the three Apollo astronauts. Below their Command Module is a Lunar Landing Module that will land two of the astronauts on the moon's surface.

Below this, the Saturn V has three parts, or **stages**. It takes a lot of power to escape the Earth's pull, called **gravity**. The spacecraft must reach a speed of almost 40,000 km per hour. The bottom, or first stage, is the largest. After each stage uses up its **fuel**, it drops off and the next stage starts. Each stage has its own fuel and **oxygen**. The fuels need oxygen in order to burn.

The astronauts are now on their 3-day journey to the moon.

Color each Saturn V section a different color. Color the key to match each section.

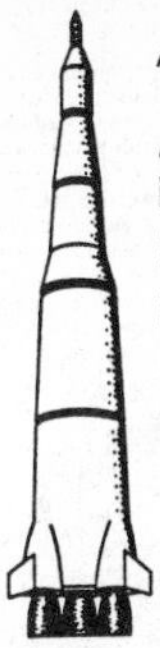

Apollo Mission Saturn V

Color Key

☐ Command Module
☐ Lunar Landing Module
☐ 3rd Stage
☐ 2nd Stage
☐ 1st Stage

Fill in the spaces with the words in bold from above. Then use the numbered letters to answer the question.

1. The Saturn V rocket has three main parts, or stages
2. Rocket engines burn fuel and oxygen
3. The Earth's pull is called gravity
4. "Lift-off." The Saturn V leaves the launch pad
5. The Apollo astronauts ride in the command module

What were the first words spoken from the surface of the moon on July 20, 1969?

"That's one small step for man, one giant leap for mankind."

Neil Armstrong, Apollo II Commander

Page 219

"Live Via Satellite"

"This program is brought to you live via satellite from halfway around the world." Satellites are very helpful in sending TV messages from one side of the world to the other. But this is only one of the special jobs that satellites can do.

Most satellites are placed into orbit around the Earth by riding on top of giant rockets. Only recently have some satellites been carried into orbit by a space shuttle. While orbiting the Earth, the giant doors of the shuttle are opened, and the satellite is pushed into orbit.

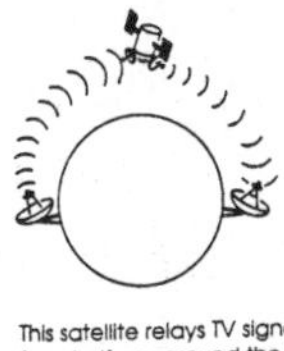

This satellite relays TV signals from halfway around the world.

Satellites send information about many things. Use the code to find the different kinds of messages and information satellites send.

television telephone

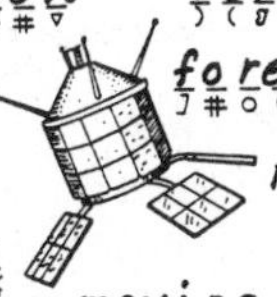

floods forest fires

weather pollution

pictures of space moving animals

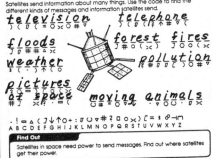

. ! ▭ △ ( ] ↓ ↑ ○ + : ʊ ◡ ▽ # ? □ ○ ><) [= ɜ 8 ⊣ ⊓
A B C D E F G H I J K L M N O P Q R S T U V W X Y Z

Find Out

Satellites in space need power to send messages. Find out where satellites get their power.

Page 220

Just Imagine . . .

Earth is a very special planet because it is the only planet known to have life. Only Earth has the necessities to support life—water, air, moderate temperatures, and suitable air pressure. Earth is about 92,960,000 miles from the sun and is 7,926 miles in diameter. Its highest recorded temperature was 136° F in Libya and the lowest was -127° F in Antarctica.

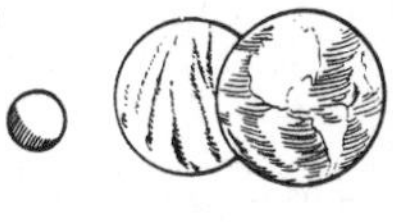

Venus is known as Earth's "twin" because the two planets are so similar in size. At about 67,230,000 miles from the sun, Venus is 7,521 miles in diameter. Venus is the brightest planet in the sky, as seen from Earth, and is brighter even than the stars. The temperature on the surface of this planet is about 850° F.

Mercury is the planet closest to the sun. It is about 35,980,000 miles from the sun and is 3,031 miles in diameter. The temperature on this planet ranges from -315° F to 648° F.

Pretend you were going to Venus or Mercury for spring break. Make a list of the things you would bring (you may have to invent them in order to survive) and draw a picture of the vehicle that would take you there. Write about your experiences on another sheet of paper.

Things I Need to Take

Answers will vary.

Vehicle

Page 221

The Large Planets

Jupiter is the largest planet in the solar system. The diameter at its equator is about 88,836 miles. It was named after the king of the Roman gods and is the fifth closest planet to the sun at about 483,600,000 miles away. This large planet also spins faster than any other. It makes a complete rotation in about 9 hours and 55 minutes.

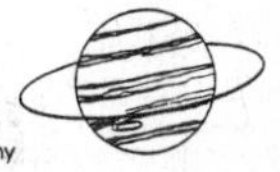

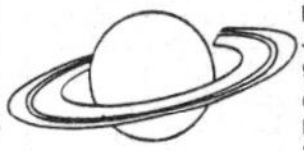

The surface of Jupiter cannot be seen from Earth because of the layers of dense clouds surrounding it. Jupiter has no solid surface but is made of liquid and gases that are held together by gravity.

One characteristic unique to Jupiter is the Great Red Spot that is about 25,000 miles long and about 20,000 miles wide. Astronomers believe the spot to be a swirling, hurricane-like mass of gas.

Saturn, the second largest planet, is well known for its seven thin, flat rings encircling it. Its diameter is about 74,898 miles at the equator. It was named for the Roman god of agriculture. Saturn is the sixth planet closest to the sun and is about 888,200,000 miles away from it. Like Jupiter, Saturn travels around the sun in an oval-shaped (elliptical) orbit, and it takes the planet about 10 hours and 39 minutes to make one rotation.

Scientists believe Saturn is a giant ball of gas that also has no solid surface. Like Jupiter, they believe it too may have an inner core of rocky material.

Fill in the chart below to compare Jupiter and Saturn. Make two of your own categories.

Categories	Jupiter	Saturn
1. diameter	88,836 miles	74,898 miles
2. origin of name	King of the Roman gods	Roman god of agriculture
3. distance from sun	483,600,000 miles	888,200,000 miles
4. rotations	one in 9hrs 55mins	10 hrs. 39mins
5. surface	liquid and gases	giant ball of gas
6. unique characteristics	Great Red Spot	7 thin, flat rings
7.		
8.		

Page 222

The Twin Planets

1. Uranus and Neptune are similar in size, rotation time, and temperature. Sometimes they are called twin planets. Uranus is about 1,786,400,000 miles from the sun. Neptune is about 2,798,800,000 miles from the sun. What is the difference between these two distances? 1,012,400,000
2. Neptune can complete a rotation in 18 to 20 hours. Uranus can make one in 16 to 28 hours. What is the average time it takes Neptune to complete a rotation? 19 hrs. Uranus? 22 hrs
3. Can you believe that it is about -353° F on Neptune, and about -357° F on Uranus? Brrr! that's cold! What is the temperature outside today in your town? Answers will vary.
   How much warmer is it in your town than on Neptune? ____ Uranus? ____

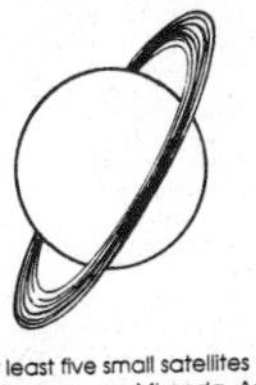

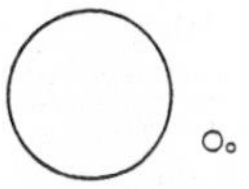

4. Uranus has at least five small satellites moving around it. Their names are Miranda, Ariel, Umbriel, Tatania and Oberon. They are 75, 217, 155, 310 and 280 miles in diameter respectively. What is the average diameter of Uranus' satellites? 207.4
5. Neptune was first seen in 1846 by Johanna G. Galle. Uranus was first discovered by Sir William Herschel in 1781. How many years ago was Neptune discovered? Will vary.
   Uranus? ____
   About how many years later was Uranus discovered than Neptune? 65
6. Both Uranus and Neptune have names taken from Greek and Roman mythology. Use an encyclopedia to find their names and their origins.
   Neptune was named for Neptune, the Roman sea god. Uranus was named for the first god of the sky.

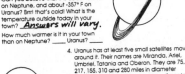

Page 223

The Moon's Many "Faces"

As the moon orbits Earth, we see different amounts of the moon's lighted part. The moon appears to change its shape. These different shapes are called phases.

1. Use words from the Word Bank below to label each of the moon's phases.
2. In the box next to each phase, draw the shape of the moon's lighted part that is visible from Earth.

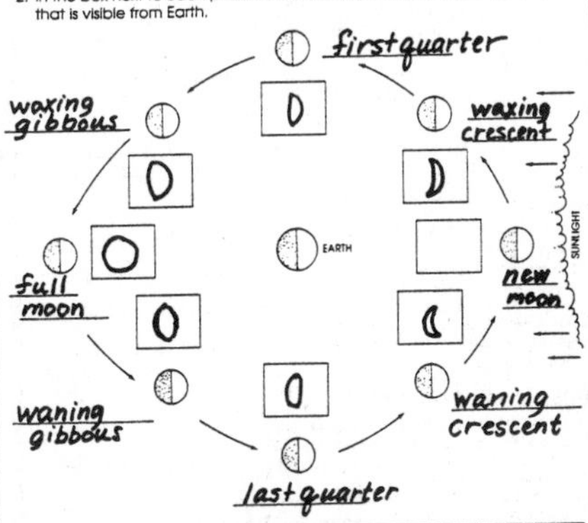

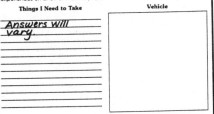

WORD BANK

new moon	waning crescent	waning gibbous	first quarter
waxing gibbous	waxing crescent	last quarter	full moon

Page 224

Comets—Dirty Snowballs

Use words from the Word Bank to label the diagram and complete the following description of a comet.

Word Bank									
Sun	nucleus	coma	dust tail	gas tail	rocks	dust	gases	orbits	tail

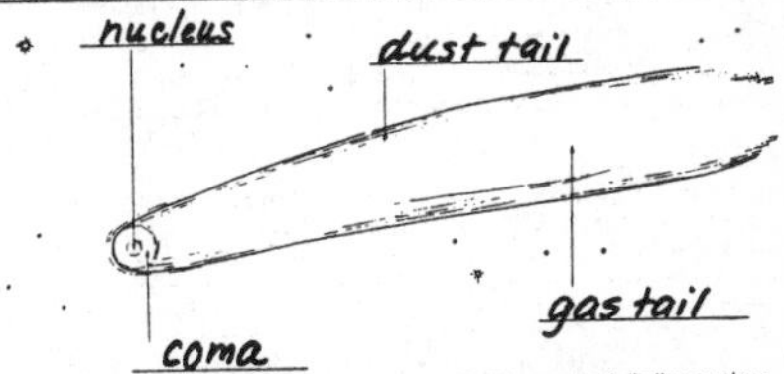

An astronomer once described a comet as a dirty snowball. Its tiny nucleus, measuring less than 10 miles in diameter, is made of dust and rocks cemented together by frozen gases. Comets travel in long, cigar-shaped orbits that take them from the outermost regions of the solar system toward the sun. As the comet approaches the sun, the ice changes into a huge, hazy gas cloud called a coma. The solar wind pushes on the coma to form a long, thin tail that is millions of miles long and glows in the sunlight.

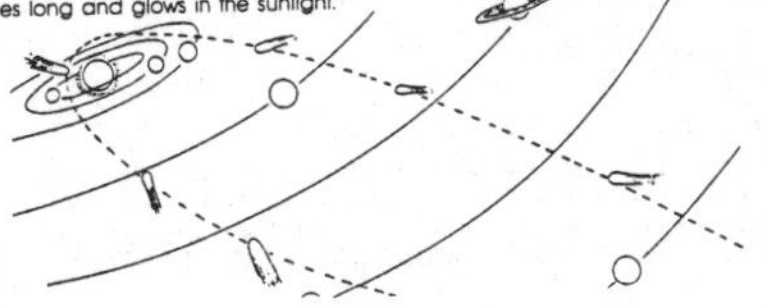

Page 225

0-7682-3794-7 Skills & Practice Gr. 4

Star Search

On a clear dark night, you can look up in the sky and see about 2,000 stars without the help of a telescope. But unless you know which stars form constellations, all you will be seeing are stars. Carefully poke holes in the *Constellation Patterns* sheet using a sharp pencil. Then tonight, when it is dark, hold a flashlight behind the paper to make the constellations appear.

Below are star charts to further help you recognize the constellations. To use the charts, turn them until the present month is at the bottom. Depending on your latitude and the time of night, you should be able to see most of the constellations in the middle and upper part of the chart. **Answers will vary.**

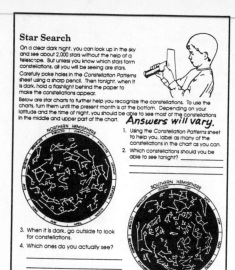

1. Using the *Constellation Patterns* sheet to help you, label as many of the constellations in the chart as you can.
2. Which constellations should you be able to see tonight? _____

3. When it is dark, go outside to look for constellations.
4. Which ones do you actually see?
_____
_____

5. On the back of this paper, draw the night sky you see. Put a small X in the center. This should be the point in the sky directly above you.

Page 226

Constellation Patterns

See pages 226 (*Star Search*) and 228 (*Class Constellation*) for directions.

The Big Dipper	Cygnus the Swan	Hercules the Hero
Orion the Hunter	Leo the Lion	Sagittarius the Archer
Draco the Dragon	Scorpius the Scorpion	Pegasus the Winged Horse
Taurus the Bull	Gemini the Twins	Virgo the Virgin
Canis Major the Dog	Andromeda the Chained Lady	Cassiopeia the Queen

Page 227

Class Constellation

Thousands of years ago, people believed that there were many gods in the heavens above. They believed that the gods made the sun rise, the weather change, the oceans move, and even made people fall in love! The people made up stories (myths) about the gods and their great powers. Many of the characters in these myths can be found in the shapes of the stars. These "star pictures" are called constellations. There are 88 constellations in the sky, but not all of them can be seen from one location. Some are only visible in the Southern Hemisphere while others can only be seen in the Northern Hemisphere. Some are also best observed only in certain seasons. Look at some of the constellations on page 227, *Constellation Patterns*. Pick one or create your own and write a myth about it. Follow the directions below.

1. On a lined sheet of 8 ½" x 11" paper, write your name, the title of your myth, and the myth.
2. Glue the paper on the right side of a 12" x 18" piece of black construction paper.
3. In the box below, design your constellation using star stickers.
4. Connect the stars to show your constellation and add details.
5. Cut out and glue your constellation on the left side of the construction paper.

Myths and constellations will vary.

Page 228

Read My Mind

Pretend you have been contacted by NASA to serve as an astronaut on a secret mission. Because of its secrecy, NASA cannot give you your destination. Instead, you must figure it out using the clues below. After each clue, check the possible answers. Your destination will soon be evident.

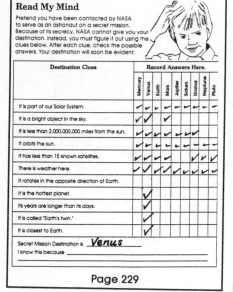

Destination Clues	Mercury	Venus	Earth	Mars	Jupiter	Saturn	Uranus	Neptune	Pluto
It is part of our Solar System.	✓	✓	✓	✓	✓	✓	✓	✓	✓
It is a bright object in the sky.	✓	✓		✓					
It is less than 2,000,000,000 miles from the sun.	✓	✓	✓	✓	✓	✓			
It orbits the sun.	✓	✓	✓	✓	✓	✓	✓	✓	✓
It has less than 15 known satellites.	✓	✓	✓	✓			✓	✓	✓
There is weather here.	✓	✓	✓	✓	✓	✓	✓	✓	
It rotates in the opposite direction of Earth.		✓							
It is the hottest planet.		✓							
Its years are longer than its days.		✓							
It is called "Earth's twin."		✓							
It is closest to Earth.		✓							

Secret Mission Destination is ___*Venus*___
I know this because _____

Page 229

Space Snowballs

Planets and moons are not the only objects in our solar system that travel in orbits. Comets also orbit the sun.

A **comet** is like a giant dirty snowball from 1 to 5 kilometers wide. It is made of frozen gases, dust, ice, and rocks.

As the comet gets closer to the sun, the frozen gases melt and evaporate. Dust particles float in the air. The dust forms a cloud called a **coma**. The "wind" from the sun blows the coma away from the sun. The blowing coma forms the comet's tail.

There are more than 800 known comets. Halley's Comet is the most famous. It appears about every 76 years. The year 1985 was the last scheduled appearance in this century. When will it appear next?

Find the words from the Word Bank in the wordsearch. When you are finished, write down the letters that are not circled. Start at the top of the puzzle and go from left to right.

Word Bank	
dust	orbit
Halley	tail
coma	ice
snowball	sky
melt	shining
solar system	

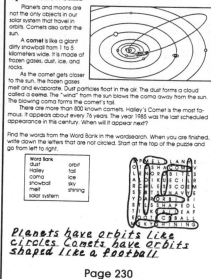

Planets have orbits like circles Comets have orbits shaped like a football

Page 230

Amazing Asteroids

Asteroids are extremely small planets that revolve around the sun. They are also called minor planets or planetoids. These small planets travel mainly between the orbits of Mars and Jupiter. There are thousands of them, and new ones are constantly being discovered.

Many asteroids are made of dark, rocky material, have irregular shapes and range widely in size. Ceres, the largest and first-known asteroid, is about 600 miles in diameter. Eros, another asteroid, is only about ⁹⁄₁₀ of a mile in diameter.

Because the asteroids' orbits change slowly due to the gravitational attraction of Jupiter and other large planets, asteroids sometimes collide with each other. Fragments from these collisions can cause other collisions. Any resulting small fragments that reach the surface of Earth are called meteorites.

Try your hand at personification. Personification means giving an inanimate (non-living) object human qualities. Draw a cartoon below of two asteroids colliding with each other. Give the asteroids names and write what they might say to each other.

Cartoons will vary.

1	2
3	4

Page 231

Star Light, Star Bright

Lay on your back. Gaze up into the night sky. Which star is the brightest? On a clear night you can see hundreds of stars—some are bright and others are dim.

Why are some stars brighter than others? Let's try to find out by looking at the picture on this page.

1. Look at the two streetlights in the picture. Which streetlight appears the brightest? *the closest*
   Why? *Because it is closest the light looks larger and brighter.*
2. Look at the bicycle and the truck. Which headlights appear the brightest? *the trucks*
   Why? *They are larger*
3. Some stars appear brighter than others for the same reasons as those stated above. What are the two reasons?
   a. *They are larger.*
   b. *They are closer to Earth.*

Color Me Hot

Stars differ not only in brightness but also in color. As a star gets hotter, its color changes.

Refer to the chart to color these stars.

Star Color Temperature	Color
20,000° C	Blue
10,500° C	White
5,500° C	Yellow
3,000° C	Red

blue	white	yellow	red
Spica 20,000°C	Sirius 10,500°C	Sun 5,500°C	Betelgeuse 3,000°C

Page 232

Pass the Profiles

How much do your classmates know about you? Give copies of this sheet to a few other students. Tell them to fill out the information about you. Fill in the blanks that they cannot complete.

Answers will vary.

Full name: _____
How my name was chosen: _____
Address: _____
Other places I have lived: _____
Parents' names: _____
Parents' occupations: _____
Brothers and sisters' names: _____
Pets (kinds and names/ present or past): _____
Kinds of clothes I like: _____
Fun things I like to do: _____
Favorite foods: _____
Favorite songs: _____
Favorite videos and TV shows: _____
Someday I'd like to be . . . _____
I'm really good at . . . _____
My favorite expression is . . . _____
States I've visited: _____
My hero or heroine: _____
Some of my closest friends: _____
What I like to do with friends: _____
Someday I'd like to try to . . . _____
My birthday is . . . _____
My favorite restaurant is . . . _____
Things at school I'm good at: _____

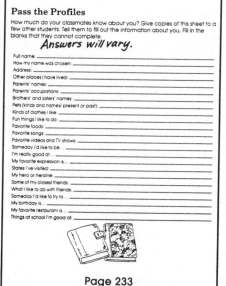

Page 233

List Bliss!

Making lists helped Harvey cope. Try some lists of your own. Each school day for one month, make a list from one of the titles given below. Keep your lists together in a special notebook or binder. You'll be surprised how well you get to know yourself in one month! Check off each list as you've used it. Make up new list titles if you run out. *Lists will vary.*

1. Big Events in My Life
2. Things That Worry Me
3. Projects I've Liked in School
4. Things I Like about Me
5. Bad Things That Have Happened to Me
6. Things I Like to Make
7. My Favorite Things To Do
8. Jobs I'd Like To Do When I'm Older
9. Gifts I Got That I Didn't Want
10. Sad Moments I Remember
11. Places I've Visited
12. Songs I've Always Liked
13. Important People in My Life
14. Months and Dates Special to Me
15. Foods I Just Don't Like
16. Games That I Play Well
17. Books I've Enjoyed
18. Things I Wish For
19. Animals I'd Like to Have
20. Things That Make Me Happy

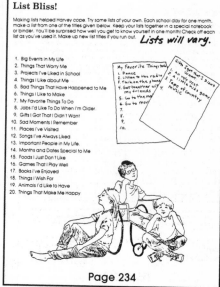

Page 234

It's a Shame!

With which children are you most likely to sympathize? Rate these characteristics from the greatest to the least with number 1 drawing the greatest amount of sympathy.

Answers will vary.

Characteristics	Rating
no father at home	___
teacher's pet	___
poor eating habits	___
overweight	___
cries easily	___
death in the family	___
rich	___
little self-control	___
poor health	___
ignorance	___
bad reputation	___
very thin	___
poor	___
adults have high expectations of	___
uncoordinated	___
little adult guidance	___

Should you be more sympathetic with some people?
Write a contract in which you make a promise you can keep.

Sympathy Contract

I, _____ (your name), do hereby promise to be more understanding and sympathetic to those who _____. I hope to show consideration by _____

_____
(signature)   (date)

Give this contract to a trustworthy friend or adult who will help you be more caring.

Page 235

Emily Post Says . . .

Emily Post's book *Etiquette*, published in 1922, established behavior guidelines for all sorts of situations. She believed good manners were based on common sense and feelings for others. She kept up with the changing times and wrote ten editions of her book during her lifetime. People still refer to it when they have a question about proper behavior in social situations. Post also gave advice in a newspaper column and on the radio.

Write a column and give advice for the following situations.

1. Jane wants to have a party. There are ten boys and twelve girls in her class. She wants to invite everyone in the class except two of the girls. She also wants to ask her neighbors Emily and Bridgette, but her Mom says she can only have fifteen guests including herself. Who should she ask? How should they be asked? Answer these questions and give reasons for your answers.
   Answers will vary.

2. Tim is one of the lucky invited guests, but he knows his best friend, Tom, was not asked. What should Tim tell Tom when Tom asks him to spend the night on the night the party is being given? Why?

3. Michael was pleased because he got one of the leading roles in the school play, but Joe was very disappointed because he did not get a part. What can Michael do to not hurt Joe further and perhaps help ease his disappointment?

Personality Plus Write a question you have concerning the polite thing to do in a certain situation. Put your question in a box with the questions of your classmates. The questions may be discussed in a small group or as a class.

Page 236

Me and My Shadow

Addie can hardly wait to have a friend. Tilla becomes that friend even though the two are different in many ways. In the chart below, compare yourself to one of your friends. You may wish to compare such things as hair color, eye color, family size, hobbies, favorite songs, and so on.

Myself	My friend	Alike or different?
Charts will vary.		

Page 237

Families

One of the things people all over the world have in common is the need to give and receive love. Love is given when you help, talk, listen and share with another person. Family members are often the ones who do these things to show love for each other.

1. List ways your family cares for you.
   Answers will vary.

2. What do you do to show your family you care? _____

3. Do you have specific chores to do at home daily or weekly? _____
   If yes, what are they? _____

4. Does your parents giving you chores to do show that they care about you? _____
   Why or why not? _____

5. List things a family member has taught you. _____

6. List things you have taught or could teach a member of your family. _____

7. List ways a family member helps you deal with a variety of emotions. _____

8. Members of a family often take on certain roles within the family structure. Which member of your family is usually the disciplinarian? _____

9. It is often said that a parent's love for a child is unconditional. What do you think unconditional love is? _____

10. On the back of this page, write two positive statements about each member of your family. Share these with the person on a day when he/she needs cheering up.

Page 238

It's All in the Family!   *Page will vary.*

Write the names of family members with whom you live. _____

Write the names of the members of your immediate family. _____

Write the names of your extended family on the correct lines in the diagram below. Fill in the names of your immediate family in the box.

great-grandparents

grandparents

mother _____ father
you and your sisters and/or brothers

aunts and uncles   aunts and uncles

cousins   cousins

Page 239

Uniforms

People on all continents wear some type of covering on their bodies. Originally, clothing was used merely to protect a person from climatic conditions. Today, the clothes a person wears tell something about his/her lifestyle or status in society. While many businesses allow people to wear their own clothes to work, others require workers to wear a uniform. Why do you think people in some jobs must wear uniforms? *To identify them as someone of a certain profession, to eliminate confusion, etc. Answers will vary.*

List several jobs that require workers to wear uniforms. *hospital staff, police officers, military, some factory workers, maids, airline workers*

Cut out pictures of people wearing uniforms from old catalogs, magazines, or newspapers. Glue the pictures on a piece of construction paper or posterboard to make a collage of uniforms.

Pretend that you are the president or CEO of your own company. Decide what your company will sell or produce. In the space below, show examples of the uniforms you would require the following workers to wear: 1) clerical; 2) executive officers; 3) assembly line; 4) maintenance.

Pictures will vary.

Should you, as president of the company, have to wear a uniform? _____
Why, or why not? _____

Page 240

Places to Live

Shelters provide a place in which people can live and keep their possessions. Early man took shelter in places provided by nature, such as a cave, hollow or hole in the ground. One of the first shelters devised by humans is still in use today — the tent. As man improved his tools and learned to farm, permanent homes were built. Today, people throughout the world live in a wide variety of shelter. List as many different types of shelter as you can think of on the lines below. *Answers will vary.*
Condominiums, apartments, tents, houses, cabins, hotel, mobile home, houseboat, treehouse

Make a list of the different types of shelter the students in your class occupy. Use the information to complete the graph below.

Types of Housing

House	
Apartment	
Mobile Home	
Condominium	
Houseboat	
Cabin	
Other	

1 2 3 4 5 6 7 8 9 10 11 12 13 14 15 16 17 18 19 20 21 22 23 24 25 26 27 28 29 30

Use the list of homes above to complete this next activity. Some types of shelter are better suited to hot climates. Others are designed for cold climates. Write the name of each type of home under the correct heading. Some may be suitable for both types of climate.

HOT CLIMATES	COLD CLIMATES	BOTH CLIMATES
tents *houseboat*		*apartments mobile homes houses, condos*

Page 241

Picture Your Life in Time

Though you have only lived a short time, many significant events have happened in your life and in the world around you. Record some of these events on this page and the next.

Write the year you were born on the first line under **YEAR**. Write every year thereafter up to the current year. Before each year, the age you were during that year is written in parentheses. On the first line after each year, use a blue pen to write something significant you did that year. (You may have to ask a family member to help you with this.) On the second and third lines, use a red pen to write an important event that happened in the world during that year. (You may refer to an almanac or another reference.) Try to find a coin minted during each year of your life. Tape it in the circle to the right of the corresponding year.

Answers will vary.

AGE   YEAR
(0-1) _____ ◯
(1-2) _____ ◯
(2-3) _____ ◯
(3-4) _____ ◯

Page 242

Picture Your Life in Time (cont.)

Answers will vary.

(4-5) _____ ◯
(5-6) _____ ◯
(6-7) _____ ◯
(7-8) _____ ◯
(8-9) _____ ◯
(9-10) _____ ◯
(10-11) _____ ◯

Page 243

Customs and Traditions

1. List several special days or occasions you observe, such as holidays or birthdays.
   Answers will vary.

2. Pick one of the above that you celebrate with your family. Write a paragraph on the back of this page about what you and your family did to celebrate this special event the last time it occurred. Was the celebration the same as it always has been or were there some differences? Write what was the same and what was different.

   Same _____ Different _____

3. Write the name of a holiday that you observed in the past year. _____
   With whom did you observe it? _____
   What did you do to celebrate? _____

   Name three things associated with the holiday that are a traditional part of its celebration. _____

4. List some traditions you and/or your family have. _____

5. What custom do you carry on today that you would like to see changed or dropped? _____
   Why? _____

6. What custom do you intend to carry on when you have a family? _____

7. What customs observed by the general population do you no longer see a need for and why? _____

8. What would you like to see become a custom and why? _____

Page 244

U.S. Patriotic Holidays

| Memorial Day | Flag Day | Columbus Day | Presidents' Day |
| Bill of Rights Day | Labor Day | Veterans Day | Independence Day |

Use the list of holidays above to write each holiday in the appropriate blank in each sentence or paragraph below.

1. *Presidents' Day*, on the third Monday in February, honors two United States Presidents, George Washington and Abraham Lincoln, born in the month.

2. *Memorial Day* originally was celebrated May 30 and honored the war dead of the Civil War. It now is observed on the last Monday in May and is dedicated to the memory of all war dead. It is also known as Decoration Day because graves of service people are often decorated.

3. *Bill of Rights Day*, December 15, honors the date in 1791 on which Congress made them law. They are the first ten amendments of the U.S. Constitution.

4. *Columbus Day*, on the second Monday in October, commemorates the discovery of America by honoring the man who sailed near its shores in 1492.

5. *Flag Day* commemorates the act of Congress on June 14, 1777, that adopted America's stars and stripes as the country's official banner.

6. *Labor Day*, observed the first Monday in September in all states, honors America's backbone, its workers.

7. *Independence Day* on July 4, perhaps the most patriotic of all America's holidays, is celebrated in all states. It observes the adoption of the Declaration of Independence.

8. *Veterans Day* was once called Armistice Day. It began in 1926 to commemorate the signing of the armistice that ended World War I in 1918. In 1954, the holiday's name was changed to honor all men and women who have served their country in the armed services.

Select one of the above holidays. Then, on another sheet of paper, do one of the following:
- Design a stamp to honor its observance.
- Write a poem about the holiday.
- Draw a mural of a parade honoring that holiday.

Page 245

An Interview
Interviews will vary.

Person interviewed _____ Date of interview _____

1. Were you my age about 20, 30, 40, 50, 60, 70 or 80 years ago?
2. Where did you live when you were my age? _____
   If not here, how long ago did you move here? _____
3. How has the community changed? _____

4. What time did you get up when you were my age? _____
   What was your morning schedule? _____
5. What did you do after school? _____

6. What was your bedtime when you were my age? _____
7. What sort of things did you eat when you were my age? _____

8. What toys did you have? What were your favorites? _____

9. What chores did you have, if any? _____

10. Did you get an allowance? _____ How much was it? _____
    Did you earn any money when you were my age? _____ Doing what? _____
    _____ About what did you make in an hour? _____
11. How did you spend your money? _____

12. What was your most favorite thing to do during "free time"? _____
    _____ Tell about it. _____

13. What games did you play? _____

14. What did you study at school? _____

Page 246

An Interview (cont.)
Interviews will vary.

15. How did you get to school? _____
16. What was school like? What did you have that was the same? Different? (i.e. physical education, cafeteria, etc.) _____

17. Do you remember any rhymes or songs? _____
    Name one. _____
18. Did you ever get in trouble? _____ Tell about one time. _____

    What happened to you when you got in trouble? _____

19. What was the best thing that ever happened to you? _____

    What was the worst? _____

20. What were some of your family customs or traditions (i.e.: birthdays, holidays, games, jokes, etc)? _____

21. What are some of the biggest changes you have seen during your lifetime? _____

Write additional questions or information given that was not asked for below or on another sheet of paper.
_____

Page 247

Other Ways to Communicate

For those people who are hearing impaired, vocal communication is not possible. People who cannot hear use sign language. Even those who can hear but do not speak the same language often use a modified form of sign language. You will often see visitors in a foreign land trying to sign to be understood.

Using the alphabet to the right, learn to sign your name, your hometown and the name of your school. Try to have a conversation with a friend using only sign language.

Braille is a system of printing and writing for the blind. It was developed by Louis Braille, a blind Frenchman, in the 1820's. Braille uses raised dots on a page. A blind person reads dots by touching with his/her fingertips. The Braille symbols are large and thick, so they can be felt easily.

Using the alphabet below, write a paragraph about your favorite hobby. After you finish, answer these questions.

1. What is unusual about the symbols used for the numbers? *They match the symbols for the first ten letters of the alphabet.*

2. The American Printing House for the Blind in Louisville, KY, issues Braille textbooks for free. Why do you think the federal government pays for the publication of these books but does not pay for your textbooks? *Answers will vary.*

Sign Language Alphabet

Page 248

Got the Message?

Hieroglyphics is a form of writing used by the ancient Egyptians in which picture symbols represented ideas and sounds. It was the Rosetta Stone, a decree carved on stone with hieroglyphics, that gave the world the key to understanding this writing when it was found in 1799.

Use the hieroglyphics below to write a secret message to your friend. Have him/her decipher your message and write a response to it in hieroglyphics. Then, write your message and his/her response in English. Note: There were no vowels in hieroglyphics. Use capital vowels to represent a vowel sound. Note also that there were many variations of this type of writing.

Your message: *Messages will vary.*

Your friend's response: _____

Translation: _____

In Egyptian archaeology, an oval frame containing the name or symbol of a ruler written in hieroglyphics is called a cartouche. They are often seen on monuments as nameplates of ancient rulers. Use hieroglyphics to make cartouches for the names listed below. Write the name in English on the line under each oval. Again, use capital vowels for vowel sounds.

your first name   your best friend's name   your teacher's name

Page 249

Community Needs

Mother Teresa of Calcutta has dedicated her life to helping "the poorest of the poor." Mother Teresa and the members of her congregation, the Missionaries of Charity, aid poor, sick, and abandoned children and adults around the world.

Think about your community. List three of its social problems or needs.
Answers will vary.

Tell how you think each problem might be solved. Include what you might do to help in each solution.
_____

Follow the Leader Find out about an organization in your community that works to solve some of the problems you listed above. How do they work to solve the problem? Is there any way you can get involved? Share your information with the class.

Page 250

Community Workers

Ask several men and women in your community what their occupations are (e.g., doctor, farmer, maintenance worker). Record their answers, without names, on another sheet of paper.

When you have completed your survey, plot the two bar graphs below. If you have too many different responses, you may want to group them by categories, such as Medical, Sales, Government, and Service.

Answers will vary.

Men   Women

Kind of Work   Kind of Work

Answer these questions to draw some conclusions from your graphs.
What kinds of jobs do most of the community's population have? _____

Are most workers skilled or non-skilled? _____
Are there differences between jobs held by men and women? _____

What types of workers are needed in the community? _____

What else have you observed? _____

Page 251

What Kind of Community?

Read the definitions of three different types of communities below.

| Rural Community country; large amount of open space; rustic; agriculture predominates | Urban Community big city or town; often at least 50,000 people; crowded with buildings and people; business center | Suburban Community largely residential; often near a large city; often incorporated separately |

Read the sentences on this page and page 253. Underline only the sentences that describe your community. Then, answer this: In what kind of a community do you live? *Answers will vary.*

1. All that can be seen from a rooftop is land criss-crossed by dirt roads and fences.
2. Neighbors may sometimes wake neighbors if they mow their lawns too early in the morning.
3. There is a feeling of open space, and yet there are shopping malls, supermarkets, schools, etc.
4. The sounds of elevated trains and honking horns are heard almost twenty-four hours a day.
5. Many families who work in the city live here because it is quieter, and the commute to the city every day is not too long.
6. During the summer, neighborhood children set up lemonade stands, and families have picnics and barbecues in their back yards.
7. Homes are very close together. Many are stacked one on top of another in buildings called apartments.
8. Streets and sidewalks are crowded with workers going to and from work and shoppers looking in store front windows.
9. Many people work at farming.
10. Mailboxes are often very far from the houses.
11. Neighbors are often miles apart.
12. It is on the outskirts of a city.

Page 252

Published by Frank Schaffer Publications. Copyright protected.

0-7682-3794-7 *Skills & Practice Gr. 4*

What Kind of Community? (cont.)

13. Residents of the community seldom see one another, so a community gathering is a real social event.
14. Hotels provide a place for visitors to stay who come for meetings at the convention center.
15. The population is over 50,000.
16. The high school's students come from several outlying communities and must ride the bus because distances are great.
17. Nights are quiet except for the occasional sound of an animal.
18. Children play in parks rather than in back yards.
19. There is a feeling of country with the conveniences of a city.

Write two or three paragraphs about your community on the lines below. Ideas to include: its population, contact with neighbors, and availability of services.

Paragraphs will vary.

Page 253

Waste Materials

Next to each picture on this page and the next, write one or two sentences about what is pictured that is harmful for the environment. Tell why or how it is harmful. Then, write ways to correct the problem.

Answers will vary.

Plastic drink holders are thrown into lakes and fish and other wild life get caught and often die.

Solutions will also vary.

Garbage continues to increase so that landfills are over-flowing. More space is needed to hold the garbage.

Noise pollution (loud stereos, etc.) invade others space and result in stress and/or animosity.

Page 254

Waste Materials (cont.)

Forests are stripped trees are cut down and animals lose more habitat.

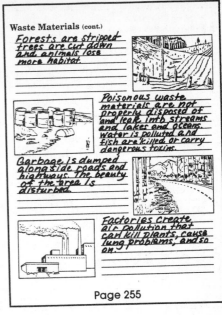

Poisonous waste materials are not properly disposed of and leak into streams and lakes and oceans. Water is polluted and fish are killed or carry dangerous toxins.

Garbage is dumped alongside roads and highways. The beauty of the area is disturbed.

Factories create air pollution that can kill plants, cause lung problems, and so on.

Page 255

Money Sources

Ask four people of different ages how they get their money. When they answer yes to a category, check the line in front of it. A person may answer yes to more than one category. Many of the categories may not apply and therefore will not be checked. If the category is "other," write the source.

Answers will vary.

Ask someone between 8-11 years old: How do you get your money?
___ allowance ___ gifts ___ full-time job ___ part-time job
___ interest ___ dividends ___ borrowed ___ pension
___ other:___

Ask someone between 15-18 years of age: How do you get your money?
___ allowance ___ gifts ___ full-time job ___ part-time job
___ interest ___ dividends ___ borrowed ___ pension
___ other:___

Ask someone between 35-45 years of age: How do you get your money?
___ allowance ___ gifts ___ full-time job ___ part-time job
___ interest ___ dividends ___ borrowed ___ pension
___ other:___

Ask someone over 65 years of age: How do you get your money?
___ allowance ___ gifts ___ full-time job ___ part-time job
___ interest ___ dividends ___ borrowed ___ pension
___ other:___

Compare findings with other class members. Tally where people's money comes from in the different age groups. If desired, make a bar graph for each group.

	8-11	15-18	35-45	65 or over
allowance				
gifts				
full-time job				
part-time job				
interest				
dividends				
borrowed				
pension				
other				

Page 256

Where Money Goes

Ask four people of different ages on what they spend their money. When they answer yes to a category, put a check mark on the line in front of it. A person may answer yes to more than one, or some of the categories may not apply and therefore will not get checked. If the category is "other," write how that money is spent.

Answers will vary.

Ask someone between 8-11 years old: On what do you spend your money?
___ rent/mortgage ___ clothing ___ food ___ utilities
___ transportation ___ vacation ___ taxes ___ savings
___ entertainment ___ insurance ___ dates ___ school
___ investments ___ presents ___ treats ___ supplies
___ medical/doctors ___ eating out ___ sports ___ hobbies
___ other:___

Ask someone between 15-18 years of age: On what do you spend your money?
___ rent/mortgage ___ clothing ___ food ___ utilities
___ transportation ___ vacation ___ taxes ___ savings
___ entertainment ___ insurance ___ dates ___ school
___ investments ___ presents ___ treats ___ supplies
___ medical/doctors ___ eating out ___ sports ___ hobbies
___ other:___

Ask someone between 35-45 years of age: On what do you spend your money?
___ rent/mortgage ___ clothing ___ food ___ utilities
___ transportation ___ vacation ___ taxes ___ savings
___ entertainment ___ insurance ___ dates ___ school
___ investments ___ presents ___ treats ___ supplies
___ medical/doctors ___ eating out ___ sports ___ hobbies
___ other:___

Ask someone over 65 years of age: On what do you spend your money?
___ rent/mortgage ___ clothing ___ food ___ utilities
___ transportation ___ vacation ___ taxes ___ savings
___ entertainment ___ insurance ___ dates ___ school
___ investments ___ presents ___ treats ___ supplies
___ medical/doctors ___ eating out ___ sports ___ hobbies
___ other:___

Compare class findings. On another page, tally how the age groups spend money.

Page 257

Needs for Your "Full Circle"

We all have physical, intellectual, emotional and social needs to live a happy and healthy life. Read each statement from the text and decide which need is being met. Write it on the blank.

1. Mattie finished the test before anyone else and turned her paper over on her desk. She reached inside for a book. *intellectual*

2. Matt had dinner started when Mattie got home—salad and leftover spaghetti. *physical*

3. Mr. Ashby had outdone himself this weekend. His homework assignments included math, spelling, a social studies essay, a book report, and vocabulary words. He was determined to make his fifth graders work. *intellectual*

4. "But Mattie, I do love you," said Mrs. Benson with tears in her eyes. *emotional*

5. When the telephone rang in the living room, Matt called to his sister. It was Toni. *social*

6. Humming softly, Mattie sat up, reached in her back pocket and un-wrapped her favorite photograph. She had decided to carry it with her today, and her father's strength seemed to reach out and hold her. *emotional*

7. Mattie started dinner—chili, rice, and salad. *physical*

8. "Oh, Toni, this sounds like a lot of maybes. I'm going to Stern's on Saturday and stopping in to see Mrs. Stamps. I wanted you to come with me." *social*

Page 258

Do You Speak My Language?

It is estimated that there are about 3,000 spoken languages in use today by the people of the world. This is not a precise figure because linguists disagree as to what constitutes a spoken language and what constitutes a dialect. A dialect is usually considered to be a variation within a language.

Language influences all aspects of a culture, including social behavior. If people can understand each other, human society tends to function smoothly. If people are not able to understand one another, society often grinds to a halt.

To the right are the most widely spoken languages in the world and the percent of the world's population that speaks each one. Use the list to complete the graph below.

Language	
German	1.5
French	1.5
Japanese	2.0
Portuguese	2.0
Arabic	2.0
Spanish	3.0
Russian	3.5
Hindi	4.5
English	6.0
Mandarin	20.0

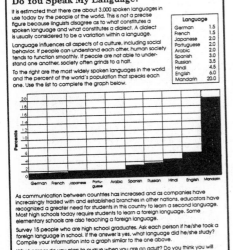

As communication between countries has increased and as companies have increasingly traded with and established branches in other nations, educators have recognized a greater need for students in this country to learn a second language. Most high schools today require students to learn a foreign language. Some elementary schools are also teaching a foreign language.

Survey 15 people who are high school graduates. Ask each person if he/she took a foreign language in school. If the answer is yes, what language did he/she study? Compile your information into a graph similar to the one above.

What career do you plan to pursue when you are an adult? Do you think you will need to know a foreign language for this career? Why, or why not?

Page 259

Where Is Wheat Grown?

Wheat grows best in dry temperate regions. The ideal climate includes a cool, moist spring, a warm dry harvest period and an annual rainfall of 9 to 30 inches. There are nine areas of the world which provide a wheat-growing climate.

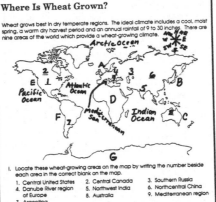

I. Locate these wheat-growing areas on the map by writing the number beside each area in the correct blank on the map.
   1. Central United States   2. Central Canada   3. Southern Russia
   4. Danube River region   5. Northwest India   6. Northcentral China
      of Europe   8. Australia   9. Mediterranean region
   7. Argentina

II. Label the seven continents on the map by placing the letter beside each in the correct location.
   A. Europe   B. Asia   C. Australia   D. Africa
   E. North America   F. South America   G. Antarctica

III. Label each of these bodies of water by writing the name in the correct location on the map: Mediterranean Sea, Pacific Ocean, Atlantic Ocean, Indian Ocean, Arctic Ocean.

IV. On the map, draw a compass rose which shows all cardinal and intermediate directions.

Page 260

The Beginning of Rome

The earliest Roman settlers were mostly shepherds. Their settlements, mainly in the Roman hills, eventually joined to form the city of Rome. It is believed Romulus and Remus were the legendary founders of Rome, but no one knows for sure if they really existed. However, their story exemplifies strength, a quality admired by ancient Romans. There are several versions of the Romulus and Remus legend. Read the one below. Follow the directions after the story.

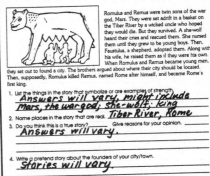

Romulus and Remus were twin sons of the war god, Mars. They were set adrift in a basket on the Tiber River by a wicked uncle who hoped they would die. But they survived. A she-wolf heard their cries and rescued them. She nursed them until they grew to be young boys. Then, Faustulus, a shepherd, adopted them. Along with his wife, he raised them as if they were his own. When Romulus and Remus became young men, they set out to found a city. The brothers argued about where their city should be located. Then, supposedly, Romulus killed Remus, named Rome after himself, and became Rome's first king.

1. List the things in the story that symbolize or are examples of strength. *Answers will vary, might include Mars, the war god; she-wolf; King*
2. Name places in the story that are real. *Tiber River, Rome*
3. Do you think this is a true story? Give reasons for your opinion. *Answers will vary.*

4. Write a pretend story about the founders of your city/town. *Stories will vary.*

Page 261

Two Great Statues

Two of the Seven Wonders of the World are statues. Both of them were in Greece: The Statue of Zeus at Olympia and The Colossus of Rhodes, near the harbor of the island in the Aegean Sea.

The statue of Zeus was made by the Greek sculptor Phidias around 435 B.C. It was dedicated to Zeus, the king of gods. It showed Zeus seated on his throne and was forty feet tall. Zeus' robe and ornaments were made out of gold and his flesh was made out of ivory. In his right hand, he held a figure of his messenger, Nike. In his left hand, he held a scepter with an eagle.

Imagine a conversation the statue of Zeus might have had with an athlete at an Olympic Game. Choose an athlete and write the conversation below.

Conversations will vary.

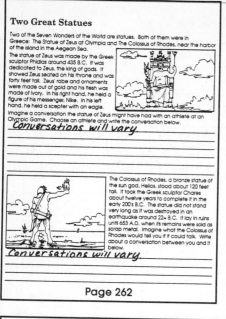

The Colossus of Rhodes, a bronze statue of the sun god, Helios, stood about 120 feet tall. It took the Greek sculptor Chares about twelve years to complete it in the early 200's B.C. The statue did not stand very long as it was destroyed in an earthquake around 224 B.C. It lay in ruins until 653 A.D. when its remains were sold as scrap metal. Imagine what the Colossus of Rhodes would tell you if it could talk. Write about a conversation between you and it below.

Conversations will vary.

Page 262

Comparing Civilizations

A Venn diagram is a great way to compare things. Use the one below to compare two leaders, gods, or civilizations of Ancient Greece or Rome. Write the names of the two things you are comparing on the lines provided. Fill in the unshared portion of each circle with characteristics common only to the subject. In the overlapped portion, write down characteristics the two subjects share. Then, write a story about your findings on the lines below.

subject name _____   subject name _____

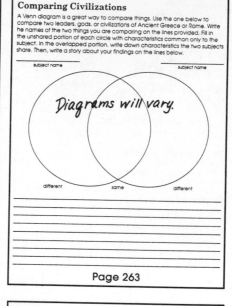

Diagrams will vary.

different   same   different

Page 263

How!

How many of these Indian names can you identify as state names? Write the name of the state by each Indian name. Then draw the matching symbol of that state on the United States map where it belongs.

★ Ute — *Utah*
◎ Emissourita — *Missouri*
△ Wishdonsing — *Wisconsin*
◁ Mishigamaw — *Michigan*
✕ Massaadchueset — *Massachusetts*
◆ Misisipi — *Mississippi*
◯ Oheo — *Ohio*
▽ Idaho — *Idaho*

◇ Dakotas — *North Dakota / South Dakota*
◁ Alashak — *Alaska*
△ Arizonac — *Arizona*
◯ Minista — *Minnesota*
≈ Illiniwek — *Illinois*
☆ Arkansaw — *Arkansas*
⊠ Alibamu — *Alabama*
✕ Tanasi — *Tennessee*

Page 264

Decision-Making Map

As the United States government began forcing the Sioux off their land, the Sioux fought to keep it. They took great care of the land and believed that it belonged to them. The white settlers believed that they were smarter and more deserving of the land. The battles between the two sides resulted in the death of many men, women, and children. Was there a better way they could have used to solve the problem? Find the best solution by working with a partner to complete the chart below.

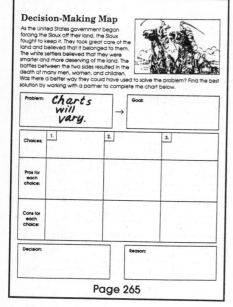

Problem: *Charts will vary.*	→	Goal:
Choices: 1.	2.	3.
Pros for each choice:		
Cons for each choice:		
Decision:		Reason:

Page 265

Welcome to the Union   ★ 39 & 40 could be reversed.

The fifty United States are listed below alphabetically. The date each one entered the Union is given after it. On the line to the left of each state, write the number that tells in what order the state joined the Union.

22	Alabama	Dec. 14, 1819		41	Montana	Nov. 8, 1889
49	Alaska	Jan. 3, 1959		37	Nebraska	Mar. 1, 1867
48	Arizona	Feb. 14, 1912		36	Nevada	Oct. 31, 1864
25	Arkansas	June 15, 1836		9	New Hampshire	June 21, 1788
31	California	Sept. 9, 1850		3	New Jersey	Dec. 18, 1787
38	Colorado	Aug. 1, 1876		47	New Mexico	Jan. 6, 1912
5	Connecticut	Jan. 9, 1788		11	New York	July 26, 1788
1	Delaware	Dec. 7, 1787		12	North Carolina	Nov. 21, 1789
27	Florida	Mar. 3, 1845		39	North Dakota	Nov. 2, 1889
4	Georgia	Jan. 2, 1788		17	Ohio	Mar. 1, 1803
50	Hawaii	Aug. 21, 1959		46	Oklahoma	Nov. 16, 1907
43	Idaho	July 3, 1890		33	Oregon	Feb. 14, 1859
21	Illinois	Dec. 3, 1818		2	Pennsylvania	Dec. 12, 1787
19	Indiana	Dec. 11, 1816		13	Rhode Island	May 29, 1790
29	Iowa	Dec. 28, 1846		8	South Carolina	May 23, 1788
34	Kansas	Jan. 29, 1861		40	South Dakota	Nov. 2, 1889
15	Kentucky	June 1, 1792		16	Tennessee	June 1, 1796
18	Louisiana	Apr. 30, 1812		28	Texas	Dec. 29, 1845
23	Maine	Mar. 15, 1820		45	Utah	Jan. 4, 1896
7	Maryland	Apr. 28, 1788		14	Vermont	Mar. 4, 1791
6	Massachusetts	Feb. 6, 1788		10	Virginia	June 25, 1788
26	Michigan	Jan. 26, 1837		42	Washington	Nov. 11, 1889
32	Minnesota	May 11, 1858		35	West Virginia	June 20, 1863
20	Mississippi	Dec. 10, 1817		30	Wisconsin	May 29, 1848
24	Missouri	Aug. 10, 1821		44	Wyoming	July 10, 1890

• Draw what comes next. △ ◇ ▽ ◈

Page 266

Figure Out Freedom

In 1861, 19 states declared themselves "Free States." People in these states were opposed to slavery. Unscramble each name to find out which states were considered "Free."

EIMNA — *Maine*
EWN SEERJY — *New Jersey*
TREOVMN — *Vermont*
WNE ROYK — *New York*
LFIINAAORC — *California*
WIOA — *Iowa*
EGROON — *Oregon*
NESNOMITA — *Minnesota*
IICHAGMN — *Michigan*
DAANIIN — *Indiana*
SILLIONI — *Illinois*
SASKNA — *Kansas*
CHASETSUTSMAS — *Massachusetts*
NOSSCIIWN — *Wisconsin*
HIOO — *Ohio*
CCUTICIENON — *Connecticut*
HODER SLANDI — *Rhode Island*
VANPIASENYNL — *Pennsylvania*
WNE SHEPRAMIH — *New Hampshire*

Page 267

Topical Titles

Pick the best title for each paragraph. Be certain to capitalize the first, last and all important words in each title. You will not use all choices listed.

the gregorian calendar
george washington's birthday
the french and indian war
schools in england
lieutenant colonel george washington
mount vernon

1. *Lieutenant Colonel George Washington*

In 1754, the Governor of Virginia made George Washington a lieutenant colonel and sent him and his troops into the Ohio River Valley to claim the land for Britain. Although the French and the Indian allies fought hard to keep this land, when the war ended in 1763, Britain was the victor.

2. *Mount Vernon*

Augustine Washington had three farms. When his son, Lawrence, returned home from school in England, Augustine asked him to manage one of the plantations for him. Lawrence later renamed his plantation "Mount Vernon" in honor of his hero, Admiral Edward Vernon, and both he and George loved living there.

3. *George Washington's Birthday*

George Washington was actually born on February 11. But in 1752, the British adopted a new calendar, and this changed his birthday to February 22. George, however, always considered February 11 to be his date of birth and preferred to celebrate his birthday on that date.

A NOW ... D The picture at the top of this page shows Mount Rushmore, a national memorial that has the largest figures of any statue in the entire world. If you were going to design such a memorial, which four faces would you choose to include? Then draw a picture of what your memorial would look like.

Page 268

Personality Profiles

All the fourth graders are doing reports on famous Americans. Jackie has gathered lots of information on John Adams. Now all she has to do is pull it together. Help her out by numbering the events below in chronological order.

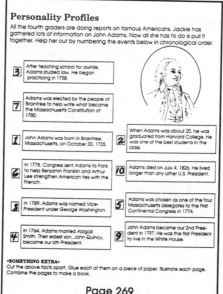

3 After teaching school for awhile, Adams studied law. He began practicing in 1758.

7 Adams was elected by the people of Braintree to help write what became the Massachusetts Constitution of 1780.

1 John Adams was born in Braintree, Massachusetts, on October 30, 1735.

2 When Adams was about 20, he was graduated from Harvard College. He was one of the best students in the class.

6 In 1778, Congress sent Adams to Paris to help Benjamin Franklin and Arthur Lee strengthen American ties with the French.

10 Adams died on July 4, 1826. He lived longer than any other U.S. President.

8 In 1789, Adams was named Vice-President under George Washington.

5 Adams was chosen as one of the four Massachusetts delegates to the First Continental Congress in 1774.

4 In 1764, Adams married Abigail Smith. Their eldest son, John Quincy, became his 6th President.

9 John Adams became our 2nd President in 1797. He was the first President to live in the White House.

•SOMETHING EXTRA•
Cut the above facts apart. Glue each of them on a piece of paper. Illustrate each page. Combine the pages to make a book.

Page 269

What a Trip!

Read the paragraphs below about Meriwether Lewis and William Clark's journey to the Pacific Coast. Then, plot their journey on the map below.

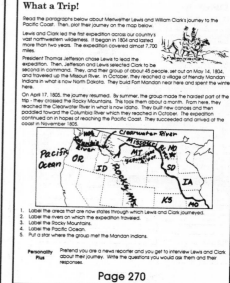

Lewis and Clark led the first expedition across our country's vast northwestern wilderness. It began in 1804 and lasted more than two years. The expedition covered almost 7,700 miles.

President Thomas Jefferson chose Lewis to lead the expedition. Then, Jefferson and Lewis selected Clark to be second in command. They, and their group of about 45 people, set out on May 14, 1804, and traveled up the Missouri River. In October, they reached a village of friendly Mandan Indians in what is now North Dakota. They build Fort Mandan near here and spent the winter here.

On April 17, 1805, the journey resumed. By summer, the group made the hardest part of the trip - they crossed the Rocky Mountains. This took them about a month. From here, they reached the Clearwater River in what is now Idaho. They built new canoes and then paddled toward the Columbia River which they reached in October. The expedition continued on in hopes of reaching the Pacific Coast. They succeeded and arrived at the coast in November 1805.

1. Label the areas that are now states through which Lewis and Clark journeyed.
2. Label the rivers on which the expedition traveled.
3. Label the Rocky Mountains.
4. Label the Pacific Ocean.
5. Put a star where the group met the Mandan Indians.

Personality Plus Pretend you are a news reporter and you get to interview Lewis and Clark about their journey. Write the questions you would ask them and their responses.

Page 270

Down with Slavery

ewrite the sentences in the paragraph below in the correct order.

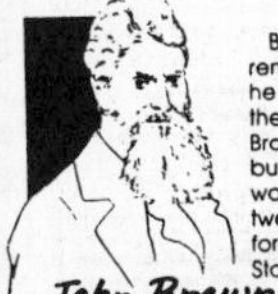

John Brown

Brown was tried for and convicted of treason. He rented a farm near Harper's Ferry, Virginia from which he led an armed group of eighteen men. They seized the town and the United States Arsenal there. John Brown spent much of his adult life opposing slavery, but he is best remembered for his final act in 1859. He was hanged in Charleston, South Carolina. Within twenty-four hours the raid was over. Brown's forces were either killed or captured by the United States Marines led by Robert E. Lee.

John Brown spent much of his adult life opposing slavery, but he is best remembered for his final act in 1859. He rented a farm near Harper's Ferry Virginia, from which he led an armed group of eighteen men. They seized the town and the United States Arsenal there. Within twenty-four hours the raid was over. Brown's forces were either killed or captured by the United States Marines led by Robert E. Lee. Brown was tried for and convicted of treason. He was hanged in Charlestown, South Carolina.

- Nat Turner is another man who was important in American history. What did he do?

Nat Turner led the most famous slave revolt in United States' history in 1831.

Page 271

Nuts About Nuts!

A famous American was responsible for the recognition of the peanut as a crop. This brilliant and creative person was George Washington Carver. Carver's research lead to the development of over 300 products made with peanuts!

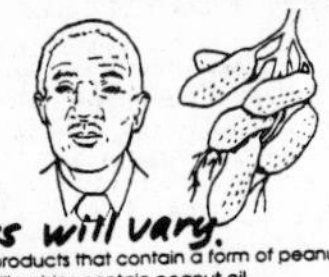

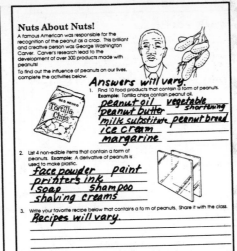

To find out the influence of peanuts on our lives, complete the activities below.

Answers will vary.

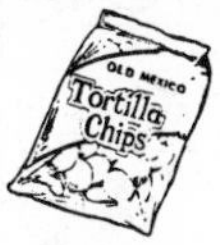

OLD MEXICO
Tortilla Chips

1. Find 10 food products that contain a form of peanuts.
   Example: Tortilla chips contain peanut oil.
   peanut oil | *vegetable shortening*
   peanut butter
   milk substitute | *peanut bread*
   ice cream
   margarine

2. List 4 non-edible items that contain a form of peanuts. **Example:** A derivative of peanuts is used to make plastic.
   face powder | *paint*
   printers ink
   soap | *shampoo*
   shaving creams

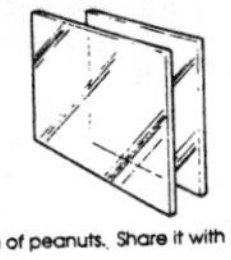

3. Write your favorite recipe below that contains a fo m of peanuts. Share it with the class.
   Recipes will vary.

Personality Plus Find another person who you think contributed something important to our society. Write what he/she contributed and why you think it was important. Share it with your class.

Page 272

A Point of View

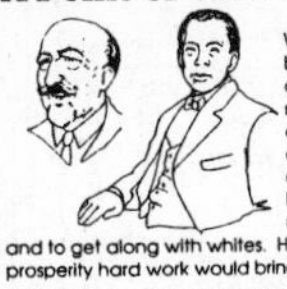

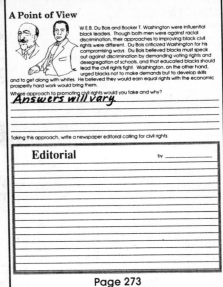

W.E.B. Du Bois and Booker T. Washington were influential black leaders. Though both men were against racial discrimination, their approaches to improving black civil rights were different. Du Bois criticized Washington for his compromising ways. Du Bois believed blacks must speak out against discrimination by demanding voting rights and desegregation of schools, and that educated blacks should lead the civil rights fight. Washington, on the other hand, urged blacks not to make demands but to develop skills and to get along with whites. He believed they would earn equal rights with the economic prosperity hard work would bring them.

Whose approach to promoting civil rights would you take and why?

Answers will vary.

Taking this approach, write a newspaper editorial calling for civil rights.

Editorial by ____________

Page 273

One Great Inventor

Rewrite the set of sentences in the correct order.
Use the proper paragraph form.

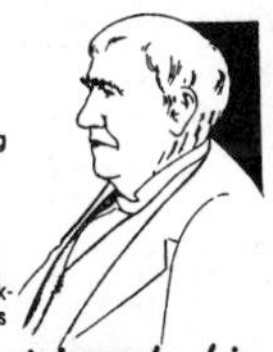

Thomas Edison

1. By the time he was twelve years old, he was selling newspapers to finance his experiments.
2. He sold the firm his patents and used the money from this sale to set himself up as a freelance inventor.
3. Thomas Edison was taught at home by his mother.
4. At the age of twenty-one, while working for a stock-ticker firm, Thomas patented various improvements on the stock ticker.

Thomas Edison was taught at home by his mother. By the time he was twelve years old, he was selling newspapers to finance his experiments. At the age of twenty-one, while working for a stock-ticker firm, Thomas patented various improvements on the stock ticker. He sold the firm his patents and used the money from this sale to set himself up as a freelance inventor.

- What other inventions are Thomas Edison noted for?

Edison invented the electric light and the phonograph and improved many other inventions.

- Name one other inventor. Tell what he invented and when.

Answers will vary.

- Draw what comes next.

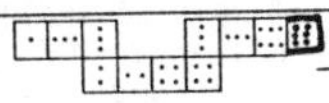

Page 274

Inventions in Time

Use the time line to help decide whether each statement is true or false.

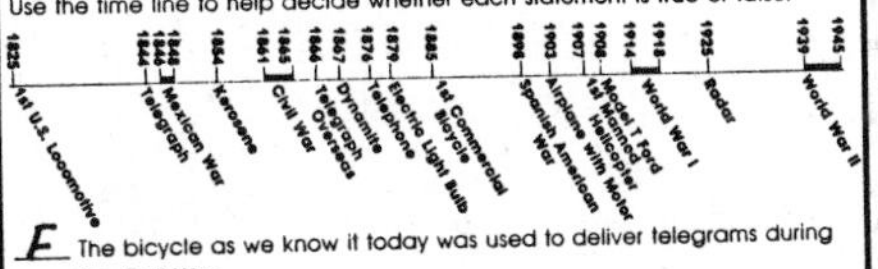

1825 1st U.S. Locomotive
1844 Telegraph
1846 1848 Mexican War
1854 Kerosene
1861 1865 Civil War
1866 Telegraph Overseas
1867 Dynamite
1876 Telephone
1879 Electric Light Bulb
1885 1st Commercial Bicycle
1898 Spanish American War
1903 Airplane with Motor
1907 1st Manned Helicopter
1908 Model T Ford
1914 1918 World War I
1925 Radar
1939 1945 World War II

F The bicycle as we know it today was used to deliver telegrams during the Civil War.
F The helicopter was used during the Spanish American War.
T People in New York could talk to people in California on the telephone during the first World War.
F Dynamite could have been used during the Civil War by the Union Army.
T Kerosene was used before the Civil War.
F In 1865 Andrew Johnson was notified by telephone that Lincoln had been shot.
F The Spanish American War was the second major war that the United States was involved in since 1840.
T When Lincoln studied law in the 1830's he sat by the fire at night in order to have light to read by.
T Planes were used in combat during World War II.
F Trains were not used until 1878.
F America fought in five wars in ninety-nine of the years shown above.
T A telegram could be sent between New York and England after the Civil War.
T World War I ended four years after it began.
T The airplane was invented before the helicopter.
T The Model T was used before World War I.

- Draw what comes next.

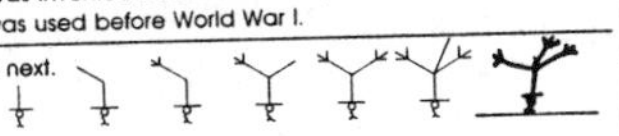

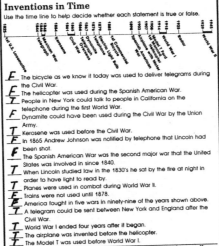

Page 275

Visiting Chile

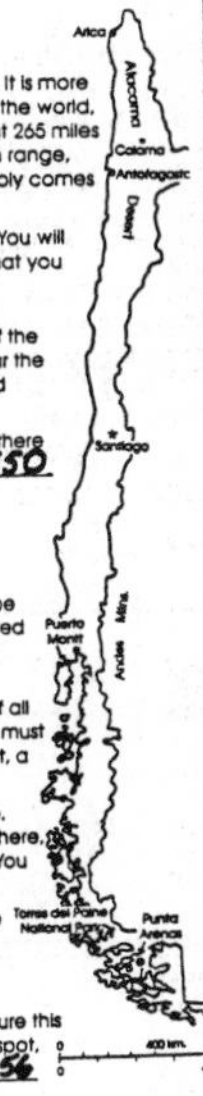

Arica
Atacama
Calama
Antofagasta
Desert
Santiago
Puerto Montt
Andes Mtns.
Torres del Paine National Park
Punta Arenas
400 km.

Chile is a long, narrow country on the west coast of South America. It is more than 10 times as long as it is wide. In fact, it is the longest country in the world, stretching 2,650 miles from north to south, yet it averages only about 265 miles from east to west at its widest section. The world's longest mountain range, the Andes Mountains, forms Chile's eastern border. Its name probably comes from the Indian word *chilli* meaning "where the land ends."

Pretend that you are on a trip from the top to the bottom of Chile. You will need your ruler and the map scale shown to figure the distances that you travel.

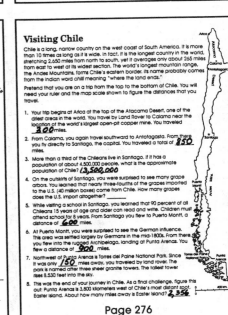

1. Your trip begins at Arica at the top of the Atacama Desert, one of the driest areas in the world. You travel by Land Rover to Calama near the location of the world's largest open-pit copper mine. You traveled *300* miles.
2. From Calama, you again travel southward to Antofagasta. From there you fly directly to Santiago, the capital. You traveled a total of *850* miles.
3. More than a third of the Chileans live in Santiago. If it has a population of about 4,500,000 people, what is the approximate population of Chile? *13,500,000*
4. On the outskirts of Santiago, you were surprised to see many grape arbors. You learned that nearly three-fourths of the grapes imported to the U.S. (40 million boxes) come from Chile. How many grapes does the U.S. import altogether? ______
5. While visiting a school in Santiago, you learned that 90 percent of all Chileans 15 years of age and older can read and write. Children must attend school for 8 years. From Santiago you flew to Puerto Montt, a distance of *600* miles.
6. At Puerto Montt, you were surprised to see the German influence. This area was settled largely by Germans in the mid-1800s. From there, you flew into the rugged Archipelago, landing at Punta Arenas. You flew a distance of *900* miles.
7. Northwest of Punta Arenas is Torres del Paine National Park. Since it was only *150* miles away, you traveled by land rover. The park is named after three sheer granite towers. The tallest tower rises 8,530 feet into the sky.
8. This was the end of your journey in Chile. As a final challenge, figure this out: Punta Arenas is 3,800 kilometers west of Chile's most distant spot, Easter Island. About how many miles away is Easter Island? *2,356*

Page 276

Rich Coast

Costa Rica is located between Nicaragua and Panama in Central America. Christopher Columbus was the first European to see and explore the region on his second voyage in 1502. He and the Spaniards who came after him called it *Costa Rica*, "rich coast." Costa Rica's fertile soil is its chief natural resource. Coffee, bananas, sugar, chocolate, and meat are its leading exports.

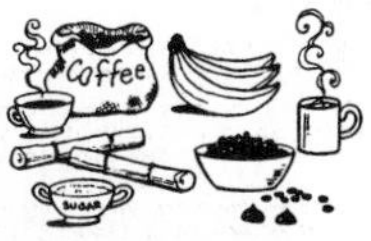

Coffee
SUGAR

Costa Rica is a small, mountainous region. Its coasts have some of the best beaches north of the equator. San José, established in 1737, is the capital and the country's environmental, artistic, educational, and cultural center.

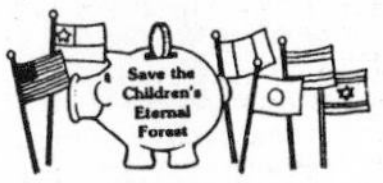

Save the Children's Eternal Forest

Significant sights include Barva Volcano in Braulio Carrilo National Park, Barra de Matina Beach, site of a leatherback turtle sanctuary, and Bosque Eterno de los Niños, the Children's Eternal Forest. This rain forest has been preserved due to the efforts of schoolchildren around the world who donated time and money.

Choose 10 words from the information above. Write the words on the lines below and then incorporate them into a wordsearch on the Costa Rican flag. Then, lightly color the flag as follows: the top and bottom stripe blue, the center stripe red. Leave the other two stripes white.

Words will vary.

blue
red
blue

Page 277

The Great Sphinx

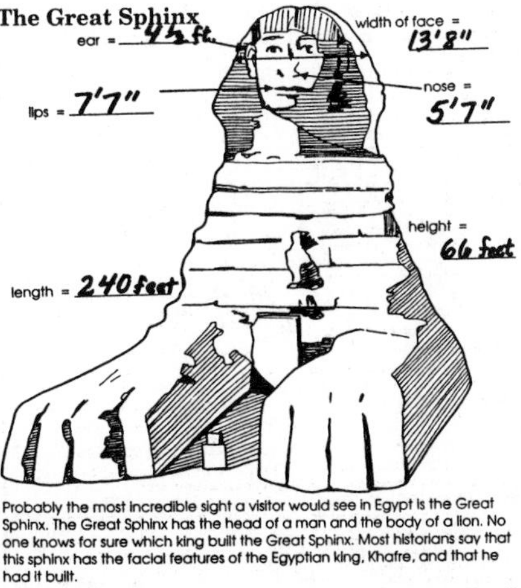

ear = 4½ ft.
width of face = 13'8"
lips = 7'7"
nose = 5'7"
height = 66 feet
length = 240 feet

Probably the most incredible sight a visitor would see in Egypt is the Great Sphinx. The Great Sphinx has the head of a man and the body of a lion. No one knows for sure which king built the Great Sphinx. Most historians say that this sphinx has the facial features of the Egyptian king, Khafre, and that he had it built.

Convert these measurements from inches to feet. Label the Great Sphinx with the new measurements.

height = 792 inches	ear = 54 inches
width of face = 164 inches	nose = 67 inches
length = 2,880 inches	lips = 91 inches

Page 278

Tour de France

The Tour de France is a 2,000-mile bicycle race that winds around France for over three weeks in July. The route changes from year to year. The map of France below shows the principal cities through which more than 100 professional bicyclists might travel. Pretend you are a rider striving for the yellow jersey. Follow the directions below.

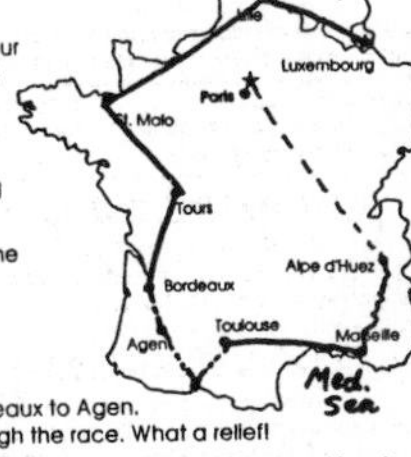

Lille
Luxembourg
Paris
St. Malo
Tours
Alpe d'Huez
Bordeaux
Toulouse
Marseille
Agen
Med. Sea

1. You live in Luxembourg. You and your bicycle fly from Luxembourg across Belgium to Lille on July 1st. Draw a solid red line from Luxembourg to Lille. You begin the race here.
2. Next travel to St. Malo. Draw a solid blue line from Lille to St. Malo.
3. Continue on to Tours. Draw a red line from St. Malo to Tours.
4. From Tours, you travel to Bordeaux. Draw a solid red line from Tours to Bordeaux.
5. Draw a blue dotted line from Bordeaux to Agen. This takes you about halfway through the race. What a relief!
6. From Agen, you ride your bicycle down to the border of Spain and back up to Toulouse. Continue your blue dotted line.
7. From Toulouse, you go east to Marseille on the Mediterranean Sea. Draw your route in red and label the sea.
8. Draw a wiggly red line from Marseille through the French Alps to Alpe d'Huez.
9. Your climb to Alpe d'Huez is nine miles long and has 21 hairpin turns. Thousands of spectators are watching you. On the back of your paper, draw what you look like when you reach the top.
10. From there you cycle to just a few miles outside of Paris. Draw a blue dotted line to that point.
11. You are first to cross the finish line! Draw and decorate your yellow T-shirt on construction paper.

Page 279

Published by Frank Schaffer Publications. Copyright protected.
319 0-7682-3794-7 Skills & Practice Gr. 4

A Maze of Chinese Terms
Use words from the Word Bank to complete the puzzle.

Across
1. famous twentieth century leader who helped form the Chinese Communist Party
5. flooded field on which rice is grown
6. well-educated man who lived 25 centuries ago and is honored by many as the greatest teacher of all times
8. medical practice of treating illness or reducing pain by inserting needles in particular parts of the body
10. art of fine handwriting
15. powerful government leader who played a major role in the push to modernize China's economy
16. fine earth carried downstream by river currents
17. excellent pottery made from a clay called kaolin
18. beads-and-wire instrument used to compute math problems

Down
2. series of rulers descended from the same ancestor
3. distinctly marked, black-and-white bear-like mammal native to China and Tibet
4. prince from India who taught that people could obtain perfect happiness if they would not be selfish
7. Chinese unit of currency
9. most populous country on Earth
11. three-wheeled vehicle powered by pedal which transports people and baggage
12. third-longest river in the world
13. capital city of China
14. series of daily exercises which help tone the muscles of the body

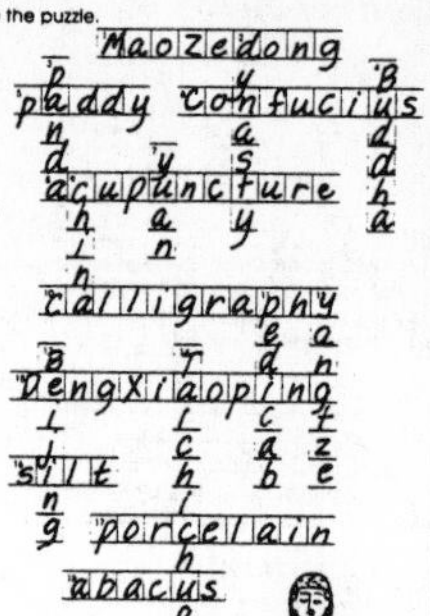

Mao Zedong
paddy
Confucius
acupuncture
calligraphy
Deng Xiaoping
silt
porcelain
abacus

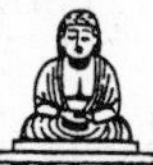

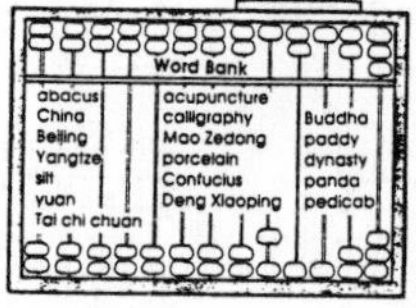

Word Bank
abacus
China
Beijing
Yangtze
silt
yuan
Tai chi chuan
acupuncture
calligraphy
Mao Zedong
porcelain
Confucius
Deng Xiaoping
Buddha
paddy
dynasty
panda
pedicab

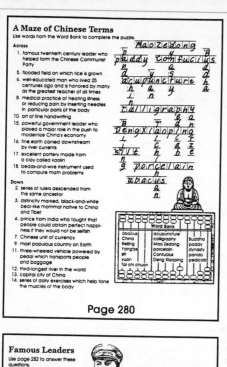

Page 280

News About Nippon
Use an encyclopedia and dictionary to research these facts about Japan. Fill the boxes with words or pictures to portray the information.

Money Unit of Japan: yen	Emperor's Name: Akihito	Number of Large Islands: four	Flag of Japan: [flag drawing]
Basic Foods of Japan: rice, fish	Shinto: Japan's oldest religion	Highest Mountain – Mount Fuji	
Kimono: traditional dress	Hibachi: earthen pot charcoal burner	The Ginza in Tokyo: shopping district	
Great Buddha: famous shrine	Two Forms of Drama: no and Kabuki	Favorite Sports: baseball, sumo wrestling	
Calligraphy: word-picture writing	Sumo: wrestling	Nippon: synonym for Japan-"source of the sun"	Obi: sash

Page 281

Famous Leaders
Use with page 283.

Ivan IV was the first czar of Old Russia. He freed his land of many foreign raiders and gained much territory for Russia. He is often called Ivan the Terrible because he was cruel to those who didn't agree with him. He even went so far as to kill his son with his own hands. He was known for being volatile and extremely paranoid about his power.

Peter I did much to modernize Russia. The Russia of 1700 was weak and backward because of its lack of information and harsh travel conditions. Peter traveled widely, often in disguise, to learn all he could. On an extensive trip to Western Europe, he studied carpentry, shipbuilding, military techniques and other Western crafts. Peter the Great, as he is usually remembered, founded the city of St. Petersburg (for a time known as Leningrad) as his "window to the West."

Catherine the Great was responsible for improving the education of the Russian people by promoting such things as art, science, education and culture. She gained power when her inept husband, Peter III, was removed from the throne and murdered. Sources say Catherine's friends murdered Peter and that she was most likely behind it. During her reign the country won land in wars with Turkey and Poland. To educate her people in modern medical practices, Catherine became the first Russian to be vaccinated against the smallpox virus.

Nicolas II was the last of the Russian czars. By the time he gained the throne, the Russian people were tired of czars. He was blamed for losing Russian territory to the Germans in World War I, and he was forced off the throne in 1917. A year later he was killed with his family.

Vladimir Ilich Ulyanov, known as **Lenin**, founded the Communist Party because he was opposed to the government which took over from Czar Nicolas II, in 1917. His party was first called the Bolsheviks (meaning majority) because he felt the majority of the people would support him. He was right. The Bolsheviks' Red Army fought mightily and drove out the government's White Army which, though aided by Western forces, was disorganized and not unified. Lenin promised the Russian people that the government would provide more food, land and peace. About the same time, the country became known as the Union of Soviet Socialist Republics.

Iosif Djugashvili, known as **Stalin**, became the dictator of the U.S.S.R. when Lenin died. The Communist government took total ownership of all farms and businesses. A "man of steel" as his adopted name implied, Stalin was ruthless in putting down his foes. Those who argued with him could quickly be sent to the Siberian frontier. Others vanished without a trace. Stalin built factories to make the U.S.S.R. independent of the West. His army became formidable in size if not in weaponry. Stalin and Hitler agreed not to fight each other and to share the takeover of Eastern Europe. The U.S.S.R. was double-crossed, however, by Hitler when Germany invaded them. Twenty-million Soviet people lost their lives in the war against Germany.

Mikhail Gorbachev, who became president of the Soviet Union in 1985, promoted change in Communist policy. He gave more rights to the Soviet allies (satellite countries). His open discussions with all the Soviet people whom he visited and conversed with surprised the Western nations. Seeing this they became more friendly with the U.S.S.R. *Glasnost* was a policy initiated by Gorbachev. With it the government publicly declared that it must be more open-minded in discussing the nation's problems.

Page 282

Famous Leaders
Use page 282 to answer these questions.

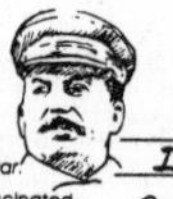

1. His nickname means "like steel." — Stalin
2. He was the first to call himself Czar. — Ivan IV (Ivan the Terrible)
3. This ruler was the first Russian vaccinated against the smallpox virus. — Catherine the Great
4. This leader's party thought that they spoke for the majority of Russians. — Lenin
5. He initiated the policy of *Glasnost*. — Gorbachev
6. He was double-crossed by Hitler during World War II. — Stalin
7. This czar was assassinated with his family in 1918. — Nicolas II
8. He was more friendly with the West than any other Soviet government during the 20th Century. — Gorbachev
9. He ordered the founding of St. Petersburg. — Peter the Great
10. He promised the Russian people that the government would provide more food, land and peace. — Lenin
11. This leader gained land for Russia in wars fought against Turkey and Poland. — Catherine the Great
12. This czar was blamed for losing territory to the Germans in World War I. — Nicolas II
13. This czar killed his oldest son with his own hands. — Ivan the Terrible
14. He was leader when his country lost 20-million people in World War II. — Stalin
15. He often put on disguises when he traveled. — Peter the Great

Research to find out whom the Russian people fought in these wars.

Crimean War — Great Britain, France, Sardinia, Turkey
World War I — Austria, Hungary, Bulgaria, Germany, Ottoman Empire (Turkey)
Seven Years' War — Great Britain, Prussia, Hanover
Napoleonic Wars — France

Page 283

Search and Rescue
Use reference materials to complete this puzzle.

Across
1. One-________ of the earth's land is covered by what was the U.S.S.R.
4. site of world's worst nuclear disaster in 1986
11. first woman in space
17. winner of Olympic women's balance beam and floor exercises in 1972
18. These tribes came from Eastern Europe to the Kiev Rus in the 6th Century.
19. unit of monetary measure
20. original republic closest to Iran and Afghanistan
21. first satellite launched into space
22. This country's Golden Horde attacked early Russians and remained in power for over a century.
23. Peter ____________ composed "The Nutcracker" and "Swan Lake."

Down
2. a cold, treeless and often frozen arctic desert
3. author of *Doctor Zhivago* whose government would not permit him to accept the Nobel Prize for literature
5. author of *War and Peace* (Hint: Use an "i" at the end of author's name instead of the more commonly used "y".)
6. capital of Ukraine; known as "the mother of Russian cities"
7. This mountain range separates Asian Russia from European Russia.
8. alphabet used in the former U.S.S.R.
9. largest freshwater lake in Eurasia
10. first human to travel in space
12. Because the U.S.S.R. invaded ________ in 1979, the U.S. boycotted the Moscow Olympic Games in 1980.
13. Czar____________ II freed serfs in 1861.
14. President of Russian Republic during 1991 attempted coup
15. the period of time when the Warsaw Pact nations and NATO nations were adversaries yet did not engage in direct combat
16. number of time zones in the former U.S.S.R.

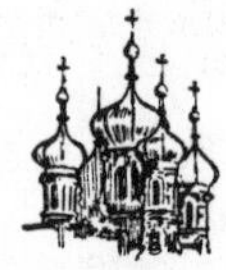

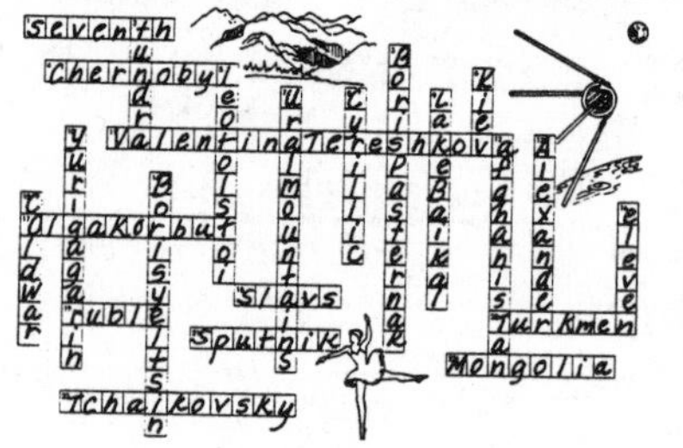

seventh
Chernobyl
Valentina Tereshkova
Olga Korbut
ruble
Slavs
Sputnik
Turkmen
Mongolia
Tchaikovsky

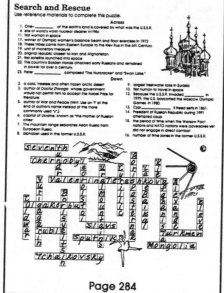

Page 284

Read All About It!
8-18-91 Coup leaders take action; Mikhail Gorbachev is placed under house arrest at his vacation dacha in the Crimea.

8-19-91 Gennady Yanayev declares himself acting president and announces a state of emergency.
The mayor of Leningrad, Anatoli Sobchak, declares the coup committee unconstitutional.
Boris Yeltsin declares the coup illegal. Many Soviet troops join him.
Yanayev tells reporters Gorbachev is ill.
Yanayev warns against Yeltsin.

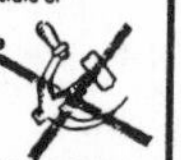

8-20-91 The president of the republic of Kazakhstan resigns from the Politburo and Central Committee to protest the coup.
Ukraine's parliament declares the actions of the coup's leaders null and void.
The coup begins to fall apart; its members quit and fall ill.
Estonia declares its independence.

8-21-91 The Soviet Parliament demands Gorbachev's return to power.
Latvia declares its independence.
Uzbekistan's president outlaws all orders made by coup leaders.

8-22-91 Gorbachev and family return to Moscow.
Lithuania outlaws the Communist Party.
In the republics of Lithuania and Estonia statues of Lenin are torn down.

8-23-91 Moldavia adopts a resolution outlawing Communist Party activities.
Georgia's president calls for a ban of the Communist Party.
Uzbekistan outlaws Communist Party activities.
Gorbachev and Yeltsin purge top officials and appoint proven reformers.

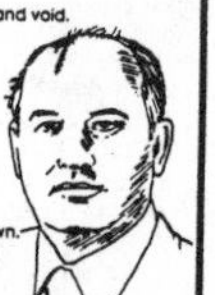

In 1991 you were a reporter assigned to Moscow by *Today's International Press* (TIP). During the coup attempt in the Soviet Union in mid-August you were on the scene. Write your news article for the world!

Include: comments from citizens on the streets, warnings from government officials, the reaction of the people around you, and a "news" photo.

Answers will vary

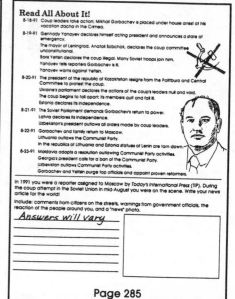

Page 285

Check It Off
Choose a country that takes/took part in the Olympics. Work alone or with others to complete the activities listed here. Check each one off when you have completed it.

_____ 1. Create a flag and make a sign to identify your country.
_____ 2. Design a display which illustrates 10 products (agriculture, industry, animals, etc.) your country is noted for.
_____ 3. Make a crossword puzzle out of at least 15 words which relate to your country.
_____ 4. Make a map of your country which shows and labels: capital city, other major cities, major rivers, lakes and oceans, neighboring countries, mountains and points of interest
_____ 5. Complete the chart of information below and be ready to share it.
_____ 6. Post all team information on the "Olympic Nations in Review" bulletin board.

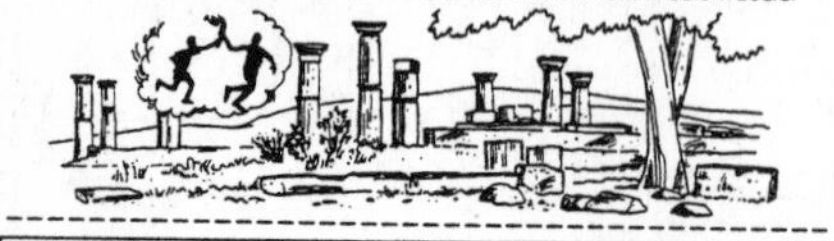

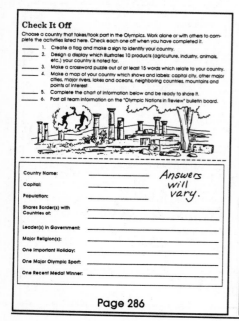

Country Name: ______ Answers will vary.
Capital: ______
Population: ______
Shares Border(s) with Countries of: ______
Leader(s) in Government: ______
Major Religion(s): ______
One Important Holiday: ______
One Major Olympic Sport: ______
One Recent Medal Winner: ______

Page 286

Who Am I?
Color each country's flag with the appropriate colors. Then fill in each blank with the letter of the country described in each sentence.

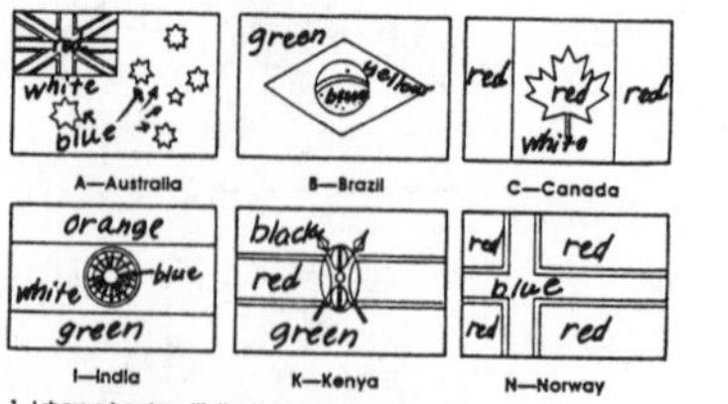

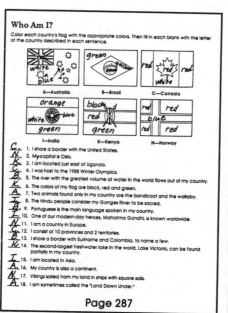

white
blue
A—Australia
green
yellow
blue
B—Brazil
red
red
white
red
C—Canada
orange
white
blue
green
I—India
black
red
green
K—Kenya
red
red
blue
red
red
N—Norway

C 1. I share a border with the United States.
N 2. My capital is Oslo.
K 3. I am located just east of Uganda.
C 4. I was host to the 1988 Winter Olympics.
B 5. The river with the greatest volume of water in the world flows out of my country.
K 6. The colors of my flag are black, red and green.
A 7. Two animals found only in my country are the bandicoot and the wallaby.
I 8. The Hindu people consider my Ganges River to be sacred.
B 9. Portuguese is the main language spoken in my country.
I 10. One of our modern-day heroes, Mahatma Gandhi, is known worldwide.
N 11. I am a country in Europe.
C 12. I consist of 10 provinces and 2 territories.
B 13. I share a border with Suriname and Colombia, to name a few.
K 14. The second-largest freshwater lake in the world, Lake Victoria, can be found partially in my country.
I 15. I am located in Asia.
A 16. My country is also a continent.
N 17. Vikings sailed from my land in ships with square sails.
A 18. I am sometimes called the "Land Down Under."

Page 287

Dear Mom, . . .
Imagine you are a contestant in this year's Summer or Winter Olympics. You are far from your family whom you haven't seen in several weeks. Write a letter home telling about your new and exciting adventure.

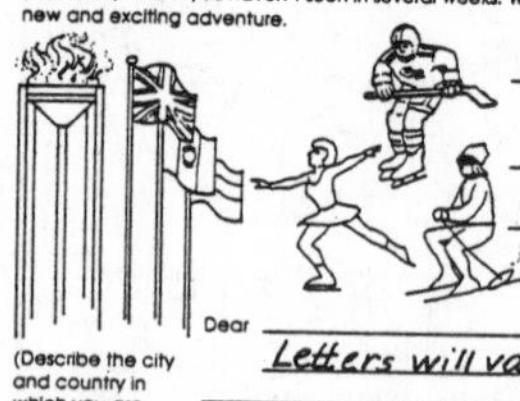

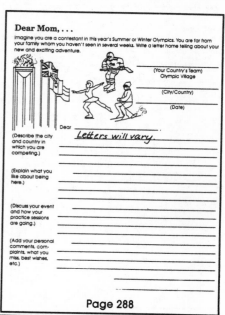

(Your Country's Team)
Olympic Village
(City/Country)
(Date)

Dear ____________

Letters will vary.

(Describe the city and country in which you are competing.)

(Explain what you like about being here.)

(Discuss your event and how your practice sessions are going.)

(Add your personal comments, complaints, what you miss, best wishes, etc.)

Page 288

Notes

Notes

Notes

Notes